Civil Litigation in a Globalising World

X. E. Kramer · C. H. van Rhee
Editors

Civil Litigation in a Globalising World

T·M·C·Asser Press

Springer

Prof. Dr. X. E. Kramer
Department of Private Law
Erasmus School of Law
Erasmus University
Burgemeester Oudlaan 50
3062 PA Rotterdam
The Netherlands

Prof. Dr. C. H. van Rhee
Faculty of Law
Maastricht University
Bouillonstraat 1-3
6211 LH Maastricht
The Netherlands

ISBN 978-90-6704-816-3 e-ISBN 978-90-6704-817-0
DOI 10.1007/978-90-6704-817-0

Published by T.M.C. ASSER PRESS, The Hague, The Netherlands www.asserpress.nl
Produced and distributed for T.M.C. ASSER PRESS by Springer-Verlag Berlin Heidelberg

Cover design: eStudio Calamar, Berlin/Figueres

Printed on acid-free paper

Springer is part of Springer Science+Business Media (www.springer.com)

Preface and Acknowledgments

In 2009, the editors of this volume developed the idea to organise a conference on the harmonisation and globalisation of civil procedure in view of the recent legislative developments in Europe and on the global level. We chose to approach this theme from different legal disciplines, including legal history, Law and Economics and legal policy as well as to articulate its interaction with private international law and private law. The harmonisation and globalisation of civil procedure also has a strong impact on national civil procedure and judicial policy. We therefore decided to dedicate a substantial part of the conference to contributions from selected jurisdictions to learn how countries deal with the challenges of globalisation and harmonisation in the area of civil procedure. The conference 'Civil Litigation in a Globalising World' took place in Rotterdam on 17 and 18 July 2010 as a joint project of the Erasmus School of Law of the Erasmus University Rotterdam and the Faculty of Law of the University of Maastricht. The present book contains the results of the conference.

We are grateful to the persons and institutions that have made this conference and the publication of the present book, possible.

In particular, we would like to thank the following persons and institutions: the Dutch Royal Academy of Arts and Sciences (KNAW), the Research School Ius Commune, the EUR Trustfonds, the University of Maastricht, the Erasmus School of Law as well as the participating ESL research programmes Lex Mercatoria and Behavioural Approaches to Contract and Tort, and their programme directors. The contributions and part of the editorial tasks by Xandra Kramer have been made possible with the support of the Netherlands Organisation for Scientific Research (NWO) within its Innovational Research Incentives Scheme.

Further, we are indebted to the secretariat of the Department of Private Law of Erasmus School of Law, in particular to Mrs. Maja Lucas, Debbie Kneefel and Margreet den Hond, for their assistance in the organisation of the conference and preparation of the book.

Mr. Randolph W. Davidson (Pavia) has rendered invaluable assistance in revising the English of the various contributions to this book. Miss Nadia Ayrir, student-assistant at the Erasmus School of Law, assisted in the sometimes difficult task of bringing literature references into line with the publisher's guidelines.

Last but not least we would like to thank all the speakers at the conference and the contributors to this book, as well as TMC Asser Press for publication.

Rotterdam/Maastricht, Autumn 2011

Xandra Kramer
C. H. (Remco) van Rhee

Contents

Chapter 1
Civil Litigation in a Globalising World: An Introduction

Xandra E. Kramer and C. H. van Rhee

Abstract Globalisation of legal matters and the inherent necessity of having to litigate in foreign courts or to enforce judgments in other countries considerably complicate civil proceedings due to great differences in civil procedure. This may jeopardise access to justice. As a result, the debate on the need for the harmonisation of civil procedure becomes ever more prominent. In recent years, this debate has gained in importance because of new legislative and practical developments both at the European and the global level. These developments require further study, amongst other things the bringing about of the ALI/UNIDROIT Principles of Transnational Civil Procedure and some recent European Regulations introducing harmonised procedures, as well as problems encountered in the modernisation of national civil procedure and in attempts for further harmonisation. This book discusses the globalisation and harmonisation of civil procedure from various angles, including fundamental (international) principles of civil justice, legal history, Law and Economics and (European) policy. Attention is also paid to the interaction with private international law and private law (Part I: Different perspectives on globalisation and harmonisation). European and global

---

Xandra Kramer—Professor at Erasmus School of Law, the Netherlands, www.xandrakramer.eu. This contribution has been made possible with the support of the Netherlands Organisation for Scientific Research (NWO) within its Innovational Research Incentives Scheme (VIDI).
C. H. (Remco) van Rhee—Professor of European Legal History and Comparative Civil Procedure at Maastricht University.

X. E. Kramer (✉)
Erasmus School of Law, Rotterdam, The Netherlands
e-mail: kramer@frg.eur.nl

C. H. van Rhee
Maastricht University, Maastricht, The Netherlands
e-mail: remco.vanrhee@maastrichtuniversity.nl

X. E. Kramer and C. H. van Rhee (eds.), *Civil Litigation in a Globalising World*,
DOI: 10.1007/978-90-6704-817-0_1,

projects that aim at the harmonisation of civil procedure or provide guidelines for the fair and efficient adjudication of justice are discussed in a subsequent part of the book (Part II: Harmonisation in a European and global context). The volume further includes contributions that focus on globalisation and harmonisation of civil procedure from the viewpoint of various national jurisdictions (Part III: National approaches to globalisation and harmonisation).

Contents

1.1 Civil Litigation in a Global Context

The present volume discusses civil litigation in a global context. During the last three decades, it has become clear that this area of legal activity has acquired more international dimensions than was ever the case in the previous period. This is in part due to the fact that attempts to harmonise substantive law, for example within the context of international bodies such as the European Union, are considerably jeopardised by the existence of extensive differences in the court procedures through which this law has to be realised and enforced.[1] In addition, according to the drafters of the ALI/UNIDROIT Principles and Rules of Transnational Civil Procedure,[2] differences in court procedures also hamper international trade.

Harmonisation of civil procedure on a worldwide level is currently mainly achieved through soft law, an example being the ALI/UNIDROIT Principles and Rules. Additionally, there are activities in the field of private international law, notably the various Hague Conventions in the field of international civil procedure. One of the latest relevant conventions is the Convention of 30 June 2005 on

---

[1] This was already noted by Cambridge Law Professor H.C. Gutteridge in 1946: 'It would, however, seem to be obvious that no scheme of unification can be regarded as satisfactory if proceedings in one of the participating countries are more dilatory and expensive than in others, or if the remedies afforded by the unified law are not the same' and 'If unification is to possess any real value it is essential that the unified rules should be applied in practice without any impediments created by procedural difficulties' (Gutteridge 1946, 35).

[2] ALI/UNIDROIT Principles of Transnational Civil Procedure, as adopted by the American Law Institute and UNIDROIT in 2004. These Principles were published, accompanied by Rules and short commentaries in ALI/UNIDROIT 2006 Principles of Transnational Civil Procedure, 2006.

Choice of Court Agreements, which came into being after the failure of the broader Hague Convention on Jurisdiction and Judgments.[3] At a European level, various legislative instruments such as directives and regulations have been promulgated, either under Article 81 of the Treaty on the Functioning of the European Union (TFEU), or on the basis of this Treaty's Article 114 (and their predecessors under the Community Treaty). The various instruments promulgated under Article 81 only concern cross-border cases, whereas the procedural rules promulgated under Article 114—these may currently only be found in Directive 2004/48/EC on the Enforcement of Intellectual Property Rights—[4] are also applicable in purely national cases. At a national level, some convergence may be noticed as a result of the adoption of international and foreign procedural rules and regulations in national law reform projects, for example in the area of international jurisdiction where the Brussels regime has had an impact on national jurisdiction rules.

The various chapters of this volume will address the need for harmonisation of civil procedural law as a result of globalisation, and the extent and various ways in which civil procedural law is currently converging on a European, global and national level. The limits of harmonisation and its pros and cons will be addressed. Additionally, national responses to the challenges of globalisation and harmonisation will be discussed.

1.2 Different Perspectives on Globalisation and Harmonisation of Civil Procedure

Part I of this volume, presenting different perspectives on globalisation and harmonisation, starts with the contribution of Neil Andrews (Chap. 2). According to this author, principles of civil justice should be of major importance in the harmonisation debate. The author states that the leading principles should be singled out and these principles should then be categorised. The following categories can in his opinion be distinguished: (1) Access to legal advice and dispute resolution systems; (2) Equality and fairness between the parties; (3) A focussed and speedy process; and (4) Adjudicators of integrity. In his opinion, by looking at civil justice from the perspective of these sets of principles, the bewildering diversity of complex, detailed and technical national rules may become manageable and proposals may be made for a further alignment of the systems of civil justice on a European or global scale. This alignment should not be confused with unification of the civil justice systems, as a model of civil justice acceptable to all jurisdictions and cultures on a global scale or even on a European level is impossible to achieve (as is emphasised by a large number of contributors to the present volume).

---

[3] Schulz 2006, 243–286.

[4] Directive 2004/48/EC on the Enforcement of Intellectual Property Rights, OJ 2004, L 143/15, with corrigendum L 195/16.

It should, however, facilitate a growing together of civil justice systems by facilitating the introduction of a variety of national rules and procedural models that meet the requirements of the sets of principles that have been identified.

Consequently, these principles would function to some extent as European directives, which state the goals that need to be achieved but leave the Member States freedom as regards the means by which they want to achieve them. An example of a well-functioning set of principles at the level of the Council of Europe may be found in Article 6(1) of the European Convention on Human Rights (ECHR), principles that are reinforced by the existence of the European Court of Human Rights. These principles may give rise to best practices which may result in a further alignment of civil justice systems. To a certain extent, the various EU directives and regulations in the field of civil procedure may also serve as best practices. Although the present directives and regulations promulgated under Article 81 TFEU and its predecessors are aimed at cases in which litigants from different Members States are involved, a number of such directives and regulations, for example the Mediation Directive[5] and the Small Claims Regulation,[6] may also serve as best practices for national lawmakers who aim at reforming their national procedural law (see also the contribution by Burkhard Hess, Chap. 8). This would certainly result in a further alignment at the EU level. On a worldwide scale the ALI/UNIDROIT Principles may serve the same goal.

Whereas the contribution of Neil Andrews focuses on future harmonisation, the contribution by C. H. (Remco) van Rhee (Chap. 3) deals with past experiences in this field. The author identifies three types of harmonisation: incidental harmonisation as a result of national law reform, harmonisation as a result of competition between civil justice systems and planned harmonisation as a result of international harmonisation projects.

The author states that incidental harmonisation as a result of national law reform has a long history, and is mainly the result of the national legislature making use of foreign experience with procedural mechanisms and rules in order to evaluate their suitability in national law reform projects. Examples can be traced back to the fifteenth- and sixteenth-century Low Countries, where the rule-making authorities often followed French legislation, and such examples continue to be present up to the present day, though as Tanja Domej (Chap. 12) illustrates Switzerland may be an exception in its hesitation to follow foreign examples in the drafting of the new Swiss Code of Civil Procedure. Especially the civil justice systems of areas that are in one way or another related to the jurisdiction in need of reform (eg economically, politically, culturally) are taken into consideration in law reform projects, and this may be good news for the further alignment of the civil justice systems of the Member States of entities such as the European Union,

[5] Directive 2008/52/EC on certain aspects of mediation in civil and commercial matters, OJ 2008, L 136.

[6] Regulation (EC) No. 861/2007 establishing a European Small Claims Procedure, OJ 2007, L 199.

States who in various ways are closely linked to each other exactly because of their involvement in these bodies.

Harmonisation as a result of competition between civil justice systems also has a long history. In his contribution, Van Rhee discusses the example of the success of the Romano-canonical procedure, originally introduced in the spiritual courts, due to its adoption as the standard procedure of various secular courts from the later medieval period onwards. The author argues that this was to a large extent the result of competition for business between spiritual and secular courts. Such competition may currently again be witnessed. An example is provided by England and Germany, where, as Stefan Huber shows (Chap. 15), brochures have been published in order to promote England and Germany respectively as jurisdictions that are, amongst other things, well suited for international business litigation. In order to overcome the language advantage of the English civil justice system, the German parliament is currently contemplating the introduction of divisions at some German courts where international business litigation can be conducted in the English language. Similar experiments are contemplated in other countries, such as France and the Netherlands (Rotterdam Court of First Instance; not discussed in the present volume).

Louis Visscher (Chap. 4) charts the pros and cons of harmonisation of civil procedural law from the perspective of Law and Economics, ie primarily from the perspective of the production of legal norms aimed at avoiding various forms of market failure; market failure occurs in situations where perfect competition is absent. The author notes that there is only a limited amount of Law and Economics literature on the harmonisation of civil procedure. He states that there is no empirical research which shows that international trade is hindered by the existence of different civil justice systems or that the number of international legal transactions would increase if the existing differences were reduced (which is the underlying assumption of the drafters of the Principles and Rules of Transnational Civil Procedure). This author comes to the conclusion that the Law and Economics arguments against harmonisation of civil procedural law are stronger than the arguments in favour of such harmonisation.

Strong arguments against harmonisation are that the availability of alternative models of civil justice (1) enables satisfying a large number of preferences and (2) facilitates learning effects. In case harmonisation or unification of civil procedure would be pursued by a central legislator, another argument against harmonisation would be (3) that such a legislator would suffer from limited information and could easily be influenced by interest groups. Also problematic is, according to the author, that civil justice systems are closely linked to the existing systems of underlying substantive law; in other words, a strong path dependency can be noted. As stated, from a Law and Economics perspective these arguments cannot be set aside by arguments in favour of harmonisation. One such argument is the need to internalise interstate externalities, but such externalities do not exist since civil procedure only takes place between the parties involved. Another argument in favour of harmonisation, the desire to avoid a race to the bottom, is again unconvincing since the chances that this will occur are limited, for example because the civil justice systems of individual jurisdictions must meet certain quality requirements, if only in order to have judgments of those systems recognised and enforced abroad. Finally, the argument that harmonisation would decrease transaction costs and allow profits of economies of scale is not convincing either. Although transaction costs are mentioned as a possible hurdle that would be taken away by harmonisation of civil procedural law, it is, according to the author, not certain that the cost savings caused by harmonisation would outweigh its costs. Therefore, the author is of the opinion that there is only limited space for the harmonisation of procedural law, and then only by way of the introduction of an additional, optional model (within a European context, a so-called 28th model). For the rest, Visscher subscribes to the view of Anthony Ogus[7] that spontaneous harmonisation is to be preferred. According to the latter author, from a Law and Economics perspective spontaneous convergence or harmonisation—eg incidental harmonisation as a result of national law reform or harmonisation as a result of competition, discussed in the contribution by Van Rhee—is to be preferred since it will only occur when the costs of convergence are exceeded by its benefits.

Gerhard Wagner (Chap. 5) discusses harmonisation of procedural law from a European policy perspective. First he mentions Article 81 TFEU, which gives rise to what is qualified as horizontal harmonisation, ie harmonisation by introducing a general set of procedural rules which apply whatever the substantive legal issue at stake may be as long as the requirements of Article 81 are met (cross-border cases, etc.). The author notes that the impact of the various directives and regulations that have been passed under Article 81 and its predecessors is very limited—an observation that is repeated by various contributors to the present volume—since for political reasons these legislative instruments are only applicable in cross-border cases, meaning cases in which litigants from different Member States are involved. Additionally, the author states that this approach results in two parallel sets of rules, one for domestic cases and another one for cross-border cases, something which may be perceived as an unnecessary burden for the judges who have to work with these rules. The author predicts that this type of law-making will not have a long future. More generally, he states that 'procedural law lacks the compromise solution of an optional system'. In his view, this would result in courts that are overburdened and in a waste of judicial resources. His view differs from that of Louis Visscher who, from a Law and Economics perspective, suggests that an additional set of rules in the sense of an optional, 28th system would be a feasible option.

Wagner continues with discussing harmonisation based on Article 114 TFEU and its predecessors. Article 114 TFEU includes a power for the EU to harmonise national procedural laws if they do not sufficiently implement substantive EU law. In other words, it sanctions a system of law enforcement and protection of subjective rights derived from EU law for specific areas of substantive EU law

7 Ogus 1999, 415–416.

governing both international and domestic cases. This system of law enforcement and protection may encompass harmonised rules of civil procedure, as is witnessed by Directive 2004/48/EC on the enforcement of intellectual property rights and possible future EU legislation on Consumer Collective Redress. This type of harmonisation can be qualified as vertical harmonisation since the harmonised rules do not concern civil disputes in general but only specific subject matter. The author holds that this approach may be fruitful since it offers a valuable tool for experimenting with harmonisation, although it is hard to justify this sectoral approach apart from referring to the competences of the EU which are not linked with an overall plan in the area of civil procedure.

Xandra Kramer (Chap. 6) focuses on the relationship between private international law and civil procedure within the context of globalisation and harmonisation. The author states that modern private international law and issues of civil procedure are closely linked. She holds that the harmonisation of civil procedural law may be facilitated by the harmonisation of private international law as an initial stage. Though private international law rules serve their own purpose, and are not merely transitional, sometimes (harmonised) private international law rules function as a preliminary phase in the harmonisation of civil procedure. This is especially the case in the EU, where in different areas there is a gradual shift from the harmonisation of private international law to a more far-reaching harmonisation of civil procedure, primarily by introducing minimum standards of civil procedure. As is demonstrated, private international law rules can also result in a gradual and spontaneous approximation of civil procedure. By coordinating different national systems of law in international cases, private international law may smoothen the way for harmonisation, for example where concepts are concerned such as *lis pendens*, or the role of *ius curia novit* in the application of foreign substantive law. Private international law and harmonisation of civil procedure are closely interwoven and both (should) aim at meeting the challenges of globalisation and realising an EU, or even a global, area of justice.

The final chapter in Part I by Matthias Storme (Chap. 7) addresses the interaction of procedural law with substantive private law, particularly in an international context. The author notes that substantive law is often drafted without paying attention to the procedural environment in which it has to function, or without paying attention to the fact that in certain cases the procedural context may be different from the national one. Procedural law should take into account that the applicable private law is often drafted or developed having regard to different rules of procedure, or without taking into consideration the existing rules of procedure. The contribution contains a series of examples illustrating the problems that may arise as a result of this. These examples are grouped under three headings: (1) The availability of the necessary procedures, powers and rules at the national forum where the enforcement of the substantive rights granted by harmonised or foreign law is sought; (2) The protection of defendants, eg against vexatious litigation; and (3) Inflexibility of national procedural rules as regards a change of parties or their rights under substantive law.

1.3 Harmonisation in a European and Global Context

Part II of this volume on harmonisation in a European and global context starts with the contribution of Burkhard Hess (Chap. 8). The author holds that during the last decade or so, EU legislation in the area of international civil procedural law has been subject to change. The EU has moved from an approach focused on the coordination of national procedures and improving traditional instruments of private international law, to an attempt to connect the procedural systems of the Member States and to realise a situation where judgments can move freely within the Union. The author states that therefore it is time for academics to develop ideas about the future architecture of civil procedural law in a European context, a discussion that might even result in the development of a European Code of Civil Procedure or another umbrella instrument.

However, first the various bases of harmonisation of procedural law (and private international law) should be deliberated on, particularly Articles 81 and 114 TFEU (referred to as horizontal and vertical harmonisation, respectively, by Gerhard Wagner in this volume). Additionally, the standards developed by the European Court of Justice for reviewing national procedural law should be taken into consideration, as well as Articles 6 ECHR and 47 of the EU Charter of Fundamental Rights. The author notes that the European Court of Justice currently emphasises the role of the Charter in the interpretation of procedural instruments of the EU and of national procedural law when European Union law is implemented by national civil courts. This results in the harmonisation of national procedures via judicial interpretation and the application of constitutional standards. This trend may become even more dominant in the future since the Stockholm programme has determined that the European Commission shall elaborate an instrument on procedural minimum standards by 2012. These standards will not only be based on the case law of the Luxemburg and Strasbourg Courts, but also on the practice of the national courts.

Chapter 9 by Alan Uzelac takes a radically different approach to harmonisation of civil procedural law in Europe than the authors of the preceding chapters. Basically, the author holds that a discussion on the harmonisation of rules of civil procedure is meaningless if one does not take into consideration that these harmonised rules depend to a large extent on the procedural structures by which they need to be implemented. Based on his experience in the work of the European Commission for the Efficiency of Justice (CEPEJ)—the first international, intergovernmental organisation systematically engaged in the collection of statistical information on the functioning of the national civil justice systems—the author highlights huge structural differences between the 47 Member States of the Council of Europe. In his contribution to the present volume, he concentrates on three core organisational structures, ie (1) courts, (2) judges and (3) lawyers.

After having shown the huge structural differences (no common European definition of 'courts', differences in the understanding of the social functions of judges, divergences in their typical tasks, something which equally applies to lawyers), the author concludes that due to the difficulty and at times even the impossibility of harmonising structures—although the CEPEJ reports seem to have triggered some structural reform and convergence—it is better to look at procedural harmonisation from a new perspective: concentrating on the issues that are of importance for the users of the judicial system instead of on the harmonisation of rules and structures. These issues may be summarised under the headings of the effectiveness and quality of the legal protection offered. Thus convergence should be aimed at the results of the national justice systems. These are, amongst other things, foreseeable time frames, clear procedural calendars, transparent time and case management, easily accessible information about the available options in the pursuit of individual and collective rights, user-friendly procedures, clearly defined fee and costs arrangements and fair legal aid systems for those who cannot afford the full costs of legal protection. Just as Visscher in the present volume, Uzelac underlines that all this does not mean that there is a need for complete harmonisation. He states: ‘But, where different procedural structures turn out to be equally effective, fair, transparent and user-friendly, the pluralism of procedural forms may even be considered as desirable, just as harmony may be better achieved by polyphonic voices than by voices chanting in unison’.

Michele Taruffo (Chap. 10) addresses the issue of the harmonisation of civil procedure where transnational litigation is concerned. The author is one of the initiators of the ALI/UNIDROIT Principles and Rules of Transnational Civil Procedure, and it is these Principles and Rules which are the focus of his contribution. Just like Andrews (Chap. 2), the author is of the opinion that the Principles and Rules could be used as a model in law reform providing standards for harmonisation of national procedures, even though they primarily focus on transnational commercial litigation. The Principles are especially useful, since they are not too general to make them completely meaningless, but also not too specific such as to make harmonisation impossible. They focus on an intermediate level and consequently represent a point of reference in the drafting of more specific, national rules and regulations. One of the problems that this author mentions is that the Principles provide a standard model and do not deal with the ‘plurality and fragmentation’ of special procedures that often exist at the national level. Additionally, when using the Principles as a model, they need to be adapted to the procedural environment provided by the various national codes, and this may, according to the author, result in cherry picking and a rejection at the national level of parts of the Principles that are not familiar to the national legal system under consideration. This will of course hamper harmonisation.

1.4 National Approaches to Globalisation and Harmonisation

Part III of the volume presents a selection of national jurisdictions and addresses the question of how these jurisdictions deal with the issues of globalisation and harmonisation. The jurisdictions under consideration are the United States, Switzerland, Scotland, the Netherlands, Germany, Belgium, France and Romania.

In the United States, following the judicial systems existing of state courts and federal courts, there are in principle as many systems of civil procedure as there are states. However, in 1938 the Federal Rules of Civil Procedure were enacted which soon spread beyond the federal judiciary. As Paul Dubinsky states (Chap. 11), already by the 1950s, one could refer with accuracy on the international stage to an 'American approach' to civil justice, consisting of a collection of practices, values, and assumptions common to all courts in the United States (federal and state), with minor differences in detail. The author analyses how in such a short period of time this degree of voluntary harmonisation was possible. In part the answer is that the establishment of the Federal Rules of Civil Procedure was not primarily an effort to bring about harmonisation but an effort at reform. From the perspective of greater access to justice and greater likelihood of justice on the merits, these Rules were an improvement over existing state law and practice. However, this is only a part of the answer. The success can also be attributed to the powerful role of emerging elites that had much to gain from the creation of a federal law of civil procedure and from its dissemination to state systems throughout the country. As Dubinsky extensively demonstrates, three powerful groups can be identified; the elite law schools, the emerging class of law firms seeking to practice law on a multistate basis, and federal judges. The author concludes that this American experience, showing that harmonisation is most likely to go forward when particular resourceful interest groups can identify clear gains from such a process, can be useful for the harmonisation movement in the EU as well.

Switzerland is an interesting case since this country witnessed a major law reform in 2011. On 1 January 2011, the 26 cantonal codes of civil procedure were replaced by one national Code of Civil Procedure. Although one would expect a keen interest in international developments in a modern codification project, this was not the case. One of the reasons may have been that the codification project was already complicated enough, having to bridge the differences between the 26 cantons, but it remains remarkable. Of course, one may expect that the involvement of 26 different procedural traditions will guarantee a code with a somewhat cosmopolitan character. However, at the same time the lack of interest in major international procedural developments can be seen as a missed opportunity. According to Tanja Domej (Chap. 12), some international influences may, however, be noticed, also in the case law of the Federal Swiss Court. An example is the influence of the rules of the Lugano Convention (and the case law of the European Court of Justice on the related Brussels Convention and the Brussels I Regulation) as regards jurisdiction in purely domestic cases, and also of Article 6 ECHR. This is, however, not a surprise given the fact that Switzerland is a signatory to these documents and therefore the rules in them can in a way be seen as internal Swiss law. The various European Union directives and regulations in the field of civil procedure have, on the other hand, not been a source of inspiration for the drafters of the new Swiss Code, and during the drafting process a considerable amount of scepticism was voiced as regards international developments, such as those in the area of class actions and mediation (in the end the Swiss legislature was, however, positive as regards mediation, most likely because of its positive budgetary consequences). One of the few elements of foreign (semi) procedural law that was considered to be suitable for adoption in Switzerland was the directly enforceable authentic instrument, due to its beneficial consequences for Swiss creditors and Swiss notaries. Another example is protective measures securing the enforcement of already existing titles (*Arrest*). Nevertheless, the author notes that for the rest Switzerland is not participating in the creation of a European area of justice. Whether this will prove to be harmful for the country in the future remains to be seen.

The opposite of Switzerland is Scotland. According to Peter Beaton (Chap. 13), Scotland is very open to international influences, something that may be facilitated by the fact that due to historical factors Scotland can be defined as a so-called mixed legal system. The author supports his thesis by discussing a selection of areas where Scotland has been influenced by and, in its turn, has influenced other legal systems. These include rules on jurisdiction, and not only those rules which have been adopted in internal Scots law as a result of the influence of the Brussels Convention (now Brussels I Regulation). If the latter would have been true, this would not have been a major achievement since even a country that is rather closed to foreign influences such as Switzerland has been influenced by this Convention, as was mentioned above. Scotland is also very liberal on recognising the jurisdiction of foreign courts where it applies the rule that the residence of the defendant is the principal connecting factor, and where the judgments of foreign courts are recognised and enforced in a liberal way: the traditional requirements of reciprocity or the existence of an international convention do not apply. The openness of Scotland is also shown by the early adoption into the domestic legal system of international arbitration law, the New York Convention, whereas unlike England and just as Switzerland it recognises the directly enforceable authentic instrument. As regards the influence of Scotland abroad, the author discusses the *forum non conveniens* rule, which is a Scottish invention that has been exported abroad, notably to the United States and other common law jurisdictions. On the basis of these and some other examples, the author concludes that 'Scotland may be seen as a bridge between the major law systems of the world'.

In her contribution on the Netherlands (Chap. 14), Paulien van der Grinten looks at the internationalisation of civil procedure from the perspective of a Dutch civil servant entrusted with this subject at the Dutch Ministry of Security and Justice. She states that '[i]n a globalising world the interaction between national and international activity is not just a choice, it is a fact of life'. As a result, she holds that national governments cannot disregard the globalisation of civil procedure but must find a way of dealing with it. She states that all national governments within the European Union are confronted with identical problems in the area of civil justice. Examples are reducing the costs of civil litigation (especially in the present times of austerity), limiting the burden of civil litigation for both citizens and governments, the introduction of an efficient way to enforce unpaid debts and how to deal with mass claims. These include class actions, a topic that the rather inward-looking Swiss legislature did not want to address in the recent Swiss law reform project, as was mentioned above. Van der Grinten warns that the inactivity of national governments in these areas is not beneficial, since in that case the European Commission will take the initiative, an option that the author does apparently not favour. In order to prevent this, governments can make use of various strategies, depending on whether they have already introduced legislation on the topic itself, are in the process of drafting such legislation or have not acted yet as regards the specific topic at hand. In the case of existing national legislation, it is, according to the author, for example, a good idea to market this legislation in order to have it adopted as a European model. Apart from a discussion of various strategies, the author notes that the Netherlands are not in favour of an approach to the harmonisation of civil procedure which Gerhard Wagner qualifies as vertical (a sectoral approach on the basis of Article 114 TFEU) because it is felt that such an approach will in the end cause confusion and hinder access to justice. The Netherlands prefer a horizontal approach and have therefore made attempts to prevent the introduction of the Enforcement Directive discussed in the contributions of Wagner and Hess, however without much success.

Germany is another jurisdiction where the changes in international civil procedure have attracted attention. According to Stefan Huber (Chap. 15), Germany participates actively in the competition between legal systems (competition that has a long history, as was shown in Chap. 3 by Van Rhee). As stated above, a brochure has been issued titled 'Law—Made in Germany' which forms a reaction to a similar brochure issued by the Law Society of England and Wales ('England and Wales: The Jurisdiction of Choice'), and which advertises Germany as the jurisdiction of choice. In addition, a bill is now pending before the German parliament in which it is proposed to create special commercial chambers in several German courts where transnational commercial disputes can be litigated entirely in the English language. The initiative goes further than the pilot at the Paris Commercial Court, where one of the chambers is staffed with judges who understand English, Spanish or German, but where the judgment needs to be issued in the national language (ie not in English). According to Huber, these developments are to be applauded, also because he agrees with Uzelac (Chap. 9) that reform of civil procedure should concentrate on the interests of the parties rather than on the idea of state sovereignty. The author holds that party autonomy in respect of procedural rules should be recognised. This would include the availability of specialised judges dealing with international commercial cases in the English language and according to a specifically drafted set of procedural rules. The use of English does, in the author's view, not result in problems as regards the fundamental principle of the publicity of the proceedings, since this principle does in his view not entail that everyone should be able to follow court proceedings in his or her own national language. Nevertheless, the use of English would mean that some other problems have to be solved, for example those concerning third parties in the proceedings.

The above developments give the impression that Germany is very open to foreign influences in the area of civil justice. However, in his contribution Huber also warns that the German attitude to this issue is biased. In order to demonstrate this he discusses the rules governing the enforcement of foreign judgments in Germany. He describes the German cooperation with foreign authorities as both efficient and reluctant. The reluctance appears when one takes into consideration the exception to the enforcement of these judgments in Germany. Different from for example Scotland, Germany strongly adheres to the reciprocity principle, whereas it gives priority to German judgments in case of a clash with a foreign judgment, without taking into consideration whether the German judgment pre- or postdates the foreign court decision. Also German courts apply their national rules on jurisdiction, and not the rules of the foreign forum, in order to determine whether the foreign court was competent to hear the issue.

One of the issues the Belgian contribution of Benoît Allemeersch and Els VandenSande (Chap. 16) addresses is the issue of regional harmonisation within the context of the Benelux countries and the reception of foreign law as options in striving for more convergence of procedural law. As regards this issue, the authors present the Benelux as a possible 'laboratory for pan-European initiatives in the field of civil justice'. They note in this respect that activities of the Benelux have come to a halt. That such activities can, nevertheless, be successful is in their opinion demonstrated by the harmonised set of rules for the civil coercive fine (*astreinte*) introduced in the three Member States of the Benelux in 1973, the uniform interpretation of which is guaranteed by the Benelux Court of Justice by way of a preliminary ruling procedure. Such an approach may in their opinion be more successful than a European approach, since they hold that Europe lacks a well thought-out concept on how the issue of procedural harmonisation should be approached. Various problems as regards the European approach are highlighted, such as the rather limited involvement of European practitioners in the harmonisation attempts, as well as problems related to the fact that civil procedure is embedded in a national structure for the administration of justice. This last point was also addressed in the contribution of Uzelac (Chap. 9). As regards the reception of foreign law, the authors are less optimistic about the Belgian situation. Just as in the Netherlands, the ALI/UNIROIT Principles have not been given much attention there. The authors also note that the manner in which legislation is drafted in that country allows little leeway for comparative law exercises. When foreign law is influential, this is less the result of legislation than of that of the initiatives of judges; within the EU, the opportunities for judges to be in touch with foreign colleagues has increased. Examples are experiments with Québec-style court-annexed 'mediation by judges' and settlement hearings following the Dutch *schikkingscomparitie* model in Belgium.

France seems to be comparable to Belgium in the sense that in that jurisdiction the influence of foreign law and developments in the area of civil procedure is to a large extent the result of the activity of judges. According to Frédérique Ferrand (Chap. 17), in case law various foreign procedural techniques and institutions have been received, such as the freezing order, the anti-suit injunction and the estoppel. This occurred first in the area of private international law, but more and more these techniques and institutions are also recognised in purely domestic cases, especially at the level of the *Cour de cassation*. However, in its judgments the court never acknowledges foreign inspiration. An example of the import of a foreign institution is the recognition of the estoppel as well as the reception of the *amicus curiae*. Sometimes comparative studies in the area of civil procedure are ordered by the *Cour de cassation*. Unlike in Belgium, the ALI/UNIDROIT Principles have been given a lot of attention. A first conference devoted to these Principles in Paris showed a very negative attitude of French lawyers since they regarded them as too American and as an example of American (legal) imperialism. The final version of the Principles was, however, well received at a conference organised by the author a few years later in Lyon. It is not clear whether the changes in the Principles caused the more positive attitude of the French audience, or a more open-minded approach to ideas from abroad.

The problems encountered by countries in transition are highlighted by Sebastian Spinei (Chap. 18). Romania is traditionally a jurisdiction that can be placed firmly in the French legal tradition, even though the Socialist period brought various changes. Romania is currently in the process of introducing a new code of civil procedure and, as Spinei shows, unlike Switzerland a lot of attention was given to international sources in the drafting process. In the Preamble of the New Code, foreign codes of civil procedure are mentioned (Québec-Canada, France, Italy, Switzerland, Germany, Finland, the Netherlands), as well as European conventions, directives and regulations, the Storme Report, the Model Code of Civil Procedure for Ibero-America, and the ALI/UNIDROIT Principles and Rules of Transnational Civil Procedure. French influence appears very clearly where the new code contains guiding procedural principles at its start. This shows that Romania, also as one of the new EU Member States, is open to foreign influences and experiences in the area of civil procedure.

1.5 Concluding Remarks

The book is concluded by Chap. 19, in which the *eminence grise* in the area of procedural law and its harmonisation, Marcel Storme, not only reflects on the various contributions in the present book, but also looks at the future. The author argues that further harmonisation within Europe should (1) start from the notion of equal access to justice, (2) not narrow the application of instruments to cross-border cases, (3) be based on horizontal harmonisation instead of vertical harmonisation, and (4) make a clear choice as to its interaction with national civil procedures with the so-called 28th model being the most feasible. The author concludes that the process of harmonisation and unification of procedural law on a European level appears to be an irreversible trend and that a harmonised or unified or globalised procedural law could help to find justice, not only in Europe, but all over the world.

While globalisation is a fact, and it is true that especially at the European level harmonisation appears to be an irreversible trend, globalisation and harmonisation still pose serious questions. In the EU, the very foundations of a European civil procedure are far from solid, as the various contributions to this book also underline. The discussion should start with a fundamental debate on the treaty and policy bases of the further harmonisation of civil procedure. Are the current bases—particularly Article 81 and/or Article 114 TFEU (the latter of which is hardly used for harmonised procedural rules)—adequate to build a European civil procedure on? Is it—if the European legislator continues to use Article 81 as a basis—acceptable that increasingly different procedures and procedural rules will be available to EU citizens, depending upon whether or not the situation concerns a cross-border case? A related issue discussed in this volume that concerns the ground layers of a (future) European civil procedure is the debate on vertical (sectoral) versus horizontal harmonisation. While from a policy perspective a sectoral approach is understandable, this may—as Van der Grinten rightfully argues—at the same time jeopardise access to justice, which, as we agree with Marcel Storme, is the very essence of European legislative action in the area of civil procedure. Other issues that need further deliberation are, amongst other things, whether—in addition to the current regulatory framework—soft law in the form of Principles of European Civil Procedure are desirable. A recent Commission policy, as is demonstrated by Kramer and Hess, is the objective to introduce minimum standards of civil procedure. This also triggers the debate on minimum versus maximum or full harmonisation, as is familiar from the discussion of (substantive) European private law. At the moment, it is not clear what exactly the Commission envisages with these standards and how these should relate to existing instruments. It is important that these fundamental issues, and in general the overriding question of what type of European civil procedure we want, are thought through, because a building without a foundation will not survive for long. Though from a political point of view compromises may be a feasible solution, the nature of procedural law may not be compatible with compromises. It is to be expected that there will also be a gradual harmonisation of civil procedure, as the example of the US has shown, where there was not even a mandate to impose procedural rules on the states. It stresses that harmonisation should start from access to justice and the desire to reform and improve civil procedure, rather than for reasons of integration or harmonisation as an objective in itself.

Harmonisation at the global level does not pose these urgent questions, for the simple reason that there is no official encompassing body to establish binding rules. At the global level harmonisation is limited to conventions that are naturally subject to national ratification, and soft law. The conventions of the Hague Conference on Private International Law aim at the coordination or bridging of the different systems, without having the pretention to create a genuine unified procedural law. The same goes for UNCITRAL. Its 1958 New York Convention is the only ‘hard law’ in the area of civil procedure and has the sole purpose of creating a basis for the enforcement of foreign arbitral awards. It is submitted that though its aim and regulatory body is modest, its success is evidently unmatched. Its 2002 Model Law on International Commercial Conciliation is also witnessing a growing number of adhering jurisdictions. Meanwhile, the 2004 ALI/UNIDROIT

Principles and Rules of Transnational Civil Procedure have created an invaluable framework that may inspire both national and EU legislators.

It is interesting to note that, as the various national contributions to the current volume show, while EU institutes and private initiatives continue, the EU Member States and countries outside the EU offer *ad hoc* solutions to tackle the challenges of globalisation, such as the introduction of English as an official court language in Germany. At the same time, national jurisdictions gradually become more open to foreign procedural institutions and international standards of civil procedure, and resistance to harmonisation of civil procedure as a matter of principle seems to slowly evaporate. These developments demonstrate that comparative, international and harmonised procedural law is no longer an academic matter for a small group of specialists, but that it has entered the courtrooms and the offices of policy makers and legislators.

The current book shows that at the same time the scholarly debate is still alive, and more important than ever. The US contribution in the current Volume underlines how crucial the involvement of an academic elite is in the harmonisation of procedural law. With the challenges of globalisation and harmonisation as outlined above, the editors hope that this book offers valuable contributions to the debate and paves the way to further discussion and, where necessary, action.

References

ALI/UNIDROIT (2006) Principles of transnational civil procedure. Cambridge University Press, Cambridge

Gutteridge HC (1946) Comparative law: an introduction to the comparative method of legal study and research. Cambridge University Press, Cambridge

Ogus A (1999) Competition between national legal systems: a contribution of economic analysis to comparative law. Int Comp Law Q 48:405–418

Schulz A (2006) The Hague convention of 30 June 2005 on choice of court agreements. J Private Int Law 2:243–286

Part I
Different Perspectives on Globalisation and Harmonisation

Chapter 2
Fundamental Principles of Civil Procedure: Order Out of Chaos

Neil Andrews

Abstract There is a wide array of fundamental and important principles of civil justice. The main suggestion has been that the leading principles of civil justice might usefully be arranged under these four corner-stones of civil justice: Access to Legal Advice and Dispute-Resolution Systems; Equality and Fairness between the Parties; A Focused and Speedy Process; and Adjudicators of Integrity. Jurists and scholars of procedure will acknowledge the need to identify fundamental norms, but outside the hallowed halls of international colloquia or the court system, general principle is not widely respected. It is regarded with suspicion, especially by politicians and officials who might feel threatened and fettered by such generalities. The European Convention on Human Rights was a post-second world war response to the horrific collapse of all civilised values. Therefore, custodians of true civil justice should not become complacent. As our democratic systems become more and more hollow, procedural rights can provide some concrete protection for ordinary people. Another value of emphasising general principles is that they are an antidote to the numbing and bewildering complexity, detail, and technicality which characterise many national procedural rule books. Finally, international scholarly discussion thrives on fundamental principle. As we continue to debate the central procedural principles, students of civil justice will be standing on the shoulders of those celebrated jurists who have already contributed to this unending task by examining matters of first principle.

N. Andrews (✉)
University of Cambridge, Cambridge, UK
e-mail: nha1000@cam.ac.uk

X. E. Kramer and C. H. van Rhee (eds.), *Civil Litigation in a Globalising World*,
DOI: 10.1007/978-90-6704-817-0_2,

Contents

2.1 Introduction

The tendency of many national procedural systems is towards a proliferation of rules, sub-rules, and sub-sub-rules. This can produce over-detailed and unsystematic procedural regulation. This is clearly true in England, barely ten years after an injection of fundamental procedural aims and principles within the CPR system (1998). We are truly in search of order out of chaos: major principle rather than minutiae.

This tendency can be counter-balanced, even in due course corrected, by reference to generally recognised principles of civil procedure. Without a firm grasp of central and fundamental principles, we are in danger of becoming lost.

Another advantage of attention to general principle is that it can help legal systems move closer together, by reference to 'best practice.' There is so much national baggage, so much domestic clutter. Local detail can have a paralysing effect.

In Europe, harmonisation can be perceived at two levels: adjustment of national systems to ensure compliance with the procedural guarantees contained in, or implied by, Article 6(1) of the European Convention on Human Rights; secondly, regulations introduced to ensure pan-European Union adoption of rather more specific procedural institutions or practices.

Because of the welter of fundamental principles of civil justice that now jostle for recognition, and as the science of procedural law becomes ever more sophisticated, we need pointers, and groupings. My main suggestion will be that the leading principles of civil justice might usefully be arranged under four headings, which I have called the four corner-stones of civil justice. These are:

(1) Regulating access to court and to justice;
(2) Ensuring the fairness of the process;
(3) Maintaining a speedy and effective process;
(4) Achieving just and effective outcomes.

2.2 UNIDROIT/American Law Institute's Principles of Transnational Civil Procedure

The ALI (American Law Institute) and UNIDROIT's (International Institute for the Unification of Private Law) joint project, 'Principles and Rules of Transnational Civil Procedure' (2004),[1] aims to combine common law and civil law approaches to civil litigation. The general aim of composing a 'soft law' fusion of common law and civilian procedure was preceded ten years before, in 1994, by Marcel Storme's innovative project in Europe, a visionary search for shared civil procedural principles, combining civil and common law learning and experience.[2]

The ALI/UNIDROIT Principles offer a balanced distillation of best practice, especially in the sphere of transnational commercial litigation. They are not restricted to the largely uncontroversial 'high terrain' of constitutional guarantees of due process. Instead the project was skilfully pitched at the difficult mid-point between uncontroversial procedural axiom and the fine texture of national codes. The Principles are accompanied by Rules. The Rules are more detailed, fleshing out the more general Principles. And so the Rules offer greater guidance to national lawmakers who wish to use the Principles as a framework for revision of their procedural rules. As Geoffrey Hazard Jr. explained, the Rules are 'merely one among many possible ways of implementing the Principles.'[3]

The Principles and Rules were drafted by a team, appointed by the ALI and UNIDROIT. This team met for a total of 20 days in Rome during the years 2000–2003 (the present author was privileged to be a member). The General Reporters in Rome were Professors Hazard and Stürner, and in Washington DC, Professors Hazard and Taruffo. Within the Working Group, the nationalities represented were Argentina, Brazil, France, Germany, Italy, Japan, and Switzerland, and (from the other side of the common law/civil law fence) the USA and England.[4]

---

[1] The official text is ALI/UNIDROIT 2006, 157 et seq containing a full bibliography of works associated with this project; for large collection of papers (2001–4) 6 Uniform Law Review, a special issue under the title 'Harmonising Transnational Civil Procedure: the ALI/UNIDROIT Principles and Rules'; Andenas and Andrews 2006 (essays and comments by many senior British judges and leading practitioners and commentators on the draft UNIDROIT/ALI project); see also Fouchard 2001; Hazard et al. 2001; Stürner 2000; Stürner 2005, 201–254.

[2] Storme 1994 (Professor Marcel Storme is the long-serving President of the International Association of Procedural Law; he retired from that office in 2007; his successors are Professor Federico Carpi, Bologna, and Professor Peter Gottwald, Regensburg).

[3] ALI/UNIDROIT 2006, 99.

[4] The members of the drafting group were: Neil Andrews, University of Cambridge, UK; Professor Frédérique Ferrand, Lyon, France; Professor Pierre Lalive, formerly University of Geneva, in practice as an international commercial arbitrator, Switzerland; Professor Masanori Kawano, Nagoya University, Japan; Mme Justice Aida Kemelmajer de Carlucci, Supreme Court, Mendoza, Argentina; Professor Geoffrey Hazard Jr, USA; Professor Ronald Nhlapo, formerly of the Law Commission, South Africa; Professor Dr iur Rolf Stürner, University of Freiburg, Germany, and Judge at the Court of Appeals of the German State Baden-Württemberg, Karlsruhe; the assistant to these discussions was Antonio Gidi (USA and Brazil).

The 'Common Law' was clearly out-numbered seven to two by the 'Civil Law' representatives. It is also fair to say that the Civil Law members of the group were strong in resisting certain Common Law ideas. Everywhere the restraining hand of the Civil Law is visible and robust Common Law tendencies (American and English) are curbed.

It was apparent throughout the drafting group's discussions in Rome 2000–2003 that there were radical differences between the USA and English systems, and between the various civil law jurisdictions represented around the table. These differences make nonsense of both the glib phrase 'Anglo-American procedure' and the crude expression 'civilian procedure.' A refrain at these intense drafting sessions was, 'we do not have that institution in our own jurisdiction, but we would be interested in considering it'; or, 'the tradition in my jurisdiction is to regard that practice as wholly inconsistent with one of our fundamental starting-points; however, perhaps we have exaggerated the value of that starting-point.' Rolf Stürner, appointed to be the General Reporter of the UNIDROIT side of this collaborative project, has chronicled the working group's elaboration of these principles.[5]

As the author has suggested elsewhere[6] the Principles operate at three levels of importance: fundamental procedural guarantees,[7] other leading principles[8] and 'framework or incidental principles.'[9]

The author suggested that the ALI/UNIDROIT Principles range from (1) quasi-constitutional declarations of fundamental procedural guarantees to (2) major guidelines concerning the style and course of procedure to (3) points of important detail.[10]

---

[5] Stürner 2005, 201–254.

[6] Andrews 2006.

[7] Andrews 2006, 23, listing: judicial independence, judicial competence, judicial impartiality, procedural equality, right to assistance of counsel, professional independence of counsel, attorney-client privilege ('legal professional privilege'), due notice or the right to be heard, prompt and accelerated justice, the privilege against self-incrimination, publicity, and reasoned decisions.

[8] Andrews 2006, 23–24, listing: parties' duty to co-operate; party initiation of proceedings; party's definition of scope of proceedings; parties' right to amend pleadings; parties' right to discontinue or settle proceedings; judicial management of proceedings; sanctions against default and non-compliance; need for proportionality in use of sanctions; parties' duty to act fairly and to promote efficient and speedy proceedings; parties' duty to avoid false pleading and abuse of process; rights of access to information; right to oral stage of procedure; final hearing before ultimate adjudicators; judicial responsibility for correct application of the law; judicial initiative in evidential matters; judicial encouragement of settlement; basic costs shifting rule; finality of decisions; appeal mechanisms; effective enforcement; recognition by foreign courts; international judicial co-operation.

[9] Andrews 2006, 25, listing: the purpose and scope of the project; jurisdiction over parties; protection of parties lacking capacity; security for costs; venue rules; expedited forms of communication; pleadings; implied admissions; joinder rules; non-party submissions; allocation of burden and nature of standard of proof; making of judicial 'suggestions'; experts.

[10] Andrews 2006, 23.

Fundamental procedural guarantees:

- judicial competence; judicial independence; judicial impartiality; procedural equality; due notice or the right to be heard; publicity; reasoned decisions;
- prompt and accelerated justice;
- professional independence of counsel; right to assistance of counsel; attorney-client privilege ('legal professional privilege');
- privilege against self-incrimination.

Leading principles concerning the style and course of procedure:

- jurisdiction over parties; venue rules; party initiation of proceedings;
- party's definition of scope of proceedings; joinder rules; allocation of burden and nature of standard of proof; pleadings; parties' duty to avoid false pleading and abuse of process;
- rights of access to information; judicial initiative in evidential matters; experts;
- judicial management of proceedings; sanctions against default and non-compliance; need for proportionality in use of sanctions;
- parties' duty to act fairly and to promote efficient and speedy proceedings; parties' duty to co-operate;
- parties' right to discontinue or settle proceedings; judicial encouragement of settlement;
- right to oral stage of procedure; final hearing before ultimate adjudicators; judicial responsibility for correct application of the law;
- basic costs shifting rule; finality of decisions; appeal mechanisms;
- effective enforcement; recognition by foreign courts; international judicial co-operation.

Points of important detail:

- protection of parties lacking capacity; security for costs; expedited forms of communication; non-party submissions; making of judicial 'suggestions.'

As mentioned, the ALI/UNIDROIT project was not the first attempt at bridging the division between Civilian and Common Law procedures. Marcel Storme (and his team, including Tony Jolowicz) had led the way.[11] But, thus far, the ALI/UNIDROIT project is the most detailed identification of points of common ground.

The ALI/UNIDROIT Principles unfold as follows:

(1) Pre-Action Stage: the ALI/UNIDROIT materials say little about this stage other than possible provision of 'provisional and protective measures,' notably orders preserving assets against dissipation, in cases of 'urgent necessity' (Principle 8.2; Rule 17.2); neither the Principles nor the Rules adopt the English scheme of pre-action protocols[12];

[11] Storme 1994.

[12] Andrews 2007a, 201–242; Andrews 2008b, paras 2.26 et seq.

(2) Court's Composition: the requirements of independence, impartiality, 'substantial legal knowledge and experience,' equality of treatment, due notice, and publicity, are listed at Principles 1, 3, 5 and 20 and Rules 3.1, 7, 10 and 24; these requirements apply whenever the court is engaged in the conduct of the case, including an oral hearing, or creating a relevant court file or giving judgment; the question of venue is addressed at Principle 3.4 and Rule 3.3; the right to engage an independent lawyer is enshrined at Principle 4;
(3) Structure of the Proceedings: a three-fold division has been adopted: the 'pleading phase,' the 'interim phase,' and the 'final phase,' see Principle 9;
(4) Commencement and Service: commencement is effected by a party, not by the court, Principle 10.1; jurisdiction is determined in according with Principle 2 and Rule 4; service of originating notices is governed by Principle 5 and Rule 7 and 11; the question of joinder and intervention, as well as amicus curiae briefs, are governed by Principles 12 and 14 and Rules 5 and 6;
(5) Pleadings: statements of claim and defences are regulated by Principle 11.3, and by Rules 11, 12 and 13; amendments to pleadings by Principle 10.4 and Rule 14; default judgment for failure to defend is covered by Rule 15; Rules 15.1 and 19 concern early dismissal of defective pleadings or hopeless cases; the scope of the proceedings is determined by the parties' pleadings, as acknowledged by Principle 10.3;
(6) Case Management by Court: Principles 7.2, 9.3, 11.2, 14, and 17 are relevant; Rule 18 provides detail on this important aspect of modern commercial practice; encouragement of 'ADR' is noted at Principle 24.2 and Rule 18.5; separation of claims is covered by Principle 12.5 and Rule 5.6;
(7) Sanctions against Parties, Lawyers, or Non-parties: this difficult topic attracts attention in Principle 17 (and Principles 5.1, 15, and 21.2) and Rule 35.2;
(8) Preparation of Evidence, including Access to Information: on the court's powers to receive evidence, or even in some situations positively to order its production, see Principles 9.3, 9.4, 16, 18, 19, 22 and Rules 20, 21 to 23, 25, 27, 28;
(9) Expert Opinion: this can be by party-appointed expert or, where appropriate, court-appointed 'neutral expert or panel': Principle 22.4, and Rule 26;
(10) 'Early Court Determinations,' 'Dismissal and Default Judgments,' and 'Provisional and Protective Measures': these very important matters are covered by Principles 2.3, 5.8, 8, 9.3.3, 9.3.5, 15, and by Rules 15, 17, 19, 36.2;
(11) Final Hearing: the 'hearing' or receipt of evidence at the final phase is governed by Principle 19 and Rules 29 to 31; the court's responsibility to apply the law is stated at Principle 22.1; the giving of reasoned judgments at Principle 23 and Rule 31.2; for the requirements of judicial independence, impartiality, the court's possession of 'substantial legal knowledge and

experience,' public access, and independent legal representation, see (2) above;

(12) Res Judicata: this matter is considered at Principle 28;

(13) Costs Decisions: these are regulated by Principle 25 and Rule 32 (on security for costs see also Principle 3.3 and Rule 32.9; and on costs in support of settlement offers, Rule 16);

(14) Possible Appeal: Principle 27 governs; for greater detail, see Rules 33 and 34;

(15) Enforcement: this is regulated by Principle 26 and Principle 29, and Rule 35;

(16) Cross-Border Recognition of Judgments and Judicial Co-operation: on this see Principles 30 and 31 and Rule 36.

The drafters of the Principles acknowledged that there is scope for radical differences of approach on aspects of practice. Such agnosticism pervades discussion of the following topics: sanctions for procedural default, receipt of expert evidence, examination of witnesses, and the system of appeal (see above at (7)–(9), and (14), for references). Should the drafting party have been more decisive on these points and less agnostic? The better view is that these were intellectually honest decisions. They reveal the radical split between different traditions based on principled contrasting approaches. This is more likely to be helpful to future advisors than a confusing statement of an illusory compromise or a mistaken statement of 'universal common ground.' In short, *vive la différence*: provided the procedural difference between one nation's system (or family of nations) and another's is real and fundamental, and no international preference or accepted compromise can be discerned.

The ALI/UNIDROIT text was widely admired by the English commentators, who found this work to be suggestive, original, and flexible. Professor Adrian Zuckerman encapsulated that English consensus as follows[13]:

> Plurality of procedure encourages experimentation and promotes evolutionary progress. Jurisdictional competition could … lead to improvement in dispute resolution. It might, therefore, be better to direct the efforts in this area not so much towards an unified procedural system for transnational cases but towards establishment of general normative standards that allow for considerable variations. Community of general standards would facilitate easier mutual recognition of judgments and … enable different jurisdictions to find their own way of providing adjudication that is effective and attractive …

Although the ALI/UNIDROIT project is relatively young (completed in 2004, published in 2006), it seems likely that it will assist greatly in the intellectual mapping of civil justice and that it will influence policy-makers. If the project is re-opened at some point, fundamental change of the existing Principles is unlikely.

[13] Zuckerman 2002, 322.

Change is more likely to take the form of addenda rather than delenda or corrigenda. Thus some new or emerging topics might be considered at a revision council:

- pre-action co-ordination of exchanges between the potential litigants[14];
- multi-party litigation (this is a 'hot' and controversial topic within the USA, Europe,[15] including England,[16] Canada, Australia, and Brazil); and greater attention might be given to:
- the interplay of mediation and litigation[17];
- costs and funding (in England, the expense of litigation is the greatest impediment to effective civil justice);
- evidential privileges and immunities (notably, attorney-client privilege, protection of negotiation and mediation discussions, and the privilege against self-incrimination)[18]; and
- transnational 'provisional and protective relief'[19] (notably, asset preservation).

On the question whether it is desirable to maintain competition between jurisdictions to maintain competition or national experiment in the fashioning and refinement of civil procedure, the consensus emerging at the discussion of the (then) draft ALI/UNIDROIT Principles and Rules held at the British Institute for International and Comparative Law in May 2002 by leading English judges and commentators was this[20]: 'international uniformity on all points of procedural detail is an unattractive goal, but agreement on fundamental values and doctrines is desirable' (the author has developed this idea elsewhere).[21] In London the ALI/UNIDROIT project was greeted as stimulating and suggestive, and as a fruitful example of 'soft law.' Beyond that, however, there should be scope for national differences in that most delicate of legal activities: administering litigation in a fair and flexible fashion, remaining true to fundamental principles of fairness, but against the background of national traditions.

---

14 Andrews 2007a, 201–242.

15 Hodges 2008.

16 Andrews 2008a, 92–97.

17 Andrews 2008b; Andrews 2005, 1–34; Andrews 2007d, 1–9; Andrews 2007c, 1–43.

18 In England this is a fast-moving and delicate topic, Andrews 2008a, b, paras 6.26–6.40; leading works include: Andrews 2003a, chs 25, 27–30; Tapper 2007, chs IX, X; Hollander 2006, chs 11–20; Matthews and Malek 2007; Howard et al. 2005, chs 23–26; Passmore 2006; Thanki 2006, Zuckerman 2006, chs 15–18; see also, Auburn 2000.

19 Andrews 2003b; published also in Andrews 2002, 48–56.

20 Andenas 2003.

21 Andrews 2008b, paras 13.24 et seq; Andrews 2007e, 829–851.

2.3 What Really Counted Before the CPR (1998)? Principles Within the Old English Civil Procedure System

Having been given an opportunity in the mid 1980s to teach civil procedure in Cambridge, I wrote Principles of Civil Procedure (1994).[22] The eleven principles selected in that text were[23]:

- due notice;
- pre-trial disclosure;
- protection against spurious claims and defences;
- justice is not to be evaded;
- accelerated justice;
- oral proceedings;
- publicity;
- promoting settlement;
- finality;
- the adversarial principle;
- the principle of privity.

Some of these had been highlighted by Sir Jack Jacob in his The Fabric of English Civil Justice (1987).[24] In Principles of Civil Procedure (1994) I said that these eleven principles 'lie within the realm of practical politics.' I then mentioned the following three 'noble aims,' and expressed doubt whether they might ever 'be fully attained'[25]:

(1) access to justice;
(2) prevention of undue delay;
(3) management of complex litigation.

2.4 'Woolf Changes' of Principle: CPR (1998)

On 28 March 1994 Lord Mackay LC of Clashfern (Lord Chancellor 1987–1997) appointed Lord Woolf to make recommendations concerning civil procedure, with the following aims[26]: (i) improving access to justice and reducing the cost of litigation (ii) reducing the complexity of the rules (iii) modernising terminology (iv) removing unnecessary distinctions of practice and procedure. Woolf's interim

---

22 Andrews 1994.
23 Andrews 1994, paras 2-003 et seq.
24 Hamlyn Lectures for the year 1986.
25 Andrews 1994, 2-013.
26 Terms of appointment cited in Woolf 1995, introduction.

and final reports appeared in 1995[27] and 1996,[28] and they stimulated a substantial literature.[29] The CPR was enacted in 1998 and took effect on 26 April 1999.

From the perspective of overarching principle, the main features[30] of this exciting fresh start involved recognition of nine leading principles, values, or aims:

- proportionality in the conduct of proceedings;
- procedural equality;
- introducing general judicial case-management responsibilities;
- accelerated access to justice by improved summary procedures;
- increasing focus and reducing cost by curbing excessive documentary disclosure;
- greater resort to the disciplinary use of costs orders;
- curbing appeals by requiring permission;
- stimulating settlement through costs incentives to induce parties to accept settlement offers; and
- judicial encouragement of resort to ADR, notably mediation.

These bare points are fleshed out in the following nine sub-paragraphs.

'The Overriding Objective' in CPR Part 1 gives prominence to the notion of 'proportionality' both in the organisation of levels of procedure—small claims, fast-track, or multi-track proceedings[31]—and in the exercise of the court's extensive case-management powers.[32]

Part 1 also emphasises the requirement of procedural equality.

The principle of party-control was modified.[33] The CPR created a general framework for active involvement of judges in the pre-trial development of moderately or extremely complex litigation. Judges are required to ensure that litigation proceeds with reasonable speed and that the issues are identified and

---

[27] Woolf 1995: it and its successor are available on-line at http://www.dca.gov.uk/civil/reportfr.htm (last consulted in May 2011).

[28] Access to Justice: Final Report (1996).

[29] Zuckerman and Cranston 1995; Cranston 2006; Andrews 2003a, Andrews 2000, 19–38; Flanders 1998, 308; Jolowicz 1996, 198; Zander 1997, 208; Zander 1998; Zuckerman 1997, 31 et seq.

[30] The author's most recent examinations of the CPR system are: Andrews 2008b (also considering the rise of ADR); and Andrews 2010.

[31] Respectively, CPR Parts 27, 28, 29.

[32] CPR 1.4(2); CPR 3.1(2); CPR Parts 26, 28, 29; Andrews 2008b, 3.13 et seq; Andrews 2007b, (see now the new Admiralty and Commercial Courts Guide 2009, Section D, 17–31; and note the anxious discussions engendered by 'rogue' 'super-cases': the Long Trials Working Party Report December 2007; and a pilot scheme during 2008; for the background, Sir Anthony Clarke MR, The Supercase-Problems and Solutions, 2007 Annual KPMG Forensic Lecture, available at http://www.judiciary.gov.uk/docs/speeches/_speech.pdf (last consulted [May 2011]).

[33] On the CPR system from the perspective of the traditional principle of party control, Andrews 2000, 19–38; Andrews 2003a, paras 13.12–13.41; 14.04–14.45; 15.65–15.72.

prioritised. At trial (and during its preparation), judges should control the volume of evidence.

But there are limits to judicial initiative: Parties still select factual witnesses and draw up witness statements[34]; parties still select party-appointed experts (they can also agree upon selection of a single, joint expert, this 'shared' expert being an innovation of the CPR system); judicial permission to use experts is required, but judicial selection of individual experts is avoided, unless the parties reach stalemate in agreeing a single, joint expert[35]; the Court of Appeal has said that excessive intervention by trial judges during the course of evidence is prohibited because it would be wrong for a judge to 'arrogate to himself a quasi-inquisitorial role,' this being something which is 'entirely at odds with the adversarial system.'[36] Summary disposal of cases is promoted by introduction of a more searching test of 'real prospect of success,' in CPR Part 24.[37]

'Standard disclosure' was intended to subject documentary discovery to a more focused notion of relevance. 'Standard disclosure'[38] covers documents on which a party will rely; or which adversely affect his case; or adversely affect the opponent's case; or support the opponent's case.

Procedural discipline would be reinforced by a more discretionary approach to costs decisions.[39] The courts could adjust costs awards and so reflect the fact that a victorious party had raised unnecessary issues. Lord Woolf MR in *AEI Rediffusion Music Ltd v Phonographic Performance Ltd* (1999), attempting to temper the perceived rigidity of the 'winner takes all' approach, said:

> too robust an application of the 'follow the event principle' encourages litigants to increase the costs of litigation'; and he suggested 'if you recover all your costs as long as you win, you are encouraged to leave no stone unturned in your effort to do so.[40]

Finality of judgment would be fortified by the requirement that an appellant would require permission to appeal.[41]

Nearly all appeals require the court to give its permission (formerly known as 'leave'),[42] in response to the appellant's speedy request to the first instance court

---

[34] Andrews 2008b, paras 8.04 et seq.

[35] On these aspects of CPR Part 35, Andrews 2008b; Dwyer, 2008.

[36] *Southwark LBC v Maamefowaa Kofiadu* [2006] EWCA Civ 281, at [148].

[37] CPR 24.2: *Swain v Hillman* [2001] 1 *All ER* 91, 92, CA; Andrews 2008b, paras 5.18 et seq.

[38] CPR 31.6; Andrews 2008b, paras 6.04, 6.22; on the pre-CPR excessive documentary disclosure system, Lord Woolf 1995, paras 1–9 (commenting on the 'Peruvian Guano' test: *Compagnie Financière v Peruvian Guano Co* 11 QBD 1882, 55, 63, CA); Steyn 1992; Cranston 2007, 190, 203.

[39] Andrews 2008b, 9.09 et seq.

[40] [1999] 1 *WLR* 1507, 1522-3, CA.

[41] Andrews 2008b, paras 8.12 et seq.

[42] CPR 52.3(1): except decisions affecting a person's liberty.

(normally within fourteen days[43]; a period which cannot be extended by party agreement).[44] If the lower court refuses permission, a fresh application for permission can be made to the appeal court.

Settlement would be promoted by the capacity of both claimants and defendants to make settlement offers backed by costs sanctions.[45]

In essence: under the English CPR system, Part 36, the claimant's costs risk arises if he does not accept the defendant's settlement offer. In that situation, if the claimant at trial 'fails to obtain a judgment more advantageous than a defendant's Part 36 offer,' then, 'unless [the court] considers it unjust to do so,' the claimant must pay the defendant's costs incurred after the date when the claimant should have accepted the settlement offer. The defendant will only be liable for the claimant's costs incurred before that date.

The defendant's costs risk arises if he does not accept the claimant's settlement offer. If 'judgment against the defendant is at least as advantageous to the claimant as the proposals contained in a claimant's Part 36 offer,' then, 'unless [the court] considers it unjust to do so,' the defendant will be liable to pay the claimant not just the ordinary measure of costs ('standard' costs) but an aggravated measure (so-called 'indemnity costs'), with the further possibility of a high level of interest on those costs.

The courts were charged with the duty to promote resort to ADR,[46] especially mediation, through use of costs orders,[47] and the staying of proceedings.[48]v

2.5 Article 6(1) European Convention on Human Rights

The (British) Human Rights Act 1998, which took effect in October 2000, rendered the European Convention on Human Rights directly applicable in English courts. Article 6(1) of the Convention states[49]:

> Right to a Fair Trial: In the determination of his civil rights and obligations or of any criminal charge against him, everyone is entitled to a fair and public hearing within a reasonable time by an independent and impartial tribunal established by law.

---

43 CPR 52.4(2); appeals out of time will only exceptionally be permitted: *Smith v Brough* [2005] *EWCA* 261; [2006] *CP Rep* 17.

44 CPR 52.6(1) (2).

45 Andrews 2008b, paras 10.15 et seq.

46 CPR 1.4(2)(e).

47 Notably, *Dunnett v Railtrack plc* [2002] 1 *WLR* 2434, CA; *Halsey v Milton Keynes General NHA Trust* [2004] 1 *WLR* 3002, CA; *Nigel Witham Ltd v Smith* [2008] *EWHC* 12 (TCC) at [36] (J Sorabji 27 *CJQ* (2008) 427); on this line of cases, Andrews 2008b, paras 11.40 et seq.

48 CPR 3.1(2)(f); Andrews, 2008b, para 11.31.

49 Cmd 8969; Human Rights Act 1998, s 1(3) Sch 1 incorporates the European Convention on Human Rights into UK law; Grocz et al. 2008; Janies et al. 2008; Clayton and Tomlinson 2008.

That important codification of fundamental principle consists of the following elements:

The right to 'a fair hearing': this is a wide concept embracing[50]:

- the right to be present at an adversarial hearing;
- the right to equality of arms;
- the right to fair presentation of the evidence;
- the right to cross examine opponents' witnesses;
- the right to a reasoned judgment[51];
- 'a public hearing': including the right to a public pronouncement of judgment[52];
- 'a hearing within a reasonable time'; and
- 'a hearing before an independent[53] and impartial[54] tribunal established by law.'

Of great interest is that the Strasbourg court divined an implicit fundamental right of 'access to court.' Lord Bingham in *Brown v Stott* (2001) explained[55]: Article 6(1) contains no express right of access to justice, but in *Golder v UK* the European Court of Human Rights said that it was 'inconceivable' that this provision should give detailed procedural guarantees without protecting access to justice.[56] The court in the Golder case conceded that this implied right was not absolute and so admitted limitations.[57]

The Court of Appeal in *English v Emery Reimbold & Strick Ltd* (2002) noted that Article 6(1) requires a court to provide a reasoned judgment[58]: The [ECHR]

50 Clayton and Tomlinson 2008, ch 11.

51 Andrews 2003a, paras 5.39–5.68.

52 Andrews 2003a, 4.59-end of chapter; Strasbourg authorities cited, Andrews 2003a, 7.21–7.79.

53 *Starrs v Ruxton* 2000 *JC* 208, 243; 17 November 1999 *The Times* (High Court of Justiciary) *per* Lord Reed; *Millar v Dickson* [2002] 1 *WLR* 1615, PC; s 3, Constitutional Reform Act 2005 (UK) states: 'The Lord Chancellor, other Ministers of the Crown and all with responsibility for matters relating to the judiciary or otherwise to the administration of justice must uphold the continued independence of the judiciary.' 'The Lord Chancellor and other Ministers of the Crown must not seek to influence particular judicial decisions through any special access to the judiciary.' 'The Lord Chancellor must have regard to (a) the need to defend that independence; (b) the need for the judiciary to have the support necessary to enable them to exercise their functions; (c) the need for the public in regard to matters relating to the judiciary or otherwise to the administration of justice to be properly represented in decisions affecting those matters.'.

54 *Porter v Magill* [2002] 2 *AC* 357, HL.

55 [2003] 1 *AC* 681, 694, PC.

56 (1975) 1 *EHRR* 524, 536, at [35].

57 Ibidem, at [38].

58 [2002] *EWCA* Civ 605; [2002] 1 *WLR* 2409, CA, at [12] (adumbrated by *Flannery v Halifax Estate Agencies Ltd* [2000] 1 *WLR* 377, CA; noted Jolowicz, [2000] *CLJ* 263 (judge must give intelligible reasons for rejecting one side's expert testimony and preferring the other side's; a common law decision which ante-dated commencement of the Human Rights Act on 2 October 2000).

… requires that a judgment should contain reasons that are sufficient to demonstrate that the essential issues that have been raised by the parties have been addressed by the domestic court and how those issues have been resolved. It does not seem … that the Strasbourg jurisprudence goes further and requires a judgment to explain why one contention, or piece of evidence, has been preferred to another.

2.6 Author's Second List of Principles: English Civil Procedure (2003)

Having participated in the ALI/UNIDROIT project, and stimulated by the first years of the brave new CPR world, in English Civil Procedure (2003) I decided to look again at the kaleidoscope of procedural principle because it was obvious that new patterns had emerged. In Chapters 4 to 6 of my 0 no fewer than twenty-four major principles.

- Judicial Independence;
- Judicial Impartiality;
- Publicity or Open Justice;
- The Principle of Due Notice;
- Judicial Duty to Give Reasons;
- Avoidance of Undue Delay;
- Litigants are Not to be Prejudiced by the Court's Culpable Shortcomings;
- Access to Justice;
- Right to Choose a Lawyer;
- Confidential Legal Consultation;
- Procedural Equality;
- Protection against Bad or Spurious Claims and Defences;
- Simplicity of Procedure;
- Judicial Control of the Civil Process;
- Proportionality;
- Disclosure;
- Oral Proceedings;
- Procedural Equity;
- Promoting Settlement;
- Accuracy;
- Fair Play Between Litigants;
- Protection of Non-Parties;
- Effectiveness;
- Finality.

2.7 Order Out of Chaos: The Four Corner-Stones of Civil Justice[59]

I suggest that principles of civil justice can be usefully arranged under four headings, which I call the four corner-stones of civil justice:

(1) Regulating Access to Court and to Justice;
(2) Ensuring the Fairness of the Process;
(3) Maintaining a Speedy and Effective Process;
(4) Achieving Just and Effective Outcomes.

In greater detail, this is how the various leading and fundamental principles of civil justice can be arranged using this four-fold classification.

REGULATING ACCESS TO COURT AND TO JUSTICE

- Access to Justice;
- Right to Choose a Lawyer;
- Confidential Legal Consultation;
- Protection against Spurious Claims and Defences;
- Promoting Settlement and Facilitating Resort to Alternative Forms of Dispute-Resolution, notably Mediation and Arbitration.

ENSURING THE FAIRNESS OF THE PROCESS

- Judicial Independence;
- Judicial Impartiality;
- Publicity or Open Justice;
- Procedural Equality (equal respect for the parties);
- Fair Play between the Parties;
- Judicial Duty to Avoid Surprise: The Principle of Due Notice;
- Equal Access to Information, including Disclosure of Information between Parties.

MAINTAINING A SPEEDY AND EFFICIENT PROCESS

- Judicial Control of the Civil Process to Ensure Focus and Proportionality (tempered, where appropriate, by Procedural Equity; the process is not to be administered in an oppressive manner);
- Avoidance of Undue Delay.

---

[59] The author's decision to seek to re-order his 2003 long list of 24 principles (Andrews 2003a, ch's 4–6) was prompted by Shimon Shetreet during conversation in Cambridge in March 2010, and at a Colloquium in Clare College, May 21, 2010, in honour of Professor Kurt Lipstein. But Shimon Shetreet and I differ on how best to arrange these principles.

ACHIEVING JUST AND EFFECTIVE OUTCOMES

- Judicial Duty to Give Reasons;
- Accuracy of Decision-making;
- Effectiveness (provision of protective relief and enforcement of judgments);
- Finality.

2.8 Conclusion

There is a wide array of fundamental and important principles of civil justice. The lists can almost overwhelm us. And so we need pointers, and groupings. My main suggestion has been that the leading principles of civil justice might usefully be arranged under four headings, which I have called the four corner-stones of civil justice. These are:

- Regulating Access to Court and to Justice;
- Ensuring the Fairness of the Process;
- Maintaining a Speedy and Effective Process;
- Achieving Just and Effective Outcomes.

Of course, jurists and scholars of procedure will acknowledge readily the need to identify the basic or fundamental norms of their field of study and practice. But outside the hallowed halls of international colloquia or outside the court system, general principle is not widely respected. Indeed it is regarded with suspicion, especially by politicians and officials who might feel threatened and fettered by such generalities. Ever more aggressive, controlling, manipulative, and cynical government systems have taught us not to take anything for granted. And of course the European Convention on Human Rights was a post-second world war response to the horrific collapse of all civilised values.

Therefore, custodians of true civil justice should not become complacent. As our democratic systems become more and more hollow, procedural rights can provide some concrete protection for ordinary people. If judges continue to display high ethical standards governed by this demanding set of procedural principles, other forms of public life might shape up.

Another value of emphasising general principles is that they are an antidote to the numbing and bewildering complexity, detail, and technicality which sadly characterise many national procedural rule books. Certainly this has become a problem in England which, since 1998, has witnessed an oppressive proliferation of pre-action protocols, procedural rules, supplemented by Practice Directions, transmuted by Guides to different branches of the High Court (the 2009 edition of the Commercial Court Guide is 222 pages long). This deluge of micro-detail has rendered the search for overarching and underpinning norms even more important.

Finally, international scholarly discussion thrives on fundamental principle.[60] It is the life-blood. As we continue to debate the membership of the canon of central procedural principles, students of civil justice will be standing on the shoulders of those celebrated jurists who have already contributed to this unending task by examining matters of first principle.[61] For these have become the heroes of procedural scholarship, and I congratulate them on the stimulating work which has already been achieved.

References

ALI/UNIDROIT (2006) Principles and rules of transnational civil procedure. Cambridge University Press, Cambridge

Andenas M et al (eds) (2006) The future of transnational commercial litigation: English responses to the ALI/UNIDROIT draft principles and rules of transnational civil procedure. British Institute of Comparative and International Law, London

Andrews N (1994) Principles of civil procedure. Thomson Professional Publishing, Canada

Andrews N (2000) A new civil procedural code for England: party-control "going, going, gone". Civ Justice Q 19:19–38

Andrews N (2002) Provisional and protective measures: towards an uniform protective order in civil matters. Unif Law Rev 6:931–949

Andrews N (2003a) English civil procedure. Oxford University Press, Oxford

Andrews N (2003b) Towards an European protective order in civil matters. In: Storme M (ed) Procedural laws in Europe: towards harmonisation. Maklu, Antwerp, pp 267–304

Andrews N (2005) Alternative dispute resolution in England. Zeitschrift für Zivilprozess International 10:1–34

---

[60] In the English language, these include: Jolowicz 2000; Cappelletti and Perillo 1965; Cappelletti 1976; Langbein 1985, 823–866; Damaska 1986; Cappelletti 1989; Storme 1994; AAS Zuckerman 1999; Rechberger and Klicka 2002; Asser et al. 2003, 329–387; Storme 2003; Storme and Hess 2003; Murray and Stürner 2004; Van Rhee 2005; Trocker and Varano 2005; Chase et al. 2007; Pellegrini Grinover and Calmon 2007, 201–242; Van Rhee 2007; Van Rhee and Uzelac 2007; Deguchi and Storme 2008; Van Rhee and Uzelac 2010. And on 'transnational principles,' Storme 1994, and ALI/UNIDROIT 2006; on this project, Kronke 2002; Andenas et al. 2006; Stürner 2005, 201–254; Walker and Chase 2010.

[61] Besides the authors listed in the preceding note, consider the following transnational or comparative works and projects (presented here in chronological order):

(1) Storme 1994; see also Storme 2003; Storme and Hess 2003;
(2) Jolowicz 2000;
(3) The contributors to ALI/UNIDROIT 2006;
(4) Shimon Shetreet, Mount Scopus International Standards of Judicial Independence (a continuing project);
(5) The Nagoya/Freiburg project on 'A New Framework for Transnational Business Litigation,' a project led by Professor Masanori Kawano; the published works in this series (so far) are: Stürner and Kawano 2009; national studies: Andrews 2007b; Ervo 2009; Eslugues-Mota and Barona-Vilar 2009; Kengyel and Harsagi 2010; Andrews 2010; Maniotis and Tsantinis 2010; Schmidt 2010; De Cristofaro and Trocker 2010.

Andrews N (2006) Embracing the noble quest for transnational procedural principles. In: Andenas M et al (eds) The future of transnational commercial litigation: English responses to the ALI-UNIDROIT draft principles and rules of transnational civil procedure. British Institute of International and Comparative Law, London, pp 21–43

Andrews N (2007a) General report. In: Pellegrini GA, Calmon P (eds) Direito processual comparado: XIII World Congress of procedural law. Editora Forense, Rio de Janeiro, pp 201–241

Andrews N (2007b) English civil justice and remedies: progress and challenges: Nagoya lectures. Shinzan Sha Publishers, Tokyo

Andrews N (2007c) I Metodi Alternativi di Risoluzione delle Controversie in Inghliterra. In: Varano V (ed) L'Altra Giustizia. Giuffre Editore, Milano, pp 1–36

Andrews N (2007d) Mediation: a pillar of civil justice in modern English practice. Zeitschrift für Zivilprozess Int 12:1–9

Andrews N (2007e) La Giustizia Civil Inglese e Il Mondo Esterno. Rivista Trimestrale di Diritto e Procedura Civile 61:829–851

Andrews N (2008a) Multi-party litigation in England: current arrangements and proposals for change. Int'l Lis 2:92–97

Andrews N (2008b) The modern civil process. Mohr Siebeck, Tübingen

Andrews N (2010) Contracts and English dispute resolution. Jigakusha Publishing, Tokyo

Asser D et al (eds) (2003) A summary of the interim report on fundamental review of the Dutch law of civil procedure. Zeitschrift für Zivilprozess International 8:329–387

Auburn J (2000) Legal professional privilege: law and theory. Hart, Oxford

Cappelletti M (1976) International encyclopaedia of comparative law, vol XVI. Civil procedure. Mohr Siebeck, Tübingen

Cappelletti M (1989) The judicial process in comparative perspective. Oxford University Press, Oxford

Cappelletti M, Perillo J (1965) Civil procedure in Italy. Martinus Nijhoff, The Hague

Chase O et al (eds) (2007) Civil procedure in comparative context. Thomson/West, St. Paul

Clarke AMR (2007) The supercase-problems and solutions. Annual KPMG forensic lecture. Available at http://www.judiciary.gov.uk/docs/speeches/kpmg_speech.pdf (Accessed May 2011)

Clayton R, Tomlinson H (2008) The law of human rights. Oxford University Press, Oxford

Cranston R (2006) How law works: the machinery and impact of civil justice. Oxford University Press, Oxford

Cranston R (2007) Complex litigation: the commercial court. Civ Justice Q 26:190–203

Damaska M (1986) The faces of justice and state authority: a comparative approach to the legal process. Yale University Press, New Haven

De Cristofaro M, Trocker N (2010) Civil justice in Italy. Jigakusha Publishing, Tokyo

Deguchi M, Storme M (2008) The reception and transmission of civil procedural law in the global society. Maklu, Antwerp

Dwyer D (2008) The judicial assessment of expert evidence. Cambridge University Press, Cambridge

Ervo L (2009) Civil justice in Finland. Jigakusha Publishing, Tokyo

Eslugues-Mota C, Barona-Vilar C (eds) (2009) Civil justice in Spain. Jigakusha Publishing, Tokyo

Flanders S (1998) Case management: failure in America? Success in England and Wales? Civ Justice Q 17:308–319

Fouchard P (2001) Vers un Procès Civil Universel? Les Règles Transnationales de Procédure Civile de L'American Law Institute. Panthéon-Assas, Paris I

Grocz S et al (eds) (2008) Human rights: the 1998 Act and the European convention. Sweet & Maxwell, London

Hazard G Jr et al (eds) (2001) Principles and rules of transnational civil procedure. NY Univ J Int Law Politics 33: 769–785

Hodges C (2008) The reform of class and representative actions in European legal systems. Hart Publishing, Oxford
Hollander C (2006) Documentary evidence. Sweet & Maxwell, London
Howard M et al (eds) (2005) Phipson on evidence, 16th edn. Sweet & Maxwell, London
Janies MW et al (2008) European human rights law: text and materials. Oxford University Press, Oxford
Jolowicz JA (1996) The Woolf report and the adversary system. Civ Justice Q 15:198–209
Jolowicz JA (2000) On civil procedure. Cambridge University Press, Cambridge
Kengyel M, Harsagi V (2010) Civil justice in Hungary. Jigakusha Publishing, Tokyo
Kronke H (ed) (2002) Special issue of the Uniform Law Review, vol VI
Langbein J (1985) The German advantage in civil procedure. Univ Chic Law Rev 52:823–866
Maniotis D, Tsantinis S (2010) Civil justice in Greece. Jigakusha Publishing, Tokyo
Matthews P, Malek H (2007) Disclosure. Sweet & Maxwell, London
Murray PL, Stürner R (2004) German civil justice. Durham, USA
Passmore C (2006) Privilege. XPL, Hertfordshire
Pellegrini GA, Calmon R (eds) (2007) Direito Processual Comparado: XIII World Congress of procedural law, Editora Forense, Rio de Janeiro, pp 201–242
Rechberger W, Klicka T (2002) Procedural law on the threshold of a new millenium XI. World Congress of procedural law. Center for legal competence, Vienna
Schmidt S (2010) Civil justice in France. Jigakusha Publishing, Tokyo
Steyn J (1992) Preface. In: Hodge C, Mathews G (eds) Discovery. Sweet & Maxwell, London
Storme M (1994) Approximation of judiciary law in the European union. Kluwer, Dordrecht
Storme M (ed) (2003) Procedural laws in Europe. Towards harmonization. Maklu, Antwerp
Storme M, Hess B (eds) (2003) Discretionary power of the judge: limits and control. Kluwer, Mechelen
Stürner R (2000) Some European remarks on a new joint project of the American Law Institute and UNIDROIT. Int Lawyer 34:1071–1086
Stürner R (2005) The principles of transnational civil procedure. Rabels Zeitschrift 69:201–254
Stürner R, Kawano M (eds) (2009) Current topics of international litigation. Mohr Siebeck, Tübingen
Tapper C (2007) Cross and tapper on evidence. Oxford University Press, Oxford
Thanki B (2006) The law of privilege. Oxford University Press, Oxford
Trocker N, Varano V (eds) (2005) The reforms of civil procedure in comparative perspective. Editori G. Giappichelli, Torino
Van Rhee CH (ed) (2005) European traditions in civil procedure. Intersentia, Oxford
Van Rhee CH (ed) (2007) The law's delay. Essays on undue delay in civil litigation. Intersentia, Antwerp
Van Rhee CH, Uzelac A (eds) (2007) Public and private justice. Intersentia, Antwerp
Van Rhee CH, Uzelac A (eds) (2010) Enforcement and enforceability. Intersentia, Oxford
Walker J, Chase O (2010) Common law, civil law: the future of categories—categories of the future. Lexis Nexis, Markham
Woolf H (1995) Access to justice: interim report. Available at http://www.dca.gov.uk/civil/reportfr.htm (Accessed May 2011)
Zander M (1997) The Woolf report, forwards or backwards for the new Lord Chancellor? Civ Justice Q 16:208–227
Zander M (1998) The government's plans on civil justice. Mod Law Rev Ltd 61:383–389
Zuckerman AAS (1997) The Woolf report on access to justice. Zeitschrift für Zivilprozess International 2:31–42
Zuckerman AAS (1999) Civil justice in crisis: comparative perspectives of civil procedure. Oxford University Press, Oxford
Zuckerman AAS (2002) Conference on the ALI-UNIDROIT principles and rules of transnational civil procedure. Civ Justice Q 21:322–325

Zuckerman AAS (2006) Zuckerman on civil procedure: principles of practice. Sweet & Maxwell, London
Zuckerman AAS, Cranston R (1995) The reform of civil procedure: essays on 'access to justice'. Oxford University Press, Oxford

Chapter 3
Harmonisation of Civil Procedure: An Historical and Comparative Perspective

C. H. van Rhee

Abstract This chapter focuses on the harmonisation of civil procedural law in Europe and on a global scale. As the title indicates, this will be done by also taking into consideration past experiences in this field. The question as to the desirability of harmonisation will not be discussed. The chapter will especially focus on (1) Harmonisation as a result of national law reform, (2) Harmonisation as a result of competition between procedural systems, and (3) Harmonisation as a result of international harmonisation projects.

Contents

Professor of European Legal History and Comparative Civil Procedure at Maastricht University, The Netherlands

---

C. H. van Rhee (✉)
Maastricht University, Maastricht, The Netherlands
e-mail: remco.vanrhee@maastrichtuniversity.nl

X. E. Kramer and C. H. van Rhee (eds.), *Civil Litigation in a Globalising World*,
DOI: 10.1007/978-90-6704-817-0_3,

3.1 Introduction

A first glance at the various civil procedural systems of our modern world shows considerable disparities. One of the explanations for this is often found in the historical differences in the approach to civil litigation in what may be called the Common Law and Civil Law families of civil procedure.[1] However, this explanation may not be sufficient anymore, since even within the two main families of civil procedure the differences are sometimes large. The author of the previous chapter has even stated that because of this the dichotomy between Civil Law and Common Law may have lost much of its relevance.[2] The truth of this statement may be demonstrated by comparing England and Wales (shortly 'England' hereafter) and the United States of America. As all comparative procedural lawyers will know, in England the jury has nearly disappeared from civil trials,[3] whereas the right to a jury trial is a constitutional right in the US.[4] It is also a known fact that the role of pre-trial discovery (currently known as disclosure in England) is radically different in these two jurisdictions. Whereas discovery in the US is still rather extensive, at least from a European perspective,[5] stringent limits have been introduced in England by the Woolf Reforms (1999).[6] At the same time, it seems that the differences between jurisdictions from different procedural families are becoming less pronounced.[7] When one compares modern English civil procedure with the procedure of various continental European jurisdictions, it appears, for example, that both in England and in large parts of the Continent the judge has become an active case manager in civil proceedings, albeit in England mainly as regards the formal aspects of litigation, whereas the judge is also active as regards the content of the case in many Continental jurisdictions.[8] In this respect, England

---

1 Van Caenegem 2005; Van Rhee 2005a, b.

2 Andrews 2009, 52: 'This project [i.e. the American Law Institute/l'Institut international pour l'unification du droit privé (ALI/UNIDROIT) Principles of Transnational Civil Procedure] also shows that a jurisdiction's historical association with the Common Law or Civil Law tradition is not an immutable genetic stamp. Arguably, this backward-looking distinction will soon have lost any clear value in modern procedural structures.' And also: 'These differences [between the US and English systems, and between the various civil law jurisdictions] make a nonsense of the glib phrase "Anglo-American procedure" and, especially, of the crude expression "Civilian procedure".' See also Chap. 2 of the present Volume and Storskrubb 2008, 285, and Trockner and Varano 2005, 244–247.

3 Andrews 2003, paras 34.08–34.10; Supreme Court Act 1981, Section 69; Stürner 2005, 225; Van Rhee 1998, 129.

4 Seventh Amendment of the US Constitution.

5 Burnham 2006, 226–259.

6 Woolf 1996, para 37 et seq (available at http://www.dca.gov.uk/civil/final/index.htm; last consulted in June 2011); Andrews 2009, paras 26.01–26.128.

7 Lindblom 1997, 20.

8 Woolf 1996, Section II; Van Rhee 2008, 11–25.

has moved away from the traditional Common Law approach and in the direction of the European Continent.[9] Additionally, various Continental systems of civil procedure continue to demonstrate an interest in English procedural devices and rules, for example English-style documentary discovery (disclosure) mechanisms, even though such mechanisms are traditionally absent in these systems, a situation which has occasionally caused concern in some countries. In the Netherlands, a draft Civil Code from 1804—at that time part of civil procedure was regulated by the Civil Code—already attempted to introduce extensive duties for litigants and third parties to allow access to documents beneficial to the case of the opposing party, even if the specific documents could only be identified in a very inexact manner,[10] whereas Franz Klein, the famous Austrian law reformer, referred to discovery as a beneficial procedural device in his *Pro Futuro*, published in the 1890s.[11] Due to the increasing conviction in many countries that civil judgments should be based on the substantive truth instead of the truth as fabricated by the parties only, it is not unlikely that documentary discovery will soon be part of most modern Continental civil procedural codes.[12] This will obviously result in a move of Continental procedural systems in the direction of England, at least in this particular respect.

In this chapter I will focus on the prospects of the harmonisation of civil procedural law in the future. As the title of my paper indicates, I will also do this

---

9 Van Rhee 2003, 217–232. See for an overview of the major similarities and differences between the world's civil procedural systems, ALI/UNIDROIT 2006, 4–7.

10 Aa et al. 1968, 459–461 (Ontwerp-Cras 1804): Art. 55. 'Gelijk elk verpligt is, daar toe behoorlijk geroepen zijnde, getuigenis der waarheid te geven, zoo moet ook elk, die eenige bewijsstukken onder zich heeft, welke tot ontlasting of bezwaar, 't zij in burgerlijke, 't zij in misdadige zaken, strekken, dezelve aan den belanghebbenden, of die daar recht op hebben, uitreiken.' (Similar to the rule that everyone who has been called to court in the prescribed manner has to testify, also everyone who has any beneficial or detrimental documentary proof under him has to provide anyone with an interest in or an entitlement to these documents with these very documents, both in criminal and in civil cases). However, even though this rule seems extremely broad, according to the draft in most cases the defendant—but only the defendant—did not have to disclose documents to the claimant; see Art. 59. 'Gelijk, in het algemeen, de eisscher met het bewijs zijner vordering belast is, zonder dat de verweerder iets daar tegen behoeft te berde te brengen, zoo kan ook deze niet genoodzaakt worden, om de bewijzen, welke hij voor de vordering van den eisscher in zijnen boezem heeft over te geven.' (Similar to the rule that, generally speaking, the claimant has the burden of proof as regards his claim, without the need for the defendant to act in this respect, also the defendant cannot be obliged to disclose documents in his power which are beneficial for the claimant's case). After the draft has listed some exceptions to this rule, Art. 62 states that in situations other than those listed as exceptions to the general rule, the judge has considerable discretion as regards the defendant's duty to disclose documents; see Art. 62. 'In welke andere gevallen een gedaagde tot overgifte der brieven, welke bij hem berusten, gehouden zij, moet de rechter beoordeelen.' (In which other cases the defendant can be obliged to disclose documents has to be determined by the judge).

11 Klein 1891, 41 et seq.

12 On the introduction of discovery devices in some Continental jurisdictions, see also Trockner and Varano 2005, 255–258; and Verkerk 2010, 37.

by taking into consideration past experiences in this field. The question as to the desirability of harmonisation will not be discussed in depth here.[13]

I will focus on three types of harmonisation:

(1) Harmonisation as a result of national law reform;
(2) Harmonisation as a result of competition between procedural systems;
(3) Harmonisation as a result of international harmonisation projects.

3.2 Harmonisation as a Result of National Law Reform

Some procedural systems have a tendency to become more alike—at least as regards the civil procedure rules, i.e. black letter law—even though this is not the primary aim of the legislature or other rule-making authorities. This is due to the fact that comparative civil procedure—explicitly or implicitly—has, since time immemorial, been used as a tool where attempts are made to reform a national procedural system. Such an approach may be wise since foreign experiences may offer information on the functioning of particular procedural rules in practice. An early example is the fifteenth- and sixteenth-century Low Countries, where explicit legislative attention for French-Burgundian procedural law resulted in a considerable alignment with that procedure. This proved to be the case not only as regards black letter law but also as regards procedural practice, as appears from the history of various courts in the Low Countries, notably the so-called Great Council of Malines, which was one of the superior courts of that area in the early modern period.[14] In more recent times, examples abound. Reference may be made to the nineteenth- and twentieth-century Netherlands[15] and Belgium.[16] Since implicit attention for foreign civil procedure—i.e. attention which is not specifically mentioned by the legislature, for example for political reasons—is more difficult to demonstrate and needs considerable additional research,[17] this chapter will concentrate on examples of explicit attention.

A first question that may be addressed is which jurisdictions are usually studied in law reform projects. It appears that often the jurisdictions that are studied are related in one way or another to the system in need of reform as it is apparently thought that these jurisdictions offer examples that may be implemented in a relatively uncomplicated manner. There are, of course, exceptions to this rule, as is shown by the introduction of the German civil procedural legislation in Japan in

[13] Miller 1997, 905–918.

[14] Van Rhee 1997, 313 et seq. See also Van Rhee 2000a.

[15] Jongbloed 2005, 69–95.

[16] Heirbaut 2009, 89–117.

[17] This topic will be the subject of a future PhD thesis, supervised by the author of this chapter at Maastricht University Faculty of Law.

1890, as part of the law reform project started after the Meiji Restoration in 1868.[18] These exceptions are, however, rare and usually only occur when an entire legal system is replaced in a single blow by another legal system and not when gradual law reform is contemplated, as is usually the case.

The relationship between the system in need of reform and the foreign legal system is usually the result of close contact, not only in the procedural field but also as regards the law in general, the economy, politics and/or culture, between the various jurisdictions. The fifteenth-century Low Countries, for example, were in various of these respects closely related to their French-Burgundian example (the Burgundian dukes ruling the Low Countries were a younger branch of the French royal house of Valois) and French influence continued—maybe surprisingly—in the sixteenth century under Habsburg rule.[19] This is also true for the nineteenth-century Netherlands and Belgium. The annexation of these territories by France had resulted in the introduction of French legislation. This legislation was not repealed after the defeat of Napoleon Bonaparte. From a legal point of view (and, before the defeat of the French emperor at Leipzig, also from the political and economic perspective), the Netherlands and Belgium were integrated into the French legal system, something that especially in Belgium was reinforced by the French cultural and linguistic orientation of the elite of that country during the nineteenth and a large part of the twentieth century. Consequently, for Belgium it was only natural to look at French procedural law and contemporary French criticism of the French Code of Civil Procedure when far-reaching reforms to the Belgian Code of Civil Procedure were contemplated in the second half of the nineteenth century (other foreign influences were at that time less important and restricted to countries which were still influenced by France even though they had their own codifications: Geneva, the Netherlands and the Kingdom of Italy)[20] and again in the second half of the twentieth century when reforms were actually introduced (at this time the list of relevant jurisdictions other than France was considerably longer, even though French influence remained dominant).[21] The same is true for the Netherlands. This country introduced its own civil procedural code in 1838 which showed a strong French influence. In later reform projects, the Dutch lawmaker looked at other jurisdictions, notably Austria and Germany at the start of the twentieth century,[22] and England and Wales at the start of the twenty-first century.[23] This, in my view, is the result of the fact that these jurisdictions had to a certain extent replaced France as the dominant force in the legal, economic, political and cultural fields in the Netherlands in this period.

---

18 Chase et al. 2007, 35–36.

19 Blok et al. 1980, 135 et seq, and idem, 311 et seq.

20 Van Rhee 2006, 129–165; Heirbaut 2009.

21 Heirbaut 2009.

22 Van Rhee 2000b, 331–346.

23 Van Rhee 2008.

The current legal, economic, political and to a certain extent cultural integration of the Member States of the European Union may serve as a strong impetus for the 'spontaneous' harmonisation or, at least, approximation of the civil procedural systems in Europe in the future.[24] An example of spontaneous approximation that may be observed in Europe is the increase in the case management powers of the judge in a large number of European jurisdictions including England (as of 1999), mentioned in the introduction of this chapter.[25] Although this development started at the end of the nineteenth century in Austria, it is not unlikely that European integration is one of the factors that has stimulated its acceptance in a growing number of current EU Member States. After all, especially during the last decades, when European integration became more intense than before, the introduction of case management powers for the judge has occurred at an increasing pace,[26] especially in Western Europe. Given the fact that the States of Western Europe have for a long time been in close contact with each other within the framework of the European Community (or the European Free Trade Association), this is in my opinion not a surprise. It is not surprising either that the judge's case management powers are more problematic in the former Eastern Bloc States that are currently members of the EU,[27] given their isolation from Western Europe during the Cold War period and their radically different political and economic make-up at that time. This may, however, change over time, not only due to the continuing integration of Europe within the context of the European Union, but also due to the increasing availability of information through the Internet and the important activities of international bodies like the International Association of Procedural Law[28] and the Council of Europe (e.g. the European Commission for the Efficiency of Justice).[29]

The example of spontaneous harmonisation in the area of judicial case management shows that this type of harmonisation is not limited to minor issues in the procedural field, but that it may influence important aspects of the existing civil procedural systems in today's world. After all, the early nineteenth-century idea, clearly expressed in the highly influential French *Code de procédure civile* of 1806, that civil litigation is a private matter and only of interest to the parties to the lawsuit was originally one of the cornerstones of most European legal systems.[30] According to the French Code, the parties were considered to be free in deciding how they would conduct their case. They could opt for litigating expediently, but

---

[24] Van Rhee 2003. The use of the term 'approximation' is based on the title of the Report of the Storme Group, discussed below (Storme 1994). See now also Art. 81(1) of the Treaty on the Functioning of the European Union.

[25] Van Rhee 2008.

[26] Van Rhee 2008; Stürner 2005, 226–227.

[27] Van Rhee 2005b, 23.

[28] http://www.uni-regensburg.de/Fakultaeten/Jura/gottwald/iapl/ (last consulted in June 2010).

[29] http://www.coe.int/T/dghl/cooperation/cepej/default_en.asp (last consulted in June 2010).

[30] On the history of the French Code of Civil Procedure, see Wijffels 2008, 5–73.

could also decide to have their case move forward at a slow pace. Although according to one nineteenth-century observer the French judge had already become rather active at the end of the nineteenth century without the need for specific procedural regulations to this end,[31] it was only after the necessary theoretical framework had been developed by this very same observer (Franz Klein 1854–1926) that the new perspective of the judge as case manager became popular, first in Austria and later elsewhere.[32]

Klein's influence in Europe may be demonstrated by the reception of his theoretical ideas in other European jurisdictions. Klein's aim was the realisation of the so-called 'social function' (*Sozialfunktion*) of civil litigation. This 'social function' may be viewed as a reaction against the nineteenth-century liberal ideal of procedure. It meant that litigation should not only be considered as a means to solve individual lawsuits between private litigants, but also as a phenomenon that affected society as a whole.[33] Civil procedure should serve the public interest (*Wohlfahrtsfunktion*), but it had to be viewed from an economic perspective as well. The economic perspective meant that one should, for example, guard against civil procedure being used as a means to postpone payment of a debt or to obtain money at a low interest rate.[34] As a result, the judge was given the task of making sure that court time was used in the right manner. His case management powers were also needed because the parties were only theoretically equal (the premise of equality lies at the basis of the French *Code de procédure civile* of 1806). Conducting litigation in an inefficient manner was, for example, usually not the result of a joint decision of the parties, but only of one party who would gain from protracted litigation and who had the money to afford this type of litigation.

---

[31] Franz Klein (1854–1926) claimed in the 1890s that even though the French Code of Civil Procedure did not grant the French judge far-reaching case management powers, such powers were, in practice, exercised by him without a legal basis in the Code. See Klein 1891, 25: 'Dem französischen Rechte ist der Richter in Prüfen, Glauben und Urtheilen eine lebendige Person mit zu achtenden intellectuellen und moralischen Bedürfnissen, nicht ein blutleerer Judicaturapparat, wie sich ihn das gemeine Recht ausgesonnen hat. Diese so unscheinbare Wahrheit [...] erklärt, warum in Frankreich freie Instructionsthätigkeit des Richters ohne besondere gesetzliche Anerkennung bestehen, die allercursorischste Normirung genügen kann.' That claim echoes an observation constantly made by French authors themselves writing on civil procedure from the latter part of the nineteenth century onwards, although of course verifying the veracity of such statements would require extensive research of the French case law and of day-to-day practice during this period.

[32] Oberhammer and Domej 2005, 103–128.

[33] Klein asked the following, rhetorical question: 'Sollte das "Processeigenthum" stärker als alles sonstige Privateigenthum sein, und muss erst gesagt werden, welches die öffentlichen Interessen sind, mit denen die uns so selbstverständliche schrankenlose Disposition über den Processinhalt collidirt, und was sich dann gerade aus der Eigenthumsanalogie ergibt?' (Klein 1891, 17).

[34] See Fasching 1988, 97–117, and Van Caenegem 2005, 97.

The new perspective was adopted in many European States, first only in Germany (especially from the 1920s onwards),[35] but in the second half of the twentieth century also in other jurisdictions.

Due to the increasing pace of internationalisation and globalisation, which results in the legal, economic, political and/or cultural integration of various parts of the world in larger entities, one may expect harmonisation as described in this section to occur on an ever larger scale in the future. After all, internationalisation and globalisation mean closer contact between a larger number of States in the legal, political, economic and cultural spheres, and this will result in an ever growing number of *relevant* foreign procedural models in national law reform projects that adopt a comparative approach, either explicitly or implicitly.

3.3 Harmonisation as a Result of Competition Between Procedural Systems

In this section, I will deal with harmonisation of civil procedural law as a side effect of the wish to create a competitive forum for civil litigation. Although this may not be the major goal of law reformers in today's world, this may change in the future for reasons stated below. Before we look at the future, however, I would like to have a look at the past and summarise the success story of the medieval Romano-canonical procedure that lies at the basis of the various systems of civil procedural law on the European Continent.[36] In my opinion, competition between procedural systems in the medieval world explains this success and, consequently, it is a good example of harmonisation of procedural models as a side effect of competition.

The Romano-canonical procedure was developed within the context of the medieval Church and its spread to secular courts can—at least in part—be explained on the basis of its attractiveness for the litigants. Much earlier than medieval secular courts, medieval ecclesiastical courts knew a written procedure which aimed at uncovering the substantive truth by way of a rational system of proof. This system of proof did not appeal to supernatural forces—as the old system did, for example by way of ordeals such as trial by battle—but was based on means of proof that are still recognised in our modern procedural systems: the emphasis was on documents, but, for example, the examination of witnesses also started to play an important role. This increased the predictability of the outcome of cases and, as a result, many litigants tended to prefer litigation before a Church court instead of litigation before a secular jurisdiction. In areas and cases where a choice of forum was possible, this was detrimental to worldly rulers in various ways, for example from the perspective of their prestige and influence, but also as

---

35 Walter 2005, 67–72.

36 For more detailed information, see Van Rhee 2000a.

regards the revenues related to court litigation. Since a choice of forum was more often possible in the medieval world than today due to overlapping jurisdictions and the absence of clear-cut jurisdictional rules, high numbers of litigants started to flock to the ecclesiastical courts quickly after the introduction of the new procedure there. As a result, the secular courts lost a considerable amount of business, and it has been held that this is one of the reasons why they started to adopt elements of the Romano-canonical procedure, first of all the superior secular courts. After all, they needed to strengthen their position in respect of the ecclesiastical courts. They did not choose for a wholesale adoption of the new procedure, however, since each secular court knew its own mix of Romano-canonical and indigenous elements. Nevertheless, this mixing must have served its purpose since as a result the secular courts in the various parts of Europe were able to increase their success vis-à-vis the Church courts. At the same time it resulted in a certain approximation of the procedural models of the various European courts.

In our modern world and especially in a national context, competition between courts on the basis of procedural rules has virtually disappeared. This is due to the introduction in most States of nationwide uniform procedural models for the courts. Nevertheless, this does not mean that the State courts do not have to fear any competition at all. After all, although litigants cannot influence the procedural law applied by the State courts and therefore have to accept the national procedural models when litigating at these courts, they can in various cases decide to avoid litigation at these courts altogether by choosing arbitration or other types of alternative dispute resolution, or opt for the court of a foreign State by way of a choice of forum. In this way, they indirectly choose the applicable rules of procedural law and, in a study by Vogenauer and Hodges,[37] it is shown that as regards choices of forum the procedural law applied by the forum is one of the factors that is taken into consideration by businesses. States that consider it important to attract international litigation will—or at least should—therefore consider whether their procedural law—either positively or negatively—affects a choice of forum. Comparative civil procedure is relevant for these States because comparing a national procedural model with foreign procedural regimes is indispensable in order to evaluate the strengths and weaknesses of a particular procedural system in an international context.[38] Such comparative research may, of course, result in a certain approximation since it may give rise to the adoption of successful procedural rules and models from abroad.

States may be interested in attracting litigation for various reasons. One reason might be that they want cases that are in one way or another linked to their own jurisdiction litigated before their national courts. Another reason might be related to attracting businesses. A preference by the international business community for

[37] Available at http://denning.law.ox.ac.uk/iecl/ocjsurvey.shtml (last consulted in July 2011).

[38] In a European context, the various reports of the European Commission for the Efficiency of Justice (CEPEJ) are of interest (http://www.coe.int/T/dghl/cooperation/cepej/default_en.asp, last consulted 3 June 2010). See Albers 2008, 9–28. See also Albers 2009, 57–74.

the courts of a particular State may be held to indicate that this community regards this State as an attractive place, not only from the perspective of litigation, but also from the perspective of doing business.[39] Most likely, businesses that choose the forum of a particular State trust the proper functioning of the organs of that State in general, i.e. not only that of the courts. Another reason for a State's interest in attracting international litigation is that such litigation may be an incentive for the development of the national legal services market, or for the development of case law for a large number of situations, and there may be many other reasons.

One step States may take in improving their competitiveness in the international litigation market is to change their rules of procedure, both for domestic cases and for international litigation. However, this is a very drastic step which—apart from its unpopularity[40]—may not be effective, since different litigants may have different preferences. Another approach is introducing some flexibility in the application of procedural rules, allowing litigants a certain choice in the applicable procedural regime, for example by allowing them to opt for the application of alternative—domestic or foreign—procedural rules as regards certain aspects of their case or packages of such rules. Especially offering a limited number of packages of rules (i.e. procedural models) at the national level is, in my opinion, an interesting option, since a choice of individual rules may result in an unworkable situation due to the high number of combinations of rules that are available, and also because it may result in a choice that is only beneficial for the economically stronger party while being detrimental to his opponent. Additionally, offering packages allows the national legislator to achieve certain policy aims, e.g. by offering combinations that are at the same time attractive to international litigants and beneficial from the perspective of these policy aims. Rules allowing the judge to be an active case manager could, for example, be combined with extended discovery mechanisms in order to cater to both the international litigant who wants an efficient administration of justice and to national policy makers aiming at litigation based on the substantive truth as opposed to the truth as fabricated by the parties.

It may even be possible to allow the parties a certain flexibility as regards the choice of some of the rules that are offered within each package. Allowing a choice of the applicable procedural rules (e.g. domestic or foreign rules or rules based on the ALI/UNIDROIT Principles of Transnational Civil Procedure) within the various packages might not be as problematic as it may seem, since not all procedural rules are closely related to the overall procedural model of a country, to the system of substantive private law or have, e.g., constitutional significance. An example is the rules on the computation of time, but also

---

[39] In this respect the *Doing Business* Reports of the World Bank are of interest. Part of the comparison made by the World Bank concerns the national justice systems of the various economies (183 in total in the 2011 Report). See the chapter on enforcing contracts in the 2011 Report, 70–76 (the report is available at http://www.doingbusiness.org/; last consulted in July 2011).

[40] E.g. Walter and Baumgartner 1998, 463–476.

various rules as regards conciliation, the commencement of the proceedings and the subject matter of the litigation.[41] In my opinion, a distinction should be made between rules that are either closely related to substantive law or the procedural system, or that have constitutional significance—such as those concerning the available means of recourse against judgments which impact on judicial organisation, i.e. a constitutional issue—and rules that can be viewed in isolation and that do not have such significance. It is unlikely that States would be willing to subject the former procedural rules to the parties' preferences. However, the story may be different regarding the latter rules.

An early example of a trend towards flexibility as regards procedural rules may be witnessed in the Nordic countries. According to Laura Ervo, in these countries '[t]he state delegates more and more disposition power to the parties concerning matters of action.' Based on the writings of P. H. Lindblom, she observes that '[i]n Sweden, parties already have quite a lot of power to decide procedural matters and, for instance, the possibility to choose written or oral preparation to some extent.' It is held by this author that the dominant trend in Swedish civil procedure is expanding flexibility, and the same kind of broad freedom on procedural forms has according to her been suggested for Finland. The author states that this freedom is viewed as positive for the competitiveness of courts.[42]

3.4 Intended Harmonisation[43]

One of the major reasons for the recent growth of interest in comparative civil procedure is the attempts to harmonise civil procedural law in various parts of the world or even on a global scale. Two such harmonisation attempts that are invariably mentioned in comparative procedural studies are the Storme Report[44] and the Principles of Transnational Civil Procedure of the American Law Institute and UNIDROIT.[45] The Storme Report is the result of such a development on a European scale, whereas the Transnational Principles are the result of a similar development in the area of commercial disputes on a worldwide scale.

---

[41] See, e.g., the various proposals for harmonisation in Storme 1994.

[42] Ervo 2009, 26.

[43] This section is based on parts of Van Rhee 2010.

[44] Storme 1994.

[45] ALI/UNIDROIT 2006. Another example is the *Código Procesal Civil Modelo para Iberoamérica* (1994). The text may be found at the website of the 'Centro de Estudios de Justicia de las Americas' (http://cejamericas.org/, last consulted in April 2010). I will not discuss various initiatives as regards arbitration and The Hague Conventions on civil procedure in this chapter.

3.4.1 Harmonisation on a European Scale

Harmonisation and even unification of civil procedural law may be required for various reasons. Although litigants may, in several cases, opt for a court with their preferred procedural regime, this is not always possible. Apart from legislation prescribing the litigants to conduct their lawsuit before the courts of a specific jurisdiction (e.g. where the case concerns immovable property), a choice of forum may not be feasible for financial reasons. In an economic area like the European Union, this may create problems from the perspective of the four freedoms (free movement of persons, goods, capital and services). Citizens may, for example, decide to abstain from purchasing certain goods outside their own jurisdiction because of (perceived) problems should litigation become necessary. Additionally, businesses may be influenced by differences in procedural law in deciding to produce and market products in the various Member States. Although the impact of differences in procedural law in this particular area may be limited, they nevertheless contribute to a fragmented market and not to the creation of the single internal market that is the objective of European cooperation.[46] Additionally, the result of this is differences as regards access to justice which, within the context of the European Union—or within the wider context of the Council of Europe—may be considered undesirable.[47]

To start with the Council of Europe: due to Article 6 of the European Convention on Human Rights (ECHR) (which is comparable to Article 14 of the International Covenant on Civil and Political Rights and Article 47 of the Charter of Fundamental Rights of the European Union) and especially the case law of the European Court of Human Rights, Member States of the Council must guarantee the observance of some fundamental procedural guarantees, in the areas of both criminal and civil litigation (obviously, I will only discuss civil litigation here). The case law of the European Court of Human Rights on Article 6 has been instrumental in laying down the minimum requirements each national procedural regime of the Member States should meet. On the basis of this case law, it has appeared that Article 6 prescribes the following guarantees[48]:

1. Access to justice[49];
2. A fair hearing (trial), which includes[50]:
    a. the right to adversarial proceedings;
    b. the right to equality of arms;

[46] See Arts. 26 et seq Treaty on the Functioning of the European Union.

[47] Storskrubb 2008, 1–3, 78.

[48] See also Andrews 2009, 54–55.

[49] *Golder v UK*, 4451/70, judgment of 21 February 1975.

[50] Van Dijk et al. 2006, 578–596.

   c. the right to be present at the trial;
   d. the right to an oral hearing;
   e. the right to a fair presentation of evidence;
   f. the right to a reasoned judgment;

3. A public hearing, including the public pronouncement of judgment;
4. A hearing within a reasonable time;
5. A hearing before an independent and impartial tribunal established by law.

Although Article 6 does not necessarily lead to unification as regards procedural rules *sensu stricto*, some 'approximating' effects of the fundamental principles of Article 6 have been witnessed during the last decades, for example as regards legal aid or other measures increasing access to justice, the reasonable time requirement, the rise of the oral element in civil litigation and the admissibility of the parties as witnesses.[51] These effects are also important within the context of the European Union, since every Member State is a party to the ECHR and because Article 6 ECHR and the case law based on it are part of the *acquis communautaire*,[52] something which is also reflected by Article 47 of the Charter of Fundamental Rights of the European Union.[53]

Even though Article 6 ECHR has had an approximating effect, this is not necessarily the aim of this Article: it only aims at laying down some fundamental guarantees. In actual fact, the need for harmonisation for a group of 47 European countries[54] that are rather diverse may not be felt as urgently as within the context of an entity such as the European Union. This is not surprising, taking into consideration that even within the European Union harmonisation of procedural law is a controversial issue. In actual fact, apart from the fundamental procedural principles of Article 6 ECHR that should be observed in all Member States, the harmonisation that has been achieved in the European Union is rather limited and expressly focused on international cases, often leaving purely national cases outside the discussion (see below).

Within the context of the European Union, Article 81 of the Treaty on the Functioning of the European Union (former Article 65 of the Treaty Establishing

---

[51] Freudenthal 2007, 269–270.

[52] I.e. the total body of European Union law accumulated thus far.

[53] Art. 6(2) Treaty on European Union (TEU); Charter of Fundamental Rights of the European Union (*Official Journal* C 364, 18/12/2000, 1–22), Art. 47: Everyone whose rights and freedoms guaranteed by the law of the Union are violated has the right to an effective remedy before a tribunal in compliance with the conditions laid down in this Article. Everyone is entitled to a fair and public hearing within a reasonable time by an independent and impartial tribunal previously established by law. Everyone shall have the possibility of being advised, defended and represented. Legal aid shall be made available to those who lack sufficient resources in so far as such aid is necessary to ensure effective access to justice.

[54] Nearly all European countries are members of the Council of Europe, the exceptions being the Vatican, and Belarus—because of this country's lack of respect for human rights and democratic principles.

the European Community),[55] introduced by the Treaty of Lisbon in 2009, is of utmost importance from a civil procedural point of view.[56] It states that:

1. The Union shall develop judicial cooperation in civil matters having cross-border implications, based on the principle of mutual recognition of judgments and of decisions in extrajudicial cases. Such cooperation may include the adoption of measures for the approximation of the laws and regulations of the Member States.
2. For the purposes of paragraph 1, the European Parliament and the Council, acting in accordance with the ordinary legislative procedure, shall adopt measures, particularly when necessary for the proper functioning of the internal market, aimed at ensuring:
   (a) the mutual recognition and enforcement between Member States of judgments and of decisions in extrajudicial cases;
   (b) the cross-border service of judicial and extrajudicial documents;
   (c) the compatibility of the rules applicable in the Member States concerning conflict of laws and of jurisdiction;
   (d) cooperation in the taking of evidence;
   (e) effective access to justice;
   (f) the elimination of obstacles to the proper functioning of civil proceedings, if necessary by promoting the compatibility of the rules on civil procedure applicable in the Member States;
   (g) the development of alternative methods of dispute settlement;
   (h) support for the training of the judiciary and judicial staff.
3. [family law]

---

[55] Former Article 65 European Community Treaty: Measures in the field of judicial cooperation in civil matters having cross-border implications, to be taken in accordance with Article 67 [Article 67 ECT lays down the procedure for the adoption of legislation under, amongst other Articles, Article 65. See Storskrubb 2008, 47–48] and in so far as necessary for the proper functioning of the internal market, shall include:

(a) improving and simplifying:

- the system for cross-border service of judicial and extrajudicial documents,
- cooperation in the taking of evidence,
- the recognition and enforcement of decisions in civil and commercial cases, including decisions in extrajudicial cases;

(b) promoting the compatibility of the rules applicable in the Member States concerning the conflict of laws and of jurisdiction;
(c) eliminating obstacles to the good functioning of civil proceedings, if necessary by promoting the compatibility of the rules on civil procedure applicable in the Member States.

[56] For a discussion of Art. 114 TFEU, which according to a new legislative approach of the European Commission includes the power of harmonising national procedural laws if the latter do not sufficiently implement substantive EU law, see the chapters by Wagner and Hess in this Volume.

Many of the fields mentioned in this Article have already resulted in European legislation[57] (applicable to all Member States, usually with the exception of Denmark) by way of either regulations or directives.[58]

The following important regulations and directives can be mentioned (I omit the Council Regulation on Maintenance Obligations 4/2009)[59]:

1. Council Regulation (EC) No. 1346/2000 of 29 May 2000 on insolvency proceedings;
2. Council Regulation (EC) No. 44/2001 of 22 December 2000 on jurisdiction and the recognition and enforcement of judgments in civil and commercial matters;
3. Council Regulation (EC) No. 1206/2001 of 28 May 2001 on cooperation between the courts of the Member States in the taking of evidence in civil or commercial matters;
4. Council Regulation (EC) No. 2201/2003 concerning jurisdiction and the recognition and enforcement of judgments in matrimonial matters and in matters of parental responsibility;
5. Regulation (EC) No. 805/2004 of the European Parliament and of the Council of 21 April 2004, creating a European Enforcement Order for uncontested claims;
6. Regulation (EC) No. 1896/2006 of the European Parliament and of the Council of 12 December 2006, creating a European order for payment procedure;
7. Regulation (EC) No. 861/2007 of the European Parliament and of the Council of 11 July 2007, establishing a European small claims procedure;
8. Regulation (EC) No. 1393/2007 of the European Parliament and of the Council of 13 November 2007 on the service in the Member States of judicial and extrajudicial documents in civil or commercial matters;
9. Council Directive 2003/8/EC of 27 January 2003 to improve access to justice in cross-border disputes by establishing minimum common rules relating to legal aid for such disputes;

---

[57] I will not discuss the European Judicial Network here, nor judicial training and some other measures. See Storskrubb 2008, 233 et seq.

[58] For non-European lawyers, it may be useful to know that a regulation is a legislative act which becomes immediately enforceable as law in all Member States simultaneously. Regulations can be distinguished from directives, which need to be transposed into national law by the Member States. Directives may give rise to different national legislative solutions in order to reach the aim of the directive. All regulations and directives mentioned in this chapter can be found on the website of the European Union: http://europa.eu/ (last consulted in May 2011).

[59] Article 81(2) sub c, as far as it deals with the conflict of laws, will not be discussed in detail here, since the topics that have so far been brought under this heading are not directly relevant for civil procedural law. The two most important topics that may be mentioned are Regulation No. 593/2008 on the law applicable to contractual obligations (Rome I), OJ 2008, L 177/6, and Regulation No. 864/2007 on the law applicable to non-contractual obligations (Rome II), OJ 2007, L 199/40.

10. Directive 2008/52/EC of the European Parliament and of the Council of 21 May 2008 on certain aspects of mediation in civil and commercial matters.

As stated, however, the harmonisation resulting from the instruments mentioned above only concerns international cases. This means that purely national cases continue to be governed by the rules of civil procedure of the Member State where the case is brought. In my opinion, this is unfortunate, especially since it would have been possible to interpret Article 81(2)f (former Article 65 sub c ECT) broadly, in the sense that it may form the basis of an alignment of the civil procedural laws of the Member States irrespective of the national or international character of litigation. After all, it could be claimed that differences between the procedural laws of the Member States always have cross-border implications, e.g. in the sense that businesses may be affected by these differences when deciding where to produce and market their products. The free movement of persons, goods, capital and services within the EU and, consequently, the proper functioning of the internal market are affected by a restrictive interpretation. In my opinion, the differences in civil procedural law can often only be removed by Union action and not by action at the respective national levels and, consequently, the principle of subsidiarity of Article 5 of the Treaty on European Union (former Article 5 ECT) does not prevent the Union from using its powers. Also, the principle of proportionality mentioned in the same Article 5 does not seem to hinder Union action. Nevertheless, this interpretation of Article 81 TEU is currently politically unacceptable for the Member States.[60]

Although the European approach excludes purely national cases, a debate on the 'approximation' of the national procedural laws of the Member States of the European Community was already underway in the late 1980s, i.e. before the introduction of Article 81 and its predecessor, Article 65 ECT. As is widely known, the initiative was taken by a working group chaired by Professor Marcel Storme from Ghent (Belgium). The report this working group produced does not distinguish between national and international cases and was aimed at the then 12 Member States of the European Community.

In his introduction to the Report, Professor Storme states that harmonisation of civil procedural law is more feasible than harmonisation of other fields of law. The author claims that this is the result, amongst other things, of the fact that in the area of procedure many of the rules are not interrelated with other rules, either procedural or substantive[61] (apart from some procedural rules which are, e.g., closely interwoven with substantive law, such as those concerning marriage and divorce, areas for which the current Article 81(3) of the Treaty on the Functioning of the

[60] Storskrubb 2008, 39, 272–273. The European Small Claims Procedure, for example, was originally envisaged as also being applicable in purely national disputes. At a late moment in the drafting process, however, it was decided that it would only cover international cases, leading to discrimination as regards purely domestic cases in jurisdictions where the national rules are less favourable than the European rules. See Storskrubb 2008, 220–221.

[61] Storme 1994, 53 et seq.

European Union contains specific provisions).[62] Consequently, an immediate, thorough overhaul of the system is not needed and harmonisation may proceed on a piecemeal basis.[63]

The original idea of the Storme Group was to produce a model code, to be implemented by way of a Directive.[64] However, it was soon realised that there were still too many differences between the procedural systems of the 12 Member States to make a generally acceptable, all-encompassing proposal possible. Therefore, the Working Group concentrated on 16 separate issues which, in their view, were fit for approximation: (1) Conciliation, (2) Commencement of the Proceedings, (3) Subject matter of litigation (pleadings, i.e. statements of case), (4) Discovery, (5) Witnesses, (6) Technology and Proof, (7) Discontinuance, (8) Default, (9) Costs, (10) Provisional Remedies, (11) Order for Payment, (12) Enforcement, (13) *Astreinte*, (14) Computation of time, (15) Nullities and (16) some general rules concerning judges and judgments (appeal and disqualification of judgments). In the Report, the rules as regards some of these issues are very detailed (e.g. commencement of the proceedings), whereas other issues are regulated in a rather sketchy manner (e.g. witnesses). Although the rules themselves are available in both French and English, the accompanying explanatory memorandum, comments and recitals are only available in either French or English (depending on the language skills of the person responsible for a certain part of the memorandum or the other documents), which is due to the limited means available to the Working Group.[65]

Criticism was soon to come. To mention but one example, in the *European Review of Private Law*, Professor Per Henrik Lindblom discussed various issues which in his opinion showed the weaknesses of the Storme report.[66] He claimed that the report did not make clear whether it meant to lay down only minimum requirements or standard rules.[67] Professor Lindblom stated that if the report was meant to formulate standard rules, it might not give rise to an improvement in countries that have higher quality rules.[68] At the same time, the author held that if only minimum rules were given, it might be questioned whether this would lead to harmonisation or approximation.[69] Additionally, Professor Lindblom observed that several of the rules suggested by the Report were rather general and often did not address the real problems in the area of civil procedural law. He demonstrated this, amongst other things, by mentioning that the Report contains only one article (Article 5) concerning witnesses, an article which in his view states the obvious,

---

[62] Storme 1994, 57–58.

[63] Storme 1994, 54.

[64] Storme 1994, 61. For a definition of a directive, see n. 58.

[65] Storme 1994, 62–63.

[66] Lindblom 1997.

[67] Lindblom 1997, 32, 45.

[68] Lindblom 1997, 45.

[69] Lindblom 1997, 32.

since it only lays down that '[a]ny person duly summoned in accordance with the law of a Member State to give evidence before a court of that State shall be under a duty to appear before that court and give evidence.'[70]

Although the criticism may be justified, the significance of this first attempt to provide a model for the approximation of procedural law in the European Union, involving the leading experts in the field at the time, should in my perspective not be underestimated.[71] One of its achievements is that it has triggered the debate on the possibility and the pros and cons of procedural harmonisation and has been a source of inspiration for other projects, notably a project initiated by the American Law Institute and later also sponsored by UNIDROIT, i.e. the Principles of Transnational Civil Procedure.[72]

3.4.2 Harmonisation on a Worldwide Scale: The Principles of Transnational Civil Procedure

In the comparative study of civil procedure, the Principles of Transnational Civil Procedure are of considerable importance. According to one author, disregarding the Principles 'might be declared a form of procedural illiteracy'.[73] They are a major achievement, considering that the majority of comparatists were of the opinion that harmonisation of civil procedure on a worldwide scale was not possible.[74] As was to be expected, the project met with fierce criticism, especially

---

[70] Lindblom 1997, 36.

[71] For some very derogative remarks, see, e.g., Biondi 2005, 233: 'The rather ponderous project (127 articles!), as it is otherwise known, was soon pilloried (complex, adding complexity to quote the kindest) and did not produce any practical effects. Its lasting notoriety is due to the fact that it is invariably quoted in any articles that deal with procedural law and European law.' It should, however, be remembered that complexity (meaning a large number of articles) is not felt by everyone as a negative aspect of procedural legislation, taking into consideration the contribution in the same Volume of Díez-Picazo Giménez 2005, entitled 'The Principal Innovations of Spain's Recent Civil Procedure Reform' (33–66), who highly praises the new Spanish Code of Civil Procedure. On the basis of his contribution, however, the least that can be said about this new Code is that it is complex (it contains 827 articles although it does not even cover many of the areas which in other Civil Law countries are usually part of the Code of Civil Procedure) and, according to the author, in various instances unclear. Sometimes the so-called 'innovations' of this new Code are even medieval in character. The following quote is rather interesting for someone with some knowledge of the history of civil procedure: 'A special device has been established [by the new Code] for issues related to jurisdiction and proper venue of the court: the so called *declinatory plea* (*declinatoria*) … Exceptions of lack of jurisdiction and proper venue have to be raised by the defendant prior to filing his answer …' It suffices to know that the declinatory plea already figures in the 13th century *Speculum Iudiciale* of Durantis.

[72] ALI/UNIDROIT 2006, 3. See for an extensive bibliography on the Principles: ALI/UNIDROIT 2006, 157 et seq.

[73] Andrews 2009, 52.

[74] Stürner 2005, 203.

in the initial stages. The most amusing book in this respect is in my opinion a volume edited by Philippe Fouchard, *Vers un procès civil universel. Les règles transnationales de procédure civile de l'American Law Institute* (Paris, Panthéon-Assas 2001), where various French authors show themselves in a rather parochial manner, to put it mildly.

The initiators of the project, Geoffrey Hazard Jr. and Michele Taruffo, originally intended to draft a code of *rules* for national courts that would set aside domestic procedural rules: (1) when litigation between parties from different States would take place or (2) whenever property in one State would be the object of litigation by a party from another country. These rules would form a code acceptable both from the Common Law and the Civil Law perspective.[75] In 1997 the American Law Institute adopted the project[76] and in 2000 UNIDROIT joined.[77] This gave rise to a change, since UNIDROIT did not feel that civil procedure rules of some detail would be acceptable to different cultures. It was of the opinion that it was better to develop a set of general *Principles*.[78] Finally, only the Principles were adopted by the American Law Institute and UNIDROIT although it was felt that the rules represented a possible example of implementation of the Principles.[79]

The final draft of the Principles of Transnational Civil Procedure dates from 2004. It was published in 2006 by Cambridge University Press in English and in French.[80] The publication also includes a commentary.

According to their drafters, the Principles must be seen as best practices and as a benchmark for national procedures.[81] Consequently, they are not necessarily only aimed at international cases, but may also be used within a national context, e.g. in national reform projects (see below). They are a blend of elements from the Civil Law and the Common Law[82]: discovery is, for example, limited in nature,[83] but this is corrected by a liberal approach towards shifting the burden of proof.[84] Additionally, the hearing of the case is concentrated, but this does not necessarily mean that there should only be a single trial.[85] The hybrid character of the Principles may also be viewed slightly less favourably. According to Neil Andrews,

---

[75] Stürner 2005, 204.

[76] ALI/UNIDROIT 2006, xxxi.

[77] ALI/UNIDROIT 2006, 4.

[78] Stürner 2005, 205–206. On the three types of Principles that may be distinguished, see Storskrubb 2008, 290.

[79] ALI/UNIDROIT 2006, 4; Stürner 2005, 205–209, 215.

[80] ALI/UNIDROIT 2006, 9. The document is also available in a number of other languages.

[81] ALI/UNIDROIT 2006, xxix.

[82] ALI/UNIDROIT 2006, 11.

[83] ALI/UNIDROIT 2006, Principle 16.

[84] ALI/UNIDROIT 2006, Principle 21.

[85] ALI/UNIDROIT 2006, Principle 9.

'[e]verywhere the restraining hand of the Civil Law is visible and robust Common Law tendencies are curbed.'[86]

The Principles aim in the first place at transnational commercial litigation.[87] This approach was adopted in order to increase the chances that the Principles would be acceptable to lawyers from various jurisdictions. After all, in commercial litigation there is no constitutional right to a jury trial and the existence of the jury in civil cases is a major issue separating the US from most other jurisdictions. By only focusing on commercial litigation, the whole subject of the jury could be excluded from consideration.[88] Additionally, it was felt that international commercial litigation was less subject to national legal traditions than other types of litigation because the existence of a body of well-developed rules of commercial arbitration offered a good common starting point.[89]

Apart from transnational commercial litigation being a field where harmonisation is feasible, there are also intrinsic reasons for concentrating on this area. In the introduction to the Principles we find the following comment: 'The explosion in transnational commerce has changed the world forever. International commerce and investment are increasing at an enormous rate and the rate of change is continuing to accelerate. The legal procedures applicable to the global community, however, have not kept pace and are still largely confined to and limited by individual national jurisdictions.'[90] Consequently, there is a need for initiatives in this area, since the current situation is said to diminish international trade and investment. In the opinion of the drafters, the existing international conventions (The Hague Conventions)[91] on civil procedure and related topics are not a solution to the problems, since they only address aspects of civil litigation (e.g. commencement and recognition) and say little about the actual procedure to be followed.[92] From this perspective, they may also be highly relevant from a European Union perspective, as many of the existing European Regulations on civil procedure show the same limitations as The Hague Conventions (see above).

Even though the Principles aim at transnational commercial litigation, this does not mean that they are without use in other fields. On the contrary, they may, for example, (1) influence the further development of the rules of national and international arbitration (to which they are themselves indebted),[93] (2) be used by national law reformers as an example of worldwide accepted guidelines and

86 Andrews 2009, 53.

87 ALI/UNIDROIT 2006, 'Scope and Implementation,' 16. The terms 'transnational' and 'commercial' are not defined precisely. See ALI/UNIDROIT 2006, Comments P-B and P-C.

88 ALI/UNIDROIT 2006, xxvii; Stürner 2005, 209–210.

89 Stürner 2005, 210.

90 ALI/UNIDROIT 2006, xxix.

91 See for an overview: http://www.hcch.net/index_en.php?act=text.display&tid=10#litigation (last consulted in May 2010).

92 Hazard et al. 2001, 770–771.

93 ALI/UNIDROIT 2006, 10–12. See also ALI/UNIDROIT 2006, Comment P-E.

standards of procedural law,[94] and (3) be consulted by national judges in the interpretation of national procedural rules and international conventions that are formulated in a way which leaves the necessary room for judicial interpretation.[95] Finally, (4) they may be used as standards against which foreign judgments and arbitral awards may be measured when a decision has to be taken as regards their recognition and enforcement.[96] The use of the Principles under (2) and (3) may give rise to spontaneous harmonisation or harmonisation as a side effect as mentioned above.

The procedural model suggested by the Principles aims to avoid favouring national parties in international litigation.[97] It is a flexible model which accommodates all of the existing national procedural models. Nevertheless, the Principles suggest a preferred model.[98] This model consists of three stages: the pleading stage (statements of case), an interim stage (scheduling) and a final stage (main hearing).[99] This model is popular in many European countries such as Germany, England and Spain. Stürner calls it the 'main hearing model'.[100] The Principles assume an active judge[101] and in this respect they take the German-Austrian model as an example (see above).[102] This active stance of the judge means that the court is also responsible for determining issues of law, including foreign law.[103] On the other hand, the Principles lay down that the court is never permitted to introduce new facts not previously advanced or at least briefly mentioned by the parties to litigation.[104] It is, however, again the court's responsibility to ensure that justice is administered promptly,[105] a responsibility that is to some extent shared with the parties.[106] There is no notice pleading like in the US, which means that the assertion of detailed facts and the submission of exactly specified means of evidence during the pleading phase is required.[107] All contentions of the parties should be considered by the court.[108] The principle of finality is adhered to.[109] The Principles do not follow the American rule as regards costs, i.e. they do not follow

94 ALI/UNIDROIT 2006, 10–11; idem, 'Scope and Implementation,' 16.

95 ALI/UNIDROIT 2006, 4.

96 ALI/UNIDROIT 2006, Comment P-A, 16; Stürner 2005, 210 et seq.

97 ALI/UNIDROIT 2006, 1-4.

98 Stürner 2005, 223, 226.

99 ALI/UNIDROIT 2006, Principle 9.

100 Stürner 2005, 224–226.

101 ALI/UNIDROIT 2006, Principle 14.

102 Stürner 2005, 226–227.

103 Stürner 2005, 228.

104 ALI/UNIDROIT 2006, Principle 10; Stürner 2005, 229.

105 ALI/UNIDROIT 2006, Principle 7.1; Stürner 2005, 227.

106 ALI/UNIDROIT 2006, Principle 11.2.

107 ALI/UNIDROIT 2006, Principle 11.3; Stürner 2005, 233.

108 ALI/UNIDROIT 2006, Principle 22.

109 ALI/UNIDROIT 2006, Principle 26.

the rule that each party pays his own expenses.[110] However, they do recognise the *amicus curiae*.[111] Appeal is not a new hearing, but limited to re-evaluating the judgment of first instance.[112] The Principles discuss sanctions on parties, lawyers and third persons for failure or refusal to comply with the obligations concerning the proceeding.[113]

According to Neil Andrews, several issues are not (sufficiently) addressed by the Principles. The author mentions (1) pre-action coordination of exchanges between the potential litigants (pre-action protocols as known in England since the Woolf reforms) and (2) multi-party litigation. Andrews also states that greater attention could be given to the interplay of mediation and litigation, costs and funding, evidential privileges and immunities, and transnational and protective relief.[114] For these and other reasons, the Principles should not be seen as the final stage in the development of procedural harmonisation on a global scale, but as an initiative which will certainly witness various follow-ups in the years to come.

3.5 Final Remarks

Attempts to harmonise civil procedure have made the study of comparative civil procedure (including the history of this area of the law) an exciting field of study during the last few decades. Although the comparative study of civil procedure was originally the domain of national law reformers, busy with drafting new or amended codes of civil procedure in a national context, mainly focusing on nearby jurisdictions, globalisation has made it a field of study for a wider audience. It is a promising area of study, for example, where national procedural systems are seen to compete with each other for litigation business. Comparative civil procedure allows these systems to evaluate their strengths and weaknesses in the international playing field when taking into consideration the preferences of litigants who have become ever more mobile where it concerns choices of forum. As has been stated in this chapter, especially businesses have certain preferences as regards the procedural model for litigation, to which jurisdictions that aim at attracting litigation before their various State courts should be aware. Additionally, attempts to approximate civil procedural law in an international context benefit tremendously from this field of study. Although successes in this field are limited, especially the Principles of Transnational Civil Procedure of the American Law Institute and UNIDROIT show us the way ahead. Parochial criticism in this field is of course possible, but as in other areas in today's world, it will quickly become apparent

110 ALI/UNIDROIT 2006, Principle 25; Stürner 2005, 251.

111 ALI/UNIDROIT 2006, Principle 13.

112 ALI/UNIDROIT 2006, Principle 27.

113 ALI/UNIDROIT 2006, Principle 17.

114 Andrews 2009, 57, and also Chap. 2 in this Volume.

that parochialism is not the way ahead to survive in our modern times in which the world is becoming smaller and smaller. It is to be hoped that the Transnational Principles will trigger further in-depth studies of civil procedure, and I am convinced that in this particular area the study of comparative law, including the study of the history of civil procedure, will continue to add new insights and show the way ahead. In this respect, the comparative study of civil procedure in action could be further developed, with the consideration that the relationship between civil procedure and (procedural) culture and the extent to which procedural reform is implicitly influenced by foreign procedural models should be focused on.

References

Aa H et al (eds) (1968) Bronnen van de Nederlandse Codificatie sinds 1798. Kemink en Zoon NV, Utrecht

Albers P (2008) Judicial systems in Europe compared. In: Van Rhee CH, Uzelac A (eds) Civil justice between efficiency and quality: from Ius Commune to the CEPEJ. Intersentia, Antwerp, pp 9–28

Albers P (2009) Quality assessment of courts and the judiciary: from judicial quality to court excellence. In: Uzelac A, Van Rhee CH (eds) Access to justice and the judiciary: towards New European standards of affordability, quality and efficiency of civil adjudication. Intersentia, Antwerp, pp 57–74

ALI/UNIDROIT (2006) Principles of transnational civil procedure. Cambridge University Press, Cambridge

Andrews N (2003) English civil procedure. Fundamentals of the new civil justice system. Oxford University Press, Oxford

Andrews N (2009) A modern procedural synthesis: the American Law Institute and UNIDROIT's 'Principles and rules of transnational civil procedure.' Tijdschrift voor Civiele Rechtspleging 52–58

Biondi A (2005) Minimum, adequate or excessive protection? The impact of EC law on national procedural law. In: Trockner N, Varano V (eds) The reforms of civil procedure in comparative perspective. Giappichelli Editore, Torino, pp 234–243

Blok DP et al (eds) (1980) Algemene Geschiedenis der Nederlanden, vol IV. Unieboek B.V., Bussum

Burnham W (2006) Introduction to the law and legal system of the United States. Thomson/West, St. Paul

Chase OG et al (eds) (2007) Civil litigation in comparative context. Thomson/West, St. Paul

Díez-Picazo Giménez I (2005) The principal innovations of Spain's recent civil procedure reform. In: Trockner N, Varano V (eds) The reforms of civil procedure in comparative perspective. Giappichelli Editore, Torino, pp 33–66

Ervo L (2009) Party autonomy and access to justice. In: Ervo L, Gräns M, Jokela A (eds) Europeanization of procedural law and the new challenges to fair trial. Europa Law Publishing, Groningen, pp 21–41

Fasching HW (1988) Die Weiterentwicklung des österreichischen Zivilprozessrechts im Lichte der Ideen Franz Kleins. In: Hofmeister H (ed) Forschungsband Franz Klein (1854–1926). Leben und Wirken. Manz, Vienna, pp 97–117

Freudenthal M (2007) Schets van het Europees civiel procesrecht. Kluwer, Deventer

Hazard GC et al (2001) Introduction to the principles and rules of transnational civil procedure. NY Univ J Law Politics 33:769–784

Heirbaut D (2009) Efficiency: the Holy Grail of Belgian Justice? In: Uzelac A, Van Rhee CH (eds) Access to justice and the judiciary: towards New European standards of affordability, quality and efficiency of civil adjudication. Intersentia, Antwerp, pp 89–117

Jongbloed AW (2005) The Netherlands (1838–2005). In: Van Rhee CH (ed) European traditions in civil procedure (Ius Commune Europaeum 54). Intersentia, Antwerp, pp 69–97

Klein F (1891) Pro Futuro. Betrachtungen über Probleme der Civilprocessreform in Österreich, Franz Deuticke, Leipzig/Wien

Lindblom PH (1997) Harmony of legal spheres. A Swedish view on the construction of a unified European procedural law. Eur Rev Private Law 5:11–46

Miller GP (1997) The legal-economic analysis of comparative civil procedure. Am J Comp Law 45:905–918

Oberhammer P, Domej T (2005) Germany, Switzerland and Austria (ca. 1800–2005). In: Van Rhee CH (ed) European traditions in civil procedure. Intersentia, Antwerp, pp 103–128

Storme M (1994) Approximation of judiciary law in the European union. Kluwer, Dordrecht

Storskrubb E (2008) Civil procedure and EU law. A policy area uncovered. Oxford University Press, Oxford

Stürner R (2005) The principles of transnational civil procedure. An introduction to their basic conceptions. Rabels Zeitschrift 201–254

Trockner N, Varano V (2005) Concluding remarks. In: Trockner N, Varano V (eds) The reforms of civil procedure in comparative perspective. Giappichelli Editore, Torino, pp 243–267

Van Caenegem R (2005) History of European civil procedure. In: International encyclopedia of comparative law, vol XVI. J.C.B. Mohr (Paul Siebeck), Tübingen, pp 16–23

Van Dijk P et al (2006) Theory and practice of the European convention on human rights. Intersentia, Oxford

Van Rhee CH (1997) Litigation and legislation. Civil procedure at first instance in the Great Council for the Netherlands in Malines (1522–1559), Archives générales du Royaume, Brussels

Van Rhee CH (1998) English civil procedure until the civil procedure rules. In: Van Rhee CH (ed) European traditions in civil procedure. Intersentia, Oxford, pp 129–159

Van Rhee CH (2000a) Civil procedure: a European Ius Commune? Eur Rev Private Law 8:589–611

Van Rhee CH (2000b) 'Ons tegenwoordig sukkelproces'. Nederlandse opvattingen over de toekomst van het burgerlijk procesrecht rond 1920, Tijdschrift voor Rechtsgeschiedenis. pp 331–346

Van Rhee CH (2003) Towards a procedural Ius Commune? In: Smits J, Lubbe G (eds) Remedies in Zuid-Afrika en Europa. Intersentia, Antwerp, pp 217–232

Van Rhee CH (ed) (2005a) European traditions in civil procedure. Intersentia, Oxford

Van Rhee CH (2005b) Introduction. In: Van Rhee CH (ed) European traditions in civil procedure. Intersentia, Oxford, pp 3–23

Van Rhee CH (2006) The influence of the French Code de procédure civile (1806) in 19th Century Europe. In: Cadiet L, Canivet G (eds) De la Commémoration d'un code à l'autre: 200 ans de procédure civile en France. Litec, Paris, pp 129–165

Van Rhee CH (2008) The development of civil procedural law in twentieth-century Europe: from party autonomy to judicial case management and efficiency. In: Van Rhee CH (ed) Judicial case management and efficiency in civil litigation. Intersentia, Antwerp, pp 11–25

Van Rhee CH (2010) Civil procedure in a globalizing world: a historical perspective. In: Faure MG, Van der Walt A (eds) Globalization and private law: the way forward. Edward Elgar, Cheltenham, pp 343–367

Verkerk RR (2010) Fact-finding in civil litigation: a comparative perspective. Intersentia, Oxford

Walter G, Baumgartner S (1998) Utility and feasibility of transnational rules of civil procedure: some German and Swiss reactions to the Hazard-Taruffo project. Tex Int Law J 33:463–476

Walter G (2005) The German civil reform Act 2002: Much Ado about nothing? In: Trockner N, Varano V (eds) The reforms of civil procedure in comparative perspective. Giappichelli Editore, Torino, pp 67–89

Wijffels A (2008) The Code de procédure civile (1806) in France, Belgium and the Netherlands. In: Van Rhee CH (ed) The French code of civil procedure (1806) after 200 years. The civil procedure tradition in France and abroad. Kluwer, Mechelen, pp 5–73

Woolf H (1996) Access to justice: final report. http://www.dca.gov.uk/cil/final/index.htm (accessed June 2011)

Chapter 4
A Law and Economics View on Harmonisation of Procedural Law

Louis Visscher

Abstract Even though there exists an extensive Law and Economics literature on the topics of procedural law and harmonisation of law, very little has been written on harmonisation of procedural law as such. This chapter starts by providing a brief overview of the economic approach to legal intervention, private enforcement and procedural law. Subsequently, the economics of harmonisation of (substantive) private law is discussed. The traditional legal arguments in favour of harmonisation (differences in legal rules between countries result in legal uncertainty and increased costs and therefore hinder cross-border trade, and harmonisation would create a level playing field) turn out to be unconvincing. The economic analysis of law provides several arguments against harmonisation (regulatory competition enables satisfying a larger number of preferences, it enables learning effects, (centralised) legislators suffer from limited information and the possible influence of interest groups should be taken into account) and in favour of it (the need to internalise interstate externalities, the desire to avoid a race to the bottom, decreasing transaction costs and profiting from economies of scale). These arguments have to be weighed in order to reach a conclusion on the desirability of harmonisation. Such a weighing shows that there is, at best, a limited scope for harmonisation of procedural law (and then only as an additional option). Harmonisation would remove the possible learning effects and does not allow satisfying a larger number of preferences. The possible arguments in favour of harmonisation of procedural law seem weak, especially now that procedural law

Associate Professor of Law and Economics, Rotterdam Institute of Law and Economics (RILE), Erasmus School of Law, Erasmus University Rotterdam

L. Visscher (✉)
Erasmus School of Law, Rotterdam Institute of Law and Economics (RILE), Erasmus University Rotterdam, Rotterdam, The Netherlands
e-mail: visscher@law.eur.nl

X. E. Kramer and C. H. van Rhee (eds.), *Civil Litigation in a Globalising World*,
DOI: 10.1007/978-90-6704-817-0_4,

is closely connected to the underlying substantive law. The only potentially strong argument is the reduction of transaction costs. It is ultimately an empirical matter whether this argument outweighs the arguments against harmonisation. The 2008 Oxford Civil Justice Survey suggests that this is not the case.

Contents

4.1 Introduction

Even though there exists an extensive Law and Economics literature on the topics of procedural law and harmonisation of law, very little has been written on harmonisation of procedural law as such. In order to be able to assess this topic from an economic perspective, it is necessary to start with both separate issues. Without knowledge of these two topics, it is impossible to provide, from an economic perspective, an answer to the question whether harmonisation of procedural law should be striven for.

Section 4.2 provides a brief overview of the economic approach to legal intervention in general and to private enforcement in particular. After that, in Sect. 4.3 economic literature regarding (civil) procedural law is discussed. This Section will make clear that legal economists do not focus solely on the dispute resolution function of civil procedures, but also on its potential to 'produce' legal norms. These norms are relevant not only for the parties involved in the procedure, but also for other actors who may derive behavioural guidelines from the outcome of the case. This law-producing feature of civil procedures can be regarded as a social benefit. However, the parties involved in the procedure are likely more interested in their private costs and benefits. In economic terms, civil procedures may create a positive externality, so that the private incentives to sue are not perfectly aligned with the socially optimal incentives.

In Sect. 4.4, attention is shifted to the economic approach to harmonisation of law in general. Most economic literature on this topic concerns harmonisation of substantive law, but the arguments which are developed pro and contra harmonisation are also relevant in the current debate on procedural law. Examples from several fields of substantive law are provided in order to make clear to what conclusions the economic arguments may lead.

Section 4.5 treats the issue of harmonisation of procedural law. The arguments from Sect. 4.4 are applied to procedural law, taking into consideration the economic role of civil procedure as sketched in Sect. 4.3. Section 4.6 contains the conclusion.

4.2 The Economic Approach to Law and Private Enforcement

4.2.1 Reasons for Legal Intervention

In the Law and Economics approach, legal intervention is primarily regarded as a way to try to correct various forms of market failure.[1] In the theoretical construct of full competition, i.e. a perfectly functioning market, social welfare is maximised. In such a market, parties transact without transaction costs on the basis of full information, so that entitlements per definition end up with the parties who value them the most. Actors incorporate all costs and benefits (both to themselves and to others) attached to their behaviour. They therefore only engage in an activity if the social costs are lower than the social benefits, so that their activities increase social welfare. Furthermore, due to competition, producers have to produce efficiently because otherwise consumers will buy the product from a more efficient and hence cheaper competitor. Therefore, resources are not wasted (which would have lowered social welfare).

In reality, several departures from the market form of full competition exist. These market failures lower social welfare and form reasons for legal intervention. The first type of market failure is *market power*. In situations where market power exists, the producer(s) is (are) not forced to produce efficiently because the necessary competition is lacking. Producers can produce inefficiently, can limit their output to below-competitive levels and can increase prices to above-competitive levels. This may result in a situation where consumers who value the product higher than its full costs, but lower than its increased price, will not buy the product anymore. This results in a loss of welfare. Furthermore, the costs of acquiring and maintaining market power as well as the reduced incentive to

[1] See, e.g., Rowley 1981, 401.

innovate lower social welfare. Competition law can be seen as a legal response to these problems; see for example the prohibition on cartel agreements (Article 101 Treaty on the Functioning of the European Union, hereafter TFEU) and the ban on abuses of dominant position (Article 102 TFEU).[2]

The second type of market failure consists of *negative externalities*. The behaviour of an actor may cause negative consequences for others, such as pollution or risk. If the actor does not bear these negative consequences, he does not incorporate these costs into his decision whether, and if yes how often, to engage in his activity. His decisions, in other words, only take his private costs and benefits into account, but not the social costs and benefits. Engaging in the activity may therefore decrease rather than increase social welfare. Besides this problem of a too high activity level, the actor may also take inadequate precautionary measures to reduce the probability and/or the severity of the negative externalities. Various legal interventions may lead to internalisation of the externality. For example, liability for harm caused by an actor may provide him with incentives to decrease the probability and/or magnitude of harm occurring, and/or it may incentivise him to reduce his activity level.[3]

The third type of market failure relates to the available *information*, which may differ between the transacting parties. If one party cannot perfectly monitor the other, the latter may decide to shirk, take excessive risks, et cetera. This problem of *moral hazard* is relevant in, for example, insurance, where the insured may take fewer precautionary measures than the uninsured who themselves face the possible consequences of their behaviour. Comparably, consumers may become less careful in using products if they can sue manufacturers under product liability for losses caused by the product. This reduces social welfare because people do not take the correct decisions regarding their behaviour. A second problem caused by information asymmetry is called *adverse selection*.[4] In a transaction, one party (for example the seller of a product) may know more about the quality of the product than the other party (the buyer) does. Given that the buyer does not know if the product is of high or low quality, he may only be willing to pay an average price. The seller, who knows the quality of the product, is only willing to sell products of at most average quality for this price. This means that the average quality of the products which are offered for this price is lower than the average of *all* products and hence the consumer lowers the price which he is willing to pay. This continues until only products of low quality are available. Hence, welfare-increasing transactions may be forgone. Trademarks may ameliorate this problem because they allow producers or sellers of high quality products to signal the quality of their product and they allow buyers to recognise products of high quality. Also consumer law can be regarded as a potential solution, for example through information duties of the producer or seller, or through the requirement of conformity.

---

2 See, e.g., Van den Bergh and Camesasca 2006, 43 et seq.

3 See, e.g., Shavell 1987.

4 See, e.g., Akerlof 1970, 488–500.

The fourth type of market failure is the fact that so-called *collective goods* are not produced in a private market. Collective goods are non-exclusive (it is not possible, or too expensive, to exclude someone from enjoying the good) and non-rivalrous (the use by a person does not affect the possibilities for use by others). Producers therefore cannot earn money with the good because potential users who do not want to pay cannot be excluded, and their ability to use the good is not affected by the use by others. Information can be regarded as a collective good, which is shown, for example, in the downloading of music and movies, and in the copying of texts. This may result in a lower than socially optimal amount of information being produced because the producer may not be able to recoup the investments. Intellectual property law can be seen as a possible solution because copyrights and patents give the producer of information a legal monopoly on the production and sale of the information, which enables them to recoup their investments.

Finally, in reality, transaction costs exist, which may prohibit welfare-increasing transactions from taking place. This implies that entitlements may not end up with the parties who value them the most, so that their initial allocation becomes important. Law plays an important role in this initial allocation. In addition, law can try to reduce transaction costs, for instance by establishing default rules in contract law. Only in the event that parties want to make a different arrangement than the default rules, do they need to draw up a more extensive contract. Besides reducing the transaction costs, this also reveals private information of the party that wants to deviate from the default, which reduces the information asymmetry.

4.2.2 Private Enforcement

Section 4.2.1 showed the economic rationale behind various bodies of law. In order for these legal rules to fulfil their role, it is necessary that they be enforced and that violations be sanctioned. The expected sanction is the instrument which may induce the potential violator to refrain from his potentially welfare-lowering behaviour.

The economic literature regarding *optimal enforcement* analyses under which conditions public enforcement may be better and when private enforcement is to be preferred. For example, anticompetitive behaviour can be targeted by the relevant competition authority in a public procedure, but alternatively the victims of this behaviour may start a civil procedure. Negative externalities may be handled through administrative law, criminal law and/or tax law, but also via private tort claims.

An important factor in the choice between public and private enforcement is the (un)availability of information regarding a norm violation and regarding the identity of the wrongdoer. If private parties have good information regarding these issues, it is not desirable to choose for (more expensive) public enforcement.[5] In a typical tort case, the victim knows that there was a norm violation and he also knows the identity of the wrongdoer.[6] This information is often not available to a public enforcer. Furthermore, the victim has an incentive to utilise his information if he wants to claim damages. In case of a breach of safety regulation, private parties often lack the necessary information, so that public enforcement may be desirable. The public enforcer may build up expertise in the relevant area and may benefit from economies of scale in investigating possible violations.[7] The same holds for the area of competition law.[8] If representative actions are allowed, also private organisations may build up the necessary expertise or benefit from economies of scale.[9] Often a mix of public and private enforcement is needed to reach the best outcome.

A second relevant aspect in the choice between public and private enforcement is the question whether the enforcer receives socially desirable incentives in his decision whether or not to start a legal procedure. Generally speaking, private parties will be more interested in their private costs and benefits of litigation than in the public costs and benefits. Given that others than the parties involved may benefit from the outcome of a certain case (a point to which I will return in Sect. 4.3), private parties may prefer others to bear the costs of litigation. They may, in other words, want to take a free ride on the efforts of others. However, if too many people behave as free riders, there may be no civil procedure to start with, which would be an argument in favour of public enforcement. Furthermore, if the expected private benefits of a case are relatively small (for example because the wrongdoer is insolvent so that he cannot pay full damages or because every individual victim has only suffered a small loss), private parties may decide not to start a lawsuit (they then remain rationally apathetic). If insolvency is the cause of the problem, public enforcement may be called for. If scattered losses are the cause of the problem, besides public enforcement, allowing collective (damages) actions may be a solution. However, given that rational victims are not willing to pre-finance legal counsel, introduction of a form of result-based remuneration will be necessary then. Alternatively, allowing a victim to recover more than only his losses (hence, *punitive damages*) may overcome the problem of victims staying rationally apathetic.[10]

---

[5] Van den Bergh and Visscher 2008, 39.

[6] Landes and Posner 1975, 31; Shavell 1993, 267.

[7] Shavell 1984, 359.

[8] Van den Bergh and Keske 2007, 471 et seq.

[9] Keske 2010, 110.

[10] Wils 2003, 476, regarding treble damages in competition law, and Visscher 2009, 219–236, for a general economic approach to punitive damages.

4.3 The Economics of Civil Procedures in a Nutshell

4.3.1 The Social Goal of Civil Procedures

In Sect. 4.2.1, the social goal of law from an economic perspective became clear: ameliorating the problems caused by different forms of market failure. Section 2.2 briefly discussed the choice between public and private enforcement of law and showed that under certain conditions private enforcement is desirable. Viewed from this perspective, the main social goal of civil procedures is to enforce legal rules which address the issues caused by market failures. For example, collective actions in antitrust cases instigated by consumers or competitors of the infringer(s) serve the goal to bring the anticompetitive behaviour to a halt and to deter the defendant(s) and others from engaging in such behaviour. Tort cases for damages or injunctions aim equally to stop the tort from continuing and to deter this and other tortfeasors from subsequent tortious acts. They also may clarify the applicable behavioural norms, for example because the court provides more information on how to concretise the negligence standard in certain circumstances. Contract cases in which damages or specific performance is being requested on the basis of breach of contract reinforce the norm that contractual parties (not only those involved in the procedure, but also others) should live up to their contractual obligations, or internalise the negative consequences in case they do not. Copyright and patent cases protect the legal monopoly which was granted to the holder in order to provide adequate incentives for production of information. Trademark cases protect the instrument with which producers can signal quality to overcome the problem of adverse selection. Hence, in all these cases, there is a clear social goal which is served: increasing social welfare by solving the problems caused by market failures.

However, as became clear in Sect. 4.2.2, the parties involved in civil litigation have private goals which may be ill-aligned with the social goals. A typical plaintiff in a tort case, for instance, is likely more interested in receiving damages than in deterring potential tortfeasors or clarifying the applicable behavioural norms. Likewise, private enforcers of competition law may be more interested in the direct (financial) outcome of the case than in deterring others from anticompetitive behaviour. To put it in more general terms, the parties involved in a civil procedure may be more interested in the dispute resolution aspect of civil litigation, whereas the economic approach to civil litigation stresses a different function of civil litigation: contributing to the production of legal norms which help to tackle the problems caused by market failures. The legal approach is more *ex post*, looking back to the case at hand, whereas the economic approach is more *ex ante*, focusing on future behaviour. There are, of course, also cases which do not have merits beyond the case at hand, such as uncontested pecuniary claims. There the difference between private and social gains is much less important.

The fact that civil procedures may produce the above-described positive externalities (clearer guidelines for behaviour, general deterrence, et cetera) implies that there may be a social value of litigation which goes beyond the private value of conflict resolution.[11] It is therefore important that civil litigation does not become too costly for potential plaintiffs (both in terms of money and of time) because otherwise substantive law will not be enforced adequately and hence will not be able to provide the desirable incentives.

4.3.2 Minimising Costs

Economic analysis of civil procedure centres on the issue of how different procedures affect the sum of *direct costs* and *error costs* and how they influence the behaviour of the parties involved in the dispute resolution process.[12] The latter topic will be discussed in Sect. 4.3.3 below.

Direct costs are the costs of adjudication itself, namely the time invested by the various actors involved (parties, lawyers, judges, (expert) witnesses), their wages, as well as the material costs (offices, office supplies, et cetera). Error costs emerge when wrong decisions are taken because the substantive law then does not provide the correct incentives (for instance cases where liability is warranted but, due to for example problems of proving causation, liability is not imposed). There exists a trade-off between both types of costs. The more resources that are invested in the procedure, for instance in hearing witnesses, the lower the probability of wrong decisions may become, so that direct costs increase while error costs decrease. The economic goal is to strike a balance between both types of costs so that the sum of error costs and direct costs is minimised. Quicker, cheaper procedures therefore have the benefit that they save on direct costs, but if the quality of the resulting rulings decreases, the overall assessment may still be negative. After all, if more errors are made, the behavioural incentives provided by the legal system are of a lower quality, which may result in more undesirable behaviour taking place. In addition, the direct costs of the legal system may increase after all, if lower-quality decisions (meaning, less in conformity with the desired outcome) are more often appealed than higher-quality decisions. Another important possible drawback of cheap and quick procedures is that the number of legal claims will probably increase. After all, the price of litigation goes down (both in terms of money and of time) and the law of demand then predicts an increase in demand. Especially in cases where the social value of litigation is limited, such an increase is undesirable.

An important procedural ‘instrument’ with which both direct costs and error costs are influenced is the burden of proof. From an economic point of view, many factors are relevant in deciding who should bear the burden of proof.[13] Obviously, the costs of producing evidence are important. If it is cheaper for the plaintiff to

---

[11] Shavell 1997, 575–612 and Shavell 2004, 283 et seq.

[12] See for early literature, e.g., Landes 1971, 61–107 and Posner 1973, 399–458. See for an overview Kobayashi and Parker 2000, 1–26.

[13] See, e.g., Hay and Spier 1997, 418.

prove the presence of something (such as negligence, breach of contract, anti-competitive behaviour, existence of a debt, or more general the presence of a factor 'X') than it is for the defendant to prove the absence of X, then it makes sense to put the burden of proof on the plaintiff. However, also the a priori possibility that factor X is present should be included. If X is an unlawful act, given the assumption that most people do not behave unlawfully, the probability that X is present is much lower than the probability that X is not present. In that case, even if the costs of proving the presence of X may outweigh the costs of proving the absence of X, it still makes sense to put the burden of proof on the plaintiff. After all, if the burden of proof is put on the defendant while it is unlikely that he has acted unlawfully, direct costs increase because the absence of X has to be proven in many cases, and error costs increase dramatically in the cases where the defendant cannot prove the absence of X. For example, if a plaintiff sues someone for damages for drunk driving, the costs of proving either drunkenness or soberness may be comparable (in both cases, a breath or blood test may be required) or may be even lower for the defendant (he can ask witnesses to testify about where he was before the accident, while the plaintiff does not have that information). However, given that the vast majority of people do not drive while being drunk, it still makes sense to put the burden of proof on the plaintiff. It is also important to include available information which affects the a priori assessment of the probability that X is present. For example, if our defendant smells of alcohol, drives erratically and has bloodshot eyes, given that (the combination of) these factors occur much more often in cases where a person is drunk than in cases where a person is not drunk, it makes sense to reverse the burden of proof.

Obviously, a procedural issue such as the burden of proof, as well as the level of certainty required, is strongly influenced by the underlying substantive law. I will return to this issue of the interconnection between procedural law and substantive law in Sect. 4.5.

4.3.3 Influencing Behaviour in the Dispute Resolution Process

The dominant economic model of dispute resolution (the 'expected value model of adjudication') evaluates the impact of procedural rules in different phases of the process. The parties involved in litigation make an assessment of the expected (private) costs and benefits in which they incorporate their beliefs on the probability of success. This assessment determines whether they file a claim, whether they proceed with a claim or drop it after new information becomes available during the dispute resolution process, whether they are willing to make or accept a settlement offer or whether they proceed to the actual trial and, if yes, how much they spend on litigation.[14]

[14] See, e.g., Shavell 1982, 55–81; Cooter and Rubinfeld 1989, 1067–1097; Hughes and Snyder 1995, 225–250; Daughety 2000, 95–158; Kobayashi and Parker, 2000.

It goes beyond the scope of this chapter to discuss these insights in detail, but the example of the way in which the litigation costs are divided between plaintiff and defendant may be instructive to illustrate the line of reasoning. Under the English Rule the prevailing party recovers some or all litigation costs from the unsuccessful party, while under the American Rule each party bears its own expenses. Under the English Rule parties are expected to spend more on litigation than under the American Rule, now there is more at stake.[15] Furthermore, the higher the subjective assessment of success of the plaintiff, the more likely he is to sue. This effect is stronger under the English Rule because a successful plaintiff under this rule does not bear the (full) litigation costs. This implies that the English Rule creates a selection effect in the direction of high-merit claims. In addition, the more risk averse a plaintiff is, the less likely he is to sue. This effect is stronger under the English Rule because the stakes there also include the litigation costs of the other party. The effect on settlement is unclear. On the one hand, the 'greater expenditure effect' makes settlements more attractive because litigation is expected to become more expensive. On the other hand, the tendency of parties to overestimate their probability of success reduces the incentive to settle under the English Rule. Empirical research suggests that this over-optimism effect dominates.[16] The overall impact on the total duration of claims is unclear. Information that becomes available during the procedure which shows a lower quality of the claim than originally expected will lead to a dropping of the claim sooner than under the American Rule because the plaintiff runs the risk of having to bear the litigation costs of the defendant as well. The settlement stage is also expected to be shorter because of the selection effect towards higher quality claims. However, cases which are not settled are expected to take longer in the adjudication phase due to the greater-expenditure effect.

The economic literature on the dispute resolution process also studies the impact of issues such as fee arrangements (no cure no pay, *quota pars litis*, no win less fee, et cetera) and possibilities of collective actions. All these issues turn out to be interrelated and they are also connected to other issues, such as the availability of legal expense insurance (after the event or before the event) or subsidised legal aid. The relevance of all these issues for this paper is that procedural law may affect the parties involved in litigation in many interrelated ways. This implies that proposals for harmonisation, which change the current procedural law, should be thought through very carefully in order to avoid adverse effects. In addition, it is important to keep in mind that the incentives provided through the rules of civil procedure are also influenced by the underlying substantive law and issues such as the availability of legal expense insurance and subsidised legal aid, the question whether collective actions are allowed, et cetera. I will return to this issue in Sect. 4.5, where I will argue that the connection between substantive and procedural law is an issue which should be carefully considered in the debate regarding

[15] Katz 1987, 159 et seq.

[16] Snyder and Hughes 1990, 366.

harmonisation of procedural law. Before returning to that point, in Sect. 4.4 I will discuss the economic approach to harmonisation of private law in general.

4.4 Harmonisation of Private Law from an Economic Point of View

4.4.1 The Limited Value of the Traditional Legal Arguments in Favour of Harmonisation

If one reads the economic literature regarding harmonisation of law, it quickly becomes clear that the traditional legal arguments in favour of harmonisation are critically assessed and that different arguments in favour of and against harmonisation are applied.

One of the main legal arguments pro harmonisation is that differences in legal rules between countries result in legal uncertainty and increased costs. This would hinder cross-border trade because the costs of getting informed about the different legal systems may outweigh the gains from cross-border trade. And even if there were still such trade, it would become more expensive due to these legal differences. In the words of the European Commission, regarding contract law[17]:

> For consumers and SMEs [small and medium enterprises] in particular, not knowing other contract law regimes may be a disincentive against undertaking cross-border transactions. This has been part of the rationale for some existing Community acts aimed at improving the functioning of the internal market. Suppliers of goods and services may even therefore regard offering their goods and services to consumers in other countries as economically unviable and refrain from doing so.
>
> Moreover, disparate national law rules may lead to higher transaction costs, especially information and possible litigation costs for enterprises in general and SMEs and consumers in particular. Contractual parties could be forced to obtain information and legal advice on the interpretation and application of an unfamiliar foreign law. If the applicable law has been chosen in the contract, this applies to the contractual party whose law has not been chosen.
>
> These higher transaction costs may furthermore be a competitive disadvantage, for example in a situation where a foreign supplier is competing with a supplier established in the same country as the potential client.

Besides the fact that it remains to be seen whether harmonised law indeed would result in more legal certainty (problems of different interpretation and application of the legal rules may still result in non-uniform law),[18] there is no empirical evidence that differences between legal systems indeed significantly impede international trade, nor that harmonisation of law would result in more

---

[17] Communication from the Commission to the Council and the European Parliament on European Contract Law, COM (2001) 398 final, No. 30–32.

[18] See also Smits 2005, 179.

international transactions. Wagner for instance argues, regarding contract law, that large, multinational enterprises will not be deterred by differences between legal rules in the countries where they are active. They have experience with this problem and they will often use local lawyers and incorporate subsidiaries in the different countries to deal with the issue of different legal rules.[19] For small and medium-size firms this may be different so that in theory the costs of dealing with different legal systems could indeed hinder international trade. However, Wagner states that in reality this may not be the case. He provides anecdotal evidence on small and medium-size enterprises that are active in many countries all over the world. More importantly, business associations representing small and medium-size firms during the consultation process on the Commission Communication of European Contract Law themselves did not regard full harmonisation as a necessary tool to promote competition within the common market.[20] According to several responses, problems in the functioning of the internal market are caused more by language barriers, cultural differences, distance, habits and divergence in other areas of law, such as tax law and, noteworthy, procedural law.[21]

A second traditional argument for harmonisation is that it would create a 'level playing field.' After all, differences in legal rules between countries could create inequality in competitive conditions across Member States, so it is argued. There are several reasons why this argument is not convincing. The first reason, that different (groups of) people may prefer different rules so that a level playing field is not desirable to start with, will be treated in more detail in Sect. 4.4.2 below where the economic arguments against harmonisation are discussed. In addition, in as far as the legal rules in a given jurisdiction hold for all actors in that jurisdiction, the playing field within every single jurisdiction already is level. There would only be a problem of unequal competitive conditions across Member States if foreign actors were held to different, more stringent norms than domestic actors. In case of for instance tort law or contract law, this problem therefore does not exist. Furthermore, if the goal of harmonisation is to remove the differences between legal rules of different countries altogether, this goal neglects that differences between countries are the basis of international trade to start with. Removing such differences may very well reduce social welfare. If legal differences enable for instance prices of goods or services to be lower in some jurisdictions, this will lower the prices on the international market, which also benefits those in the jurisdictions with the stricter rules.[22] Finally, harmonisation of law will not result in a level playing field because other aspects, such as infrastructure, wages, labour productivity, et cetera will stay non-harmonised.

[19] Wagner 2002, 1014. Also see Smits 2005, 167.

[20] Ott and Schäfer 2002, 213; Wagner 2002, 1015; Smits 2005, 170.

[21] Smits 2005, 170.

[22] See, e.g., Ogus 1999, 417; Van den Bergh and Visscher 2006, 515.

4.4.2 Economic Arguments Against Harmonisation

4.4.2.1 Satisfying a Greater Number of Preferences

The starting point of the economic approach to harmonisation is that legal diversity in principle is desirable because different people may have different preferences regarding the goals of law, they may differ in wealth, in social norms, et cetera. Uniform law, equally applying to everybody, is not able to take such differences into account. For example, countries with a higher national income per capita may prefer a higher safety standard or a different allocation of risks than less wealthy countries, for the simple reason that the level of safety and the allocation of risk influence the price of products and services, as well as the type of insurance necessary to cover those risks. Diverging social norms may impact what is regarded as desirable and acceptable behaviour, so that the legal norms governing this behaviour may differ per country or region.

This idea was first expressed by Tiebout, who illustrated it by the choice of people regarding where to locate. Depending on their preferences, one community will be more attractive to person A, while another community may be more attractive to person B. Tiebout argues that 'the greater the number of communities and the greater the variance among them, the closer the consumer will come to fully realizing his preference position.'[23] Under certain conditions (among which full information about the different communities and full mobility of consumers), people will move to the community which is best for them. The parallel to the topic of harmonisation of law is clear: by having different legal systems co-existing, a greater number of preferences can be satisfied because people can move to the jurisdiction which best fits their preferences (which is called 'voting with their feet'). Alternatively, legislators may be induced to change the law if it turns out that competing jurisdictions meet the preferences of actors better.

Wagner extensively discusses this idea and the assumptions made. In reality, people do not have full information about different jurisdictions. Furthermore, moving from one jurisdiction to another is anything but costless and it is unlikely that people would move to another Member State because they prefer the legal rules there. However, in areas of law such as contract law where it is possible to choose the applicable law, it may still be possible that the existence of different legal systems facilitates satisfaction of a greater number of preferences (provided that foreign law is recognised and enforced in domestic courts).[24] In Wagner's view, incomplete information about the different legal systems is still problematic, so that it is highly doubtful whether choice of law can act as a substitute for voting with one's feet.[25]

---

23 Tiebout 1956, 418.

24 See also, e.g., Ogus 1999, 408, 416.

25 Wagner 2002, 1007–1011.

4.4.2.2 Enabling Learning Effects

A second possible advantage of legal diversity is that competition between legal systems enables learning effects.[26] Different solutions to similar problems and different interpretations of vague legal concepts may all yield valuable information of how legal rules influence human behaviour. It is therefore possible to learn from the solutions applied in other countries, which may help in finding a better solution in the domestic legal system.[27] Van den Bergh describes the example of competition law, where different instruments may be used to assess the anti-competitive effects of market concentration. The fact that different experiences exist, enables improving competition law.[28] It is also possible to 'import' legal concepts from other jurisdictions if they enable solving certain problems in a more satisfactory way. For example, the concept of 'loss of a chance' was already known in French law for a long time before it was accepted in Dutch law.[29]

Ogus explains that a possible spontaneous convergence due to these learning effects has an important advantage over imposed harmonisation: the former will happen if the benefits of convergence exceed the costs. Imposed harmonisation on the other hand, with the focus on the possible benefits of cost reduction, may have more costs (formulating uniform principles, adapting national legal systems, et cetera) than benefits (reduction in for example information costs).[30] Obviously, this possibility of learning effects is lost in case of harmonised law. It is very doubtful whether the centralised legislator is able to make up for this loss of learning possibilities by providing a higher quality of law. The next topic, limited information and the potential influence of interest groups, strengthens these doubts.

4.4.2.3 Limited Information of the Legislator and Influence of Interest Groups

There are additional reasons why legislation should take place at the lowest level possible, rather than at a higher level and hence also why competing national legal systems in principle are preferable to harmonised law (possible reasons why legislation should nonetheless take place at a higher level are discussed in Sect. 4.4.3). First, the 'local' legislator presumably will have better information regarding the local issues, problems and preferences than the legislator on a higher

[26] See, e.g., Van den Bergh 2000a, 437, 438.
[27] See also Wagner 2002, 1012.
[28] Van den Bergh 2000a, 455.
[29] Kerkmeester and Visscher 2003, 5.
[30] Ogus 1999, 415–416.

level. This implies that local regulation is better able than centralised legislation to deal with the issues and problems and to satisfy the preferences.[31]

The second issue is more complicated. The starting point is that regulators may be influenced by interest groups. Regulation hence does not by definition always serve 'the general interest' (whatever that may be) in an optimally balanced way. Interest groups, for example in the way in which they provide information to the regulator regarding the issue under regulation, may try to influence the regulator in such a way that the resulting regulation serves their private interests. As Wagner puts it: 'the democratic process is surrounded by and embedded in a world of intensive rent-seeking behaviour of societal groups, fighting to secure legislation furthering their particular interests.'[32] In order to try to reduce the possible problems caused by the influence of pressure groups, competition between different sets of regulations is preferred.

There exists a complication, though. Regarding the topic of harmonisation of law, some groups will have an interest in keeping non-harmonised law while others on the contrary benefit from harmonisation. This is the case irrespective of the answer to the question whether harmonisation is desirable from a societal point of view. For example, academics specialised in their national legal system have different interests than academics specialised in international and comparative law.[33] The same is true for practising lawyers in the different fields of law.[34] Furthermore, European bureaucrats, whose prestige and influence depend also on the level of centralisation of law-making in Europe, have a private interest in harmonisation. Finally, firms may have different interests. A firm located in a jurisdiction with a high level of consumer protection which has already spent resources on meeting those high demands will have an interest in avoiding harmonisation which would lower the standard. After all, the fact that this firm already meets the demands is a competitive advantage when compared to potential newcomers who still have to invest.[35] On the other hand, firms that already meet the more demanding requirements may benefit from harmonisation which would increase the standard because this forms a barrier to entry.[36]

Hence, even though the impact of interest groups is in principle an argument in favour of competition between legal systems, one should not forget that interest groups may oppose harmonisation also in cases where there are good arguments for it.[37] These arguments are discussed in the following Section.

---

[31] See, e.g., Faure 2003, 38.

[32] Wagner 2002, 1000.

[33] Wagner 2002, 1012.

[34] Ogus 1999, 412.

[35] Van den Bergh 2000a, 448, 449.

[36] Faure 2003, 44.

[37] Ogus in this respect also argues that if interest groups can obstruct the process of competition between jurisdictions which could lead to spontaneous harmonisation, mandatory harmonisation may be required. Ogus 1999, 416.

4.4.3 Economic Arguments in Favour of Harmonisation

4.4.3.1 Internalising Interstate Externalities

In Sect. 4.4.2, the issue of satisfying a larger number of preferences was discussed, which resulted in an argument for decentralised rule-making. This argument, however, assumes that all costs and benefits of the regulation under consideration are borne by those living in the relevant jurisdiction. If costs of the regulation can be externalised to actors in other jurisdictions, social welfare may decrease because in deciding on the regulation not all costs are taken into account. If, for example, country A had lenient rules regarding protection of the environment and if the pollution caused by actors in country A mainly materialised in country B (for example because the pollution is transported there through the air or through rivers), then the joint welfare of country A and B might increase if both countries together decided on the appropriate level of environmental protection.

If voluntary negotiations between the countries involved do not result in the optimal outcome, for instance because property rights are not clearly defined or because parties behave strategically in negotiations, top-down harmonisation may be required.[38] However, first it has to be assessed whether national laws are able to cope with the externality. For example, in the case of product liability, differences in the level of consumer protection in principle could result in an interstate externality if producers in a lenient State sold their (unsafe) products in other countries. However, given that the manufacturer can be held liable according to the law of the importing state, there is no problem of interstate externalities and hence no need for harmonisation after all.[39]

If national laws cannot cope with the problem adequately, regulation should take place on the level which is able to cover the area in which the externality exists.[40]

4.4.3.2 Avoid a 'Race to the Bottom'

The basic argument of the 'race to the bottom' is that competition between jurisdictions may lead to 'bad law.' The idea is that States, in deciding on regulation, may try to attract actors to their jurisdiction by offering rules which are attractive to them. For instance by lowering the level of protection of employees, consumers and/or the environment, et cetera, States try to attract firms because this is to the benefit of the State (e.g. through more foreign investment and/or by increased tax returns). In competing with each other, States would continuously lower the standards of protection to become more attractive, which would result in

[38] See Van den Bergh 2000b, 80 et seq.

[39] Van den Bergh and Visscher 2006, 518–519.

[40] Faure 2003, 38.

very low standards which would only be to the benefit of firms. Centralisation (including harmonisation), so it is argued, may be necessary to avoid this problem.[41]

Besides the fact that it is difficult to argue on a theoretical level why competition between States would lead to adverse effects whereas competition in general is regarded positively,[42] empirical evidence for this alleged race to the bottom is also weak. Ogus offers some possible explanations. First, in order for the race to the bottom to occur in cases of negative interstate externalities, legislators have to find activities which generate 'significant transborder effects but little or no domestic effects.'[43] Second, it may be beneficial for firms to operate in jurisdictions with higher rather than lower standards because this may induce them to technological improvements which provide competitive benefits. Ogus' first point can be generalised: a race to the bottom may occur only if States are able to attract industry with lenient rules. Faure discusses this issue for environmental law, where firms may locate in 'pollution havens' with low environmental standards. He shows, referring to a multitude of publications, that empirical support in this area again is weak: pollution control costs are relatively low so that firms do not base their location decision on this issue; environmental regulation turns out not to induce existing firms to relocate, although location decisions of new firms may be influenced by it somewhat; other issues such as taxes, public services and the way in which the labour force is organised are much more important in the location decision. According to Faure, a 'race to the top' is more likely than a race to the bottom in cases of environmental liability because States may choose to protect the interests of victims rather than industry and because more stringent rules may enable the States to sue for damages in cases of, for example, soil pollution.[44] Similar doubts regarding the alleged race to the bottom hold for the topic of product liability. If harm occurs in export markets, the firm is liable according to the rules of those jurisdictions, and not to those of the more lenient exporting State. Furthermore, it is doubtful whether States can charge the industry for using lenient tort law. This is an important difference with the often-used example of corporate law where a large proportion of American firms incorporate in Delaware. Here, Delaware receives incorporation fees, but in the field of tort law there is no comparable benefit for States offering attractive rules.[45] Of course, the mere fact that the firms locate in a jurisdiction already may be beneficial because it may reduce unemployment, increase wages, et cetera. This does not change the fact that empirical support for the race to the bottom argument is at best weak. Besides, even if harmonisation were justified by the danger of a race to the bottom, there is

---

41 Wagner 2002, 1003–1004; Faure 2003, 47; Van den Bergh and Visscher 2006, 519–520.

42 See, e.g., Revesz 1992, 1236 et seq.

43 Ogus 1999, 415.

44 Faure 2003, 48–49.

45 Van den Bergh and Visscher 2006, 520.

still the problem that not all States are equally strict in enforcing the regulation, so that differences between countries would still exist.[46]

4.4.3.3 Decrease Transaction Costs and Profit from Scale Economies

A last possible argument in favour of harmonisation is that it may achieve economies of scale and it may reduce transaction costs. Scale economies exist if it is cheaper to have one (international) regulator rather than more lower-level regulators. This may be the case if the information that is required for regulation is relevant not only for one national jurisdiction, but also on a higher level, for example a group of countries or the entire European Union. Scale economies are likely important for the design of efficient rules of public law (such as product safety standards), but they may be much smaller, if not negligible, in other fields of law such as private law (including for example product liability).[47]

The transaction cost argument is closely related to the traditional legal argument of reducing legal uncertainty and reducing costs of international transactions, although that traditional legal argument is often set in the context of hindering cross-border trade. The line of reasoning is, in principle, quite simple. The currently existing differences in legal systems add to the costs of international transactions, for example of getting informed about the legal systems, of drawing different contracts for different countries, of litigation, et cetera. Wagner writes that 'legal diversity places a tax on European business, a tax that creates no benefits either for firms or for consumers but only benefits for lawyers.'[48] Even if firms were not deterred from international transactions due to the higher costs caused by having to cope with different legal systems, there still would be such additional costs. Harmonisation would reduce those costs because one would not need to have knowledge of several different legal systems anymore. Again in the words of Wagner: 'Harmonisation would eliminate a considerable part of the transaction costs … and thus benefit society as a whole by abolishing a tax on international businesses.'[49]

Ribstein and Kobayashi distinguish several types of costs, which are reduced by uniformity[50]:

- *Inconsistency costs*: an actor that is active in several jurisdictions will have to meet the requirements posed by these different jurisdictions. These requirements will likely differ, which creates additional costs for the actor. Uniform law does

---

46 See, e.g., Gatsios and Holmes 1998, 274.

47 Van den Bergh 2000a, 445; Van den Bergh and Visscher 2006, 521.

48 Wagner 2002, 1014.

49 Wagner 2002, 1017.

50 Ribstein and Kobayashi 1996, 138 et seq. See also Ott and Schäfer 2002, 207 et seq and Wagner 2005, 31–32.

not necessarily remove these costs, in so far as it is not applied and/or interpreted uniformly;

- *Information costs*: actors need to determine the law which applies in every jurisdiction in which they are active. Uniform law reduces these costs because it is clearer which law applies, but also the interpretation may be easier if judicial decisions regarding the correct interpretation become available. Smits argues that the information costs decrease only if all relevant rules are unified because otherwise the actor still has to get informed about the other relevant, non-unified rules.[51] Ribstein and Kobayashi furthermore state that reduction of information costs is less relevant in situations where parties are able to choose the applicable law themselves;
- *Litigation costs*: under uniform law, parties no longer need to deal with issues regarding choice of law and also do not spend resources on forum shopping. Smits adds the point that parties no longer have to obtain information about how to bring a claim against the other party. In my view, this is already 'covered' under information costs;
- *Instability costs*: if the law that governs a transaction changes, this forces the transacting parties to incorporate this change. According to Ripstein and Kobayashi, uniform law reduces these costs by focusing public attention on changes that reduce uniformity. Smits adds that information on changes in the uniform law will be more readily available than information on changes in a foreign legal system;
- *Externalities*: this issue was already discussed above. Decentralised regulators may be able to enact legislation that serves the interests of the people living in its own jurisdiction, thereby externalising costs on people outside the jurisdiction. Uniform law avoids this problem because the legislator has to take the interests of all constituents in all jurisdictions into consideration. Possibilities of 'voting with their feet' and choice of law, however, limit the relevance of this cost-reducing ability of uniform law; and
- *Drafting costs*: uniform law-making agencies can concentrate their resources on drafting particular laws and can hire experts in particular fields or in statutory drafting. Decentralised legislators, on the other hand, 'are often part-time generalists who have little incentive to spend time finely crafting legislation in particular areas and lack resources to hire advisors.'[52] Smits rightfully doubts whether this is an accurate description of the comparison between legislation on a European level and on the level of the Member States.[53]

Obviously, these benefits of uniform law have to be compared with the costs thereof. Ribstein and Kobayashi in this respect state that regulatory competition enables satisfying a greater number of preferences, that it enables learning effects

[51] Smits 2005, 168.

[52] Ribstein and Kobayashi 1996, 140.

[53] Smits 2005, 169.

(they call this ‘innovation and experimentation’) and that local legislators have better information regarding the local conditions.[54]

There are several reasons why the potential of uniform law to save on transaction costs should not be overestimated.[55] First, it is doubtful whether harmonised law would indeed remove transaction costs to a large extent. After all, the harmonised rules will have to be translated into the different languages of Member States. The interpretation of the provisions might not be the same in all Member States, especially if vague concepts are used, so that differences could still exist.[56]

Second, the harmonisation process itself causes transaction costs. Actors in all Member States have to switch from their own national legislation to the new, harmonised legislation. Smits argues that these costs are considerable. They include the costs of political decision making, of implementing the reform and of adaptation to the new legislation (amending contracts, educating lawyers and judges, et cetera).[57] Especially if differences between national legislations are rooted in the respective legal cultures, harmonisation will be difficult and costly.[58]

4.5 Harmonisation of Procedural Law from an Economic Perspective

Looking at the role of civil procedures as discussed in Sect. 4.3 and at the economic approach to harmonisation which was treated in Sect. 4.4, it is now possible to bring both lines of reasoning together and to discuss harmonisation of civil procedural law from an economic viewpoint.

The point of departure has to be, just as with any other type of law, that economists in principle prefer diversity because it enables satisfying a larger number of preferences as well as a learning process towards ‘better law.’ Hence, the subsidiarity principle from an economic point of view is relevant not only for substantive law, but also for procedural law.

An additional reason why especially harmonisation of procedural law may be problematic is the fact that it is so closely connected to the substantive law of the different countries. After all, civil procedures are the instruments with which rights and obligations which result from substantive law are enforced. Differences in substantive law, legal culture, the relative importance of public versus private enforcement and social norms may have a strong impact on procedural law. For example, in countries where consumers are predominantly regarded as ‘weak’ parties who need protection against firms, procedural law may be used to

54 Ribstein and Kobayashi 1996, 140, 141.

55 Van den Bergh 1998, 146–148.

56 See, e.g., Van den Bergh and Visscher 2006, 521.

57 Smits 2005, 178. Also see, e.g., Weber-Rey 2006, 233.

58 Faure 2003, 59–60.

strengthen this protection in the form of information duties for the defendant-firm, shifting the burden of proof, applying different statutes of limitation, et cetera to a larger extent than in countries where consumers are regarded as 'normal' parties in contractual settings who do not need additional protection. In tort law, questions about whether certain risks are governed by strict liability or negligence, whether proportional liability is accepted, what the required proof of for instance causation is ('more likely than not' or 'beyond a reasonable doubt') and which losses are regarded as recoverable (think of issues such as pure economic loss, pain and suffering damages, hedonic damages in fatal accidents) all influence the way in which a trial is conducted. A last example regards the difference in cost shifting rules. As was shown in Sect. 4.3, these rules may impact civil procedures in many aspects, such as the decision to settle or sue, the resources spent on litigation, the quality of the claims being brought, et cetera. Cost shifting rules therefore have an impact on access to justice. The optimal rules on who ultimately bears litigation costs are strongly influenced by other issues, such as whether legal expense insurance and/or subsidised legal aid is available, whether fee arrangements are possible and what types of collective claims are possible. Hence, certain aspects of procedural law may be closely connected to many other aspects.[59] In other words, there exists a strong 'path dependency' of procedural law. Harmonising procedural law therefore might not only be more difficult than harmonising substantive law, it is also even doubtful whether harmonisation of procedural law in these areas where substantive law differs makes much sense. After all, the combination of substantive law and procedural law provides the behavioural incentives to actors. Procedural law is the instrument with which to effectuate claims arising from substantive law. Given the reservations Law and Economics has against harmonisation of substantive law, it does not seem to make much sense to focus on harmonisation of procedural law.

Summarising, differences in substantive law which reflect differences in preferences, social norms, et cetera make harmonisation of procedural law with which substantive law is enforced problematic. In order to be able to satisfy more preferences, it is preferable to allow actors to choose which legal system they want to apply to their relationship. Hence, choice of law is in principle preferred over harmonisation. This nicely connects to the presentation which the Secretary General of the Council of Bars and Law Societies of Europe gave at the 2008 Conference on Civil Justice Systems in Europe of the Institute of European and Comparative Law, where he stressed the importance of subsidiarity and mutual recognition.[60]

A possible 'middle ground' between the desire to harmonise on the one hand and the benefits of regulatory competition on the other hand can be reached by

[59] See also Parker 2009, 12.

[60] Goldsmith, Civil Justice Systems, Choice of Forum and Choice of Contract Law in Europe, available at http://denning.law.ox.ac.uk/news/events_files/Civil_Justice_Systems,_Choice_of_Forum_and_Choice_of_Contract_Law_in_Europe_-_Jonathan_Goldsmith_.pdf (last consulted 1 August 2011).

offering harmonised law as an additional choice. Especially in the debate on harmonisation of contract law, this option is often mentioned as an attractive alternative.[61] It enables parties to choose a legal system which is the same (or at least comparable) in different countries, but it does not force them to do so if they prefer specific national legislation. The European Order for Payment Procedure[62] and the European Small Claims Procedure[63] provide examples of this idea in the area of procedural law. The fact that the proper functioning of the internal market, avoiding distortion of competition within the internal market and the need for Community legislation that guarantees a level playing field for creditors and debtors throughout the European Union are all mentioned as rationales behind the regulation is not convincing from a Law and Economics point of view, as became clear in the above analysis of harmonisation in general. However, Article 1 of the European Order for Payment Procedure states that it 'shall not prevent a claimant from pursuing a claim … by making use of another procedure available under the law of a Member State or under Community law' and Article 1 of the European Small Claims Procedure states that it 'shall be available to litigants as an alternative to the procedures existing under the laws of the Member States.' This optional character fits nicely into the economic line of reasoning because regulatory competition is actually increased by adding an additional choice. Experience with how often this additional option is chosen provides valuable information about the relative magnitude of the different costs and benefits associated with harmonisation which were discussed above.

The risk of a race to the bottom does not seem very realistic in the case of procedural law, especially now that actors cannot directly choose the applicable procedural law but have to do this via the 'detour' of choice of forum. Such a race would imply that countries try to attract actors with cheap and quick procedures. This in itself is no problem and could even be seen as a race to the top. After all, if the costs of civil procedures as well as the time involved in them decrease, transaction costs will go down, which is desirable. The economic approach to civil procedures as discussed in Sect. 4.3 strengthens this point because private enforcement of law is necessary in order to provide actors with the correct behavioural incentives. Barriers to civil litigation therefore are undesirable. This holds even stronger for small claims, where low barriers can already result in rational apathy. It is therefore positive that the European Small Claims Procedure provides a relatively inexpensive procedure, which results in a judgment that is recognised and enforceable in other Member States without the need for a declaration of enforceability and without any possibility of opposing its recognition.

Obviously, stimulating civil procedures should not go at the expense of the quality of the procedure. Low quality of civil procedures will itself result in costs

---

[61] Although the danger exists that this 'European option' is chosen more often due to its prestige rather than its contents.

[62] Regulation No. 1896/2006 creating a European order for payment procedure, OJ 2006, L399/1.

[63] Regulation No 861/2007 establishing a European Small Claims Procedure, OJ 2007, L199/1.

(for instance the costs of appeal but also the costs of producing wrong behavioural norms), so that producing bad law is not attractive for countries anyway. In addition, it is doubtful whether countries would derive benefits from attracting international actors with 'bad' procedural law, besides stimulating their domestic legal profession. Furthermore, Article 6 of the European Convention on Human Rights poses several requirements on civil procedures, which further reduce the possibilities for a race to the bottom. The requirement of recognition and execution of foreign court rulings can also play a role in avoiding the race to the bottom problem. Hence, the race to the bottom argument is, to say the least, no more convincing than in the different areas of substantive law.

The possible problem of interstate externalities does not play a role in procedural law, especially now that the civil procedure takes place between the parties involved. Of course there is a positive externality of civil litigation in the sense that it produces behavioural norms which are also valid to actors who are not involved in the procedure. This is, however, not an interstate externality which calls for harmonisation. On the contrary, given that the procedure can help in clarifying legal concepts, in fine-tuning vague terms, et cetera, it is important that the procedure fit the underlying substantive law and that all relevant circumstances of the case, including local circumstances, customs, et cetera, be dealt with. Procedures that are specifically designed to fit these circumstances will probably result in better rulings than procedures which are based on a common denominator of several different systems.

Given that harmonisation of procedural law does not benefit from economies of scale, especially now that substantive law may differ per country, we have reached the last possible economic argument in favour of harmonisation of procedural law: reduction of transaction costs. Clearly, on the one hand, harmonisation of procedural law leads to a reduction of transaction costs because lawyers from all countries involved no longer have to deal with and get informed about different legal systems. It is especially noteworthy that in the Commission Communication of European Contract Law, several responses stated that problems in the functioning of the internal market were not so much caused by differences in contract law, but more by language barriers, cultural differences, distance, habits and divergence in other areas of law, such as tax law and procedural law. Hence, procedural law is explicitly mentioned as a possible hurdle.

On the other hand, it is far from certain that the transaction cost savings by harmonising procedural law outweighs its costs. Given that the underlying substantive law still differs, it is very doubtful whether harmonised procedural law truly leads to uniform law, or whether differences in interpretation would still result in substantial non-uniformity. Furthermore, the transition from the currently existing systems of national procedural law to the new harmonised law also causes transaction costs. As was explained in Sect. 4.4, it remains to be seen whether the reduction in transaction costs due to harmonisation outweighs the costs of harmonisation, including losing the possibility of learning effects and of satisfying a larger number of preferences.

In the 2008 Oxford Civil Justice Survey of the Institute of European and Comparative Law it was examined 'to what extent businesses in Europe were influenced by their perceptions of national civil justice systems and contract laws when choosing the applicable law and the forum of litigation for cross-border transactions.'[64] From this Survey it becomes clear that many of the respondents find it very important (61 per cent) or important (36 per cent), when conducting cross-border transactions, to be able to choose the dispute resolution forum.[65] With the statement that variations in European civil justice systems deter the respondent's company from doing business in certain jurisdictions, 51 per cent disagree strongly, 25 per cent disagree mildly, 19 per cent agree mildly and 1 per cent agrees strongly.[66] With the statement that such differences constitute, overall, a barrier to trade, 25 per cent disagree strongly, 35 per cent disagree mildly, 33 per cent agree mildly and 6 per cent agree strongly.[67] In my view, these results suggest that the transaction cost savings argument does not outweigh the arguments in favour of regulatory competition. Granted, the respondents are positive about the idea of a harmonised European civil justice system (36 per cent very favourably, 40 per cent favourably, 19 per cent not very favourably and 4 per cent not at all favourably), especially because it reduces costs.[68] However, only 22 per cent would choose for the option of a European civil justice system which replaces national civil justice systems, while 25 per cent would choose for this European system to be an additional choice. Most respondents (37 per cent) would opt for a greater alignment of civil justice systems.[69]

4.6 Conclusion

Evaluated from an economic perspective, there do not seem to be many arguments in favour of harmonisation of procedural law. In order to be able to learn from experiences and solutions in other jurisdictions, to meet more diverging preferences and to better connect procedural law to the underlying substantive law, clear rules regarding choice of law and regarding recognition and execution of foreign titles seems like a much better approach. To the extent that 'best practices' exist which could also be used in other jurisdictions, regulatory competition enables bottom-up harmonisation because other jurisdictions may incorporate similar solutions.

---

[64] Hodges et al. 2009, 8.

[65] See Question 28 of the Survey, available at http://denning.law.ox.ac.uk/iecl/ocjsurvey.shtml (last consulted 1 August 2011).

[66] See Question 41 of the Survey.

[67] See Question 42 of the Survey.

[68] See Question 43 and 46 of the Survey.

[69] See Question 45 of the Survey.

Does this mean that there is no scope for harmonisation whatsoever? Not necessarily. In Sect. 4.5, the possibility of harmonised procedures as an additional option to choose from was already mentioned. This approach fits in an economic line of reasoning. Furthermore, as has become clear in the above Sections, Law and Economics identifies the potential costs and benefits of harmonisation. Generally speaking, the benefits seem to be restricted to possible transaction cost savings. The Oxford Civil Justice Survey suggests that differences in civil justice systems do not deter international trade, so it is questionable whether the transaction cost savings outweigh the social costs of harmonisation.

For specific topics this may be different. For example, in a case of uncontested pecuniary claims, the fact that the underlying substantive law which determines whether there is a debt and how large it is may differ, is irrelevant. After all, the debt is uncontested. Furthermore, given that there is no substantial precedent-value of rulings in such uncontested pecuniary claim cases, it is desirable to process such cases at the lowest possible costs. Hence, uncontested pecuniary claims are an area where the costs of harmonisation are relatively low while the benefits may be substantial. However, it remains far from clear whether the benefits outweigh the costs of shifting to a new system and whether the centralised legislator is better able than the decentralised legislator to design an optimal system of handling uncontested pecuniary claims.

The question whether the benefits of harmonisation outweigh the costs is ultimately an empirical question which I cannot answer in this chapter. The Oxford Civil Justice Survey suggests that differences between civil justice systems are a relevant factor for businesses, but they do not deter them from international trade, nor are they generally regarded as a barrier to trade. In my opinion, the scope for harmonisation of procedural law from a Law and Economics point of view is hence at best limited and it should have an optional character.

References

Akerlof G (1970) The market for lemons: qualitative uncertainty and the market mechanism. Q J Econ 84:488–500

Cooter RD, Rubinfeld DL (1989) Economic analysis of legal disputes and their resolution. J Econ Lit 27:1067–1097

Daughety AF (2000) Settlement. In: Bouckaert B, De Geest G (eds) Encyclopedia of law and economics, vol V: the economics of crime and litigation. Edward Elgar, Cheltenham, pp 95–158

Faure MG (2003) How law and economics may contribute to the harmonisation of Tort law in Europe. In: Zimmermann R (ed) Grundstrukturen des Europäischen Deliktsrecht. Nomos Verlagsgesellschaft, Baden-Baden, pp 31–82

Gatsios K, Holmes P (1998) Regulatory competition. In: Newman P (ed) The new Palgrave dictionary of economics and the law, vol 3. MacMillan Reference Limited, London, pp 271–275

Goldsmith J (2010) Civil justice systems, choice of forum and choice of contract law in Europe. http://denning.law.ox.ac.uk/news/events_files/Civil_Justice_Systems,_Choice_of_Forum_

and_Choice_of_Contract_Law_in_Europe_-_Jonathan_Goldsmith_.pdf (Accessed 31 August 2010)
Hay BL, Spier KE (1997) Burdens of proof in civil litigation: an economic perspective. J Leg Stud 26:413–431
Hodges C et al (2009) Costs and funding of civil litigation: a comparative study. University of Oxford Legal Research Paper Series, Paper No. 55/2009
Hughes JW, Snyder EA (1995) Litigation and settlement under the English and American rules: theory and evidence. J Law Econ 38:225–250
Katz AW (1987) Measuring the demand for litigation: is the English rule really cheaper? J Law Econ Organ 3:143–176
Kerkmeester HO, Visscher LT (2003) Learned hand in Europe: a study in the comparative law and economics of negligence, German working papers in law and economics, Paper 6
Keske SE (2010) Group litigation in European competition law. Intersentia, Antwerp
Kobayashi BH, Parker JS (2000) Civil procedure: general. In: Bouckaert B, De Geest G (eds) Encyclopedia of law and economics, vol V: the economics of crime and litigation. Edward Elgar, Cheltenham
Landes WM (1971) An economic analysis of the courts. J Law Econ 14:61–107
Landes WM, Posner RA (1975) The private enforcement of law. J Leg Stud 4:31–55
Ogus A (1999) Competition between national legal systems: a contribution of economic analysis to comparative law. Int Comp Law Q 48:405–418
Ott C, Schäfer HB (2002) Die Vereinheitlichung des europäischen Vertragsrecht—Ökonomische Notwendigkeit oder akademisches Interesse? In: Ott C, Schäfer HB (eds) Vereinheitlichung und Diversität des Zivilrechts in transnationalen Wirtschaftsräumen. Mohr Siebeck, Tübingen, pp 203–236
Parker JS (2009) Comparative civil procedure and transnational 'harmonization': a law-and-economics perspective. George Mason University Law and Economics Research Paper Series, Paper 09-03, 12
Posner RA (1973) An economic approach to legal procedure and judicial administration. J Leg Stud 2:399–458
Revesz RL (1992) Rehabilitating interstate competition: rethinking the 'Race-to-the-Bottom' rationale for federal environmental regulation, New York University Law Rev 67:1210–1254
Ribstein LE, Kobayashi BH (1996) An economic analysis of Uniform State Laws. J Leg Stud 25:131–199
Rowley CK (1981) Social sciences and the law: the relevance of economic theories. Oxf J Leg Stud 1:391–405
Shavell S (1982) Suit, settlement, and trial: a theoretical analysis under alternative methods for the allocation of legal costs. J Leg Stud 11:55–81
Shavell S (1984) Liability for harm versus regulation of safety. J Leg Stud 13:357–374
Shavell S (1987) Economic analysis of accident law. Harvard University Press, Cambridge
Shavell S (1993) The optimal structure of law enforcement. J Law Econ 36:255–287
Shavell S (1997) The fundamental difference between the private and social motive to use the legal system. J Leg Stud 26:575–612
Shavell S (2004) Foundations of economic analysis of law. The Belknap Press of Harvard University Press, Cambridge
Smits J (2005) Diversity of contract law and the European internal market. In: Smits J (ed) The need for a European contract law. Empirical and legal perspectives. Europa Law Publishing, Groningen
Snyder EA, Hughes JW (1990) The English rule for allocating legal costs: evidence confronts theory. J Law Econ Organ 6:345–380
Tiebout CM (1956) A pure theory of local expenditures. J Political Econ 64:416–424
Van den Bergh R (1998) Subsidiarity as an economic demarcation principle and the emergence of European private law. Maastricht J Eur Comp Law 5:129–152
Van den Bergh RJ (2000a) Toward an institutional legal framework for regulatory competition in Europe. Kyklos 53:435–466

Van den Bergh RJ (2000b) Economic criteria for applying the subsidiarity principle in European environmental law. In: Revesz R et al (eds) Environmental law, the economy, and sustainable development. Cambridge University Press, Cambridge, pp 80–95

Van den Bergh R, Keske SE (2007) Private enforcement of European competition law: quo vadis? Eur Rev Contract Law 3:468–486

Van den Bergh RJ, Camesasca PDN (2006) European competition law and economics: a comparative perspective. Sweet & Maxwell, London

Van den Bergh RJ, Visscher LT (2008) Optimal enforcement of safety law. In: De Mulder RV (ed) Mitigating risk in the context of safety and security. How relevant is a rational approach? Erasmus University, Rotterdam, pp 29–62

Van den Bergh RJ, Visscher LT (2006) The principles of European Tort law: the right path to harmonization? Eur Rev Private Law 14:511–543

Visscher LT (2009) Economic analysis of punitive damages. In: Koziol H, Wilcox V (eds) Punitive damages: common law and civil law perspectives. Springer, Vienna, pp 219–236

Wagner G (2002) The economics of harmonization: the case of contract law. Common Mark Law Rev 39:995–1023

Wagner H (2005) Economic analysis of cross-border legal uncertainty. In: Smits J (ed) The need for a European contract law. Empirical and legal perspectives. Europa Law Publishing, Groningen, pp 25–51

Weber-Rey D (2006) Harmonisation of European insurance contract law. In: Vogenauer S, Weatherill S (eds) The harmonisation of European contract law. Hart Publishing, Oxford, pp 207–234

Wils WJP (2003) Should private antitrust enforcement be encouraged in Europe? World Compet 26:473–488

Chapter 5
Harmonisation of Civil Procedure: Policy Perspectives

Gerhard Wagner

Abstract European civil procedure is a rapidly growing field, judging by the numbers of directives and regulations churned out by the European Commission over the past decade. However, the practical impact of legislative acts passed under the provision of Article 81 TFEU remains very limited. These measures of 'horizontal harmonisation' create uniform rules for disputes of every kind, yet they remain confined to cross-border cases. As the Commission moved beyond the issues of international jurisdiction and enforcement of foreign judgments, it placed European institutions alongside the national ones, which continued to govern domestic disputes. This results in duplicative sets of procedural rules which place a heavy burden on the judges who have to work with them. Another thread of European legislation does not bear the label of civil procedure at all, but purports to harmonise the domestic system of law enforcement and protection of subjective rights in selected substantive areas, such as intellectual property rights, competition law and consumer law. Such measures of 'vertical harmonisation' remain confined to specific kinds of disputes, but they apply regardless of whether the dispute is international or domestic. In so doing, their practical impact is much greater than that of horizontal measures. For European lawmakers, it is essential to bear in mind that the policies of law enforcement and protection of property rights

---

Professor of German and European Private Law and Civil Procedure, University of Bonn (Germany) and Professor of Fundamentals of Private Law, Erasmus University Rotterdam (the Netherlands).

G. Wagner (✉)
University of Bonn, Bonn, Germany
e-mail: wagner@jura.uni-bonn.de

G. Wagner
Erasmus University Rotterdam, Rotterdam, The Netherlands

X. E. Kramer and C. H. van Rhee (eds.), *Civil Litigation in a Globalising World*,
DOI: 10.1007/978-90-6704-817-0_5,

deeply involve principles of civil procedure and that account must be taken of this when drafting pertinent legislation.

Contents

5.1 The Current State of European Civil Procedure

To an observer, the image currently conveyed by European civil procedural law suggests that the field is rapidly growing. Since the European Union (EU) gained the competence to legislate in this field of the law through the Treaty of Amsterdam of 2 October 1997,[1] which introduced Article 65 of the then Treaty establishing the European Community (EC Treaty), we have seen a rapid expansion of European legislation.

Before the Treaty of Amsterdam was agreed, the stronghold of European law in the area of civil procedure was the Brussels I Convention dating back to 1968, which has been in force since 1973. The Convention on Jurisdiction and the Recognition and Enforcement of Judgments was agreed and signed by the Member States in the course of intergovernmental cooperation under the former Article 293 (fourth point) EC Treaty. Given such a framework it was impossible to react quickly to new challenges, as even the mere accession of new Member States triggered a protracted and cumbersome process of revision, after which the dust settled only when a fresh version of the Brussels I Convention was negotiated and

[1] OJ 1997 No. C 340, 1 et seq.

agreed between the old and the new Member States and the several processes of ratification had been completed. As ratification never occurs at the same time by every signatory State, it was not unusual that different versions of Brussels I happened to be in force within the European Community (later, the European Union) at any given time. Obviously, such a state of affairs was highly unsatisfactory from a policy point of view. Instruments like Brussels I aim at harmonisation, or rather unification, of divergent rules in force in the several Member States.[2] The goals associated with the policy of unification cannot be achieved if different versions of the same legal instrument are floating around in the Member States and are applicable in one case or another. This makes life harder for the judges and lawyers preparing cases for litigation in the courts of any given country. In addition, and more importantly, it eats away at one central goal of the unification of civil procedure, i.e. the foreseeability and predictability of outcomes from the perspective of the parties.[3] If the parties cannot readily foresee which set of jurisdictional rules will be applied should a dispute arise between them in the future, they will be unable to draft their contracts and set their prices accordingly.

Against this backdrop, the switch of civil procedure from the so-called 'third column' of European Union law, i.e. intergovernmental cooperation, to the 'first column,' i.e. a direct competence of the Union itself, was a major step towards 'real' harmonisation, or rather unification. Article 65 EC Treaty provided a competence to legislate in the area of 'judicial cooperation in civil matters with cross-border implications' and particularly included measures to improve and simplify the system of cross-border service and notification of judicial and extrajudicial documents, cooperation between courts in the collection of evidence, recognition and enforcement of decisions in civil and commercial cases, including non-judicial decisions, the promotion of the compatibility of rules applicable in the Member States concerning jurisdictional conflicts, and the elimination of obstacles hindering the proper functioning of civil proceedings including, if necessary, by promoting the compatibility of the rules on civil procedure applicable in the Member States.

After the Treaty of Amsterdam had come into force, the Commission immediately used its new powers to regulate and legislate in this area. Up to the present day, eleven legislative acts have piled up which may be grouped under the rubric of civil procedure:

- Regulation No. 44/2001 on jurisdiction and the recognition and enforcement of judgments in civil and commercial matters (Brussels I)[4];
- Regulation No. 1346/2000 on insolvency proceedings (Insolvency Regulation)[5];

---

[2] ECJ 1 March 2005, Case C-281/02, ECR I-1383 (*Owusu v Jackson*) paras 34, 38 et seq.

[3] ECJ 23 April 2009, Case C-533/07, ECR I-3327 (*Falco Privatstiftung v Weller-Lindhorst*) para 21.

[4] Regulation No. 44/2001 on jurisdiction and the recognition and enforcement of judgments in civil and commercial matters, OJ 2001, L 012.

[5] Regulation No. 1346/2000 on Insolvency Proceedings, OJ 2000, L 160.

- Regulation No. 1206/2001 on cooperation between the courts of the Member States in the taking of evidence in civil or commercial matters (Evidence Regulation)[6];
- Directive No. 2003/8/EC to improve access to justice in cross-border disputes by establishing minimum common rules relating to legal aid for such disputes[7];
- Regulation No. 805/2004 creating a European enforcement order for uncontested claims[8];
- Regulation No. 1896/2006 on a European order for payment[9];
- Regulation No. 861/2007 on a European small claims procedure[10];
- Regulation No. 1393/2007 on the service in the Member States of judicial and extrajudicial documents in civil or commercial matters (Service Regulation), which repealed and replaced Regulation No. 1348/2000[11];
- Directive No. 2008/52/EC on mediation in civil and commercial matters.[12]

And relating to family matters

- Regulation No. 2201/2003 concerning jurisdiction and the recognition and enforcement of judgments in matrimonial matters and in matters of parental responsibility (Brussels IIA), which repealed Regulation No. 1347/2000 (Brussels II),[13]
- Regulation No. 4/2009 on maintenance obligations.[14]

The Lisbon Treaty did nothing to alter, expand or scale back the powers of the EU in the area of civil procedure. Rather, Article 65 EC Treaty was transformed more or less 'as is' into Article 81 of the Treaty on the Functioning of the European Union (TFEU). The latter continues to vest the Union with the power to develop cooperation in civil matters with cross-border implications. To this end, and for the purpose of the 'proper functioning of the internal market,' the Union may adopt 'measures for the approximation of the laws and

---

[6] Regulation No. 1206/2001 on Cooperation between the Courts of the Member States in the Taking of Evidence in Civil or Commercial Matters, OJ 2001, L 174.

[7] Directive No. 2003/8/EC to Improve Access to Justice in Cross-border Disputes by Establishing Minimum Common Rules relating to Legal Aid for such Disputes, OJ 2003, L 26.

[8] Regulation No. 805/2004 creating a European Enforcement Order for uncontested claims, OJ 2004, L 143/15.

[9] Regulation No. 1896/2006 creating a European Order for Payment Procedure OJ 2006, L 399.

[10] Regulation No. 861/2007 establishing a European Small Claims Procedure, OJ 2007, L 199.

[11] Regulation No. 1393/2007 on the Service in the Member States of Judicial and Extrajudicial Documents in Civil or Commercial Matters (service of documents), OJ 2007, L 324/50, and repealing Regulation No. 1348/2000 (OJ 2007 L 324).

[12] Directive 2008/52/EC on Certain Aspects of Mediation in Civil and Commercial Matters, OJ 2008, L 136.

[13] Regulation No. 2201/2003 concerning Jurisdiction and the Recognition and Enforcement of Judgments in Matrimonial Matters and in Matters of Parental Responsibility, OJ 2003, L 338.

[14] Regulation No. 4/2009 on Jurisdiction, Applicable law, Recognition and Enforcement of Decisions and Cooperation in Matters relating to Maintenance Obligations, OJ 2009, L 7.

regulations of the Member States,' and it may do so by using the ordinary legislative procedure set out in Article 294 TFEU. Article 81(2) TFEU provides a non-exhaustive list of subject-matter areas that are open to legislation by the European Union, namely:

- Mutual recognition and enforcement of judgments and non-judicial decisions;
- Cross-border service of judicial and non-judicial documents;
- Compatibility of Member States' rules on jurisdiction;
- Cooperation in the taking of evidence;
- Effective access to justice;
- Elimination of obstacles to the proper functioning of civil proceedings, including the promotion of the compatibility of the rules on civil procedure applicable in the Member States;
- Development of alternative methods of dispute settlement;
- Support for the training of judicial staff.

Article 81(3) TFEU goes on to impose special hurdles in terms of the legislative process for such measures in the field of family law.

5.2 The Limitations of Horizontal Harmonisation

5.2.1 Application to Cross-Border Disputes Only

The list supplied by Article 81(2) TFEU is impressively long and comprehensive. However, it must not be overlooked that the subject-matter areas listed in Article 81(2) TFEU must still be related to the 'purposes of paragraph 1,' i.e. the development of judicial cooperation in civil matters with cross-border implications. Even under the TFEU, the authority of the European Union in the area of judicial cooperation remains limited to international civil procedure, i.e. conflicts of jurisdiction. Put differently, it does not extend to domestic disputes that have no cross-border aspect to them, like those involving parties resident in the same Member State. Accordingly, the jurisdictional scheme of the Brussels I Regulation, for example, remains limited to cases that involve a cross-border element.[15]

For the time being, this restriction of the legislative power of the European Union must be taken seriously. The Commission was forced to acknowledge this when it suggested defining the scope of application of new legislative acts based upon the former Article 65 EC Treaty more broadly. The initial proposals of the

[15] Recitals (2) and (3) Regulation 44/2001 on jurisdiction and the recognition and enforcement of judgments in civil and commercial matters, OJ 2001, L 012; ECJ 1 March 2005, Case C-281/02, ECR I-1383 (*Owusu v Jackson*) (1456) para 25; ECJ 7 February 2006, ECR I-1145 Opinion 1/03, para 145.

Commission for regulations introducing a European payment order[16] and a European small claims procedure[17] were not limited to cross-border disputes but were supposed to apply equally to domestic ones. The inherent expansion of the legislative powers of the European Union met with so much resistance that these plans had to be abandoned. In the current versions, which were finally enacted, both instruments apply only to cross-border disputes. As their respective Articles 2 explain, both regulations remain limited in scope to 'civil and commercial matters in cross-border cases.'

As the Commission explained in its original proposal for a regulation introducing a European payment order, there are 'vast differences between national systems' regarding the mechanism for the swift enforcement of monetary claims while 'an efficient procedure for the recovery of undisputed debts' is of 'fundamental economic significance' for the internal market.[18] While this certainly involves an exaggeration, there is also a grain of truth to it. If the goal is to create a uniform system of debt recovery across the Union and thus to supply creditors with an equally efficient mechanism in every Member State, then it does not make a difference whether the legal relationship which gave rise to the dispute extended across the border or not. The interest of a creditor in the speedy and efficient enforcement of a monetary claim is undiminished if the dispute grew out of a domestic transaction rather than involving a cross-border element.

For the time being, the distinction between domestic and cross-border disputes remains a cornerstone of the system of competences under the EU Treaties and of the underlying constitutional principle of conferral. However, it makes no sense at all for a potential creditor who operates within the European Union and has a keen interest in the speedy and efficient enforcement of his or her claims. The limitation placing domestic disputes beyond the reach of the legislative powers of the Union is based on the constitutional law of the European Union, not on any logic inherent in the subject matter concerned.

5.2.2 Limited Impact

However well-founded the distinction between international and domestic disputes may be as a matter of the constitutional make-up of the EU and of the division of labour between the Union and the Member States, it takes much of the practical steam out of the legislation referenced above. The growing number of legal instruments stands in sharp contrast to the small difference these instruments make

[16] Proposal for a Regulation of the European Parliament and of the Council creating a European order for payment procedure, 25.05.2004, COM(2004) 173 final/3, 7 et seq, 20.

[17] Proposal for a Regulation of the European Parliament and of the Council establishing a European Small Claims Procedure, 15.3.2005, COM(2005) 87 final, 11.

[18] Proposal for a Regulation of the European Parliament and the Council creating a European order for payment procedure, 25.05.2004, COM(2004) 173 final/3, 7.

with regard to real-world transactions and the legal disputes growing out of them every day.

The diminished practical impact of European civil procedure is particularly striking with regard to the two regulations which received praise not only for alleviating cross-border judicial cooperation but also for setting up distinct 'European' proceedings on the merits. In this vein, Regulation No. 1896/2006 on a European order for payment designs and sets up a legal mechanism for the enforcement of monetary claims,[19] and Regulation No. 861/2007 on a European small claims procedure[20] even carries its main characteristic, i.e. the introduction of a separate track for proceedings involving small claims, in its name. Both regulations go beyond the mere coordination of the civil justice systems of the Member States, as they supply procedures that directly recommend themselves for use by creditors seeking enforcement of their claims.[21]

Far-reaching as the Regulations on orders for payment and on small claims may be, their impact is still a far cry from the one enjoyed by national law. This may be exemplified by the Regulation on a European payment order. In German law, this instrument exists alongside the traditional and well-established domestic procedure for a payment order (*Mahnverfahren*). Strikingly, the latter is not limited to domestic disputes but equally covers the enforcement of monetary claims established elsewhere, outside of Germany (Section 703d, German Code of Civil Procedure—*Zivilprozessordnung*, ZPO), against a debtor. The German procedure for a payment order, which has been in place for many decades, works like a well-oiled machine and continues to attract many users. Why then should a creditor seeking enforcement of a monetary claim turn to the European payment order, even if it may offer advantages in terms of facilitated cross-border enforcement?[22]

5.2.3 Limitations for Future Development

Assuming that European procedural institutions, which supplement the national systems and are placed alongside domestic institutions, work well and are in fact utilised in practice, it seems obvious that there are limits as to the scale to which this approach may be carried. With every European regulation or directive supplementing the national systems, another layer of complexity is being added. There is no doubt that little harm is done if national procedures for a payment order are in fact duplicated by a European regulation which in essence provides

[19] Regulation No. 1896/2006 creating a European order for payment procedure, OJ 2006, L 399.

[20] Regulation No. 861/2007 establishing a European Small Claims Procedure, OJ 2007, L 199.

[21] Kramer 2008, 253 et seq; Kramer 2010, 17 et seq.

[22] The court order made under the domestic procedure may even be enforced in other Member States under Regulation No. 805/2004 as a European enforcement order for uncontested claims. As to modifications of Section 703d ZPO in the European context, cf. Voit 2009, para 2.

for the same mechanism but offers numerous variations in detail. On the other hand, it seems equally clear that this rationale must not be maximised. If the European Union continued to legislate using this model, large chunks of the national systems of civil procedure would be supplemented by neighbouring European institutions for procedures involving cross-border disputes. The result, taken to its extreme, would be double-tracked systems of civil procedure in which domestic and European procedures, essentially serving the same purpose existed alongside each other. Such a world may be interesting to scholars but it is loathed by judges, as they would have to switch back and forth between different procedural frameworks. The loss in terms of procedural efficiency caused by such a double-tracked system must not be underestimated. Throughout Europe, courts have tried to avoid the costs and losses associated with operating different systems of procedure by stubbornly applying their respective *lex fori*, even to disputes involving a foreign element.[23] This is all the more striking as courts have shown no reluctance in applying another legal system's rules in the area of substantive law. For centuries, foreign substantive law has been applied by European courts without hesitation where the applicable choice of legal rules so required. Their unwillingness to follow the same course in the area of procedure is striking evidence of the considerable loss in litigation efficiency associated with such a move.

5.2.4 No Optional System

For these reasons, the recent trend in European law-making in the area of civil procedure, to supplement the national systems by European instruments, which in effect introduce distinct procedural frameworks even though they perform essentially the same functions as their domestic counterparts, has no long-term future. Carrying this argument only a little further generates the insight that—as opposed to substantive law—procedural law lacks the compromise solution of an optional system.[24] In the area of substantive law, it may be possible to bridge the controversy between the proponents of legal diversity in the form of different national systems and the promoters of harmonisation by the compromise-solution of a 28th legal system, which the parties may opt into if they so wish.[25]

---

[23] Wagner 1998, 353 et seq.

[24] Max Planck Institute for Comparative and International Private Law, Policy Options for Progress Towards a European Contract Law, Comments on the issues raised in the Green Paper from the Commission of 1 July 2010, COM (2010) 348 final, 2011, paras 69 et seq.

[25] Cf. Green Paper on policy options for progress towards a European Contract Law for consumers and businesses, 1.7.2010, COM (2010) 348 final, 9 et seq; Beale 2007, 260 and 269 et seq.

With regard to procedural law, such an intermediate solution is not available. The courts would be overburdened if they were required to alternate between two different procedural systems on a day-to-day basis. This is not because judges are too silly, lazy or hardwired to work with different sets of procedural frameworks. They could certainly do so if they tried hard enough. The crucial point is that judicial resources are limited and thus must be put to their most efficient use. Given that civil procedure is no end in itself but rather serves the function of enforcing and protecting legal rights, there is a general interest that judges focus on the resolution of the dispute on the merits rather than wasting whatever analytical and legal capacities they have for the purpose of operating different systems of civil procedure. Therefore, the duplication of procedural institutions, which essentially serve identical purposes, does not seem to propose a fruitful strategy for the future.

5.3 Vertical Harmonisation

5.3.1 The Concept of Vertical Harmonisation

The limitations of the former Article 65 EC Treaty and the current Article 81 TFEU are the real cause for the exploration and development of additional bases for European legislation in the area of civil procedure. European legislation in the area of civil procedure is no longer confined to the foothold of the chapter on judicial cooperation in civil matters. Rather, the legislative acts passed under these titles are being supplemented by others, which were based on Treaty provisions conferring powers in particular 'substantive' policy areas. In this context, the term 'substantive' is used in opposition to 'procedural.' It thus denotes a title of authority, which is not concerned with the procedural treatment of claims and the resolution of disputes involving private rights, but with substantive rights created or protected by European law. As they remain confined to distinct subject-matter areas only, these policies shall be labelled as 'vertical harmonisation.'

The concept of vertical harmonisation is employed to designate those areas where the EU introduces procedural rules without legislating in the area of civil procedure and, therefore, without relying on the authorisation granted by Article 81 TFEU. Instruments of this type of community legislation focus on specific subject-matter areas for which the EU has a competence other than that granted by Article 81 TFEU. The subject-matter area where the European Treaties bear the closest relation with rights and obligations between private parties is the case of competition law. The former Articles 85 and 86 EC Treaty (which have become Articles 101 and 102 TFEU) directly regulate the behaviour of companies in the market. However, there are other examples as well.

5.3.2 The Enforcement Directive

5.3.2.1 Scope

Directive 2004/48/EC on the enforcement of intellectual property rights introduces an array of procedural rules, particularly with regard to fact-gathering, evidence and injunctive relief. The so-called Enforcement Directive was not based on the predecessor of then Article 65 EC, which is now Article 81 TFEU, but on ex-Article 95 which has become Article 114 TFEU. Under Article 114 TFEU the EU has the power to take legislative measures for the approximation of the laws of the Member States 'which have as their object the establishment and functioning of the internal market.' While the availability of judicial protection and assistance in the enforcement of legal rights certainly has some bearing on the 'functioning of the internal market' it would be a stretch to maintain that the harmonisation of rules of civil procedure as such constitutes a valid function of Article 114 TFEU. If it were otherwise, Article 81 would be rendered obsolete.

For this reason, it seems, the Commission did not even try to sell the Enforcement Directive as an instrument for harmonising certain aspects of civil procedure. Taken as such, ex-Article 95 EC would have been unavailable. Similarly, under the heading of civil procedure, it was impossible to bring the Enforcement Directive within the ambit of ex-Article 65 EC too, as it applies indiscriminately to international and to domestic disputes, while Article 65 EC was, and Article 81 TFEU remains, limited to measures aimed at facilitating and improving judicial cooperation in civil matters that 'have cross-border implications.'[26] The only option left was to classify the directive not as a means of harmonising certain aspects of civil procedure, but of improving the enforcement of intellectual property rights. In substance, the directive is not really about the 'enforcement' of property rights but about their protection from infringements, or even more precisely: about the enforcement of claims for compensation for the harm caused by infringements of intellectual property rights, as well as, for enjoining future infringements.

5.3.2.2 Contents

Outcome-determinative

Whereas the procedural directives and regulations passed under ex-Article 65 EC remain confined to international cases involving some foreign element, the Enforcement Directive—like all measures passed under the predecessors of Article 114 TFEU—covers both domestic and international cases. But not only is the scope of the Enforcement Directive exceptional, the same is true for its contents. Whereas

[26] See Sects. 5.2.1 and 5.2.2.

the truly 'procedural' legislative acts passed under what is now Article 81 TFEU tend to focus on rather marginal issues like debt collection and undisputed claims, the Enforcement Directive covers a range of topics which lie close to the heart of any system of civil procedure and are often determinative of the outcomes reached in individual cases. While it is true that the Enforcement Directive contains provisions dealing with issues of a substantive-law nature, epitomised by Article 13 on damages, for the most part its provisions sit close to the core of civil procedure.

Access to and production of evidence

Pursuant to Article 6(1) (cl. 1) of the Enforcement Directive, Member States must ensure that 'on application by a party which has presented reasonably available evidence sufficient to support its claims, and has, in substantiating those claims, specified evidence which lies in the control of the opposing party, the competent judicial authorities may order that such evidence be presented by the opposing party, subject to the protection of confidential information.' Article 6(2) of the Enforcement Directive goes on to explain that the opposing party may even be ordered to produce banking, financial or commercial documents relevant to the resolution of a dispute involving the infringement of intellectual property rights on a commercial scale.

Even though these obligations to produce evidence may seem harmless and are well understood by scholars from jurisdictions embracing rather broad duties to disclose, they are by no means self-evident. Some jurisdictions in Europe, among them Germany, are far more restrictive in requiring the parties to a legal dispute to contribute to the establishment of the true facts of the case.[27] The German Federal Supreme Court (*Bundesgerichtshof*—BGH) even committed to the view that a party need not disclose information that is relevant to the resolution of the dispute to which the other side lacks access but which would harm the interests of the party controlling the information.[28] In effect, the court allows a party to frustrate a potentially meritorious claim brought by its less informed opponent.[29] Against this background, Article 6 of the Enforcement Directive appears to be a major step in the direction of a general duty to disclose and produce evidence.

Preservation of evidence

There are more provisions in the directive that suggest that the framers saw the judicial process as a means of establishing the true facts of the case and to

---

[27] Wagner 2007, 711.

[28] BGH, NJW (*Neue Juristische Wochenschrift*) 1958, 1491, 1492; NJW 1990, 3151 = ZZP (*Zeitschrift für Zivilprozess*) 104 (1991), 203 with critical note Stürner = JZ (*Juristenzeitung*) 1991, 630 with critical discussion Schlosser, JZ 1991, 599; BGH, NJW 1997, 128, 129; 2000, 1108, 1109; BAG (*Bundesarbeitsgericht*), NJW 2004, 2848, 2851; in the same vein Leipold 2005, paras 26 et seq.

[29] For a critical account, cf. Wagner 2007, 706 et seq.

force both parties to contribute to the attainment of this aim. Thus, for example, Article 7 of the Enforcement Directive authorises the courts (or rather requires the Member States to ensure that their courts are authorised) to take provisional measures to preserve relevant evidence in respect of the alleged infringement of an intellectual property right. Pursuant to Article 7(1) (cl. 3) of the Enforcement Directive, such measures may be taken without the other party having been heard where this is necessary in order to fend off irreparable harm to the rightholder. In this case, Article 7(2) of the Enforcement Directive requires the court to inform the parties immediately after the protective order becomes effective, and to schedule a hearing at the request of the aggrieved party. In appropriate circumstances, the applicant may be required to provide security ensuring that any harm suffered by the respondent as a consequence of the measure will be compensated. Where the applicant fails to institute proceedings on the merits within a reasonable time, the court must revoke the protective measure at the request of the respondent under Article 7(3) of the Enforcement Directive. In cases of revocation and in cases where the applicant fails with his or her claim on the merits, the respondent must be compensated for any losses incurred (Article 7(4), Enforcement Directive). Finally, Article 7(5) of the Enforcement Directive authorises the Member States to take measures for the protection of the identity of witnesses.

The provisions of Article 7 of the Enforcement Directive were set out in such detail in order to dispel any doubts that the real subject matters of major parts of the directive are in fact within the domain of civil procedure—and nowhere else. If the language derived from the intellectual property world were eliminated or, rather, replaced by the general concepts of applicant and respondent, Article 7 of the Enforcement Directive would fit in well with any decent Code of Civil Procedure, under a subchapter on preservation of evidence.

Interim relief

Any list of illustrations of the procedural nature of the Enforcement Directive will include Article 9, pursuant to which Member States must authorise their courts to issue interlocutory injunctions against alleged infringers 'where appropriate' (para 1). Article 9(3) of the Enforcement Directive specifies that the judicial authorities must 'have the authority to require the applicant to provide any reasonably available evidence in order to satisfy themselves with a sufficient degree of certainty that the applicant is the rightholder and that the applicant's right is being infringed, or that such infringement is imminent.'

The contrived language employed by Article 9(3) and many of the other provisions of the Enforcement Directive must not conceal the fact that it defines the requirements for granting interim relief and sets the necessary threshold of probability for the establishment of these requirements. It seems that Article 9(3) could not say so explicitly for the sole reason that the EU lacks the competence to legislate in the area of civil procedure. If this were otherwise, the European lawmakers could have addressed the issue head-on and said that the court may issue an interim injunction where the applicant has provided reasonable evidence, establishing with a sufficient degree of certainty that the applicant is the right-holder, and that his or her rights are being infringed or that such infringement is imminent. Article 9(3) of the Enforcement Directive instead says that the judicial authorities of the Member States shall behave in this way, probably because the relevant perspective was one of protection of intellectual property rights. From this perspective courts are mere enforcement agencies of the respective Member State, operating in much the same way as 'market police.' For this reason, the Directive is not framed in terms of defining requirements for obtaining interim relief from courts of law, but in terms of the obligation of Member States to intervene against infringers through the strong arm of their courts.

It is not the aim of the present analysis to argue that the Enforcement Directive was outside the scope of Article 95 EC (Article 114 TFEU) but rather to show that it clearly operates within the domain of civil procedure. This point immediately comes to the fore with some minor editing of Article 9(3). It is even possible to go one step further and to purge all language related to the world of intellectual property rights from Article 9(3) in order to arrive at a fairly general and operational formulation of the standard for granting an interim injunction:

> The court must grant such an interlocutory injunction where the applicant establishes with a sufficient degree of certainty that his or her rights are being infringed or that such infringement is imminent.

Such a provision would be more precise than, for instance, their counterparts in the English Civil Procedure Rules of Part 25 CPR,[30] and it would come very close to those governing interim relief in continental legal systems, such as Sections 920 and 936 of the German Code of Civil Procedure (ZPO).[31] To carry this a little further, Article 9(4) on ex-parte interim relief resembles Sections 924 and 944 ZPO, Article 9(5) on the repeal of interim measures upon failure to institute an action on the merits appears to have been modelled on Section 926 ZPO, Article 9(6) on the provision of security by the applicant has a parallel in Section 921 ZPO, and Article 9(7) on granting a right to compensation in cases where the provisional measure in question was revoked, had lapsed due to an act or omission of the applicant, or turned out to have been unfounded because there was no infringement or threat of infringement of a right of the applicant, is predicated in Section 945 ZPO.

In summary, Article 9 of the Enforcement Directive supplies a comprehensive framework for measures of interim relief which may easily be generalised and applied to cases other than those involving intellectual property rights. In order to arrive at a general scheme one would simply have to remove the language of enforcement and insert a specification of the requirements of interim relief, written

[30] For their interpretation, cf. Andrews 2003, ch. 18.

[31] Wagner 2004, 69 et seq.

from the perspective of the court or, what amounts to the same thing, from the perspective of a potential applicant seeking a protective measure from the court. If such a general scheme were in place, lawmakers could still add provisions addressing issues particular to the area of intellectual property rights such as Articles 10–12 of the Enforcement Directive, which set out particular categories of interim relief.

Fee-shifting

The same exercise could be administered with regard to other sections of the Enforcement Directive. The procedural nature is particularly obvious for Article 14 of the Directive which orders Member States to ensure that legal costs and other expenses incurred by the successful party, to the extent that they are reasonable and proportionate, shall be borne by the unsuccessful party, unless equity requires otherwise.

5.3.3 Collective Redress

5.3.3.1 Current Proposals

A second area where vertical integration may work its way into national systems of civil procedure is collective redress. The term collective redress is meant to include procedural mechanisms to aggregate damages claims for harm caused by the same behaviour or event or by a series of similar and related actions or events. It covers more or less the same ground as the famous or, to many European observers infamous, U.S.-style class action.[32] Plans developed within the Commission to adopt or introduce legal institutions paralleling the American class action have progressed farthest within the Directorate General for Competition (DG COMP) which, in April 2008, produced a White Paper on Damages Actions for Breach of the EC Antitrust Rules that envisages the introduction of two separate mechanisms: representative claims brought by consumer associations and other qualified entities and, in addition, opt-in class actions brought by the victims themselves.[33]

The objective of improving mechanisms of collective redress has not remained confined to competition law. The European Commission Directorate General for Health and Consumers (DG SANCO) intends to move further, as the Green Paper on Consumer Collective Redress of 27 November 2008 has made clear.[34] There, the Commission outlines a range of measures for strengthening consumer

[32] Cf. Issacharoff and Miller 2009.

[33] White Paper on Damages actions for breach of the EC anti-trust rules, COM (2008) 165 final, 4.

[34] Green Paper on Consumer Collective Redress, COM (2008) 794 final.

confidence in the functioning of the internal market and stimulating cross-border trade. Among those, the proposal to introduce EU legislation establishing mechanisms of collective redress is by far the most interesting—and the most controversial. In particular, DG SANCO is considering the introduction of class actions, representative actions, e.g. of consumer associations, and of test-case procedures.[35] Whether such instruments should take the form of an opt-in mechanism or rather follow the opt-out approach is left open.

5.3.3.2 Competence of the European Union

As to the legislative competence of the EU in the area of collective redress, it must be noted that both projects of DG COMP and DG SANCO, respectively, would remain outside the ambit of Article 81 TFEU. Again, the Commission is not concerned with improving the cooperation between the courts and judges in the several Member States or the jurisdictional and procedural rules governing the resolution of cross-border disputes. Rather, the objective is to improve the enforcement of, and compliance with, EU law, be it the law regulating business-to-consumer transactions or the rules safeguarding competition within the internal market. As a consequence, the legislative measures envisaged, which would introduce mechanisms of collective redress, would have to be based on the competence for the 'substantive' policy in question, i.e. Articles 101 and 102 TFEU for mechanisms enhancing the collection of damages caused by infringements of competition law[36] and on Articles 114 and 169(2) (b) TFEU with regard to collective redress in consumer law.

5.3.3.3 Procedural Nature of the Proposals

This is not the right place to discuss the merits of these proposals.[37] In the present context, the interesting question to ask is how they relate to the advancement of European integration in the area of civil procedure. In answering this question, it is submitted that one must distinguish between representative actions brought by associations and opt-in class actions or, to use a better term, group actions, which join together a multitude of actions brought by claimants who suffered similar harm.[38] The former would amount to an extension of the Injunctions Directive of

---

[35] Green Paper on Consumer Collective Redress, COM (2008) 794 final, 16, paras 54 et seq.

[36] Cf. White Paper on Damages actions for breach of the EC anti-trust rules, COM (2008)165 final, 2 et passim, referring to then Arts. 81 and 82 EC.

[37] Wagner 2011.

[38] For a thorough discussion, cf. Wagner 2011, 61 et seq.

May 1998 into the area of claims for damages.[39] Even though this directive created something like a representative action of associations for the 'protection of the collective interests of the consumer,' it remains limited to the remedy of injunctive relief, excluding damages actions from its purview.

More importantly for present purposes, the Injunctions Directive remains an isolated legal instrument in the sense that it does not have a great connection with the law and practice of civil procedure. The genuine procedural problems raised by representative actions are essentially confined to the doctrines of standing and *res judicata*. Extending the entitlement of consumer associations to the remedy of redress for harm caused raises difficult issues of the calculation of damages and distribution of proceeds, but does not involve the general rules of civil procedure significantly more than the Injunctions Directive did. Nonetheless, even the introduction of representative actions into civil practice in the aftermath of the Injunctions Directive amounted to a small-scale revolution for some legal systems and therefore was not met with open arms but sometimes with outright hostility.[40] This illustrates how a purportedly 'substantive' policy of improving the enforcement of, and compliance with, substantive rules of consumer protection may upset the community of practitioners and scholars active in the area of civil procedure.

The plans of the Directorate General for Competition to introduce an opt-in class action mechanism into European law will prove to be much more disruptive for the national systems of civil procedure. This characterisation does not imply that these plans are flawed from the outset or that the attempt must be abandoned in order to avoid the harm done to civil practice otherwise. Rather, it is meant to suggest that the introduction of a group action mechanism into the national legal systems, if it is going to work efficiently, needs careful fine-tuning with the procedural frameworks in place in the Member States. Group actions touch upon many more procedural topics and doctrines than representative actions and pose problems that are much more difficult to resolve. Lawmakers must answer questions such as how the multitude of claims will be joined together, how the lead case or the several test cases singled out for full trial are to be selected, what the appeals process with regard to the test case should look like, or how the findings reached within the proceedings on the test case relate to the deferred cases that are still pending at first instance. In addition, the intricate problems of remuneration of counsel, fee-allocation between winners and losers and within groups of claimants must be answered consistently and with great care because mistakes in these areas are likely to destroy the effectiveness of the mechanism altogether.

The legislative history of the German 'Act on the Initiation of Model Case Proceedings in Respect of Investors in the Capital Markets' (*Kapitalanleger-*

[39] Directive 98/27/EC of the European Parliament and the Council of 19.05.1998 on injunctions for the protection of consumer interests (OJ 1998 L 166/51).

[40] For the problems raised in German law, cf. Greger 2000, 399, 406 et seq.

Musterverfahrensgesetz—KapMuG)[41] provides ample illustration of the many controversial problems that need to be solved along the way.[42]

Again, the fact that there are many difficulties does not in itself imply that the project should be abandoned. What must be kept in mind, however, is the fact that the introduction, by European legislation, of a class action mechanism of the opt-in variety, allowing the grouping together of related claims of a multitude of victims, would cut deeply into the national systems of civil procedure. Lawmakers must be aware of the nature of the problems they face and be alert to the ramifications that a solution to an isolated problem may have for neighbouring fields of practice. Even if the opt-in class action mechanism remained confined to the field of competition law, it would still require the harmonisation of important parts of civil procedure. This may not be a bad thing, since harmonisation of civil procedure with regard to discrete subject-matter areas allows lawmakers to experiment with particular solutions, to receive feedback, to gather experience and ultimately to learn from their successes and failures. As long as the experiment remains confined to a particular subject area, the harm caused by mistakes may be easier to bear.

5.3.4 *Problems of Vertical Harmonisation*

5.3.4.1 Focus on Law Enforcement

For some scholars of civil procedure it will be a source of unease and consternation that the harmonisation of key features of civil procedure is approached from the political angle of enforcement of European law in specific subject-matter areas and not regarded as a subject in itself, worthy of undivided attention. The danger exists that in the course of developing and improving the procedures providing for the efficient enforcement of European competition and consumer law, as well as, for the efficient protection of intellectual property rights, milestones are placed in spots where they would not have been placed if a broader perspective had been taken which focused on civil procedure as an end in itself, and not as a tool for law enforcement. One may even argue that the Commission started from the wrong principle as civil justice is not about law enforcement at all, but about striking the right balance between vindication and protection of entitlements and denial of judicial protection for unwarranted claims.

---

[41] An English translation of the statute may be found on the homepage of the Federal Ministry of Justice, at http://www.bmj.bund.de/files/-/1110/KapMuG_english.pdf (last consulted in June 2011).

[42] For details, cf. Wagner 2006, 115 et seq; Wagner 2011, 66 et seq.

5.3.4.2 The View Towards Generalisation

However plausible these worries about the proper focus of vertical harmonisation in selected subject-matter areas may sound, they are not borne out in reality, i.e. by the legal instruments and proposals which are currently on the table. Presently, the true concern is not that vertical integration moves the law of civil procedure in the wrong direction, but that it precipitates harmonisation in selected areas only, even though these subject-matter areas have nothing special about them. The Enforcement Directive is the most straightforward example to demonstrate this. If one believes that fee-shifting along the principle of 'loser pays' is appropriate, why is it confined to disputes involving the infringement of intellectual property rights as Article 14 of Directive 2004/48/EC implies? If there is a need for a European framework of interim relief, including the authority of the court to order the applicant to provide security, to revoke the measure in case the applicant fails to institute proceedings on the merits, and to award damages to the respondent where the measure turns out to have been unwarranted—if all this is needed, then why are Articles 9, 11, 12 and 13 of Directive 2004/48/EC confined to the protection of intellectual property rights within the meaning of Article 1 of Directive 2004/48/EC? The same questions must be asked with a view towards the provisions dealing with evidence and its preservation (Articles 6 and 7, Directive 2004/48/EC) and access to information (Article 8, Directive 2004/48/EC). The procedural provisions made in the Enforcement Directive may be controversial at one point or another, but all in all they seem well balanced and are thus suitable for generalisation.

From this perspective, rather than from the point of view of enforcement of intellectual property rights, it is perplexing that Article 2(1) of Directive 2004/48/EC allows Member States to deviate from the provisions made in the directive and introduces measures that are 'more favourable to the rightholders.' Assuming that the procedural rules of Article 6 et seq of Directive 2004/48/EC strike a fair balance between the interests of both parties, Member States should not be allowed to depart from them in any direction. On the assumption that the framers of the Enforcement Directive got it wrong at one point or another, these mistakes call for correction at the European level, and not for a one-sided intervention by some Member States. Finally, under the theory that there are no single right answers to the problems addressed in the Enforcement Directive and that legal diversity should be allowed in the interest of natural variation and adaptive evolution of legal systems,[43] Member States should have discretion to depart in both directions, by introducing rules which are either more or less favourable to 'rightholders' as potential claimants. Whichever way one looks at the problem, the solution embraced by Article 2(1) of Directive 2004/48/EC is never justified. The simple explanation for its existence is that lawmakers were concerned with the enforcement of intellectual property rights and not with the harmonisation of civil

[43] For details, cf. Wagner 2002, 995 et seq, 999.

procedure and therefore implicitly accepted the proposition that 'more is better' and that Member States should be free to protect intellectual property rights as intensively and comprehensively as they might wish to.

This proposition is wrong even on its own premise as intellectual property rights confer monopoly powers on their holders and thus lend themselves to abuse for the purpose of restricting competition.[44] For example, patents are sometimes used as 'weapons' launched at competitors who strive to enter the market formerly dominated by the owner of the patent. Of course, such use of the patent is perfectly legitimate if the new entrant actually takes a free ride on the technology protected by the patent. However, the new entrant is free to replicate the result achieved by the patent owner by adopting another technological route that does not draw on the development protected by the patent. Problems with procedure and law enforcement arise in the familiar situation that it is difficult for a court or other decision maker to distinguish between the two cases and to quickly resolve the case in one direction or the other. To counteract the incentive of patent owners, and holders of other intellectual property rights, to blackmail competitors for the purpose of defending their monopoly more broadly than is warranted, the German courts have developed a category of quasi-strict liability of rightholders who wrongfully enforce intellectual property rights against competitors.[45] This may serve as an illustration of the point, made earlier, that in disputes involving intellectual property rights 'more' is not always 'better.' Rather, lawmakers must try to strike the right balance and devise rules that ensure that the true facts of the case are brought to the fore and that up to the time when these facts have been gathered interim relief is available on the basis of a preliminary and tentative establishment of the facts. In essence, this is what Article 6 et seq of Directive 2004/48/EC provide for, and thus Member States should not be allowed to add more on top of it in a misguided attempt to favour rightholders.

With regard to collective redress, an argument along the same lines can be made. Where a multitude of victims each incurred serious losses, the problem for lawmakers is how to aggregate those claims in order to prevent the courts from bottlenecking. Contrary to the impression that may have been raised by the White Paper on Damages Actions for Breach of the EC Antitrust Rules, such cases are by no means restricted to competition law. While some categories of 'mass torts' may primarily be an affair of competition law, airplane and train crashes, shipwrecks, as well as mass torts involving design defects of certain product categories, raise exactly the same problem of an avalanche of claims involving roughly the same facts and legal issues which would clog the judicial system for years if they were disposed of on a claim-by-claim basis. If the European Union were to introduce a mechanism allowing for the joining and aggregation of damages claims, which are related in the sense just described, then there would be no reason to limit this

---

[44] For a critical discussion, cf. Dam 1994, 247, 249 et seq.

[45] BGHZ 62, 29, 36 et seq = NJW 1974, 315, 317; BGH NJW 1976, 916; NJW-RR 1998, 331, 332; RGZ 94, 248, 250; cf. also Wagner 2009, paras 199 et seq.

group-action-type mechanism to the field of competition law. Rather, it should encompass damages claims of any kind, provided only that they satisfy the criteria justifying joint trial and decision-making.

The same reasoning applies to the ambit of the Green Paper on Consumer Collective Redress. Capital markets fraud, for example, is by no means an exclusive affair of consumer protection as institutional investors will be the victims most seriously affected. It would be absurd to divide the cake in two and to offer aggregate proceedings to victimised consumers only, to the exclusion of victims who incurred losses in the course of running their businesses.

5.3.4.3 Preliminary Conclusions

To sum up, vertical integration is a valuable tool for experimenting with harmonisation. It allows lawmakers to limit their decisions to particular fields of law only and to gather feedback from them before settling on a general solution governing the full range of civil disputes. The downside of this process of trial and error is that it may dissect general issues into particular ones which are resolved for a limited group of cases only, without any justification except the catalogue of EU competences enshrined in the TFEU and the principle of subsidiarity safeguarding it. From the point of view of civil procedure, the limitation of EU competences is just happenstance which needs to be overcome by comprehensive solutions. In the meantime lawmakers should be conscious of their actions, i.e. be aware of the fact that they are legislating in the area of civil procedure, even if the constitutional basis for their actions is some substantive policy of the EU, like competition law, consumer protection and the approximation of laws for the benefit of the internal market. Therefore, it is inappropriate to subscribe exclusively to a perspective of law enforcement and to ignore the dangers that may result from over-enforcement of rights enjoyed by the parties. Rules of civil procedure must strike the right balance between enforcement of valid rights and rejection of alleged claims that turn out to be unfounded.

5.4 Privatisation of Dispute Resolution

5.4.1 The Range of Options

Another basic choice faced by European lawmakers is the one between public and private forms of dispute resolution. The courts of law of the Member States are but one institution to which the parties may turn for a resolution of their dispute. There are plenty of alternatives to the public courts, which may be ordered on a continuum that ranges from dispute resolution by the authoritative decision of a judge, holding public office and exercising sovereign power to a privately negotiated settlement which involves and concerns only the parties to the dispute. In between are mechanisms like arbitration, where the decision is made by a private judge or judicial panel charged with establishing the facts and applying the relevant law in the same manner as a court of law would, and mediation, where a neutral third party—the mediator—steps in and assists the parties in reaching a consensual settlement of their dispute.

5.4.2 Virtues of Alternative Dispute Resolution

If national lawmakers look at this spectrum, the best solution clearly remains litigation in public courts because this mode of dispute resolution ensures optimal degrees of fairness and law enforcement, given that lawmakers have the power to adjust the procedures followed by their courts so that they fit these goals. Nonetheless, the turn towards 'alternative'—namely private—modes of dispute resolution has been one of the dominant trends in recent decades in almost all European countries. The major driving force for this development was the high cost of litigation and the resulting demands on the public purse which were increasingly difficult to meet, even for comparatively rich countries.

On the European level, institutions of private dispute resolution out of court may be a different matter. Compared to courts of law, their major advantage is that they are not creatures of the Member States and thus may be more amenable to European regulation and more willing to enforce the substantive law of the Union. It is hard to say whether this view of alternative dispute resolution as a mechanism largely independent from the Member States figures prominently in the minds of Brussels lawmakers. However, it may be one of the reasons why mechanisms of alternative dispute resolution receive increasing attention at the European level. In fact, the landscape of alternative dispute resolution is rather diverse across Europe. With some generalisation it may be said that there is a North/South downward slope, with non-judicial dispute resolution particularly strong in Scandinavia, but also in the Netherlands, and to a lesser degree in the United Kingdom, and particularly weak in southern Europe.

5.4.3 The Mediation Directive

Against this background, the Directive 2008/52/EC on Certain Aspects of Mediation in Civil and Commercial Matters is not only, and not even, primarily an instrument of harmonisation of otherwise divergent laws.[46] There are so few statutes on mediation in the Member States that there simply was not enough

[46] Directive 2008/52/EC, OJ 2008, L 136, 3 et seq.

divergence requiring harmonisation in any meaningful sense. Consequently, the directive is cheerfully open-hearted in regard to its objectives. Article 1(1) of Directive 2008/52/EC describes them in the following terms:

> The objective of this directive is to facilitate access to alternative dispute resolution and to promote the amicable settlement of disputes by encouraging the use of mediation and by ensuring a balanced relationship between mediation and judicial proceedings.

To this end, Article 9 of Directive 2008/52/EC obliges Member States to inform the public about the availability and the virtues of dispute resolution via mediation as compared to litigation.[47] If the use of mediation in fact needs and deserves encouragement because it provides better access to justice, as the Recitals to Directive 2008/52/EC suggest, such support should not be limited to cross-border cases. The same problems the directive tries to solve—arresting limitation periods and prescription, ensuring confidentiality of the proceedings, enabling enforceability of settlements—affect mediation in domestic cases in exactly the same way as cross-border cases.[48] Not surprisingly, therefore, the Commission initially wanted a broader scope of application, including domestic cases, but was forced to abandon this plan for the sake of remaining within the limits of Article 81 TFEU. Still, Recital No. 8 of Directive 2008/52/EC encourages Member States to extend the scope of their transposition statutes to purely domestic disputes. It is to be expected that this option will be utilised by many European lawmakers. Germany is one example.[49]

5.4.4 Vertical Harmonisation, ADR, the Objective of Law Enforcement

The Green Paper on Consumer Collective Redress draws on these considerations when it pulls alternative dispute resolution into the context of vertical harmonisation, which does not need to be restricted to cross-border disputes:

> The EU could encourage Member States to establish collective consumer alternative dispute resolution schemes making sure that such schemes are available on their entire territory for all consumer claims and accessible to consumers from other Member States.[50]

The price for the possibility to broaden the scope of application of vertical instruments comes at the expense of the dominance of policy objectives other than those particular to civil procedure. In the case now under consideration the policy is again the one of law enforcement. Mechanisms of alternative dispute resolution are portrayed as facilitating access to justice and therefore allow for the

---

[47] Cf. also Recital No. 24 to Directive 2008/52/EC.

[48] Wagner 2010, 794.

[49] Wagner 2010, 794.

[50] Green Paper on Consumer Collective Redress, COM (2008) 794 final, para 39.

enforcement of small claims which would never be brought in public court because the costs of litigation are prohibitive.

While it is certainly true that mechanisms of alternative dispute resolution may be more accessible than courts of law, it seems problematic to combine this goal with the objective of improving the enforcement of the law or of subjective rights in the hands of consumers.[51] This is particularly striking with regard to mediation because it does not even purport to imitate the result that would have been obtained had the parties litigated the case in public court. The very idea of mediation is to seek out the potential for a consensual resolution of the dispute, regardless of the outcome a court would have reached had it decided the case on the merits after a full-blown trial. To the extent that this is true, mediation is simply incompatible with the function of law enforcement. A mechanism that is prepared to compromise the law for the benefit of the parties involved is anathema to the vindication of subjective legal rights. Of course, matters are entirely different if one envisages mechanisms of alternative dispute resolution to reflect the outcome of court proceedings, or at least to represent the expected value of a civil claim, i.e. the amount of a potential court award, multiplied by the probability that it would in fact be rendered. To illustrate this, imagine that a potential plaintiff believes he or she has a claim for €100 against the other party, and that a thorough legal analysis of the case reveals that a court would enter a judgment against the potential defendant in the amount of €90. Then, in order to achieve the same result, a mediator who helps the parties to negotiate a settlement would have to make sure that the settlement amount is set at €90. This assumes that the costs of litigation and mediation are equal, which they tend not to be in practice. Assuming that the total costs of court proceedings, to the extent that they must be borne by the parties, exceed the costs of mediation, the settlement amount would have to be reduced accordingly. The reverse correction would be appropriate if the 'winner' were entitled to recover the fees he or she incurred from the losing party. Even in theory, these calculations are not always obvious, and in practice they are too difficult to manage effectively. If a mediator had to know what the outcome of the case would have been had it been litigated in court, then he or she would have to be omniscient or would have to engage in a trial of the factual issues and in analyses of the legal issues involved. It goes without saying that mediation operating under such a demand would be meaningless and far too costly to be utilised in practice.

If one abandons the idea that mediation or other modes of alternative dispute resolution simply replicate, or rather imitate, the result that would have been reached in court, it is still possible to rescue the law enforcement function of alternative dispute resolution by assuming that the results reached reflect the expected value of a court judgment. Assuming again that the hypothetical judgment would have amounted to €90 but that it was uncertain whether a court would rule in favour of the claimant, the mediator could simply determine the probability of success, multiply the amount in judgment by that probability and see to it that the parties settle on this amount. In the present hypothetical, if both sides

[51] Wagner 2011, 81 et seq.

nominated witnesses to prove their case, instead of hearing all the witnesses and making a decision based on their testimony, the mediator might hear no witness at all and just estimate the probability of success. Assuming the probability that the claimant would have prevailed is 60 per cent, the mediator would help the parties settle for €54 ($90 \times 0.6 = 54$). Elegant as this approach might seem, it still ascribes supernatural powers to the mediator. How would a neutral observer know what the odds were without thorough information on the testimony of witnesses and the analyses of legal issues?

It may well be that the perspective of dispute resolution at bargaining prices blinded DJ SANCO thus making it hard to realise that mechanisms of alternative dispute resolution may be faster and cheaper than litigation in court precisely because they dispense with the idea of accurate 'enforcement of legal rights' and instead count on a reconciliation of the parties beyond the enforcement of each and every legal entitlement. While it remains possible to include the law in the array of concerns that are brought to bear in alternative proceedings such as mediation, this comes at a cost and still remains a far cry from the objective to enforce the law or subjective legal rights. It is for good reason that Directive 2008/52/EC mandates that courts must enforce settlement agreements reached in mediation only up to the point where their content is contrary to the law of the Member State in which enforcement shall take place (Article 6(1), Directive 2008/52/EC). It is understood that this proviso reflects the public policy exception known from the law of arbitration, as represented by Article V(2) (b) of the New York Convention on the Recognition and Enforcement of Foreign Arbitral Awards.[52] By no means does it require the court asked to enforce the agreement to compare it to the outcome that would have been reached had the case been resolved in litigation. Were this otherwise, mediation would not make sense at all.

It seems that the European Court of Justice (ECJ) shares these concerns about the compatibility of mechanisms of alternative dispute resolution and the objective to enforce EU law. On the one hand, the Court views the courts of the Member States as enforcement agencies of the European Union[53] which have to ensure that EU law is complied with and that remedies for violations of EU law honour the principles of equivalence and effectiveness.[54] On the other hand, the Court did not jump on the train favouring alternative dispute resolution insofar as it has denied arbitral tribunals the privilege to use the referral procedures under Article 267

[52] For the interpretation of the public policy proviso in International Arbitration, see ECJ 1 June1999, Case C-126/97, ECR I-3055 (*Eco Swiss China Time Ltd v Benetton International NV*) (3092 et seq) paras 38 et seq.

[53] ECJ 10 April 1984, Case C-14/83, ECR I-1892 (*von Colson and Kamann v Land Nordrhein-Westfalen*) (1908) paras 23 et seq; ECJ, 30 September 2003, Case C-224/01, ECR 2003, I-10239 (*Köbler v Republik Österreich*) (10310) paras 50 et seq.

[54] ECJ 30 September 2003, Case C-224/01, ECR I-10239 (*Köbler v Republik Österreich*), paras 32 et seq; ECJ 10 April 1984, Case C-14/83, ECR 1892 (*von Colson and Kamann v Land Nordrhein-Westfalen*) (1909) para 28.

TFEU, refusing to place them on the same footing as courts of law.[55] In addition, the ECJ has displayed a hostile attitude towards arbitration agreements in consumer contracts, treating arbitration not as an equally qualified mode of dispute resolution, but as a way to abridge the rights conferred upon the consumer by European law.[56] If this scepticism is warranted, then why does the Commission encourage the use of mediation and other mechanisms of alternative dispute resolution in settling disputes over EU law? If arbitration is not good enough to ensure the correct application of EU law and the vindication of the rights created by the European treaties and by legislation, why would the Union encourage the use of mediation and other modes of alternative dispute resolution which are much farther removed from the function of applying the law to the true facts of the case and thus reaching an outcome prescribed by the law?

The two policies of improving the enforcement of EU law and of expanding and encouraging the use of mechanisms of alternative dispute resolution are incompatible with one another. A lawmaker who focuses on strict enforcement of the laws that he or she has put in place must be zealous in ensuring that whatever disputes arise end up in courts of law that apply whatever rules govern the particular case. On the other hand, legislators whose primary aim is to let the parties have their way, particularly their peace, regardless of the teachings of the applicable law, should encourage the use of alternative ways of dispute resolution. It is not possible to pursue both goals at the same time. This is particularly true in the field of consumer law where disputes usually involve small claims. Where sums of less than €1,000 are at stake, it is a challenge for any mediator to work in the best interest of the parties and provide them some benefit without moving beyond the price these parties are willing to pay for his or her services. With stakes so low, it is simply impossible for a third party to engage in any kind of legal and factual analysis of the issues involved and to approximate—at least broadly—the outcome that would have been reached in court. Therefore, contrary to the suggestion of the Green Paper, damages claims for breach of consumer law are particularly unsuited for alternative dispute resolution, at least if the overriding goal is law enforcement—and not the satisfaction of the parties involved regardless of the commands of the law.

5.5 Conclusion

In the current state of European law-making, horizontal and vertical harmonisation co-exist alongside each other. The anchor of horizontal harmonisation is within Article 81 TFEU, which explicitly allows for measures approximating the laws

[55] ECJ 23 March 1982, Case C-102/81, ECR 1982, 1095 (1110) (*Nordsee v Reederei Mond*) para 10; ECJ 1 June 1999, Case C-126/97, ECR 1999, I-3055 (*Eco Swiss China Time Ltd v Benetton International NV*) (3092 et seq) paras 34, 40.

[56] ECJ 26 October 2006, Case C-168/05, ECR 2006, I-10421 (*Mostaza Claro v Centro Móvil Milenium SL*) (10445 et seq) paras 24 et seq = SchiedsVZ 2007, 46 with note G. Wagner.

and regulations of the Member States. During the first decade of the twenty-first century, the Commission has made intensive use of this authority and passed almost a dozen regulations and directives that harmonise important aspects of the law of civil procedure. However, the impact of these instruments on civil practice in the Member States remains limited because the competence conferred by Article 81 TFEU is restricted to 'civil matters with cross-border implications' and thus does not allow for the harmonisation of the rules of procedure governing domestic cases. In addition, the directives and regulations already on the books cover a wide range of minor issues and—perhaps with the exception of the Brussels I Regulation on Jurisdiction and the Recognition and Enforcement of Foreign Judgments—never touch upon the heart of civil practice, i.e. the complicated and controversial topics of fact gathering, case management, judgments, appeals and interim relief.

For a naïve reader of the EU Treaties it may come as a surprise that some of these important and controversial issues have in fact been the subject of European legislation or will be in the near future. However, these legislative acts remain confined to specific subject-matter areas for which the Union has the competence to legislate, e.g. competition law and—arguably—intellectual property. As a consequence they do not bear the label of a measure harmonising the law of civil procedure. Instead, their aim is, or is said to be, the protection of the substantive legal rights involved, e.g. intellectual property rights. The same approach may soon be followed by European legislation introducing mechanisms of collective redress in the field of competition law and potentially even in consumer law. Thanks to the fact that the 'substantive' powers of the Union are not limited to cross-border trade, instruments of vertical harmonisation remain confined to specific subject-matter areas but in these areas they reach domestic and international cases indiscriminately.

The fact that, in terms of practical impact and significance, vertical harmonisation has overrun horizontal harmonisation may be a source of unease for scholars harbouring the ideal of a well-defined system of Union powers. From a pragmatic point of view, it looks rather attractive as it allows Europe to follow the same piecemeal process of integration that has worked so well in the past. In addition, a process that allows for a limited trial and therefore limited consequences of error offers more chances of success than bold leaps forward which may eventually end in a crash. However, it remains crucial for European lawmakers to realise that even if they engage in vertical harmonisation they still legislate in the area of civil procedure and that for the law of civil procedure, the vindication of legal rights is an important objective—but not the only one involved.

References

Andrews N (2003) English civil procedure. Oxford University Press, Oxford
Beale H (2007) The future of the common frame of reference. Eur Rev Contract Law 3:257–276
Dam KW (1994) The economic underpinnings of patent law. J Legal Stud 23:247–271

Greger R (2000) Verbandsklagen und Prozeßrechtsdogmatik. Neue Entwicklungen in einer schwierigen Beziehung. Zeitschrift für Zivilprozeß 113:399–412

Issacharoff S, Miller G (2009) Will aggregate litigation come to Europe? New York University law and economics working papers, paper 156

Kramer XE (2008) A major step in the harmonization of procedural law in Europe: the European small claims procedures. In: Jongbloed AW (ed) The 13th world congress of procedural law: the Belgian and Dutch reports, Intersentia, Antwerp, pp 253–283

Kramer XE (2010) Enhancing enforcement in the European union. In: Van Rhee CH, Uzelac A (eds) Enforcement and enforceability, tradition and reform. Intersentia, Antwerp, pp 17–39

Max Planck Institute for Comparative and International Private Law, policy options for progress towards a European contract law, comments on the issues raised in the Green Paper from the commission of 1 July 2010, COM (2010) 348 final, 2011

Voit W (2009) In: Musielak Z (ed) Kommentar zur Zivilprozessordnung. Franz Vahlen, Berlin

Wagner G (1998) Prozessverträge—Privatautonomie im Verfahrensrecht. J.C.B Mohr (Paul Siebeck), Tubingen

Wagner G (2002) The economics of harmonization: the case of contract law. Common Market Law Rev 29:995–1023

Wagner G (2004) The purpose and importance of preliminary and summary proceedings. In: Gilles P (ed) Prozessrecht und rechtskulturen. Nomos Verlagsgesellschaft, Baden-Baden, pp 69–96

Wagner G (2006) Neue perspektiven im schadensersatzrecht: kommerzialisierung, strafschadensersatz, kollektivschadensersatz. In: Verhandlungen des 66. Deutschen Juristentags Stuttgart

Wagner G (2007) Urkundenedition durch prozessparteien-auskunftspflicht und weigerungsrechte, Juristenzeitung, pp 706–718

Wagner G (2009) Münchener kommentar zum BGB. C. H. Beck, München

Wagner G (2010) Grundstrukturen eines deutschen Mediationsgesetzes. Rabels Zeitschrift für ausländisches und internationales Privatrecht 74:794–840

Wagner G (2011) Collective redress—categories of loss and legislative options. Law Q Rev 127:55–67

Chapter 6
Harmonisation of Civil Procedure and the Interaction with Private International Law

Xandra E. Kramer

Abstract Traditionally, private international law and civil procedural law are separate disciplines. Even today, many proceduralists seem not to be fully acquainted with the area of private international law, while many private international law experts lack thorough knowledge of (harmonised) civil procedure. However, modern private international law is closely interwoven with civil procedure. Firstly, harmonisation of private international law may be viewed as a preliminary stage in the harmonisation of civil procedure. Secondly, and in connection with the previous point, harmonisation of private international law rules may result in a spontaneous approximation of civil procedure. Thirdly, the harmonisation of private international law rules and civil procedure are dependent upon each other and go hand in hand. Particularly in the EU, there seems to be a gradual shift from harmonising private international law to harmonising civil procedure, by means of establishing minimum standards of civil procedure and introducing uniform European procedures. The lessons learnt from the more advanced harmonisation of private international law could benefit the process of approximation of civil procedure. As long as true common standards of civil procedure are not established, private international law rules will remain to be the primary object of harmonisation.

Professor at Erasmus School of Law, the Netherlands, www.xandrakramer.eu. This contribution has been made possible with the support of the Netherlands Organisation for Scientific Research (NWO) within its Innovational Research Incentives Scheme (VIDI).

X. E. Kramer (✉)
Erasmus School of Law, Rotterdam, The Netherlands
e-mail: kramer@law.eur.nl

X. E. Kramer and C. H. van Rhee (eds.), *Civil Litigation in a Globalising World*,
DOI: 10.1007/978-90-6704-817-0_6,

Contents

6.1 Introductory Remarks and Terminology

Traditional borders between the various legal areas are becoming less distinct due to the increasing complexity of today's business world and globalisation of the law. This certainly holds true for modern private international law, which covers issues of both the applicable substantive law (choice of law) and of international civil procedure. The last category covers, in particular, the international jurisdiction, the recognition and enforcement of foreign judgments as well as the cross-border service of documents, the taking of evidence abroad, and general issues of international legal cooperation. Scholarly and legislative activities in the area of private international law thus require not only at least a basic knowledge of the underlying substantive law issue, as is generally accepted, but also basic knowledge of civil procedure.[1] On its turn, civil procedure of course cannot be studied in isolation either, since it undisputedly serves the main purpose of enforcing substantive law, and due to globalisation, procedural experts and practitioners are confronted increasingly often with issues involving private international law and foreign substantive law.

The interaction between private international law and civil procedure is not always clearly articulated. This contribution aims at exploring the relationship

[1] Due to the Europeanisation of private international law since the Treaty of Amsterdam, EU scholars and practitioners in particular evidently also require knowledge of EU law.

between, on the one hand, private international law and, on the other hand, civil procedure, within the context of globalisation and harmonisation. Private international law should be understood as including rules concerning choice of law (applicable law), as well as those on international civil procedure: namely, international jurisdiction, recognition and enforcement of foreign judgments, cross-border service of documents, and cross-border taking of evidence. Contrary to rules of harmonised civil procedure, the rules of international civil procedure, within the meaning of private international law, do not aim at harmonisation as such, but are intended to coordinate the different legal systems, and to enable legal acts and documents that are by nature confined to the national borders to take place or have an effect in another country. Particularly within the EU context, procedural rules of private international law and the rules of harmonised 'substantive' civil procedure are sometimes both gathered under the term European civil procedure.[2] Though this is perfectly legitimate, there is a fundamental difference between the coordinating rules of private international law and rules that establish true harmonised standards of civil procedure itself or uniform procedures, such as the European Order for Payment Procedure and the European Small Claims procedure. The last categories are not private international law rules as such, but are harmonised civil procedure.[3]

In this Chapter, attention will be paid to the position of private international law and civil procedure as 'opposites', harmonisation of private international law as a preliminary stage in the harmonisation of civil procedure, private international law as a moderator of 'spontaneous' approximation of civil procedure, and the interdependence and cooperation between private international law and civil procedure.

6.2 Private International Law and Harmonisation of Civil Procedure: Two Opposites?

Private international law obviously has gained importance in the past decades due to increased international trade and the mobility of persons. Private international law regulation nowadays has a prominent place at the national level, as well as at a regional and global level. Many countries have separate private international law acts in place, or devote part of their Civil Code to choice of law rules.[4]

---

[2] See, inter alia, Hess 2010.

[3] It is for the same reason that for example the UNCITRAL Convention on the International Sale of Goods of 1980 is not a private international law convention but simply uniform (substantive) law.

[4] Examples of more recent and well-known codifications are the private international Acts in the Netherlands, China, Turkey, Belgium, Germany, Italy, Austria, and Switzerland. Some of these Acts only cover choice of law (applicable law) aspects, others cover all aspects of private international law, notably the Turkish, Belgian, and Swiss Acts.

In particular, at the regional level the stormy developments of the last decade in the EU—as a consequence of the extended competence after the Treaty of Amsterdam—need to be mentioned.[5] The Hague Conference on Private International Law provides the increasingly important global framework for conventions in the area of private international law.[6]

Private international law is regarded by some as one of the most elusive areas of the law. It is neither substantive nor procedural; it is a body of law that aims at coordinating the different legal systems in international cases. Thus, its aim is not to harmonise the law, but merely to 'bridge' or overcome the differences by pointing out the applicable law or the court having jurisdiction, by applying certain—primarily geographically orientated—connecting factors.

Private international law and harmonisation of civil procedure (likewise for uniform substantive private law) may even be regarded as opposites: private international law to a large degree owes its existence to the lack of harmonisation. Where civil procedure is harmonised, private international law rules relating to international civil procedure become to a certain extent obsolete. The *lex fori processus* rule implies that a court will always apply its own procedural rules, as a consequence of the public policy nature of these rules, or of the embodiment of sovereignty.[7] Where these rules are uniform, the consequences of the *lex fori processus* rule are of little practical relevance.

As long as there is no full harmonisation, and this is likely to be the case in the near but also the more distant future, the two closely interact. Firstly, harmonisation of private international law may be viewed as a preliminary stage in the harmonisation of civil procedure (Sect. 6.3). Secondly, and in connection with the previous point, harmonisation of private international law rules may result in the spontaneous approximation of civil procedure (Sect. 6.4). Thirdly, it is clear that in current (EU) regulation, private international rules and civil procedure are dependent upon each other and go hand in hand (Sect. 6.5).

---

[5] Several books are dedicated to European private international law as a special discipline, most notably Bogdan 2006 and Stone 2010 (revised version of the first edition of 2006).

[6] See the website of the Hague Conference on Private International Law, http://www.hcch.net/index_en.php (last consulted in July 2011).

[7] See, inter alia, Hartley 2009, 505, and from an English perspective, Fawcett and Carruthers 2008, 75–76. This rule is seldom codified, but it is said that the very nature of civil procedural rules, which embody the national sovereignty and identity of countries, imply that a court will always rely on its own rules of civil procedure. In the Netherlands, this rule is codified in the general principles of the tenth book of the Civil Code, devoted to private international law, which was adopted in 2011; see Art. 10:4 Dutch Civil Code (*Burgerlijk Wetboek*). See, for example, also Art. 8 Italian Civil Code (*Código Civil*). In most countries, it is generally accepted that, as a consequence of the private international law principle of application of the *lex causae*, foreign substantive law may be applied.

6.3 Harmonisation of Private International Law As a Preliminary Stage

6.3.1 Private International Law as a Transitional Phase?

At the beginning of the last decade, a Dutch scholar in the area of European (substantive) private law posed the question of whether European private international law, for which the ground layers were developed at that time, may be regarded as a transitional stage in a uniform European private law.[8] The same question may be put forward in relation to procedural private international law rules and European harmonised civil procedure. However, there is a difference. In the case of substantive private law, a full harmonisation may indeed render private international law superfluous. On the contrary, a full harmonisation of civil procedure would still necessitate private international rules relating to, amongst other things, international jurisdiction as well as recognition and enforcement of judgments. But it is evident that the more civil procedure is harmonised, the less (procedural) private international law rules will be needed. A full harmonisation of civil procedure at a regional (EU) level or at a global level is however even less likely than full harmonisation of substantive private law. For this reason, it would be too rigid to view the harmonisation of private international law as only a transitional or preliminary stage in 'real' harmonisation.

In many cases, harmonisation of private international law rules may be enough to align or bridge the differences between legal systems. In other cases, harmonisation of civil procedural rules is not feasible, or maybe not even desirable.[9] This leaves unimpeded the fact that harmonisation of private international law may be the preliminary stage in further procedural harmonisation.

6.3.2 Harmonisation of Private International Law and Onwards

The harmonisation of private international law has made considerable progress in recent years.[10] At the global level, the Hague Conference on Private International Law has played an important role. The Hague Conference has expanded from

[8] Erp 2002. The author concludes that it may very well be that resolving private international law issues is enough, and that the unification of private international law may well be the final stage in this process.

[9] In Chapter 4 of the current volume, Visscher argues that from a law and economics point of view, harmonisation in civil procedure is not necessarily desirable. See on the harmonisation of civil procedure to facilitate the harmonisation of substantive law in Europe, inter alia, Kerameus 2011, 261–275.

[10] Over the past several years, there has also been a certain degree of harmonisation of private international law through bilateral conventions.

some 40 member countries at the beginning of the 1990s—mostly European countries, the United States, Canada, Australia, and several Southern American countries—to 72 members in 2011, covering all continents.[11] It has meanwhile established 39 conventions in the area of private international law. Since 1999, the European Union[12] has created a wide-ranging framework of private international law rules, on the basis of Article 81 of the Treaty on the Functioning of the European Union (TFEU) (formerly Article 65 EC Treaty).[13] A dozen instruments have been established on the basis of this provision. The Hague Conventions and most of the EU instruments are traditional private international law instruments, in the sense that they aim primarily at regulating cross-border cases by providing coordination rules between the different systems, and not at introducing uniform procedural rules or harmonised procedures.[14] They include rules on international jurisdiction, recognition and enforcement, the applicable law (choice of law rules), cross-border service et cetera. For example, the Hague Service Convention[15] and the EU Service Regulation[16] do not introduce uniform rules on the service itself, but merely establish a framework of judicial cooperation to secure the cross-border transmission of judicial documents. The differences between the various national ways of service (through courts, bailiffs, postal services et cetera) remain in existence.

However, these instruments do institute certain procedural standards. For example, the rules on recognition and enforcement include—more or less specific, dependent upon the instrument—grounds of refusal, which at the same time indicate which international standards are acceptable for judgments. Usually these are not precisely formulated, but refer merely to 'proper notice' or 'public policy'. But especially in the EU context these are further described in the specific instrument or in the case law of the European Court of Justice (ECJ).

---

[11] See www.hcch.net (last consulted in July 2011). This number includes the European Union as a Regional Economic Integration Organisation (since 2007).

[12] Until 1 December 2009, the date of the entry into force of the Lisbon Treaty, this was the European Community.

[13] Art. 65 EC Treaty was introduced by the 1997 Treaty of Amsterdam, which came into force on 1 May 1999, and was as a result of the Lisbon Treaty replaced by Art. 81 of the Treaty on the Functioning of the European Union on 1 December 2009. This provision differs from its predecessor, but does not include substantial changes. See on the development of the EU competence, Kramer 2008a, 254–260. Before 1999 there were only two multilateral conventions in the EU: the Brussels Convention on Jurisdiction and the Enforcement of Judgments in Civil and Commercial Matters of 1968, OJ 1972, L 299/32, and Convention 80/934/EEC on the Law Applicable to Contractual Obligations of 1980 (Rome Convention), OJ 1980, L 266/1.

[14] See also on this distinction Kramer 2008a, 254.

[15] Convention of 15 November 1965 on the Service Abroad of Judicial and Extrajudicial Documents in Civil or Commercial Matters.

[16] Regulation No. 1393/2007 on the Service in the Member States of Judicial and Extrajudicial Documents in Civil or Commercial Matters, OJ 2007, L 324/79 (replacing Regulation No. 1348/2000).

Article 81 TFEU does not only provide the EU basis for rules on recognition and enforcement of foreign judgments, international jurisdiction, applicable law, and cross-border service and taking of evidence[17]—it also provides for measures on the elimination of obstacles to the proper functioning of civil proceedings, if necessary by promoting the compatibility of the rules on civil procedure in the Member States.[18] In addition to this competence, which was also included in Article 65 EC Treaty, this provision establishes explicitly the basis for measures to ensure the effective access to justice, the development of ADR, and support for the training of the judiciary and judicial staff. Private international law issues are thus coupled with rules on the approximation of 'substantive' civil procedure, as is also evident from Article 81(1), stating that this may include the adoption of measures for the approximation of the laws.

It must be noted that, in accordance with Article 81, these measures are limited to judicial cooperation in civil matters having *cross-border implications*. In that sense, the competence is more limited than Article 114 TFEU (former Article 95 EC Treaty), the general basis for the harmonisation of legislation concerning the institution and functioning of the internal market. This last provision is mostly used as the basis for directives on substantive private law issues.

6.3.3 The Gradual Shift to Harmonisation of Civil Procedure and 'Minimum Standards'

In the legislative policy and practice of the EU, several private international law instruments are indeed used as a preliminary stage in more far-reaching instruments amounting to the harmonisation of civil procedure, or that gradually result in a certain degree of harmonisation.

The European Enforcement Order of 2004[19] may be seen as an instrument that is 'in between' private international law and harmonised civil procedure. It marks the beginning of a new era for the recognition and enforcement of decisions as well as for harmonised European civil procedure. In the first place, it abolishes the exequatur (declaration of enforceability) for uncontested claims, where upon the request of a party the court certifies its judgment as a European enforcement order. In the second place, it establishes minimum requirements for the service of

---

[17] See Art. 81(2), sub (a)–(d) TFEU. In the EC Treaty, these were laid down in Art. 65(1), sub (a) and (b).

[18] See Art. 81(2), sub (f). In the EC Treaty, this was provided in Art. 65(1), sub (c).

[19] Regulation No. 805/2004 creating a European Enforcement Order for Uncontested Claims, OJ 2004, L 143/15. See, inter alia, Rauscher 2004.

documents, the provision of due information to the debtor about the claim, and for review (see Articles 12–19 of this Regulation).

The European Enforcement Order was followed by two regulations introducing genuine harmonised procedures: the European Order for Payment Procedure[20] and the European Small Claims Procedure.[21] These regulations build upon the traditional private international law rules, going beyond the function of private international law and entering the realm of true harmonisation of civil procedure, though limited to cross-border cases.[22] In addition, in July 2011 the European Commission adopted its proposal to establish a Regulation instituting a European procedure for the preservation of bank accounts.[23]

Apart from these particular instruments, in the EU there is a general trend towards the introduction of harmonised civil procedure and 'minimum standards'. For example, in 2009 the Commission tendered a study on minimum standards for provisional measures.[24] In the 2010 Stockholm Action Plan the Commission considers that mutual trust requires minimum standards and a reinforced understanding of the different legal traditions and methods.[25] It specifically mentions the possibility of the introduction of minimum standards in relation to the service of documents and the taking of evidence, as well as for the Brussels IIA Regulation.[26] A (general) Green Paper on the minimum standards for civil procedures is scheduled for 2013.[27] Lastly, in 2011 a Consultation Paper on collective redress was put forward, which may result in harmonised rules and/or minimum standards for this particular type of procedure as well.[28]

---

20 Regulation No. 1896/2006 creating a European Order for Payment Procedure, OJ 2006, L 399/1. See, inter alia, Kramer 2010, 17–39.

21 Regulation No. 861/2007 establishing a European Small Claims Procedure, OJ 2007, L 199/1. See, inter alia, Kramer 2008b, 355–373.

22 See Art. 3 of both regulations. The European Commission proposed to have these instruments applicable to national cases as well, but this was not acceptable to most Member States, as they were seen to run counter to the wording and scope of Art. 65 EC Treaty (currently Art. 81 TFEU). See on this issue, inter alia, Kramer 2007, 20–21.

23 Proposal for a Regulation Creating a European Account Preservation Order to facilitate cross-border debt recovery in civil and commercial matters, COM (2011) 445.

24 Tender on the Study of Minimum Standards of Procedural Law (2009/S 107-153954), 6 June 2009.

25 European Commission, Action Plan Implementing the Stockholm Programme, COM(2010) 171 final, 4.

26 Regulation No. 2201/2003 concerning Jurisdiction and the Recognition and Enforcement of Judgments in Matrimonial Matters and in Matters of Parental Responsibility, OJ 2003, L 388/1.

27 Stockholm Action Plan, see n. 25, 22–23.

28 Commission staff working document. Public Consultation: Towards a Coherent European Approach to Collective Redress Brussels, SEC(2011)173 final, 4 February 2011.

6.4 Private International Law and 'Spontaneous' Approximation of Civil Procedure

6.4.1 General Observations

Private international law rules may also result in a gradual and 'spontaneous' approximation of civil procedure. This may be the consequence of the inclusion of necessary definitions of procedural issues or measures. These definitions are seldom found in the Hague conventions, and these conventions of course lack a uniform interpretation by an international court.[29] The EU private international law instruments contain explicit definitions, and the ECJ has also played an important role in this regard. One example of a definition is the determination of the date for *lis pendens* in Article 30 Brussels I.[30] In its case law, the ECJ provided autonomous definitions for several other procedural terms, amongst other things, counter-claims[31] and provisional measures.[32] It goes without saying that not all of these definitions are automatically taken over in the national procedure of the Member States—although there is a reflex effect—but within the context of application of the EU instruments, these are uniform procedural concepts.

In some instances, private international law makes a distinction between procedural law and substantive private law as regards determination of the scope of choice of law rules that naturally only cover substantive law issues. To these, the *lex causae* applies, whereas for procedural law issues, the *lex fori processus* applies.[33] For example, Article 1(3) of the Rome I Regulation on the applicable law to contracts excludes evidence and procedure from its scope.[34] Pursuant to Article 18, however, questions on the burden of proof are included, and thus not regarded as procedural. The same goes for the Rome II Regulation on the law applicable to non-contractual obligations.[35] The Rome II Regulation further characterises prescription and limitation periods as substantive law and not as procedural law.[36]

---

[29] In the process of establishing a worldwide convention on jurisdiction and enforcement, and the consequent more narrow Hague Choice of Court Convention of 2005, the lack of uniform concepts was a reason to avoid definitions as much as possible. See on this Convention, inter alia, Schulz 2006, 243–286.

[30] Though this provision includes a compromise on the two existing systems, and is thus not fully harmonised.

[31] ECJ 13 July 1995, Case C-341/93, ECR I-2053 (*Danværn Production v Schuhfabriken Otterbeck*).

[32] See further Sect. 6.4.2.

[33] See Sect. 6.2 above.

[34] Regulation No. 593/2008 on the Law Applicable to Contractual Obligations (Rome I), OJ 2008, L 177/6. Weller, in Calliess 2011, 53 and Klöhn, in Calliess 2011, 301–306.

[35] Regulation No. 864/2007 on the Law Applicable to Non-Contractual Obligations (Rome II), OJ 2007, L 199/40, see Art. 1(3) and 22. See, inter alia, Dickinson 2008, 591–597.

[36] See Art. 15 Rome II Regulation on the scope of the applicable law. Dickinson 2008, 587–591.

Private international law rules also have an impact on national civil procedure, and to a certain extent result in converging standards. As was mentioned in the previous section on private international law as a preliminary stage in a harmonised civil procedure, the regime of cross-border recognition and enforcement of judgments at the same time set certain international minimum standards for judicial decisions, particularly in the area of service of documents and, more in general, fair trial. These are partially open norms, and of course are also influenced by another external international source, Article 6 of the European Convention on Human Rights (ECHR). The rules on international jurisdiction have created an awareness of fairness of adjudication, for example under the regime of Brussels I, where certain national grounds of jurisdiction are excluded as exorbitant.[37]

In the following, two examples will be discussed in further detail, relating to the status of provisional measures and anti-suit injunctions under Brussels I, and to the service of documents and the taking of evidence.

6.4.2 Example of Brussels I: Provisional Measures and Anti-Suit Injunctions

Provisional and protective measures are important in international litigation: for example, in the area of intellectual property rights and transport and maritime law. These have been subject to international regulation, amongst other things in the context of Brussels I. Due to their importance, and to the great divergences between the legal systems, provisional measures were also the subject of the Storme project[38] and are included in the 2004 ALI/UNIDROIT Principles on Transnational Civil Procedure.[39] Within the context of the attempt to bring about a worldwide convention on jurisdiction and enforcement under the auspices of the Hague Conference on Private International Law, a definition relating to these measures was proposed, though it was submitted that it might complicate rather than simplify the interpretation.[40]

The Brussels I Regulation provides a special jurisdiction rule for these measures in Article 31. The Reichert ruling[41] defined these as measures that are

[37] See Art. 3 Brussels I Regulation.

[38] Storme 1994, 203-207 and Art. 10.

[39] Art. 8 of the ALI/UNIDROIT Principles of Transnational Civil Procedure, as adopted by the American Law Institute and UNIDROIT in 2004. These Principles were published, accompanied by Rules and short commentaries in ALI/UNIDROIT Principles of Transnational Civil Procedure 2006.

[40] Issues paper for the agenda of the Special Commission of June 1999, 17 (No. 14.4) and Work Doc. No. 95 E & F, Commission II, Jurisdiction and Foreign Judgements in Civil and Commercial Matters, Nineteenth Session, 18 June 2001, available on www.hcch.net (last consulted in July 2011), discussed by Kramer 2003, 315–316.

[41] ECJ 26 March 1992, Case C-261/90, ECR I-2149 (*Reichert v Dresdner Bank*).

'intended to preserve a factual or legal situation so as to safeguard rights the recognition of which is otherwise sought from the court having jurisdiction as to the substance of the case'. In a series of cases concerning the Dutch *kort geding procedure* (*référé*), the ECJ further distinguished and defined these measures.[42] From the famous *Van Uden v Deco-Line* ruling,[43] it is clear that at least within the context of the special jurisdictional provision of Article 31, interim payments are not to be regarded as a provisional measure. This is different where the repayment to the defendant is guaranteed if the main proceedings are unsuccessful, and the measure relates only to specific assets of the defendant (to be) located within the territory of the court seized.

Another important ruling of the ECJ on the Brussels I Regulation concerned the status of the anti-suit injunction: the (common law) order to prohibit parties from initiating or continuing litigation in another (foreign) court. In the Turner case,[44] the Court ruled that the granting of an anti-suit injunction relating to proceedings brought in another EU-Member State is irreconcilable with the Brussels I Regulation, since this would affect the authority of each State to rule on its own jurisdiction. At the same time, this injunction is contrary to the principle of mutual trust that underlies the Regulation. This means that this typically common law procedural tool is no longer allowed within the European context, not even—as the ECJ has clarified in the more recent and often criticised Westtankers ruling[45]—where parties had agreed upon arbitration, a matter that is excluded from Brussels I.[46]

Within the European context, through the prism of private international law, these rulings have resulted in a certain degree of harmonisation of civil procedure and international litigation practice.

6.4.3 Example of Service of Documents

The Hague Service Convention and the European Service Regulation do not aim at harmonising methods involving the internal service of documents, but focus on a secure transmission between countries. However, these did establish a modest

---

42 See Kramer 2003, 312–315.

43 ECJ 17 November 1998, Case C-391/95, ECR I-7091 (*Van Uden v Deco-Line*).

44 ECJ 27 April 2004, Case C-159/02, ECR I-3565 (*Turner v Grovit*).

45 ECJ 10 February 2009, Case C-185/07, ECR I-663 (*Allianz v Westtankers*).

46 Referring to the Hagen ruling (Case C-365/88, ECR I-1845), the ECJ argued that even if it were assumed that an injunction could be regarded as a measure of a procedural nature intended to safeguard the integrity of the proceedings pending before the court which issues it, and therefore as being a matter of national law alone, the application of national procedural rules may not impair the effectiveness of this EU instrument.

approximation of service and notification. This is especially true for the European Service Regulation. This Regulation aims not only at increasing procedural efficacy by providing a transmission framework but is also part of the area of freedom, security, and justice in which litigants should be able to assert their rights in the same manner as in their own courts.[47]

Both regimes prescribe certain methods of transmission, with a primary role for the transmission between Central authorities and competent judicial officers (Convention) or transmitting and receiving agencies (Regulation). Documents will be served to the defendant by the local authorities/competent agency in accordance with national law, or by way of exception, by a particular method requested by the applicant/transmitting agency.[48] Both regimes provide for optional alternative ways of transmission, such as diplomatic channels, and postal or direct service. The new Service Regulation is more compulsory in this regard, particularly since it provides that postal service by registered letter with acknowledgement of receipt or equivalent, is a valid method of service. Further, it provides a uniform period for effecting the service, as well as uniform language requirements.[49] Both regimes introduced the same standards for reviewing the service where a defendant does not enter an appearance, though they do allow for a certain discretion.[50]

The Regulation on the European Enforcement Order is taking the service issue a step further. For the purpose of ensuring the uncontested nature of the claim and certification of the judgment, it prescribes a set of eleven methods of service as minimum standards.[51] This system is completed by uniform minimum standards for a review remedy in the court of origin in the situation where service was effected without proof of receipt by the debtor.[52] The application of these provisions is sometimes problematic.

Though none of these instruments have actually resulted yet in a complete uniform system of service of documents, there is no doubt that in this regard they have important normative implications for the national law. As was mentioned above, the European Commission considers the actual introduction of minimum standards for service of documents within the context of the Service Regulation.[53]

---

[47] See also Storskrubb 2008, 93–94.

[48] See Art. 5 Hague Service Convention and Art. 7 EU Service Regulation.

[49] See Art. 7 and 8 EU Service Regulation.

[50] Art. 15 Hague Service Convention and Art. 19 EU Service Regulation.

[51] See Arts. 13, 14, and 15 European Enforcement Order.

[52] Art. 19 European Enforcement Order.

[53] See Sect. 6.3.3.

6.5 Interdependence and Collaboration of Private International Law and Civil Procedure

6.5.1 General Observations

Sometimes private international law rules do not function well, and they raise serious questions of interpretation due to the differences between the 'underlying' rules of civil procedure. In the previous section, this point was touched upon where the rules on cross-border service of documents were discussed. Furthermore, particularly in the EU context, harmonisation of private international law rules is not always sufficient. Private international law rules bridge the differences between the legal systems and put in place a system of legal cooperation between countries and in the EU member States. However, this system cannot solve all the problems relating to the high costs, delays, complexities, substantial differences in procedural law, and language issues inherent to international litigation. As was mentioned above, on the basis of Article 65 sub (c) EC Treaty, currently Article 81(2) sub (f) TFEU, several instruments introducing uniform procedures have been established.[54] That rules on private international law issues and civil procedure go hand in hand is also illustrated by the ALI/UNIDROIT Principles on Transnational Procedure; these have harmonised civil procedural rules as its core, but also include several rules on private international law issues, particularly on international jurisdiction.[55]

Two examples will be presented below to illustrate the interdependence of rules of private international law and civil procedure, more in particular showing the need for more harmonised rules of civil procedure, in order to have a proper functioning of harmonised rules of private international law in Europe.

6.5.2 Example of Application of Foreign Law

An issue that was raised in the context of bringing about the Rome I and II Regulations on the law applicable to contractual and non-contractual obligations concerns the application of conflict of law rules and foreign law. There is a difference in this regard, in particular between common law countries on the one hand—where foreign law is to a certain extent on the same footing as the facts—and civil law countries on the other hand—where the general approach is that the court applies the conflict rules and foreign law *ex officio*. These opposing approaches and all the variations thereof are largely inherent to the principally different tasks of the judge in these systems, and also vary with respect to the

[54] See Sect. 6.3.3.

[55] See Kramer 2009, 77–86.

practical difficulties experienced in the ascertainment of foreign law.[56] Since the issue could not be resolved in the context of Rome II, a review clause provides that further study will be done on the effect of the way in which foreign law is treated.[57] A Commission Statement attached to the Regulation adds that appropriate measures will be taken if necessary. An exhaustive comparative study as a result hereof was published in 2011.[58] It is clear that it is counter to the harmonisation of private international law if on the basis of differences in procedural law, to which the *lex fori* applies, these rules are automatically applied in one Member State but not in the other. Thus, this procedural issue will have to be resolved in order for private international law to function properly.

It is noteworthy that the 2004 ALI/UNIDROIT Principles on Transnational Civil Procedure provide in Principle 22.1 that the court is responsible for the determination of the correct legal basis of the claim, also where foreign law applies. Furthermore, the practical side of the application of foreign law is also the object of attention of the Hague Conference on Private International Law.[59]

6.5.3 Example of Abolition of Exequatur

Permission for enforcement, particularly in civil law traditions signified as *exequatur*, is generally regarded as a natural prerequisite for the enforcement of judgments emanating from the courts of another country. It may be seen as an exponent of national sovereignty. The purpose of exequatur proceedings is to review a foreign judgment on its compatibility with the legal order of the state of enforcement or with standards included in a particular convention or—in the EU context—regulation.

In the EU, the recognition and enforcement of foreign judgments, as part of private international law, has been regulated since 1968 by the Brussels I Regulation[60] and its predecessor, the Brussels Convention. More recently, similar regimes for the cross-border enforcement of judgments in the EU have been established, most notably for parental responsibility (the Brussels IIA Regulation[61]) and for

---

[56] Some countries simply have a better infrastructure than others.

[57] See Art. 30 Rome II Regulation.

[58] Esplugues et al. 2011.

[59] Following a 'Feasibility Study on the Treatment of Foreign Law' by the Permanent Bureau in 2007, in March 2009 a further Study was announced on 'Accessing the Content of Foreign Law and the Need for the Development of a Global Instrument in this Area—A Possible Way Ahead,' available at http://www.hcch.net/upload/wop/genaff_pd11a2009e.pdf (last consulted in July 2011).

[60] Regulation No. 44/2001 Regulation No. 44/2001 on Jurisdiction and the Recognition and Enforcement of Judgments in Civil and Commercial Matters, OJ 2001, L 12/1.

[61] See n. 26.

insolvency (the Insolvency Regulation).[62] Since the Treaty of Amsterdam and the Tampere conclusions of 1999,[63] EU policy aims at abolishing the exequatur.[64] Meanwhile, several instruments provide for a system of cross-border enforcement within the EU, without the requirement of exequatur. These are the aforementioned Brussels IIA Regulation with regard to certain decisions on parental responsibility, and the (optional) European Enforcement Order, the European Order for Payment Procedure, and the European Small Claims Procedure,[65] as well as the recently enacted Maintenance Regulation.[66]

In 2009, a Green paper[67] on the revision of Brussels I was published, followed by the Commission Proposal[68] on the Recast of Brussels I by the end of 2010. A key element of this revision is the full abolition of exequatur. The Commission argues that in an internal market without frontiers it is difficult to justify citizens and businesses having to undergo the expenses in terms of costs and needing to assert their rights abroad, particularly since it seems that in practice the exequatur is rarely refused.[69] The abolition of the exequatur is underpinned by the premise of mutual trust.[70] Though in several other recent instruments the exequatur has also

---

[62] Regulation No. 1346/2000 on Insolvency Proceedings, OJ 2000, L 160/1. There are several other special regulations that include rules on cross-border recognition and enforcement in the EU, including Regulation No. 4/2009 on Jurisdiction, Applicable Law, Recognition and Enforcement of Decisions and Cooperation in Matters Relating to Maintenance Obligations, OJ 2009, L 7/1. In the area of succession and wills and matrimonial property, the European Commission has adopted proposals; succession and wills: COM(2009)154 final; matrimonial property and registered partnerships: COM(2011) 126 final and COM(2011) 127 final.

[63] Tampere European Council: Presidency Conclusions, 15 and 16 October 1999 (Presidency Conclusions, No. 200/1/99). See also the Programme of measures for implementation of the principle of mutual recognition of decisions in civil and commercial matters, 30 November 2000, OJ 2001, C 12/1.

[64] See, inter alia, Cuniberti and Rueda 2011, 286–317; Beaumont and Johnston 2010, 249–279; Oberhammer 2010, 197–203; Schlosser 2010, 101-104; Cuniberti 2008, 371–376; Malatesta 2008, 1–8; Van der Grinten 2006, 71–83; Stadler 2004, 2–10.

[65] See Sect. 6.3.3.

[66] See n. 62.

[67] Green Paper on the review of Council Regulation (EC) No. 44/2001 on jurisdiction and the recognition and enforcement of judgments in civil and commercial matters, COM(2009)175 of 21 April 2009.

[68] Proposal for a Regulation of the European Parliament and of the Council on the jurisdiction and the recognition and enforcement of judgments in civil and commercial matters (Recast), COM(2010) 748 final of 14 December 2010.

[69] Green Paper (n. 67), 2. Data research was conducted and published by Hess, Pfeiffer & Schlosser. See Hess et al. 2008, 126–167. This report was presented, in a slightly different form, to the European Commission in 2007. It must be noted that it includes scant data from the new Member States.

[70] As the Commission optimistically notes in its Explanatory Memorandum, 6: 'Today, judicial cooperation and the level of trust among Member States has reached a degree of maturity which permits the move towards a simpler, less costly, and more automatic system of circulation of judgments, removing the existing formalities among Member States'.

been abolished, this proposal is more far-reaching, since Brussels I is the key instrument that covers a wide range of subject matters and types of decisions.

Throughout the preparation of this proposal, it has been emphasised that the abolition of exequatur should be accompanied by the necessary procedural safeguards.[71] These are needed to guarantee the right to a fair trial ensured by Article 6 ECHR and Article 47 of the EU Charter on Fundamental Rights, since the existing grounds of refusal will no longer be available.[72] Particularly the abolition of the grounds of refusal relating to procedural public policy and proper service of documents are noteworthy in this regard. The general exclusion of the public policy defence has been especially criticised in literature.[73] The Commission proposal provides for various remedies, one of which concerns default judgments where service was not properly effected or where the defendant by reason of force majeure or other extraordinary circumstances could not contest the claim. In this case, a remedy should be available in the country of origin.[74] Another rule provides that a party shall have the right to apply for refusal of recognition and enforcement where such recognition and enforcement would not be permitted by fundamental principles underlying the right to a fair trial.[75] However, apart from the principal question of whether the time is ripe for a full abolition of the exequatur, the lack of uniform rules on service of documents, and the lack of minimum standards of civil procedure—apart from the defective protection offered by the open norms stemming from Article 6 ECHR—creates a loophole in the desired EU private international law system and in the area of fair judicial treatment.

Not only is it unclear what exactly is to be qualified as proper notice and fundamental rights of civil procedure, particularly when it comes to day-to-day court practice in the 27 Member States, it is also to be expected that the effectiveness of the abolition of the exequatur is undermined by the differences between the national laws at the level of enforcement in the individual Member States. Even under the European Enforcement Order, the European Order for Payment Procedure, and the European Small Claims Procedure, the actual enforcement of the judicial decision is left to national law, which could mean that national enforcement measures may still be invoked.[76] Enforcement measures differ greatly from one Member State to another, and some allow for a review that may even go beyond the grounds of refusal laid down in the current Brussels I Regulation. This may result in a uniform exequatur procedure being replaced by 27 national enforcement regimes.

---

[71] See, for example, the Green Paper (n. 67), 2–3 and also the Commission Proposal (n. 62), 6–7.

[72] The existing grounds of refusal, included in Articles 34 and 35 Brussels I, relate to the offence of public policy (including procedural public policy), proper notice, irreconcilability, and the violation of jurisdiction rules relating to insurance and consumer contracts and certain exclusive grounds of jurisdiction.

[73] See the literature included in n. 64.

[74] Art. 45 of the Commission Proposal (n. 68).

[75] Art. 45 of the Commission Proposal (n. 68).

[76] See, inter alia, Hess 2010, 582 (No. 106).

It is noteworthy that in this Commission Proposal the exequatur is, *inter alia*, retained for group actions.[77] The Commission considers that these procedures vary too much, and that further consultation is needed. As was mentioned above, a consultation paper was circulated in 2011.[78]

It is not sure what the result of the negotiations will be, since there is criticism and scepticism relating to the 'salami technique' of abolition of the exequatur in recent years, both by scholars and by national governments. From the example of the abolition of the exequatur—a private international law issue—it is clear that a certain degree of harmonisation of civil procedure is necessary in order to take the cross-border enforcement of judgments a step further. As long as there is no evident common understanding and practice as to what pertains to fundamental principles of civil procedure, the abolition of exequatur will leave a gap where particular care is most needed due to the complex nature of cross-border litigation. Under the regime of Brussels IIA, abolition of the exequatur for decisions relating to parental responsibility has already created a serious challenge to the protection of human rights, since the ECJ upheld the strict premise of mutual trust even where a gross violation of human rights (the right to be heard) was invoked.[79]

6.6 Concluding Remarks

Private international law owes its existence to the differences in substantive and procedural law. As long as the international harmonisation of civil procedural rules is limited, private international law rules will be decisive. Private international law rules, particularly those concerned with procedural issues, will naturally become less important where there are more harmonised rules. At the same time, the private international law rule of the *lex fori processus* is of little practical relevance if the procedural law systems involved are harmonised.

In order to meet the requirements of globalisation of legal traffic, a certain degree of harmonisation is necessary. Within the EU, the proper functioning of the internal market is also invoked to justify further harmonisation. Until recently, the solution was the establishment of private international law rules, and—partially at the same time—the creation of a framework of harmonised private international law rules at the global and the EU level.

Private international law cannot be regarded merely as a transitional stage in a uniform law system. It serves its own purpose, and—even more than for substantive private law—a future where procedural laws are harmonised is still distant, and perhaps not even desirable. Especially in the EU, however, there is a gradual shift from the harmonisation of private international law to a more

---

[77] See Art. 37 Commission Proposal (n. 68) and Explanatory Memorandum, 7–8.

[78] See Sect. 6.3.3 and n. 28.

[79] ECJ 22 December 2010, Case C-491/10 (*Aguirre Zarraga v Pelz*) (not yet published in ECR).

far-reaching harmonisation of civil procedure, primarily by introducing or proposing minimum standards. In this regard, private international law may indeed function as a preliminary phase in the harmonisation of civil procedure.

Private international law can also result in a gradual and spontaneous approximation of civil procedure, as has been demonstrated by the various examples concerning international jurisdiction and recognition, and enforcement of the service of documents under the Brussels I Regulation.

The on-going harmonisation of private law does not have implications only for substantive law; in some cases, the harmonisation of private international law also requires a certain degree of harmonisation involving civil procedural rules. This, for example, is the case in the process of abolition of the exequatur under Brussels I. The trend towards the introduction of minimum standards is also primarily to be understood within the context of the proper functioning of the various private international law instruments.

Private international law and the harmonisation of civil procedure are no longer strangers, but close companions with the common goal to achieve an (EU) 'area of justice', and in the long run maybe even global justice.

References

ALI/UNIDROIT (2006) Principles of transnational civil procedure. Cambridge University Press, Cambridge

Beaumont P, Johnston E (2010) Can exequatur be abolished in Brussels I whilst retaining a public policy defence? J Priv Int Law 6(2):249–279

Bogdan M (2006) Concise introduction to EU private international law. Europa Law Publishing, Groningen

Calliess G-P (ed) (2011) Rome regulations. Commentary on the European rules of the conflict of law. Kluwer Law International, Alphen aan den Rijn

Cuniberti G (2008) The first stage of the abolition of the exequatur in the European Union. CJEL 14(2)3:71–376

Cuniberti G, Rueda I (2011) Abolition of exequatur. Addressing the commissions's concerns. Rabels Zeitschrift 75(2):286–317

Dickinson A (2008) The Rome II regulation. The law applicable to non-contractual obligations. Oxford University Press, Oxford

Esplugues C et al (2011) Application of foreign law. Sellier, Munich

Fawcett J, Carruthers JM (2008) Cheshire, North and Fawcett private international law, 14th edn. Oxford University Press, Oxford

Hartley TC (2009) International commercial litigation. Text, cases and materials on private international law. Cambridge University Press, Cambridge

Hess B (2010) Europäisches Zivilprozessrecht. Ein Lehrbuch. C.F. Müller Verlag, Heidelberg

Hess B et al (2008) The Brussels I-Regulation (EC) no. 44/2001: the Heidelberg Report on the application of regulation Brussels I in 25 member states (Study JLS/C4/2005/03). Hart Publishing, Oxford

Kerameus KD (2011) Procedural implications of civil law unification. In: Hartkamp S et al (eds) Towards a European civil code. Kluwer Law International/Ars Aequi Libri, Nijmegen, pp 261–275

Kramer XE (2003) Harmonisation of provisional and protective measures in Europe. In: Storme M (ed) Procedural laws in Europe. Towards harmonisation. Maklu, Antwerp/Apeldoorn, pp 305–319

Kramer XE (2007) Eenvormige Europese procedures voor de inning van vorderingen. De Europese betalingsbevelprocedure en de Europese procedure voor geringe vorderingen. Kluwer, Deventer

Kramer XE (2008a) A major step in the harmonization of procedural law in Europe: the European small claims procedure. Accomplishments, new features and some fundamental questions of European harmonization. In: Jongbloed AW (ed) The XIIIth world congress of procedural law: the Belgian and Dutch reports. Intersentia, Antwerp, pp 253–283

Kramer XE (2008b) The European small claims procedure: striking the balance between simplicity and fairness in european litigation. ZEuP 2:355–373

Kramer XE (2009) De IPR-bepalingen in de ALI/UNIDROIT Principles of transnational civil procedure. Een bruikbaar model voor harmonisatie? TCR 1:77–86

Kramer XE (2010) Enhancing enforcement in the European Union. The European order for payment procedure and its implementation in the member states, particularly in Germany, the Netherlands and England. In: Van Rhee CH, Uzelac A (eds) Enforcement and enforceability. Tradition and reform. Intersentia, Antwerp-Oxford-Portland, pp 17–39

Malatesta A (2008) Towards the abolition of the exequatur in Europe: an overview of the EC regulations, Liuc Papers n. 219, Serie Imresa e Istituzioni, 25, agosto 2008

Oberhammer P (2010) The abolition of exequatur. IPRax 30:197–203

Rauscher T (2004) Der Europa Vollstreckungstitel für unbestrittene Forderungen. Sellier/Verlag Recht und Wirtschaft, München/Heidelberg

Schlosser PF (2010) The abolition of exequatur proceedings—including public policy review? IPRax 30:101–104

Schulz A (2006) The Hague convention of 30 June 2005 on choice of court agreements. J Priv Int L 2:243–286

Stadler A (2004) Das Europäische Zivilprozessrecht—Wie viel Beschleunigung verträgt Europa? 24:IPRax 2–10

Stone P (2010) EU private international law: harmonization of laws. Edward Elgar Publishing, Cheltenham

Storme M (1994) Approximation of judiciary law in the European Union. Kluwer, Dordrecht

Storskrubb E (2008) Civil procedure and EU law: a policy area uncovered. Oxford University Press, Oxford

Van der Grinten P (2006) Abolishing exequatur in the European Union: an alternative. In: Heukels T (ed) Crossing borders: essays in European and private international law in honour of Frans van der Velden. Kluwer, Deventer, pp 71–83

Van Erp (2002) Editorial: European private international law as a transition stage? EJCL. Available at http://www.ejcl.org/. Accessed in July 2011

Chapter 7
Harmonisation of Civil Procedure and the Interaction with Substantive Private Law

Matthias E. Storme

Abstract This chapter deals with the interaction between procedural law and substantive private law in the context of a partially harmonised but mainly non harmonised substantive law. It also discusses civil proceedings dealing with matters not exclusively governed by domestic law. Procedural law should take into account that the applicable private law is often drafted or developed having regard to different rules of procedure (foreign private law) or without taking into consideration the existing rules of civil procedure. The author illustrates more specifically the possible problems with regard to (1) procedural rules concerning the availability of and access to procedures and the powers of courts, (2) the protection of defendants and (3) a change of parties or their rights under substantive law during the course of the proceedings.

Contents

Professor of civil and commercial law and jurisprudence at the KU Leuven; member of the Brussels Bar.

M. E. Storme (✉)
KU Leuven, Brussels, Belgium
e-mail: matthias@storme.be

X. E. Kramer and C. H. van Rhee (eds.), *Civil Litigation in a Globalising World*,
DOI: 10.1007/978-90-6704-817-0_7,

7.1 Introduction

As a contribution to a conference on the globalisation and harmonisation of civil procedure, this paper is mainly addressed to proceduralists. Its main purpose is to ask proceduralists to direct attention to a range of issues of substantive law that are affected by the rules and practices of civil procedure due to the choices made by proceduralists. Although the reverse exercise is as important, I will devote only a few paragraphs to it, given the focus and aim of this contribution.

The context I use for my remarks is that of a partially harmonised but mainly unharmonised substantive law and civil proceedings dealing with matters not exclusively governed by domestic law; the substantive law to be taken into account may include harmonised or common[1] private law, or just foreign law. In a globalising or at least Europeanising context, drafters of rules of civil procedure, indeed, have to take into account that the applicable private law is often drafted or developed having regard to different rules of procedure (foreign private law) or making, to a very large extent, abstraction from—the existing rules of—civil procedure (harmonised private law).

It is true that the function of procedural law should not be reduced to merely making effective the legal effects stated by substantive law—i.e. mainly protecting and enforcing subjective rights—; its role is also to make the effects of substantive law in a concrete case acceptable, to legitimise them to a certain extent.[2] But it is, nevertheless, one of the functions of the rules of civil procedure to effectuate substantive law; in that sense civil procedure is an *ancilla iuris*, a helper of the (substantive) law.

[1] Harmonised or 'common' private law in the sense of supranational or European common law (and clearly not meaning the common law of England and Wales or any other form of Anglo-American common law).

[2] I do not mention 'dispute resolution' as a specific purpose of civil procedure, as it is rather a purpose of the law as such: the capability of ending disputes by their acceptance when applied to a dispute is one of the criteria for good rules in general (as well for substantive rules as for procedural rules). But it is one of the purposes of rules of civil procedure specifically to legitimise the outcome of the proceedings, or at least to legitimise the fact that those substantive law rules which have been applied were applied.

7.2 Taking into Account Civil Procedure when Drafting and Interpreting Substantive Law

As stated, it is certainly important to draw the attention of drafters of substantive rules to the limitations of their effectiveness which necessarily follow from the fact that in the event of dispute these rules will have to be applied in the framework of proceedings governed by rules of procedure and especially by rules of evidence. For the reasons mentioned, I will not develop this perspective at length but will limit myself to some examples, the first one dealing with the rules on initiating proceedings, the second dealing with evidence.

The fact that judicial proceedings and/or dispute resolution proceedings and/or enforcement proceedings have been started is a relevant fact for the application of several rules of substantive law. My main examples come from the rules on prescription (or limitation of actions): in most systems of substantive law, the course of prescription will be suspended and/or interrupted by initiating proceedings. However, different systems of civil procedure may use different categories of proceedings and may have different rules on the way proceedings are initiated and on the way the date of commencement of proceedings is determined. The relevant rule should take this into account, and the drafter should try to use neutral terms in order to cover the functional equivalents existing in different systems of civil procedure. It may be that the drafters judge that the initiation of certain types of proceedings is not functionally equivalent and should, therefore, not have the same effect (e.g. proceedings which aim at collecting evidence but cannot as such lead to a decision on the merits of a claim). But the rules should not be drafted in such a way that the initiation of functionally equivalent proceedings does not have the same effect simply because of the way the rule is drafted, not taking into consideration the formulations used in civil procedural law in other countries and the types of dispute resolution available there.

The authors of the Draft Common Frame of Reference (DCFR) have taken this into account in drafting Article III-7:302 on the effect of judicial and other proceedings on the running of prescription of rights to performance. Paragraph (3) provides that the rules of paragraphs (1) and (2) on suspension of prescription in the event of judicial proceedings to assert the right 'apply, with appropriate adaptations, to arbitration proceedings, to mediation proceedings, to proceedings whereby an issue between two parties is referred to a third party for a binding decision and to all other proceedings initiated with the aim of obtaining a decision relating to the right.'[3] As to acquisitive prescription, another criterion has been

---

[3] The 1980 New York Convention on the Limitation Period in the International Sale of Goods, on the other hand, basically deals only with judicial proceedings and arbitration proceedings (see Artt. 13 to 15).

used in the corresponding Article VIII-4:203 paragraph (4) DCFR: 'These provisions apply, with appropriate adaptations, to arbitration proceedings and to all other proceedings initiated with the aim of obtaining an instrument which is enforceable as if it were a judgment.'

Apart from the rules of prescription, there may be other instances where rules of civil procedure should be taken into account—depending on the chosen solution—such as certain rules on plurality of debtors or on dependent personal security (suretyship), on the running of interest, et cetera.

In general, drafters of rules of substantive law should pay attention to the appropriateness, in the light of the rules of evidence, of the facts chosen as conditions for subjective rights or other legal effects. This is already the situation in a purely domestic setting, but even more so when one takes into account that the rule may have to be applied in a foreign court using the rules of evidence of the *lex fori*. One can probably not take into account all the possible peculiarities of the laws of evidence, but one can at least try to give preference to facts that can generally be proven more easily or with more certainty. I limit my examples again to the rules on prescription of rights to performance.

A first example concerns the effect of the initiation of judicial or other proceedings on the running of prescription. In comparing laws, one finds mainly three solutions as to the situation when the proceedings have ended: prescription was merely suspended and the creditor disposes only of the period which remained at the date of initiation of the proceedings; or prescription is also interrupted or renewed and a new period of prescription of the same length as the original period begins to run; or prescription is extended and a new period of a fixed length begins to run, which is usually shorter than the original one. In all three solutions, it is necessary to determine the exact date the proceedings ended, but only in the first solution it is also necessary to determine the exact date the proceedings were started. The first solution (two points in time to be determined) thus creates twice as many possible disputes as the two other solutions.[4]

A second example concerns the commencement of prescription in the event of defective performance. The modern rule for the commencement of prescription in general is to let prescription begin to run when the creditor knows or can reasonably be expected to know of the facts giving rise to the right to performance and the identity of the debtor (e.g. Article III-7:301 DCFR). However, that moment in time

[4] The drafters of the DCFR have chosen a mixed solution in Art. III-7:302 (2): in principle, judicial proceedings only suspend the running of prescription, but 'where the proceedings end within the last six months of the prescription period without a decision on the merits, the period of prescription does not expire before six months have passed after the time when the proceedings ended.' In my opinion, a simpler solution has to be preferred, but at least the solution is better than Art. 14:302 PECL (Principles of European Contract Law), which provided a mere suspension without any fixed period of extension.

is often difficult to prove with certainty. In the event of defective performance of an obligation to supply goods or services, many systems of substantive law provide that the creditor may not rely on the lack of conformity unless the creditor gives notice to the debtor within a reasonable time after the creditor discovered or could reasonably be expected to have discovered the non-conformity. In the event of dispute about the prescription of the right of the creditor, it is much easier to obtain certainty on the date of notification by the creditor than on the date the creditor discovered or could reasonably be expected to have discovered the non-conformity. As certainty is of the essence of rules of prescription, it is wiser to provide that in cases where there is such a duty to notify and there has been a timely notification, prescription only commences at—or is suspended until—the date of notification. Unfortunately, this wisdom has not been implemented in contemporary harmonisation projects such as the New York Convention on the Limitation Period in the International Sale of Goods (see Article 9 (2)(a); see, however, also Article 11) or the DCFR (Article III-7:301).

7.3 Taking into Account Substantive Law when Drafting and Interpreting Procedural Law: General Remarks

Let me now turn to my main topic, that being the expectations towards procedural law from the perspective of substantive (particularly private) law, especially harmonised and foreign substantive law.

Generally speaking, these expectations are evidently the same whether the applicable substantive law is domestic law or common/harmonised law or foreign law. One expects from procedural law the rules required to protect and enforce subjective rights, wherever self-help is not an option, in an effective way within an appropriate time and at reasonable cost. But one also expects from procedural law the rules required to protect defendants against the burdens and costs of procedures for unfounded claims.

Nevertheless, as national procedural law was (and is) evidently developed in relation with national substantive law, it usually does not take into account substantive law rules and remedies foreign to its national law. This may affect the protection offered by substantive law as well as the protection offered by remedies that have to be sought in a foreign court, as the protection against interference by plaintiffs resorting to a foreign court.

In Sect. 7.4, I will check possible problems with procedural rules concerning the availability of and access to procedures and the powers of courts. In section V, I will devote some attention to the protection of defendants. In section VI, I will check how procedural law responds to a change of parties or their rights under substantive law, especially when a change happens during the course of proceedings.

7.4 Availability of Procedures and Powers and Rules on Their Initiation and Scope

7.4.1 Powers of the Court

The first and most evident requirement is the availability of courts and of accessible procedures before these courts to give legal protection to private law rights. Most private law rights are, indeed, effective only when they can be protected—by recognition and where necessary enforcement—by courts in procedures accessible to the holders of those rights. Courts should in general have the power to order a party to do something which is due (including an order not to do something), to make a declaration on the existence or non-existence of a right and to modify a legal relationship where substantive law provides that a party is entitled to have the relationship modified by the court. Given the length of normal procedures, summary proceedings and/or the possibility to obtain provisional measures (interim relief) are necessary where substantive rights would become meaningless or illusory without quick protection.

The main problems arising in this respect are of a general nature and are not specific to cases where foreign or harmonised law has to be applied: duration, costs, unequal quality of judgments, difficulty to enforce judgments. Nevertheless, there are cases where substantive rights granted by common/harmonised or foreign law are not protected because they are unknown in the country of the forum and courts do not have the power to grant them or at least believe they do not have such power, based on limitations in the law on the organisation of the judiciary or civil procedure (whether based on constitutional, statutory or just customary rules or ideas).

A first example concerns immunities of jurisdiction and enforcement and similar rules, which can be found especially in favour of public authorities. Whereas in some cases they are of a substantive nature (in the sense that in that case there simply is no subjective right against the public authority), in others the applicable substantive law (e.g. foreign contract law, European Union law) does grant a subjective right, probably unknown to domestic law. The most famous example where domestic limits to jurisdiction have been set aside in favour of the effective legal protection of subjective rights derived from European Union law is the judgment of the European Court of Justice (ECJ) in the first *Factortame* case[5] in which the Court ruled that a rule of national law which would prevent a court seised of a dispute governed by Community law from granting interim relief—*in casu* suspending an Act of Parliament—must be set aside where this is necessary in order to ensure the full effectiveness of the judgment to be given on the existence of the rights claimed under Community law.

[5] ECJ 19 June 1990, Case C-213/89, ECR I-2433 (*Factortame*).

As to immunity against enforcement, the Belgian Court of Cassation ruled in three judgments of 21 December 2009[6] that the traditional rule of immunity of international organisations must be set aside as contrary to Article 6 of the European Convention on Human Rights where it is disproportional, i.e. where there are no other reasonable possibilities for the effective protection of the rights of the creditor. Although these cases were not specifically dealing with rights granted by harmonised or foreign law, the decision is also relevant for them.

Rights granted by harmonised or foreign law are, on the other hand, directly affected by procedural rules limiting the content of remedies that can be granted by courts. The most typical example is a rule exempting courts from granting the remedy of specific performance even if the applicable substantive law grants it. There is no problem for harmonised or foreign law where the rule is not a rule of civil procedure, but of domestic substantive law, as it would precisely then not be applied where domestic law is not the law to the merits of the case. However, it is not always clear in national law how such limitations are qualified. The applicable substantive law may grant a party a right to obtain certain documents from another party, which may be unknown under domestic law and exceed the possibilities granted by the procedural law of the forum in the form of a procedural right (*actio ad exhibendum*). Parties may be entitled by the applicable substantive law to remedies preventing damage to be caused by another future party but not obtain it because in the country of the forum it is considered as a matter of civil procedure and not recognised in the case. A party may be entitled to an adaptation of the content of a contract by the court, whereas the country of the forum ignores this possibility. Or the applicable substantive law may provide that where a court imposes a judicial penalty (*astreinte*) in the event of non-compliance with the court order the penalty shall be paid to the aggrieved party (this is the principle in, e.g., Article 7.2.4 of the UPICC (UNIDROIT Principles for International Commercial Contracts)) and by doing so may come into conflict with the law of the forum which considers this to be a matter of procedural law and has a procedural rule that the *astreinte* does not have to be paid to the aggrieved party (but to the public authorities).

A possible simple solution would be to have a rule in the civil procedural law stating that nothing in the rules on civil procedure forbids national courts from applying such rules of the applicable harmonised or foreign law granting remedies that the court would not grant under its own law in respect of similar legal relationships. This form of comity was, however, not accepted when the UN Convention on Contracts for the International Sale of Goods (CISG) was concluded in 1980, as it contains exactly the opposite rule in its Article 28: 'If, in accordance with the provisions of this Convention, one party is entitled to require performance of any obligation by the other party, a court is not bound to enter a judgement for specific performance unless the court would do so under its own law in respect of similar contracts of sale not governed by this Convention.'

[6] Cass. (B) 21 December 2009, *Journal des Tribunaux* 2010, 129 note E. David.

The solution just proposed could also have the following disadvantage: that the court would still remain free to grant injunctions or other remedies in cases where such a remedy is precisely excluded by the applicable substantive law. In the light of the considerations I will develop under section V, it would be better to solve the problem on the basis of conflict of law rules qualifying a number of rules on such questions as questions of substantive law.

Civil procedural law traditionally classifies claims and judgments by categories such as (claims for) 'condemnations', declaration of rights (or declaration of the absence of a right, the so-called *negatoria*) and constitutive judgments. Such qualifications should, however, again not affect the subjective right as granted by substantive law, especially by harmonised or foreign law. This may happen, for example, in the event of the termination of a contractual relationship for non-performance: in some systems of contract law the intervention of a judge is seen as merely declaratory, i.e. as confirming that the contract was correctly terminated by the plaintiff; whereas in other systems it may be qualified as constitutive, i.e. the contract is terminated only by the judgment itself. But the rights and obligations of the parties in the event of termination should be determined by the applicable substantive law.

7.4.2 Standing

Substantive rights granted by common or foreign law may also be affected by the rules of civil procedure on standing. Again, these rules have largely been developed in harmony with domestic substantive law, but may sometimes prevent the exercise of subjective rights conferred by common or foreign law. The ECJ has, therefore, dealt with this question in several judgments. In *Verholen*,[7] the ECJ decided that

> (24) While it is, in principle, for national law to determine an individual's standing and legal interest in bringing proceedings, Community law nevertheless requires that the national legislation does not undermine the right to effective judicial protection (see the judgments in Case 222/84 *Johnston v Chief Constable of the Royal Ulster Constabulary* [1986] ECR 1651 and in Case 222/86 *UNECTEF v Heylens* [1987] ECR 4097) and the application of national legislation cannot render virtually impossible the exercise of the rights conferred by Community law (judgment in Case 199/82 *Amministrazione delle Finanze dello Stato v San Giorgio* [1983] ECR 3595).

Again, preferably, civil procedure should have rather open rules which, to a large extent, leave the question of standing to substantive law. Where substantive law allows a person to exercise the rights of another person (e.g. his debtor), procedural law should allow this and grant this person standing; an example is the so-called *action indirecte* of Article 1166 of the French and Belgian Civil Codes

---

7 ECJ 11 July 1991, Case C-87-89/90, ECR I-3757 (*Verholen*).

(allowing a creditor to exercise the rights of his debtor in the event of inactivity of the debtor).

Procedural law should in principle allow subjective rights to 'appear' in court as they are under substantive law rather than to try to fit them into the categories of domestic law. A trustee should be able to sue in a foreign court in his capacity as trustee (see Article 11 of the 1985 Hague Trusts Convention: 'A trust created in accordance with the law specified by the preceding Chapter shall be recognised as a trust. Such recognition shall imply, as a minimum, that the trust property constitutes a separate fund, that the trustee may sue and be sued in his capacity as trustee, and that he may appear or act in this capacity before a notary or any person acting in an official capacity.'). Where, however, the applicable substantive law does not use the model of the trust (granting legal title to the trustee) but an alternative model, such as the model of a collective investment fund based on co-ownership, whereby the administrator may equally sue (and be sued) for the common interest of the joint owners, an administrator of such a foreign fund should equally have standing although he has no legal title and the fund has no legal personality. And a foreign insolvency administrator or liquidator should in principle have standing to exercise the collective rights of the creditors of the insolvent person or estate (see in this respect Article 18 of the Insolvency Regulation[8]).

More generally, it is advisable to allow persons not entitled to the substantive right themselves but authorised by contract or law to act for the owner of the right to figure as plaintiff or defendant in the proceedings (to be a 'party' in the formal sense). Evidently some formal requirements of legitimation and identification could be imposed by procedural law; but the old adage '*nul ne plaide par procureur*' restricts judicial protection unnecessarily. Where under substantive law a person has the authority entitling him to exercise a right without being the 'owner' (without having legal title), procedural law should not deny standing as this would merely require the 'owners' to transfer or assign assets or rights in a fiduciary

---

[8] Regulation No. 1346/2000 on insolvency proceedings, OJ 2000, L 160, Art.18:

'1. The liquidator appointed by a court which has jurisdiction pursuant to Art. 3(1) may exercise all the powers conferred on him by the law of the State of the opening of proceedings in another Member State, as long as no other insolvency proceedings have been opened there nor any preservation measure to the contrary has been taken there further to a request for the opening of insolvency proceedings in that State. He may in particular remove the debtor's assets from the territory of the Member State in which they are situated, subject to Art. 5 and 7.

2. The liquidator appointed by a court which has jurisdiction pursuant to Art. 3(2) may in any other Member State claim through the courts or out of court that moveable property was removed from the territory of the State of the opening of proceedings to the territory of that other Member State after the opening of the insolvency proceedings. He may also bring any action to set aside which is in the interests of the creditors.

3. In exercising his powers, the liquidator shall comply with the law of the Member State within the territory of which he intends to take action, in particular with regard to procedures for the realisation of assets. Those powers may not include coercive measures or the right to rule on legal proceedings or disputes'

manner, whereas under substantive law the mere granting of authority is sufficient. Typical examples are the authority to collect a debt, the authority to administer copyrights or other intellectual property rights, et cetera. Summarising, I would say that standing in the sense of authority is a matter of substantive law, whereas the identification of the parties and the other formalities to be fulfilled are in principle a matter of procedural law.

7.4.3 Plurality

The effective protection of substantive rights may also be affected by the procedural rules on plurality of parties. Here again, procedural law should be sufficiently flexible to allow a plurality of plaintiffs or defendants where a plurality of parties to the substantive relationship is invoked, such as a plurality of debtors (joint debtors, solidary debtors (joint and severally), et cetera) or a plurality of creditors or of co-owners. This also concerns the rules of (personal) jurisdiction.

7.4.4 Counterclaims

Substantive rights may also be affected by the procedural rules on—especially restrictions on—counterclaims. I take an example from the different systems of set-off. Under some legal systems, set-off can only be invoked by way of defence (*exceptio*) where the active right is already ascertained, whereas a counterclaim is necessary if the right is still unascertained; in other systems, set-off may, nevertheless, be declared (sometimes when other requirements are met—see, e.g., III-6:103 DCFR). There may be some substantive differences, especially as to the question whether invoking set-off has a retrospective effect or not. But, preferably, procedural law should not prevent set-off where a set-off would be effective in the country of the applicable law given the combination of substantive and procedural law which would be applied there. This does not exclude that the judge may, on the basis of the procedural law of the forum, divide the lawsuit and deal first with the original claim and postpone the counterclaim (where the first is sufficiently certain and the second is not).

7.4.5 Evidence

Evidence is another topic where the delimitation between the provinces of civil procedure and substantive law is unclear and varies from country to country. Specific evidential requirements for specific acts or facts will normally be a matter for substantive law. The procedures for obtaining evidence allowed by substantive law will be governed by the procedural law of the forum, but should not render the obtaining of evidence allowed by substantive law excessively difficult. The burden of proof is, in my opinion, primarily a matter of civil procedure, but where the law imposes upon a party specific 'pre-procedural' burdens of proof (the burden to pre-establish proof), this is again rather a matter of substantive law. Drafters of substantive law should, therefore, take into account the procedural rules that may apply elsewhere, and drafters of procedural law should take into account the different substantive law rules that may be applicable. It would, however, require an additional chapter to develop this question in more detail.

7.4.6 Rules on the Task of the Judge and on Belated Submissions by a Party

At first sight, the rules on the task of the judge, and especially on the question whether the judge may or even should invoke certain defences *ex officio*, is purely a matter of procedural law.

Nevertheless, at least in some countries substantive law will contain some specific rules, especially rules dictating that a certain defence should not be raised *ex officio* by the judge. Thus, Article 2223 of the Belgian Civil Code (and of the Code Napoléon) provides that a judge is not allowed to invoke *ex officio* that a right is prescribed, and a similar rule is found in most European legal systems. In the DCFR, it is not explicit, but follows from the rule in Article III-7:501 that the expiry of prescription only gives the creditor a right to refuse performance and does not end the obligation *ipso iure*. Where the applicable substantive law makes a defence dependent upon a declaration of the party entitled to assert it, procedural law should not allow or even oblige the court to raise it *ex officio*.

On the other hand, substantive law may in some cases impose upon procedural law an obligation for the courts to apply certain legal provisions *ex officio* in order to protect certain substantive rights or interests. This is clearly the situation with a number of rules of European Union law. Thus, European consumer law, as interpreted by the ECJ, contains an obligation for judges to invoke certain rules of consumer protection *ex officio*—a rule which I believe is rather a rule of substantive law. One of the roles this doctrine plays is to allow a consumer to request avoidance of an unfair term even where according to national procedural law the consumer should have already done this in an earlier stage—see the ECJ judgment in *Mostaza Claro*,[9] where the consumer requested annulment of an arbitral decision because of the unfairness of the arbitration clause, although the consumer had not pleaded that invalidity during the course of the arbitration proceedings, but only in that of the action for annulment.

---

9 ECJ 26 October 2006, Case C-168/05, ECR I-10421 *(Mostaza Claro)*.

There is evidently much more case law of the ECJ on the duty of the judge to invoke European Union law *ex officio* and/or to set aside national rules of procedural law restricting the possibilities for the judge to invoke European Union law.[10] But among these decisions, consumer law cases such as *Mostaza Claro* are, in my opinion, probably the clearest examples of setting aside the autonomy of civil procedure.

7.5 Protecting Defendants

The doctrine of effective judicial protection of subjective rights, especially in the case law of the ECJ, plays an important role for the effectiveness of substantive law in general. However, there is a serious risk that it leads to a one-sided view giving too much preference and protection to the claims—founded or unfounded—of parties asserting certain types of rights to the detriment of the defence of the other party, equally asserting a right, be it a subjective right in the strict sense or a freedom or privilege, an immunity or a similar right.[11] Procedural law should as far as possible enable the protection of the rights of the plaintiff, but equally of those of the defendant. It must maintain the blindfold, meaning that the assertions of both parties have to be taken into account in an impartial manner. It is true that, in the interest of social peace and security, 'innocent' defendants do have to bear the burden of a lawsuit and will have to defend themselves as much as 'innocent' plaintiffs do have to bear the burden of a lawsuit[12] and cannot take the law into their own hands. The interest of the 'innocent' defendant not to be sued (or at least to be compensated when unjustly sued) must be protected as much as the interest of the 'innocent' plaintiff to obtain legal protection (and to be compensated if suing is necessary to obtain his right).

Certainly, there is also an important responsibility of substantive law itself here. Substantive law cannot make it impossible for plaintiffs to start lawsuits for unjustified claims, but lawsuits should not become lotteries due to the unclearness of substantive law. Furthermore, where rules of substantive law are too harsh or of a punitive nature, even defendants who are quite convinced of their innocence will prefer a bad settlement over the small risk of incurring such a sanction, and the substantive rules become an instrument of blackmail. The 'chilling effect' of vague or imprecise rules has been identified especially in criminal law (e.g. a criminal law rule restricting free speech)—and is one of the reasons why the legality principle, understood as requiring also a precise description of a punishable

---

[10] See especially ECJ 14 December 1995, Case C-312/93, ECR I-4599 *(Peterbroeck, Van Campenhout v. Belgische Staat).*

[11] In using privilege and immunity, I am implicitly referring to the terminology of Hohfeld 1913/1917.

[12] Degenkolb 1877.

offence, is so important—but is not absent from private law either, especially where private law contains punitive elements.

Nevertheless, procedural law also plays a role in limiting legal harassment and more generally in limiting the procedural burden of 'innocent' defendants. I would like to mention three topics.

The first concerns the rules on verifying jurisdiction. Procedural rules should help to settle issues of jurisdiction as quickly as possible, and they should, therefore, in principle already be settled in a preliminary stage. An effective protection of defendants against lawsuits started before a court that lacks jurisdiction requires that courts check their jurisdiction *ex officio*. Some of the case law of the ECJ on the duty of the court to apply consumer protection rules on their own motion precisely concerns the protection of consumers against unfair jurisdiction clauses—the judgment in *Pannon*[13]—and unfair arbitration clauses—the judgment in *Asturcom*.[14]

Secondly, while the requirement of effective legal protection of rights implies that procedural law should not render the obtaining of evidence allowed by substantive law excessively difficult, nevertheless procedural law could still have rules to dismiss quickly claims which are not based on evidence as required by substantive law for such rights.

Thirdly, it is important to have good rules on the costs of legal proceedings and on cost shifting. On the one hand, there are the costs the judiciary may charge for the public service. This is no doubt a matter of procedural law. On the other hand, legal systems differ as to the question whether the rules on the shifting of attorney's fees and similar costs are a matter of procedural law or rather of substantive law. The procedural solution has the advantage that it can shift costs to any party winning the lawsuit, irrespective of the type of legal relationship; substantive law solutions are usually only partial and one-sided, often providing relief only to creditors that win their case and not to defendants against whom unfounded claims have been addressed. Moreover, the matter is complex, as uniform substantive law tends to contain such partial rules as is, for example, the situation with the European Late Payment Directive. The old Directive 2000/35[15] provided that 'unless the debtor is not responsible for the delay, the creditor shall be entitled to claim reasonable compensation from the debtor for all relevant recovery costs incurred through the latters' late payment' (Article 3, 1e). The new Directive 2011/7[16] provides, 'The creditor shall, in addition to the fixed sum referred to in paragraph 1, be entitled to obtain reasonable compensation from the debtor for any recovery costs exceeding that fixed sum and incurred due to the debtor's late

[13] ECJ 4 June 2009, Case C-243/08, ECR I-4713 (*Pannon GSM*), annotated by Ancery and Wissink 2010, 307–316.

[14] ECJ 6 October 2009, Case C-240/08, ECR I-9579 (*Asturcom*), annotated by Ebers 2010, 823–846; Schebesta 2010, 847–880.

[15] Directive 2000/35/EC on combating late payment in commercial transactions, OJ 2000, L 200/35.

[16] Directive 2011/7/EU on combating late payment in commercial transactions, OJ 2011, L 48/1.

payment. This could include expenses incurred, inter alia, in instructing a lawyer or employing a debt collection agency' (Article 6, 3). The Directive only deals with late payments in commercial transactions. But in legal systems where statutes can be reviewed under a constitutional principle of non-discrimination, it is very difficult to justify that plaintiffs recovering a late payment can shift their legal fees to the defendant when they win their case, whereas there would be no shifting in all other cases. Thus, the Belgian legislator was obliged to introduce a general rule on cost shifting as a consequence of the European Directive. This may be, after all, a reasonable solution in general, but nevertheless it is not a good thing that the general solution for this difficult question is dictated by a very specific rule strengthening the effective legal protection of just one type of subjective right.

7.6 Taking into Account the Changes During the Proceedings Relevant Under Substantive Law

My last topic concerns the question of how procedural law responds to a change of parties or their rights under substantive law, especially when a change happens during the course of the proceedings.[17] Preferably, procedural rules should be drafted in such a way that proceedings simply continue in the event of a change of one or more parties in the substantive legal relationship at stake. A substitution of the creditor or other holder of the subjective right at stake during the lawsuit should have no adverse effect, and in particular not terminate the lawsuit nor influence the jurisdiction of the court.

As the applicable substantive law may differ as to the different modes of transmission of rights or succession in rights, procedural law should again use as far as possible neutral formulations, not confined to the specific form of, for example, assignment of a right under the *lex fori*. The 'new' creditor should have an easy possibility to substitute himself as a party to the lawsuit for the old creditor and the 'old' creditor should have an easy possibility to get out of the lawsuit and be substituted by the new creditor. The form of such a procedural substitution will be determined by procedural law. But procedural law should not prevent, for example, an assignment of a right by a consumer to a non-consumer by terminating the jurisdiction of the forum of the consumer in such a case.

On the other hand, as long as there is no substitution, procedure should continue between the original parties, who are presumed to have the authorisation from their successors. The fact that the plaintiff has assigned his rights should not prevent the

---

[17] Most of the relevant questions have at some length in an article dealing with Belgian and Dutch law by Storme 1994, 178.

plaintiff from continuing the proceedings, even if he thus acts on the hidden assignee's account. And a defendant should not be obliged to take an initiative when the plaintiff remains passive.

The problem arises more specifically when appellate proceedings or similar proceedings are started. Under Belgian law, the typical case is one where a minor is represented by his or her parents in the first instance, and reaches majority during the lawsuit or after the judgment, but before the other party starts appellate proceedings. The first judgment will indicate the parents as the opponent, but procedural law may, nevertheless, require the appellant to direct the appeal against their child, as the parents have no authority anymore in appeal. Also in a case such as this, I would plead that a change in the position of a party under substantive law should not adversely affect the other parties in the proceedings as long as the change has not been notified.

Finally, a flexible procedural law will also use neutral formulations for the rules dealing with the adaptation of the 'content' of the lawsuit to new facts and circumstances. A similar factual change may be qualified in different ways by different substantive laws. I found an illustration of the necessary flexibility in a decision of the Belgian Court of Cassation of 1994[18] in a dispute concerning a right-of-way easement: during the lawsuit, the plaintiff, who was co-owner of a tract of land, became sole owner of part of the land; the plaintiff was allowed to change his claim (to modify the cause of action) during the proceedings. Different substantive laws may qualify the change differently; whether the lawsuit can be continued or a new lawsuit should be initiated should as far as possible not depend upon these qualifications.

7.7 Conclusion

The interaction between procedural law and substantive law is a vast and fascinating topic, which I have evidently not exhausted. I have merely tried to illustrate with a variety of issues that it is important for drafters of substantive law rules to take into account the various procedural contexts in which the rules may apply and for drafters of procedural rules to take into account the variety of substantive law solutions that may have to be applied in the procedures. Because, as Darbellay put it so nicely: 'La procédure conditionne la saisie du droit au fond, la perception et la délimitation du droit matériel comme la lumière conditionne la perception des couleurs.'[19]

[18] Cass. (B.) 6 May 1994, annotated by Storme 1995, 43–44.

[19] Darbellay 1964, 427.

References

Ancery AGF, Wissink MH (2010) ECJ 4 June 2009, Pannon GSM Zrt. v. Erzsébet Sustikné Győrfi. Euro Rev Priv Law 18:307–316

Darbellay J (1964) Le droit d'être entendu, 98. Referate und Mitteilungen des schweizerischen Juristenvereins, Helbing und Lichtenhahn, Basel

Degenkolb H (1877) Einlassungszwang und Urteilsnorm, Beiträge zur materiellen Theorie der Klagen, insbesondere der Anerkennungsklagen. Breitkopf and Hartel, Leipzig

Ebers M (2010) From Océano to Asturcom: Mandatory Consumer Law, Ex Officio Application of European Union Law and Res Judicata. Eur Rev Priv Law 4:823–846

Hohfeld H (1913/1917) Fundamental legal conceptions, Yale Law Journal 1913 and 1917, reprinted in Fundamental legal conceptions as applied in judicial reasoning and other legal essays by W N Hohfeld, Yale UP New Haven 1919

Schebesta H (2010) Does the national court know European law? A note on ex officio application after Asturcom. Euro Rev Priv Law 4:847–880

Storme ME (1994) Rechtsopvolging onder bijzondere titel tijdens het burgerlijk geding in België en Nederland, Rechtskundig Weekblad (RW) 1993–94, 169–186. Available at http://storme.be/rechtsopvolging.html (accessed July 2011)

Storme ME (1995) De Lebbeekse uitweg uit een processuele valstrik: ten processe optreden in een andere hoedanigheid en optreden krachtens een ander recht, Proces & Bewijs 1995, 43–44. Available at http://www.storme.be/lebbeekseuitweg.pdf (accessed July 2011)

Part II
Harmonisation in a European and Global Context

Chapter 8
Procedural Harmonisation in a European Context

Burkhard Hess

Abstract This chapter analyses the procedural landscape in the European Union, and the extent of harmonisation. The legislative activities of the EU started in the context of international procedural law, for which Article 65 EC Treaty (now Article 81 TFEU) provided the legal basis. The second area of legislative activity of the EU relates to the domestic procedures of the Member States, where a sectoral approach is taken. The principles of effectiveness and equivalence regarding the enforcement of EU law also have an impact on civil procedure, including the new competence to harmonise procedural laws if these do not sufficiently implement substantive EU law, laid down in Article 114 TFEU. Further harmonisation is reached through the minimum requirements laid down in specific instruments, such as the European Enforcement Order Regulation. It is clear that the legislative approach in international civil procedural law has changed during the last decade, from the coordination of national procedures and improved traditional instruments of private international law, to connecting the procedural systems of the Member States and to overcoming obstacles to the free movement of judgments. Furthermore, there is a trend towards the constitutionalisation of European civil procedure. In the present period of transition, it is high time for procedural scholarship to start a broad discussion within academia on the future architecture of European procedural law.

Professor of Private Law, Civil Procedure, Private International Law and Comparative Law, University of Heidelberg.

B. Hess (✉)
Private International Law and Comparative Law,
University of Heidelberg, Heidelberg, Germany
e-mail: hess@ipr.uni-heidelberg.de

X. E. Kramer and C. H. van Rhee (eds.), *Civil Litigation in a Globalising World*,
DOI: 10.1007/978-90-6704-817-0_8,

Contents

8.1 The Present Procedural Landscape in the European Union

What does harmonisation in the context of European civil procedural law mean? When beginning the preparation of this paper, I was puzzled by the concept of 'harmonisation' which was supposed to be the topic of this contribution. In European Union law, however, the concept of harmonisation is well defined: it refers to the alignment of the legal systems of the Member States by directives under Article 288(2) of the Treaty on the Functioning of the European Union (TFEU). In this regard, harmonisation describes the usual European law-making process, especially in the internal market, which operates in two steps. In the first, the Union adopts a directive which sets standards for the legal systems of the Member States. In the second, the directive is implemented and the Member States must adapt their respective legal systems to the standards of the directive.[1]

However, the present research project obviously places harmonisation in a broader context; and the term shall designate all kinds of external influences to procedural systems. This approach encompasses the adaptation and reform of existing legal systems which are triggered by the competition between the national systems. This broad approach corresponds to the situation in European procedural law, where harmonisation as such is not the predominant concept.[2] In European procedural law, a heterogeneous terminology is found ranging from approximation, coordination, cooperation, and harmonisation to unification.[3] Finally, even a codification might be an option for future development.[4] Accordingly, this paper uses the term 'harmonisation' in its broad meaning. However, particular attention will be paid to the operation of the specific concept of EU harmonisation in procedural law.

---

[1] Prechal 2005, 5 et seq.

[2] Under Art. 65 EU Treaty/Article 81 TFEU only two directives have been adopted so far; see Directive (EC) 2003/8 on Legal Aid, OJ 2003, L 26 and Directive (EC) 2008/52 on Mediation in Civil and Commercial Matters, OJ 2008, L 136/3.

[3] Kerameus 2002, 1 et seq.

[4] Hess 2010a, para 13, Nos. 17 et seq.

Against this background, it seems to be appropriate to take a short look at the present state of European procedural law. As we all know, a genuine or uniform European law of civil procedure does not exist. At present, there are two different fields of legislative activity in the Union: the more prominent and visible one relates to cross-border litigation. The pertinent head of competence is Article 81 of the TFEU which addresses 'judicial cooperation in civil matters.'[5] The second field is closely related to the application and the enforcement of EU law by national courts. According to the case law of the European Court of Justice (ECJ), the judiciaries of the Member States must efficiently enforce EU law on the basis of their respective domestic procedures.[6] In this field (which is not limited to civil procedure) a genuine harmonisation of procedural laws takes place which shall reinforce the proper implementation of EU law. Before addressing the specific functions and concepts of procedural harmonisation in Europe, it seems advisable to delineate the two different fields of legislative activity.

8.1.1 Judicial Cooperation in the Field of Cross-Border Litigation

The legislative activities of the European Community (EC) started in the context of international procedural law. Beginning in 1958, the EC Commission stressed the need for coordinating the autonomous procedures of the Member States in cross-border settings.[7] The Brussels Convention of 1968 was framed as an international convention on the jurisdiction and recognition of judgments, drafted according to the models of existing bilateral and multilateral conventions in this field. Although the Convention was aimed at the coordination of the national procedural systems, it provided for a uniform regime of rules on jurisdiction and recognition. Thus, the Brussels Convention made use of the unification of international procedural law to establish a basic coordination of the autonomous procedural systems of the Member States.

However, on the eve of the Amsterdam Treaty, the EU Commission went a step further and presented a Communication which proposed to align the procedural and enforcement laws of the Member States in cross-border situations. According to the Commission's view, the Union should no longer restrict itself to simply coordinating the procedural laws of the Member States, but ensure that judgments would be enforced equally efficiently in both domestic and cross-border settings.[8] Thus, the proposal included genuine procedural norms related to the unfolding

[5] Grabitz et al. 2011, Nos. 19 et seq.

[6] ECJ 13 July 2006, Case C-295/04 - C-298/04, ECR I-6619 *(Manfredi v Lloyd Adriatico Assicurazioni SpA.* et al.*)*, Slg. 2006, Nos. 62, 77 et seq.

[7] Hess 2010a, para 1, No. 1.

[8] OJ EC 1998 C 33, 3; Hess 1998, 1021, 1032; Wagner 1998, 241, 243 et seq. See on the political impact Storskrubb 2008, 33 et seq.

of the proceedings, provisional relief and the enforcement of judgments. This proposal was the first attempt by the Commission to harmonise civil procedures.

Although the predominant opinion of academia criticised this initiative as being premature or even 'crazy,'[9] the Communication paved the way for the next step in Europeanisation. Since 1999, Article 65 of the Amsterdam Treaty has provided for a specific Community competence in the field of 'judicial cooperation.'[10] However, this term has not yet been specifically defined, but rather circumscribed by the elements of the second paragraph which refer to a number of existing instruments of private international and procedural law. Up to today, a valid circumscription has not yet been elaborated by legal literature; case law of the ECJ is equally lacking.[11] The Tampere political programme of May 1999 implemented a rather broad approach and focussed on setting several instruments in the field of cross-border litigation which should overcome evident obstacles in this field. Most of the instruments adopted under Article 65 of the EC Treaty are regulations providing for uniform rules which directly replace or complement the existing procedural norms in the Member States.[12]

In practice, legislation under Article 65 of the EC Treaty (now Article 81 TFEU) has not been very influential because it was quickly restricted (after some political quarrels) to so-called cross-border situations. According to a compromise between the EU Council and the European Commission of 2003, 'cross-border situations' presuppose that the parties of the litigation are domiciled in different Member States.[13] Accordingly, the scope of the legal instruments adopted since 2003 is strictly limited to direct cross-border situations.[14] In practice, only a considerably small number of the cases that are dealt with by the civil courts of the Member States concern cross-border situations: the Heidelberg Report shows that the Brussels I Regulation is being applied in only 1–3 per cent of all civil proceedings in the Member States.[15]

Against this background, it is no surprise that the underlying legislative concepts in the field of Judicial Cooperation are currently unsettled: on the one hand, the Union adopted several instruments providing for specific procedures

[9] Schack 1999, 805.

[10] Hess 2010a, para 2, Nos. 7 et seq.

[11] Grabitz et al. 2011, No. 19.

[12] Some of the regulations in the procedural law contain provisions which prescribe Member States to adapt their internal systems to the standards of the regulation. These provisions operate like directives, see Hess 2010a, para 4, Nos. 21–23.

[13] Tulibacka 2009, 1527, 1561 et seq.

[14] A comprehensive survey of legislation on judicial cooperation is provided by the Compendium of Community Legislation on Judicial Cooperation in Civil and Commercial Matters edited by the European Commission (2009). The development of European Procedural Law is described by Paulino Perreira 2010, 1 et seq.

[15] Thus, there is a clear disparity between the number of cross-border transactions (up to 30 per cent in the Internal Market) and the number regarding cross-border litigation. Hess et al. 2008, paras 39 et seq.

(small claims, payment orders). These instruments adopt innovative concepts of procedural law and shall equally serve as models for the reform of national procedures.[16] In this respect, the Regulations on the Payment Order[17] and on Small Claims[18] may entail subsequent legislation in the Member States, enlarging their application to domestic proceedings. The most striking example is the Directive on Mediation[19] which is limited to cross-border mediation which hardly ever takes place in practice. Despite its 'international character,' this instrument is designed as a basic model for both cross-border and domestic mediation proceedings.[20] Accordingly, the German government recently presented a draft of implementing legislation which also includes domestic settings.[21]

On the other hand, several new instruments adopted a different approach by combining rules on international procedural and private international law.[22] The underlying concept is the plan to create a genuine European private international law composed of pertinent procedural rules and of rules on conflict of laws.[23] Prominent examples are the Maintenance Regulation combined with The Hague Protocol on Applicable Law on Maintenance[24] and the proposed Rome III Regulation.[25] At present, the legislative concept of Judicial Cooperation under Article 81 of the TFEU stands at a crossroads: it remains to be seen whether Article 81 of the TFEU will be applied as the (genuine) competence for procedural legislation or primarily as a competence for European private international law.[26]

[16] Hess 2010a, b, para 13, No. 14.

[17] Regulation No. 1896/2006 creating a European order for payment procedure, OJ 2006, L 399, Hess 2010a, para 10 II, Nos. 48 et seq.

[18] Regulation No. 861/2007 establishing a European Small Claims Procedure, OJ 2007, L 199, Hess 2010a, para 10 III, Nos. 87 et seq.

[19] Directive 2008/52 on Mediation in Civil and Commercial Matters, OJ 2008, L 136/3.

[20] This objective is openly enunciated by Recital 8 of the Directive 2008/52 on Mediation in Civil and Commercial Matters, OJ 2008, L 136/3.

[21] Referentenentwurf für ein Mediationsgesetz of 8.4.2010.

[22] Cf. the proposed instrument relating to successions and wills, COM (2009) 154 final of 10.14.2009, see MPI Working Group 2010, 522–720; Lein 2009, 107–141.

[23] In Europe, conflicts of laws and international civil procedural law have always been regarded as closely related disciplines. In 1980, the Rome Convention was adopted with the objective of limiting forum shopping under the Brussels Convention, see Wiedmann and Gebauer 2011, chap. 1, Nos. 104–105.

[24] Andrae 2010, 196 et seq.

[25] Hess 2010a, para 7, Nos. 112 et seq.

[26] Würdinger 2011, 102, 112 et seq.

8.2 Harmonisation of National Procedures

The second area of legislative activity of the European Union relates to the domestic procedures of the Member States. The starting point here was different: according to the case law of the ECJ, the courts of the Member States are acting as decentralised European courts. Therefore, they must implement European law efficiently. However, this implementation is effected on the basis of the national procedures—eventually supported by the ECJ in the proceedings for preliminary references (Article 267 TFEU).[27] As a matter of principle the national procedures remain unaffected. However, the procedural autonomy of the Member States is subject to the controlling principles of non-discrimination and efficiency which were elaborated by the ECJ. For a long time, however, these principles were rarely applied.

A genuine harmonisation of the national laws on civil procedure was initially proposed by Marcel Storme and his working group almost twenty years ago.[28] The basic idea of the working group was to elaborate an EU directive which should harmonise and modernise some core parts of the civil procedures of the EU Member States. According to the explanation of the proposal, the growing Community law should be aligned and modernised through a correspondent approximation of the civil procedures of the Member States.[29] Consequently, the working group identified several issues of procedural law where harmonisation by an EU directive seemed to be feasible. The proposed instrument was not limited to cross-border settings, but should generally apply to and improve the situation of private litigants in domestic and cross-border situations. Although the proposal has not been immediately taken up, many proposals of the Storme project are now found in the new EU instruments in the field of judicial cooperation.[30]

Recently, the harmonisation of procedural laws in Europe has gained ground. However, the EU legislator did not take up the comprehensive approach of the Storme working group, but adopted a sectoral course of action which relates to specific areas of substantive law. This new approach is based on two different but related concepts. There is the general concept of EU law that the courts of the Member States must enforce Union law efficiently on the basis of their domestic procedures.[31] This general concept was recently reinforced by the related concept that specific substantive laws should be implemented efficiently, because an

---

[27] Fredriksen 2009, 156 et seq.

[28] Storme 1994.

[29] Storme 1994, 37 et seq.

[30] The most prominent examples are the Regulations on the Payment Order and on Small Claims, see Storme 2009, Current Issues of European Civil Procedure—Which Way for Europe, paper presented at Budapest 4.12.2009.

[31] This concept is based on three principles: efficiency, non-discrimination and procedural autonomy of the EU Member States, see Hess 2010a, para 11, Nos. 4–16; Ward 2007.

underlying public interest requires their efficient implementation.[32] The combination of these two enforcement concepts entails a need for reforming the procedural laws of the EU Member States.

The first and most prominent example of this new development was the adoption of the Enforcement Directive (EC) 48/2004[33] which applies to litigation pertaining to infringements of Intellectual Property (IP) rights. Its main objective is to efficiently combat product piracy using the procedural laws of the EU Member States.[34] Accordingly, Articles 5–16 of the Directive address such core procedural issues as the gathering of information (disclosure), the preservation of evidence, provisional measures and interim relief, injunctions and the costs of litigation (the loser pays rule). Consequently, the Directive addresses core issues of procedural law and implements a uniform concept which shall improve the efficiency of the national procedures. The main challenge of such a sectoral approach is its limited reach: if the EU adopts an efficient and working instrument, why should it be restricted to a small scope of application? The answer to this question is self-evident: the sectoral instruments tend to extend into other fields.

Recently, the European Commission has taken up the sectoral approach of the Enforcement Directive and proposed an extension of its core concepts to additional areas of EU law: current projects relating to collective redress in cartel and consumer protection law are partly directly modelled on the Enforcement Directive.[35] In these fields, the legislative approach is genuinely aimed at harmonisation: the proposed legislation directly refers to existing substantive EU law and provides for common standards for their efficient implementation. As a result, the national procedures are not simply coordinated, but their content is changed.[36] The current development demonstrates how the legislative activities of the Union shift from specific fields to additional areas; existing (successful) instruments are used as models for additional legislation. Finally, a comprehensive harmonisation or at least a comprehensive adaptation of national procedures will be necessary in order to preserve the coherence and the transparency of the system.[37] The recent initiative of the European Commission regarding the elaboration of a comprehensive instrument on collective redress demonstrates the expansion of the sectoral approach of European law-making to other areas.[38]

---

[32] The enforcement concept has been developed in the context of economic law, especially competition law, see Mansel et al. 2008.

[33] OJ 2004 L 195/16 et seq.

[34] Hess 2010a, para 11, Nos. 17–27.

[35] Hess 2010b, 493, 494 et seq; Zimmer and Logemann 2009, 489 et seq.

[36] In this respect, the influence of the Enforcement Directive is considerable.

[37] Storskrubb 2008, 284 et seq.

[38] European Commission: Public Consultation: 'Towards a Coherent European Approach to Collective Redress,' SEC (2011)173 of 2.4.2011.

8.3 The European Context of Procedural Harmonisation

The law-making activities of the Union cannot be explicated without referring to the specific functions of procedural law in the context of the integrative processes of the Union.[39] In this regard, the harmonisation by the Union differs from the traditional unification of private and procedural law by international organisations. The main reason is found in the function of European law itself. According to the Treaties, European law pursues specific goals and policies. It is aimed at setting up a Single Market and an Area of Security, Freedom and Justice. Seen from this perspective, the procedural laws of the Member States are used as tools for the implementation of Union law, and the courts and the judges of the Member States are regarded as Community courts.[40] Although the courts of the Member States apply their domestic procedures when implementing EU law, the ECJ has developed standards for reviewing the national procedures. This concept is based on procedural autonomy, non-discrimination and efficiency. Accordingly, Member States must fully implement EU law; although national courts apply their domestic procedures, they must efficiently implement EU law without any discrimination. In addition, under Article 267 of the TFEU any EU Member State court may directly refer a preliminary (and decisive) question to the ECJ and ask the Court for an interpretation of EU law. Thus, there is a procedural framework between the ECJ and the national courts which guarantees the efficient implementation of EU law by national courts and its uniform interpretation by the ECJ.[41]

In practice, the application of these standards offers much flexibility for the ECJ to evaluate the specific circumstances of individual cases under its consideration. As a result, the case law of the ECJ is not always consistent and sometimes the Court refrains from interfering in sensitive areas of the national procedures. One recent example is case C-279/09, *Deutsche Energiehandels- und Beratungsgesellschaft v Germany*.[42] In this case, the Court was asked by the *Kammergericht* whether the exclusion of moral persons from legal aid according to German procedural law was compatible with the principle of effectiveness. In that case the plaintiff, a German limited company, had become bankrupt because (according to the allegations of the plaintiff), Germany had failed to implement several EU directives on the liberalisation of the market for gas and electricity. As the company wanted to profit from the liberalisation of these markets, the delayed implementation of the directive entailed its bankruptcy. The company relied on State liability under EU law and sued for damages. Before initiating the proceedings, it applied for legal aid which was not granted by the Court of First Instance. According to the pertinent provisions of the German Code of Civil

---

[39] Storskrubb 2008, 19 et seq.

[40] Tulibacka 2009, 1527 et seq.

[41] Hess 2010a, para 11, Nos. 4 et seq and para 12, Nos. 5 et seq.

[42] ECJ 22 December 2010, Case C-279/09 *(Deutsche Energiehandels- und Beratungsgesellschaft v Germany)* (not yet published).

Procedure (ZPO), moral persons are not entitled to legal aid, unless there is a public interest to pursue the claim.[43] On appeal, the *Kammergericht* referred to the ECJ the question whether the German provision on legal aid (which directly refers to the 'public interest') had to be interpreted in a way that permitted the moral person to start proceedings for the (direct) enforcement of EU law. In addition, the court relied on Article 47 of the Charter of Fundamental Rights of the European Union which guarantees access to justice.

From the perspective of effectiveness one might have expected that the ECJ would give a positive answer. Surprisingly, the ECJ avoided a clear decision. The Second Chamber stressed the principle of effectiveness and the constitutional right of access to justice. But it referred to the case law of the European Court of Human Rights (ECtHR) under Article 6 of the European Convention on Human Rights (ECHR), where the Court had held, that the exclusion of moral persons from legal aid was justified by the difference between profit-making and non-profit-making legal persons. Finally, the ECJ adopted an approach which focussed on the individual case under consideration: the national court should ascertain whether it would be a disproportionate restriction of the right to access to justice if the plaintiff would not be able to pursue his claim. Making the assessment, the national court should also take into consideration the subject matter of the litigation, the prospects of success and the importance of the proceedings for the applicant. The *Kammergericht* has not yet decided the case, but the solution will not be easy to find. The example demonstrates the practical difficulties of the concept of private enforcement of EU rights which sometimes requires a new interpretation of national procedural laws. However, in the case under consideration the ECJ was well aware of the financial implications of its decision. Not only in Germany but in many Member States the costs of legal aid have become a matter of considerable concern.[44] Against this background, the Court avoided any intrusion into the national systems although the case demanded the efficient enforcement of the EU law of State responsibility. However, it seems predictable that legal aid and the costs of the national proceedings will become an issue in the case law of the ECJ on the principle of effectiveness and on Article 47 of the Charter of Fundamental Rights.[45]

While the case law of the ECJ regarding the principles of effectiveness and equivalence is still evolving, the European legislator has taken up the issue: according to a new legislative approach by the European Commission, the general competences of the Union (Article 114 TFEU) include the power of harmonising national procedural laws if the latter do not sufficiently implement substantive EU

---

[43] Under Section 116 ZPO a (domestic) legal person shall receive legal aid if the costs can be paid neither by the party nor by any party which is economically involved in the subject matter of the proceedings, and where such failure to pursue the action would run counter to the public interest.

[44] Hess 2008, 189 et seq.

[45] Parallel cases are pending at the ECtHR (see *Granos v Germany* case No.) and in the EFTA Court (see *X. v Liechtenstein*, case No.).

law.[46] In this respect, European law-making is not limited by the principle of procedural autonomy of the Member States, which was stressed by the ECJ in the landmark decisions *Manfredi* and *Courage*, but on the idea that Union law must be enforced efficiently by national courts. The Enforcement Directive was the first instrument which comprehensively adopted this approach in the specific sector of IP litigation. The current proposals on collective redress in antitrust and consumer matters are equally based on the concept of private enforcement of EU law.[47] Seen from this perspective, the harmonisation of European procedural law can be regarded as a typical example for the application of the concept of integration: the growing Europeanisation of the substantive laws in Europe triggers a parallel need for a better enforcement in specific sectors. Finally, the growing impact of procedural harmonisation in specific areas may entail a need for a comprehensive instrument for the harmonisation of the national procedures in specific sectors (as in provisional relief, the obtaining of information, and the preservation of evidence).[48]

Similarly, the legislative approach in international civil procedural law has changed during the last decade. At the beginning, the Community focussed on the coordination of national procedures and improved the traditional instruments of private international law. The current objective is to link the procedural systems of the Member States and to overcome obstacles to the free movement of judgments. In this regard, even devices aimed at alleviating the free flow of judgments are sometimes viewed as obstacles.[49] Today, the implementation of the EC concepts of mutual trust, access to justice and the free movement of judgments entail an intensified approach which shall build up networks of cooperation among the judicial authorities of the Member States. As a result, the procedures of the Member States for cross-border litigation have been increasingly replaced by genuine EU procedural law during the past decade. However, the EU lawmaker did not adopt a comprehensive approach, but progressed in specific sectors (uncontested claims, small claims). Even so, the solution adopted in one sector is continuously expanded to other fields of law. Progressing step by step, from one sector to another, is a genuine approach of EU law-making in procedural matters.

One example of these developments is the service of documents. Several EU instruments address this issue which is crucial for the protection of the defendant's rights of defence in cross-border litigation. Originally, Article 27 No. 2 of the Brussels Convention provided that a default judgment was not recognised if the

---

[46] The new approach is clearly expressed in the White Paper on Cartel Damage Claims, COM (2005) 672 final and the Commission's Staff Working Paper (SEC 2005) 1732, see Zimmer and Logemann 2009, 489, 495 et seq; Tulibacka 2009, 1527, 1529 et seq.

[47] It remains to be seen whether the Council and the Parliament will take up this approach as a general base for legislation in procedural matters.

[48] Storskrubb 2008, 78 et seq.

[49] The most prominent example is the abolition of exequatur proceedings which is currently proposed by the European Commission with regard to the Brussels I Regulation, COM (2010) 748 final, Hess 2011, 125 et seq.

document instituting the proceedings (the complaint) had not been served properly on the defendant. However, the conditions of service were determined by The Hague Service Convention and by the procedural laws on service of the requested Member State. As a result, the recognition of default judgments often failed for improper service.[50] Consequently, Article 34 No. 2 of the Judgments Regulation provides that service must be effected in such a way that the defendant is able to defend himself efficiently. Thus, proper service is no longer a requirement for recognition, although a control of the efficiency of the service in the Member State of recognition still takes place.[51] The next step was the abolition of exequatur by the European Enforcement Order (EEO) Regulation.[52] Articles 13-15 of the Regulation contain detailed provisions on the service of the lawsuit.[53] However, these provisions are not directly applicable, but are conceived as control provisions when the European Enforcement Order is granted. Service is still effected according to the domestic provisions of the Member State where the service takes place.[54] The final step of this development is found in Article 13 of the Small Claims Regulation: according to this provision, direct service on the defendant is normally done by post. However, if postal service fails, Article 13(2) of the Small Claims Regulation directly refers to Articles 13 and 14 of the EEO Regulation as provisions governing service.[55] As a result, these provisions, which had been initially adopted in the context of reviewing whether the service (governed by national law) met the minimum EU standards (before issuing the form on the EEO), are used as directly applicable provisions for the service of documents. Consequently, the scope of the EEO provisions on service (and the corresponding scope of EU law) has been largely extended and finally unified—the example demonstrates how the growing integration of procedural law entails a deeper influence of EU law on national procedures.

8.4 The Growing Constitutionalisation of European Procedural Law

The interpretation and the development of European procedural law will be largely influenced by Article 6 of the ECHR and Article 47 of the Charter of Fundamental Rights. Article 6(1) of the Lisbon Treaty confers binding force to the Charter. According to its Article 51, the provisions of the Charter apply to the Member

[50] Hess 2010a, para 8, Nos. 97–98.

[51] Hess et al. 2009, Nos. 474–477.

[52] Regulation No. 805/2004, creating a European Enforcement Order for uncontested claims, OJ 2004, L 143; Crifò 2009, 103 et seq.

[53] Hess 2010a, para 10, Nos. 20 et seq.

[54] Crifò 2009, 74 et seq.

[55] Hess 2010a, para 10, Nos. 95 et seq.

States when they are implementing EU law. Since December 2009, the Court has been reinforcing its case law on the application of the Charter to the interpretation of the EU procedural instruments and the national procedures when Union law is implemented by civil courts. Recent case law of the ECJ demonstrates that the Court is going to enlarge its review to national procedural (and substantive) law closely related to EU instruments. As a result, this case law entails a harmonisation of the national procedures via judicial interpretation.

One example of the growing constitutionalisation under the Charter is case C-400/10 *PPU McB v L.E.* on the interpretation of Regulation (EC) 2201/2003 (Brussels IIbis).[56] In this case, the Irish Supreme Court asked the ECJ about the notion and concept of 'rights of custody' with regard to unmarried parents. The applicant sought the return of his three children from England to Ireland. His application was rejected by the Irish Court because the (unmarried) father had no right of custody under Irish law. On appeal, the Irish Supreme Court referred to the ECJ the question whether Article 2 No. 11 of Regulation (EC) 2201/2003 has to be interpreted according to Article 7 of the Charter in order to recognise a right of custody of the unmarried father. The ECJ held that the Regulation provides for a definition of the right of custody which refers to the Member State of the child's place of residence. However, the Court did not stop there, but equally addressed the issue whether Article 7 of the Charter (and Article 8 ECHR) required a different interpretation of the Regulation. The Court definitively rejected this approach and referred to Article 52(2) of the Charter which clearly states that the Charter does not extend the powers of the Union with regard to the Member States. However, the Court stated that the Regulation must be interpreted according to the Charter. Therefore, the Court went on to ask whether Article 7 of the Charter and Article 8 of the ECHR require the recognition of an autonomous concept of custody which includes the natural father.[57] Finally, the Court came to the conclusion that European constitutional law does not demand any extension of the concept of a common custody to unmarried parents.

Although the outcome of the case was no surprise, the methodological approach of the Court seems to be far-reaching: by interpreting the reference of the Regulation to national law according to the requirements of the Charter, it demonstrated its willingness to apply constitutional standards to national laws which are closely related to the European instruments. However, it remains to be seen whether and to what extent the constitutional requirements of Article 47 of the Charter and Article 6 of the ECHR will influence the application of national procedures which are closely related to the implementation of EU instruments. Nevertheless, the elaborated standards of the Charter (and the parallel case law of the ECtHR to the corresponding provisions of the Human Rights Convention) principally permit the Court to extend its control to additional fields.

---

[56] ECJ 10 May 2011, Case C-400/10 PPU *(McB v L.E.)* (not yet published).

[57] ECJ 10 May 2011, Case C-400/10 PPU *McB v L.E.*, (not yet published). Nos. 45 et seq.

In procedural law, the constitutional influences may grow even further. According to the Stockholm Programme, the European Commission shall elaborate an instrument on procedural minimum standards by 2013.[58] These standards shall be derived from the case law of the Courts in Luxembourg and in Strasbourg and from the practice of the national courts. However, the compilation of such standards in a systematic and coherent instrument will certainly contribute to a further assimilation of the procedural systems of the Member States. The practical impact of this instrument will surely transcend the scope of cross-border situations and equally influence the threshold of fundamental fairness in domestic proceedings.

8.5 The Way Forward for Procedural Science

The examples mentioned demonstrate that the autonomous procedural laws of the EU Member States are being more and more influenced and (finally) harmonised by EU law. The present developments are taking place at different levels and are influencing different areas: on the one hand, the competence of Article 81 of the TFEU on judicial cooperation has been extended by a wide array of instruments. However, the legislative activity of the Union in this field is (still) restricted to cross-border situations.[59] On the other hand, the legislative concept of the efficient enforcement of Union law by civil courts entails a far-reaching harmonisation of the national procedures. This development is reinforced by the constitutionalisation of the procedural laws of the Member States by the Charter of Fundamental Rights. However, the present developments come at a price as the multitude of European procedural legislation (especially the instruments adopted under Article 81 TFEU) lacks sufficient transparency. Thus, there is a compelling need for a more coherent and systematic legislative approach, and the new Commissioner for Justice should—in the long term—envisage the elaboration of an 'umbrella instrument' providing for a coherent and systematic set of rules of European procedural law.[60]

At the level of the national systems, there is a growing awareness in the EU Member States that procedural law is changing considerably.[61] Today, the national procedural systems are in a situation of open competition to attract litigation, and

[58] Stockholm Programme, OJ 2010 C 155/1, Wagner 2010, 483 et seq.

[59] The better solution would be a reconsideration of Art. 81 TFEU and a careful redefinition of the compromise of 2003 relating to the interpretation of the 'cross-border' threshold: the wording of Art. 81 TFEU permits a broader reading which would empower the Union to enact legislation in procedural matters for the swift and efficient enforcement of Union law, especially with regard to the Internal Market and the free movement of persons in the European Judicial Area.

[60] This perspective is also envisaged by the Stockholm Programme.

[61] Jauernig and Hess 2011, paras 1 and 4. See Huber in the present volume.

the national legislatures are adapting their respective systems to the new European framework of the procedural systems.

In the present period of transition, procedural science also stands at a crossroads. It seems to be high time to start a broad discussion within academia on the future architecture of European procedural law—about its functions with regard to the implementation of subjective rights and the implementation of additional objectives; about its different layers (national, European and global) and institutions (national courts, ECJ, ECtHR); about its coherence (with different procedures) and last, but not least, about the role and the function of procedural science in a period of transition and growing openness. It goes without saying that European procedural law deserves a corresponding European community (and organisation) of procedural science, and in looking forward the elaboration of a coherent European procedural law does seem possible. Accordingly, procedural science should address the wider perspective and start a discussion on the pros and cons of codifying procedural law in Europe.

References

Andrae M (2010) Zum Beitritt der Europäischen Gemeinschaft zum Haager Protokoll über das Unterhaltsrecht, Zeitschrift für Gemeinschaftsprivatrecht (GPR), pp 196–205

Crifò C (2009) Cross-border enforcement of debts in the European Union. Kluwer Law International, London/Alphen a/d Rijn

Fredriksen H (2009) Europäische Vorlageverfahren und nationales Zivilprozessrecht. J.C.B. Mohr (Paul Siebeck), Tübingen

Grabitz E (ed) (2011) Commentary on Article 81 TFEU. C. H. Beck, Munich

Hess B (1998) Der Binnenmarktprozess, JuristenZeitung, pp 1021–1032

Hess B (2008) EU trends in access to justice. In: Van Rhee CH, Uzelac A (eds) Civil justice between efficiency and quality: from Ius commune to the CEPEJ. Intersentia, Antwerp, pp 189–206

Hess B (2010a) Europäisches Zivilprozessrecht. C.F Müller, Heidelberg

Hess B (2010b) Kartellrechtliche Kollektivklagen in der Europäischen Union—Aktuelle Perspektiven. Wirtschaft und Wettbewerb (WuW) 5:493–501

Hess B (2011) Die Reform der EuGVVO und die Zukunft des Europäischen Zivilprozessrechts, Praxis des Internationalen Privat- und Verfahrensrechts (IPRax), pp 125–130

Hess B et al (eds) (2008) The regulation Brussels I—report on its application in 25 member states, institute fur Auslandisches und Internationales Privat- und Wirtschaftsrecht, Study JLS/C4/2005/03. Available at www.ec.europa.eu/civiljustice/news/docs/study_application_brussels_1_en.pdf (accessed in May 2011)

Hess B et al (eds) (2009) Report on the application of regulation Brussels I in the member states, Ruprecht-Karls-Universität Heidelberg, Heidelberg. Available at www.ec.europa.eu/civiljustice/news/whatsnew_en.htm (accessed May 2011)

Jauernig O, Hess B (2011) Zivilprozessrecht. C.H. Beck, Munich

Kerameus D (2002) Angleichung des Zivilprozessrechts in Europa—einige grundlegende Aspekte. Rabels Zeitschrift 66:1–17

Lein E (2009) A further step towards a European code of private international law. Yearb Priv Int Law 11:107–141

Mansel HP (ed) (2008) Zugang zum Recht: Europäische und US-amerikanische Wege der privaten Rechtsdurchsetzung. Nomos, Baden-Baden

MPI Working Group (2010) Max Planck institute for comparative and international private law, comments on the European commission's proposal for a regulation of the European parliament and of the council on jurisdiction, applicable law, recognition and enforcement of decisions and authentic instruments in matters of succession and the creation of a European certificate of succession, Rabels Zeitschrift, pp 522–720

Paulino Perreira F (2010) La coopération en matière civile dans l'UE: bilan et perspectives, Revue Critique de Droit International Privé, pp 3–36

Prechal A (2005) Directives in EU Law, 2nd edn. Oxford University Press, Oxford

Schack H (1999) Die EU-Kommission auf dem Holzweg von Amsterdam, Zeitschrift für Europäisches Privatrecht, pp 805–808

Storme M (ed) (1994) Rapprochement du Droit Judiciaire de L'Union européenne Approximation of Judiciary Law in the European Union. Martinus Nijhoff Publishers, Dordrecht

Storme M (2009) Current issues of European civil procedure—which way for Europe, paper presented at Budapest 4.12.2009

Storskrubb E (2008) Civil procedure and EU law, a policy area uncovered. Oxford University Press, Oxford

Tulibacka M (2009) Europeanization of civil procedure: in search of a coherent approach. Common Market Law Rev 46:1527–1566

Wagner R (1998) Die geplante Reform des Brüsseler und des Lugano- Übereinkommen, Praxis des Internationalen Privat- und Verfahrensrechts (IPRax), pp 241–244

Ward A (2007) Judicial review and the rights of private parties in the European union. Oxford University Press, Oxford

Wiedmann T, Gebauer M (2011) Zivilrecht und Europäische Integration. In: Gebauer T, Wiedmann M (eds) Zivilrecht unter europäischem Einfluss. C.H. Beck, Munich

Würdinger M (2011) Das Prinzip der Einheit der Schuldrechtsverordnungen im Europäischen Internationalen Privat- und Verfahrensrecht. Rabels Zeitschrift 75:102–126

Zimmer D, Logemann H (2009) Der private Rechtsschutz im Kartellrecht—Zum Weißbuch der Kommission über Schadensersatzklagen wegen Verletzung des EG-Wettbewerbsrechts, Zeitschrift für Europäisches Privatrecht, pp 489–516

Chapter 9
Harmonised Civil Procedure in a World of Structural Divergences? Lessons Learned from the CEPEJ Evaluations

Alan Uzelac

Abstract The efforts to harmonise civil procedure in Europe have to take seriously the fact that procedural rules depend on the procedural structures that implement them. This chapter presents, on the basis of the CEPEJ evaluation, the divergences of procedural structures regarding three core organisational structures: courts, judges and lawyers. After showing the drastic differences of these structures, a change of perspective is proposed. Instead of focusing on harmonisation of rules and structures, focus should be shifted to issues important for the users of the justice system: the results of judicial activities, in the first place the effectiveness and quality of legal protection. However, the current pool of information in this respect is insufficient. Pointing to on-going efforts of the CEPEJ to stimulate the uniform collection of data about judicial timeframes and the quality of court work, the author draws conclusions regarding the desirable direction of future harmonisation efforts.

Contents

Professor of Procedural Law, University of Zagreb (Croatia).

A. Uzelac (✉)
University of Zagreb, Zagreb, Croatia
e-mail: auzelac@gmail.com

X. E. Kramer and C. H. van Rhee (eds.), *Civil Litigation in a Globalising World*,
DOI: 10.1007/978-90-6704-817-0_9,

9.1 Introduction

Is the harmonisation of civil procedure a noble, but elusive goal? While the notion of a 'United States of Europe' has somewhat started to turn into reality, just as Churchill predicted in his bold speech of 1946,[1] the civil procedure of European countries is still to a large extent a parochial matter, which suffers from a significant level of 'Balkanisation.'

Yes, some harmonisation trends are well visible, in particular among legal scholars. Some of them, like Marcel Storme, have devoted to harmonisation a remarkable opus of work,[2] fighting, *inter alia*, against 'a hallucinating number of regulations in the procedural field.' Advocating an 'approximation' of the laws concerning the judiciary and civil procedure,[3] Storme was following the paths of the great international proceduralists who, like Mauro Cappeletti, wanted to see in Europe 'a sort of renewal and reinforcement of the *ius commune* to which local contradicting law must give precedence.'[4]

At the European level (or, in narrower terms, at the European Union level), we are today still far from such a 'precedence' of harmonised, 'Europeanised' rules and practices. United Europe should, so the politicians say, eventually become 'a genuine area of justice, where people can approach courts and authorities in any Member State as easily as in their own.'[5] However, procedural harmonisation has been rather successfully stopped at the doorstep of the 'cross-border' requirement, and by various techniques and methods, including insisting on the promotion of their own domestic procedural principles and rules, the European States have demonstrated their reluctance to harmonise civil procedure.[6] Regulating isolated and largely secondary matters, the 'uniform' procedural law of the European Union has not produced much real harmonisation; rather, instead of harmonisation, it is threatening to produce a hallucinating number of European legislative acts and instruments (regulations, directives, decisions, resolutions, et cetera).[7]

---

[1] In the famous speech delivered on 9 September 1946 at the University of Zurich, Switzerland.

[2] See, e.g., Storme 1994.

[3] Cf. Storme 1994.

[4] Trocker 2005, 35.

[5] Tampere Conclusions, *Towards a Union of Freedom, Security and Justice: The Tampere Milestones*, at 5 (Presidency Conclusions of the European Council held in Tampere on 15 and 16 October 1999).

[6] Cf. Freundenthal 2010, 10–14.

[7] As an illustration, just the list of legislative instruments ('acquis') of the EU Directorate for Justice, Liberty and Security (DG JLS) dated October 2009 stretches over 58 pages. See http://ec.europa.eu/home-affairs/doc_centre/intro/docs/jha_acquis_1009_en.pdf (last consulted in May 2011).

This chapter will deal with another aspect of harmonisation—the harmonisation of *procedure,* rather than the harmonisation of *procedural law.* Difficult as it might seem, the harmonisation of procedural laws in Europe is only the easier part of the job. Laws should not only be unified, harmonised or at least 'approximated,' they should be implemented in the same, or at least compatible, way. The ideal of an area of justice with equal or compatible standards of legal protection for all European citizens creates an obligation of result, not an obligation of formal adherence to the same values or legal norms.

So far, most of the harmonisation efforts aimed at the approximation of civil procedure in Europe had to face the sheer fact of the incommensurability of the starting organisational premises. The colourful variety of inter-linked institutions and players in the field of civil justice has made genuine procedural harmonisation difficult, if not impossible, since the similarity of rules (or even the enactment of the same rules) was no guarantee for the harmonised practices. This was, *inter alia*, on many occasions proved by differences in the implementation of the current body of rules of European civil procedure.[8]

In this text, I will employ empirical analysis in order to discuss the prospects for future harmonisation of civil procedure. The arguments are presented in two steps. In the first step, I will present some illustrations of the divergent procedural structures that exist in Europe, in particular with respect to the organisational framework entrusted with the conduct of civil proceedings. The data used in this part of the paper will mainly rely on the findings of the European Commission for the Efficiency of Justice (CEPEJ), which is the first international inter-governmental organisation that is systematically engaged in the collection of statistical information relevant for the functioning of the national civil justice systems. After showing that the procedural structures which should apply the future 'uniform' procedural law in Europe are dramatically different, in the second step a change of perspective will be proposed. Instead of focusing on the harmonisation of rules (and, partly, on the harmonisation of structures), the focus should be shifted to the issues that are of principal importance to the users of the justice system—to the harmonisation of the results of judicial activities. Harmonisation of the outcomes is thereby an issue of substantive law; the procedural harmonisation that would need to be achieved relates to the effectiveness and the quality of legal protection. The current pool of information about the issues relevant to the comparative assessment of the effectiveness of legal protection is incomplete and insufficient. Therefore, pointing to the on-going efforts of the CEPEJ to stimulate the uniform collection of data on procedural duration and to monitor judicial timeframes (which have also started to show certain weaknesses and limitations), a suggestion for the need to develop capacity to monitor the results of civil procedure and to start harmonisation from there will be made.

---

[8] See, e.g., examples from several countries published in a recent book: Freudenthal 2010, 11–12; Kramer 2010, 17–36; Betetto 2010, 103–110.

9.2 Can it be More Different? Divergent Structures as a Basis for Harmonised European Civil Procedure

In this part of the chapter, an inquiry into the differences between the procedural structures of various European civil justice systems is made. I use the term 'procedural structures' to indicate the organisational framework of civil procedure, which consists of various institutions and actors that participate in the process. The procedural structures that are at the core of the system of civil justice are the courts, the judges and the lawyers; further procedural structures would also encompass other legal professionals (enforcement agents, notaries), paralegals (e.g. court clerks or *Rechtspfleger*), other participants such as experts or interpreters, as well as the professional organisations and State authorities that play a bigger or smaller role in the administration of justice. All in all, these institutions and actors form a procedural landscape within which civil justice is dispensed.

For a long time the European procedural landscape was not a subject of systematic examination, though valuable research was sporadically undertaken, often under the auspices of the International Association of Procedural Law (IAPL).[9] A significant obstacle to systematic research was the difficulty of obtaining accurate, comparable and comprehensive data on the relevant aspects of the functioning of civil justice. The situation changed after the establishment of the European Commission for the Efficiency of Justice (CEPEJ) in 2003. This standing body of the Council of Europe was formed with the mandate 'to enable the European countries to examine the results achieved by the different judicial systems … by using, amongst other things, common statistical criteria and means of evaluation.'[10] This mandate may be taken as another manifestation of the idea that procedural comparisons should go beyond comparisons of abstract rules. Superficial study of the similarities of statutory regulation in various jurisdictions is not enough for the proper understanding of the functioning of the European justice systems. Comparison of organisational elements that form the national procedural landscape is the first step in the realisation of the idea that (also) law in action, and not (only) law in books, has to be studied and evaluated. In such a context, the main aim of the CEPEJ was defined as 'improving the efficiency and the functioning of the justice system of [European] States, with a view to ensuring that everyone within their jurisdiction can enforce their legal rights effectively.'[11] The main tasks of the CEPEJ included the analysis of the 'results of the judicial systems'; 'identifying difficulties they meet' and proposing concrete ways of

---

[9] Among many comparative studies concerning European and global procedural landscapes published by the IAPL members and under its auspices see Rechberger and Klicka 2002; Trocker and Varano 2005; Van Rhee 2005.

[10] From Resolution No. 1 'Delivering justice in the 21st century' of the 23rd Conference of European Ministers of Justice, 8–9 June 2000, London.

[11] Council of Europe Resolution, Res. (2002) 12 of 18 September 2002 establishing the CEPEJ, Art. 1 (Aims).

improving both the evaluation of the results of the justice systems, and their functioning.[12]

The three guiding 'principles' upon which the resolution establishing the CEPEJ was grounded were *access to justice*, the *efficiency* of judicial proceedings, and the proper *enforcement* of court decisions. All of these principles could only be implemented through the organisational structures and the actors in those structures: courts, judges, lawyers, bailiffs, et cetera. Therefore, the indicators and statistical comparisons that were developed in the course of the CEPEJ's work dealt primarily with the structural, quantitative data, such as the data on the number of courts, judges, cases, et cetera. Being an inter-governmental organisation composed of experts from 47 European countries, the CEPEJ secured for the first time the collection of data that were relatively complete and—at least in some areas—fairly accurate. An insight into developments and trends is also gradually becoming possible, as four evaluation rounds were conducted in the 2004–2010 period, each producing an ever growing corpus of data.

For the purpose of this chapter, I will present only a section of relevant findings extracted from the CEPEJ evaluation reports and suggest conclusions that may be drawn from them. The starting premise is that the first step to harmonisation is the objective assessment of similarities and the open acknowledgment of differences. To that extent, an analysis of the data collected by the CEPEJ can provide illuminative insights that are important for future harmonisation plans.

I will concentrate on three elements which form the core of the organisational structures necessary for civil proceedings: *courts, judges* and *lawyers*. For each of these structures, some tentative results of comparisons arising from the CEPEJ evaluation rounds which might have an impact on the harmonisation efforts will be presented.

9.2.1 Courts

There is no common European definition of a 'court'

In the first evaluation round, the CEPEJ collected information about the 'total number of courts in each country, the number of general jurisdiction courts at first instance and the number of specialised courts at first instance.' What had to be counted were the 'main seats' only, and not sub-locations.[13] The very notion of what a 'court' was in the first round was not defined, in spite of some preliminary efforts to indicate possible differences in the understanding of this notion.[14] However, it turned out that the court definitions and structures were not at all

12 Ibidem, Art. 2(1).

13 CEPEJ 2005, 29.

14 So, e.g., Pim Albers pointed out in his preparatory study produced for the CEPEJ that '[t]he counting of the numbers of courts seems "at first glance" to be simple. However, for this indicator there are also various options to define what a court is. Courts can be defined as "a meeting room" in an office to settle a dispute between parties or on the other hand as a fully

uniform. The result was that variations were huge, starting with the simplest forms, such as the courts of general jurisdiction. The finding for 2002 was that 'the average number of inhabitants served by one general jurisdiction first instance court' ranged 'from 18,600 (Spain) to 842,000 (the Netherlands).'[15] At the same time, methodological problems with such a comparison were noted, such as:

- the difference in counting the number of the 'smallest' type of courts (in some countries they were within the definition of the 'main seats,' in others they were not);
- regarding the special courts, some countries had courts that suited all the definitions of a court, but were not part of the normal court system and its budget;
- there was a big difference in the concept of special courts (some of the countries had barely one type of special courts, others had a large number of specialised courts—e.g. Turkey with 12 different types of specialised courts).[16]

Trying to cope with some of the problems spotted in the first round, in the next round the explanatory notes clarified that 'a court can be considered either as a legal entity or [as] a geographical location.' The distinction was explained by provisional definitions: *courts as administrative structures* were defined as 'bodies established by law appointed to adjudicate on specific type(s) of judicial disputes within a specified administrative structure where one or several judge(s) is/are sitting, on a temporary or permanent basis,' which should be distinguished from *courts as geographic locations*, defined as 'premises or court buildings where judicial hearings are taking place.'[17]

These definitions did not quite resolve all outstanding issues, but at least in some countries led to dramatically different ranking. A good example is the record holder Spain that reported for 2002 a total number of 3,083 courts[18] with a total number of 4,109 professional judges, then two years later reported 2,548 first instance courts but only 683 'court offices or buildings' and 431 judicial districts. At the opposite end of the spectrum, the Netherlands reported for 2002 altogether the total number of 28 courts in the entire country with 1,809 judges sitting in them. It was, however, noted that there were a further 61 sub-offices (i.e. separate court locations or court buildings) of the 'main seats' of the 19 district courts.[19]

In any case, it is clear that the concept and understanding of a 'court' is not harmonised, which is partly due to the fact that it is ambiguous even from the

(Footnote 14 continued)
equipped office with a court staff and a court administration. In the first situation the court operates as a sub office from the main court office,' Albers 2003, 4.

[15] EJS 2005, 32.

[16] EJS 2005, 32–33.

[17] CEPEJ 2008, 318.

[18] Out of which 2,249 are general jurisdiction first instance courts. See CEPEJ report Spain, 2004, 7 (available at http://www.coe.int/cepej; (last consulted in May 2011).

[19] CEPEJ report the Netherlands, 2004, 8 (available at http://www.coe.int/cepej; (last consulted in May 2011).

perspective of individual jurisdictions. In some countries, the organisational meaning of a 'court' is close to the procedural meaning of the word—it is a tribunal (a panel or even a sole judge) that adjudicates individual matters. In other countries, the courts are more or less synonymous with the location or physical placement (the place where judicial offices and hearing rooms are concentrated). Finally, the definition of the court may be linked to strictly administrative considerations, such as single leadership, defined territorial jurisdiction, common budget, and joint court services and employees.

Further differences may be traced with respect to the matters submitted to a particular 'court.' In fact, the strict application of the CEPEJ reference to a court as a body which 'adjudicates on specific type(s) of judicial disputes' would need to exclude a number of specialised courts in a number of countries which deal with extra-contentious matters, or to undertake activities of a merely administrative nature, such as the holding of company registers or registers of immovables.[20] Such 'courts' (sometimes operating on their own premises, sometimes within the same buildings as other courts) are basically incomparable with the organisational structures in other countries, where such administrative tasks may be given to bodies outside of the judiciary (or, even if they are in the court jurisdiction, they may be ancillary activities of the courts of general jurisdiction or other specialised courts).

The different purposes for which courts are being used in different European countries may also be indicative of the different understanding of the social role and aim of judges and civil procedure as such (for more detail see Sect. 9.2.2).

The density of the court network and the level of differentiation of the courts within European court systems are rather different

The methodological difficulties regarding the definition of courts may make the comparisons more complicated, but they do not make them impossible. After the corrections made in the course of the first evaluation exercises, the CEPEJ produced a more refined scheme; however, the results again revealed considerable differences. In particular a difference in the approach of the North-western and South-eastern jurisdictions could be seen, which is easily identifiable in the following figure, reproduced from the CEPEJ report published in 2008, showing the number of courts of general jurisdiction per 100,000 inhabitants in 2006.[21] The Northern countries (the United Kingdom, Ireland, the Scandinavian countries, the Netherlands, Germany and Poland) have a considerably smaller number of

[20] In 2002, Turkey was the second European State according to the total number of courts per inhabitant. This was, however, partly due to the existence of a large number of land registration courts (848); separate categories of 'enforcement courts' (civil and criminal) are also a part of the official judicial landscape. See CEPEJ report Turkey, 2002, 6 (available at http://www.coe.int/cepej; (last consulted in May 2011).

[21] EJS 2008, 77, Figure 23. The information relates to the courts in the meaning of 'administrative structures.'

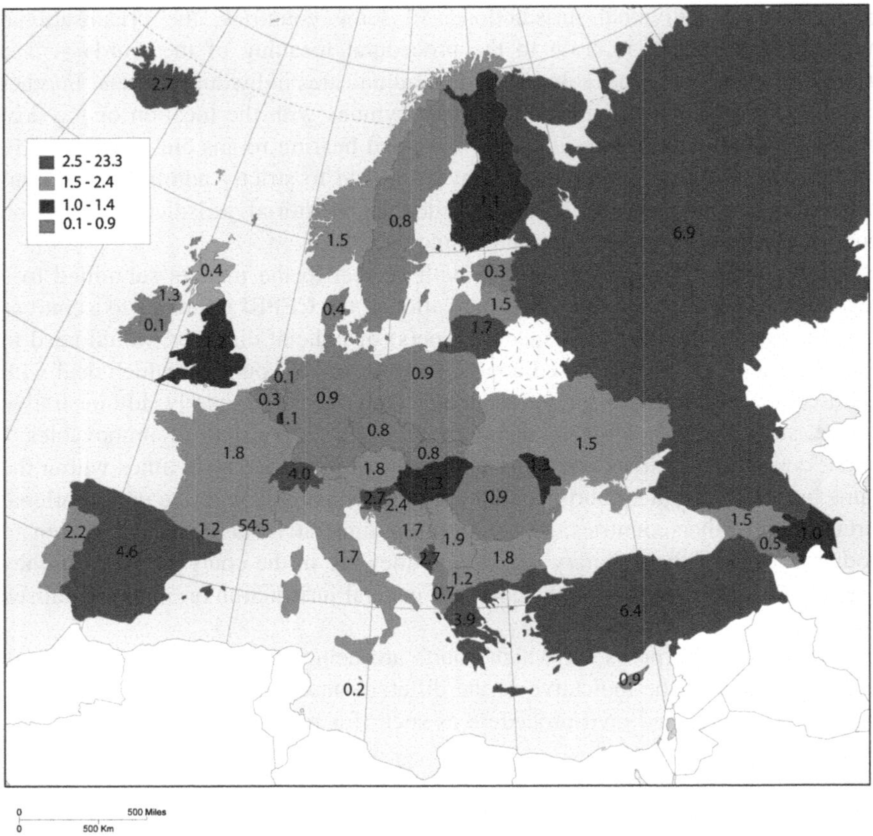

Fig. 9.1 Number of courts of general jurisdiction per 100,000 inhabitants in 2006

courts per capita (from 0.1 to 1.5 general jurisdiction courts per 100,000 inhabitants), while the Southern and Eastern countries (Spain, France, Italy, Austria, the successor countries of the former Yugoslavia, the Russian Federation and Turkey) have considerably higher figures (more than 1.5, with the highest figures of 6.9 in the Russian Federation and 6.4 in Turkey) (Fig. 9.1).

The picture was only slightly different regarding the comparison of the courts in the meaning of 'court locations.' Again, in particular the countries of the European South (from Italy to Turkey) had a 'density' of the court network which was several times higher than the density in the North.[22]

Even greater differences existed in the level of specialisation within the court structures. While some European countries have only one layer of courts—the

[22] Compare, e.g., the Netherlands with 0.3 court locations per 100,000 inhabitants to Turkey with 7.9. See EJS 2008, 78.

courts of general jurisdiction—in other countries the specialised courts make up to ninety per cent of the overall number of courts. Therefore, the calculated figure which reported that 'as a European average, specialised first instance courts represent 19 per cent of all the first instance courts considered as legal entities'[23] has very little real meaning, except that it warns that already at the conceptual level one should be careful, since the meaning of 'specialised' can be rather different. For example, the statement that 'the court system in Belgium is mainly based on specialised first instance courts (90.7 per cent of the first instance courts)' relies on the fact that the largest number of 'courts' is related to the institution of the Justice of the Peace. Such 'specialised' courts are quite different from specialised structures for dealing with administrative, commercial or labour cases. Before speaking about harmonisation, one should clarify the starting points and make an in-depth inquiry regarding the different systematisation of court structures in the European countries.

This analysis should, however, be narrowed down to the matters relevant for the harmonisation of civil procedure. Are there any conclusions that we can draw from the considerable organisational differences? Do the statistical comparisons regarding the numbers of courts, their jurisdiction, differentiation and population-coverage have any real impact at the level of court functioning? Do they reflect on the course of civil procedure and have important consequences on the prospects for harmonisation?

It is obvious that any discussion based on the bare figures and incomplete information should be extremely cautious and avoid jumping to conclusions. Still, I would suggest that the analysis of the organisational differences is important for an understanding of the differences in the functioning of civil justice systems, and that it has important consequences for an understanding of the varying procedural styles and approaches to civil procedure in different European countries. Some tentative conclusions are already possible, and may be derived from the 'big picture' presented in the CEPEJ reports.

The first conclusion is that the organisational differences create a background which sometimes contains invisible impediments for pan-European debates on the harmonisation of civil procedure. Perceptions regarding what is meant to be harmonised are not the same in the environment which is rather specialised, and in the environment composed of only one layer of courts. Equally, perceptions about a desirable 'uniform' style of procedure are different in a decentralised environment of many smaller courts than in an environment where adjudication is concentrated in a smaller number of larger courts. The same procedural norms may function differently in different organisational structures. Therefore, the harmonisation of civil procedure at the European level would also imply the approximation of organisational structures, starting first with the creation of the same conceptual framework (uniform definitions of 'courts,' 'specialisation,' et cetera). At a later

[23] CEPEJ 2010, 84.

stage, the reduction of structural differences may also be instrumental for reducing the options for failures in the harmonisation process.[24]

Another conclusion relevant for the harmonisation of civil procedure relates to the cultural and civilisational changes that also affect the organisational framework for the judicial processes. At first sight, one can be tempted to discuss the density of the court network in terms of right of access to a court, which is among the fundamental aspects of the right to a fair trial. The access to justice argument would require a higher density of the court network: the more courts, the better access to them. In the light of collected empirical evidence, it seems that this equation does not work. On the contrary, those countries which have the fewest courts per capita (e.g. the Netherlands, Denmark or Finland) are not among those which would normally be accused of having poor access to justice.[25] Interestingly, those countries which have a high number of courts (also in terms of physical facilities, i.e. court locations) are often among the countries that have more problems with securing the right to a fair trial than others (e.g. Croatia, Slovenia, Italy, Greece, Bulgaria and Turkey). The explanation for this may be twofold. On the one hand, this indicates that the development of transportation and infrastructure (faster and easier travel), but also of the procedural routines and styles (new methods of communication, use of recorded and written materials, increased use of legal representatives) have made the availability of a 'local' forum much less necessary, and even desirable, than in the nineteenth and most of the twentieth century. On the other hand, the problems faced by some jurisdictions which still have a relatively high number of courts may be an indication that the whole justice system has difficulties adjusting to the needs of the changed social environment. Finally, the high number of courts may as such have a negative impact on the fairness and effectiveness of trials. Fewer courts may mean more efficiency, but also better quality of adjudication. Small courts with very few judges, operating in small, closed environments, may be vulnerable to local pressures affecting their independence and impartiality; even if this is not the case, the high number of independent court structures could also produce different procedural routines, and impair the uniform application of the law. At the same time, the atomisation of the court network may negatively affect the efficient use of resources, for example by uneven case-load and burden on various courts, as well as by more difficult case management and court administration practices. Of course, even in such an

---

[24] The prospects for such *rapprochement* of procedural structures are ambiguous. On the one hand, the example of the United Kingdom—which has in the past decade reformed some of its peculiar judicial structures which existed for centuries (introducing, *inter alia,* bodies such as the Supreme Court and the Ministry of Justice), making them much more similar to structures on the European Continent—shows that reduction of structural differences is possible. However, the CEPEJ reports also indicate that reforms in Europe do not go in a uniform direction: the number of countries that have reduced the number of courts is not very different from the number of those that have increased them; the situation is the same with respect to the increase and reduction in the number of specialised courts. See EJS 2008, 72–73.

[25] Again, another indication may be the small number of violations of Art. 6 of the ECHR established in respect to those countries before the ECHR.

atomised and particularised environment the courts can still fulfil their social function, but it will come at high costs—the case of Switzerland being a good example.[26] The 'ideal' size of the courts may also be an important matter of discussion.[27] Although the perceptions about it may vary (which can also be a product of different concepts of civil and other judicial procedures), the style of work, or even the perception of the judicial function, is inevitably different in the very small and very large courts.

Finally, the different levels of specialisation of courts also have far-reaching procedural implications. The specialisation of courts tends to produce a specialisation of procedures, and indeed in most countries with specialised systems civil procedure before courts of general jurisdiction differs in a number of ways from the procedure before the commercial, labour or family courts. Different procedures are, of course, possible or even desirable before the same courts, if they deal with different types of matters. However, while the one-layer court types stimulate convergence, the multi-type court structures are an incentive for divergence of procedural rules. In a conventional perception of a 'modern' civil procedure of the twentieth century, there was one standard (default) type of litigation, which was a model that was applied with a very small number of departing rules in specific, non-standard types of matters. With a growing number of 'specialised' courts and 'specialised' procedure, one may begin to doubt whether there is a standard type of civil procedure, or a uniform concept of trial any more, or whether the judicial process in civil matters has splintered into a number of independent specialised fragments adjusted to smaller specific areas. In the two scenarios, the approach to the harmonisation of civil procedure would need to be poles apart. In the context of a non-specialised, generalist approach, the harmonisation efforts may proceed through the harmonisation of fundamental procedural rules and principles (just as suggested by the Hazard-Taruffo project). In the specialised universe of fragmentary proceedings, the main path to harmonisation might be through a mosaic of partial *rapprochement* of small individual areas (which, in a way, is happening with the EU civil procedure regulations).

A separate, and to date not sufficiently researched aspect of the differentiation of courts, is the one regarding the different methods of dealing with cases of lower importance or value, and the resulting implications for the court structures. So far, the CEPEJ has only started to collect data regarding the definition of small claims and the

---

[26] Switzerland is among the countries with the highest density of the court network, with 6 courts (geographic locations) per 100,000 inhabitants, but also one of the countries with the highest expenses of the justice system—see EJS 2010, 86 (courts) and 21 (public budget allocated to courts). In spite of high expenses, there is also a feeling that Swiss civil procedure should gain in efficiency—see on this account Domej 2009, 75–88.

[27] The CEPEJ held discussions on the topic: 'Does the size of the court matter?' at the SATURN meeting with the members of the Network of Pilot Courts held in Geneva on 13 April 2010. Although no strong conclusions could be drawn from the reports presented at that event, it was shown that the size of the court may definitely have an impact on productivity (Dutch research indicated, e.g., that courts smaller or larger than 300 FTEs (Full Time Equivalents) are less productive).

corresponding monetary thresholds. In this aspect, significant variations were found: while in Lithuania small claims are those equal to or not exceeding €72.40, in San Marino every claim up to (and including) €50,000 is regarded as being of a minor value.[28] The CEPEJ report notes correctly that 'these differences may partly be caused by the specific economic situation of the countries, the civil procedural rules that are applied and the level of specialisation of courts in this area.'[29] However, the impact that value or importance of a civil claim may have on the organisational structures has not been properly reflected in the present findings of the CEPEJ.[30] In any case, there are indications that the court structures in some countries take all civil cases, irrespective of their value and social importance, by the same layer of courts of general jurisdiction. Although virtually all judicial systems have some special rules regarding litigation in small claims, the one-layer approach may lead to a procedural philosophy that requires more or less the same or comparable efforts for the litigation of all cases, irrespective of their value,[31] whereas a differentiated approach may be a sign that the civil justice system adopts the principle of proportionality, which requires that the level of court efforts and engagement of judicial authorities should correspond to the 'amount of money involved…, importance of the case,… complexity… and financial position of each party.'[32] These differences may create divergence in procedural practices, very significant for the end-users which may for the same case get a fast-track summary proceeding in one jurisdiction, and a full-fledged lengthy court litigation in another.

The court budgets of different European countries are radically different

Stating that the different judicial systems in Europe have considerably different budgets may seem to be a kind of platitude. Of course, in this group of States with different economic and industrial power, it is only normal that the judiciaries of Europe do not enjoy the same level of economic wealth. The data collected

---

[28] EJS 2010, 89.

[29] Ibidem.

[30] Although some questions were asked about the 'first instance courts competent for debt collection in small claims,' the distinction between the courts handling cases of lower or higher social importance has not been separately defined. Rather, it seems that the lowest courts (such as Justices of the Peace) were added to the category of specialised courts if this was the self-understanding of the reporting country. In other systems in which two types of courts (lower and higher) dealing with 'smaller' or 'bigger' matters were both understood to belong to general jurisdiction courts, they were reported differently. Another problem with the CEPEJ scheme may be in the fact that the litigious handling of small cases was not clearly distinguished from the non-litigious collection of small monetary debts.

[31] As argued in procedural doctrine of the former Yugoslavia, the principle *de minimis non curat praetor* should be treated with caution, since 'there are no "small" and "big" matters in civil adjudication.' Triva and Dika 2004, 822. Accordingly, in the practice of civil procedure there are barely any differences in the style and length of litigation between cases of marginal social importance, and those in which significant social and economic issues are at stake.

[32] So Lord Woolf, defining the principle of proportionality as one of the most essential elements of the 'Overriding Objective' embodied in Part 1 of the Civil Procedure Rules 1998.

through the CEPEJ evaluation rounds have, however, shed a new light on the differences of the court budgets in Europe, and the results may be disturbing for the prospects of harmonisation.

Comparing the annual budget of all courts in different European jurisdictions, scaled in proportion to the number of inhabitants, reveals the fact that about one-third of all Council of Europe members have a budget of up to €30 per inhabitant, one-third from €30 to €60, and one-third over €60 per inhabitant. The extremes are extraordinarily far apart: while some countries, like Moldova or Armenia, still spend only about €2 or €3 per inhabitant, the budget of the Swiss judiciary is over €100 per inhabitant (see Fig. 9.2).

The impact of the different budgets of national judiciaries on the ability to harmonise European procedural practices should not be underestimated. The economic situation and the costs of living may be different from State to State. But, there are several common issues which do not depend much on the local differences. One is connected to the running costs of the operation of the justice system, where minimum conditions should be secured to guarantee minimal effectiveness. It may be difficult to secure any acceptable standard of justice if the courts are not able to pay postal costs, maintenance of the court buildings or advances on costs of proceedings borne by the courts (e.g. costs of evidence taken *ex officio*); all of this is still happening, and not infrequently, in some of the countries with low court budgets.

For the future, an even more important issue will be the capacity for modernisation. The costs of the introduction of information technology (IT) equipment and other modern tools of court work (e.g. embracing the new forms of 'e-justice,' automated summary proceedings, et cetera) are similar and comparable everywhere, and they are not inconsiderable. If the overall court budget is low, it is probable that the investment in new technologies will be even lower. A case in point is provided by a comparison between Greece and the Netherlands: while the former spends only 0.1 per cent of the court budget on computerisation, the latter devotes to IT the whole of 8 per cent of the overall budget for courts.[33] With such a state of affairs, not only will harmonisation be more difficult, but it is quite likely that the differences will grow larger, as the reforms in regard to facilitating the speed and quality of processing civil cases are today to a great extent connected with the introduction of new technical tools. They are becoming indispensable as a medium of the mass-processing of certain claims (e.g. the automated processing of payment orders issuance), as a facilitating factor in all processes (new methods of service or delivery of documents, evidence-taking by IT means, electronic recording of court hearings, holding of e-files, et cetera) and as a universal tool for court administration and case management (introduction of Integrated Case Management Solutions). Such new tools also play an important analytical role in the collection and processing of relevant statistical data, which in turn enables

---

[33] EJS 2010, 26 (data for 2008). At the same time, Greece had a total annual court budget of about €32 and the Netherlands of about €89 per inhabitant.

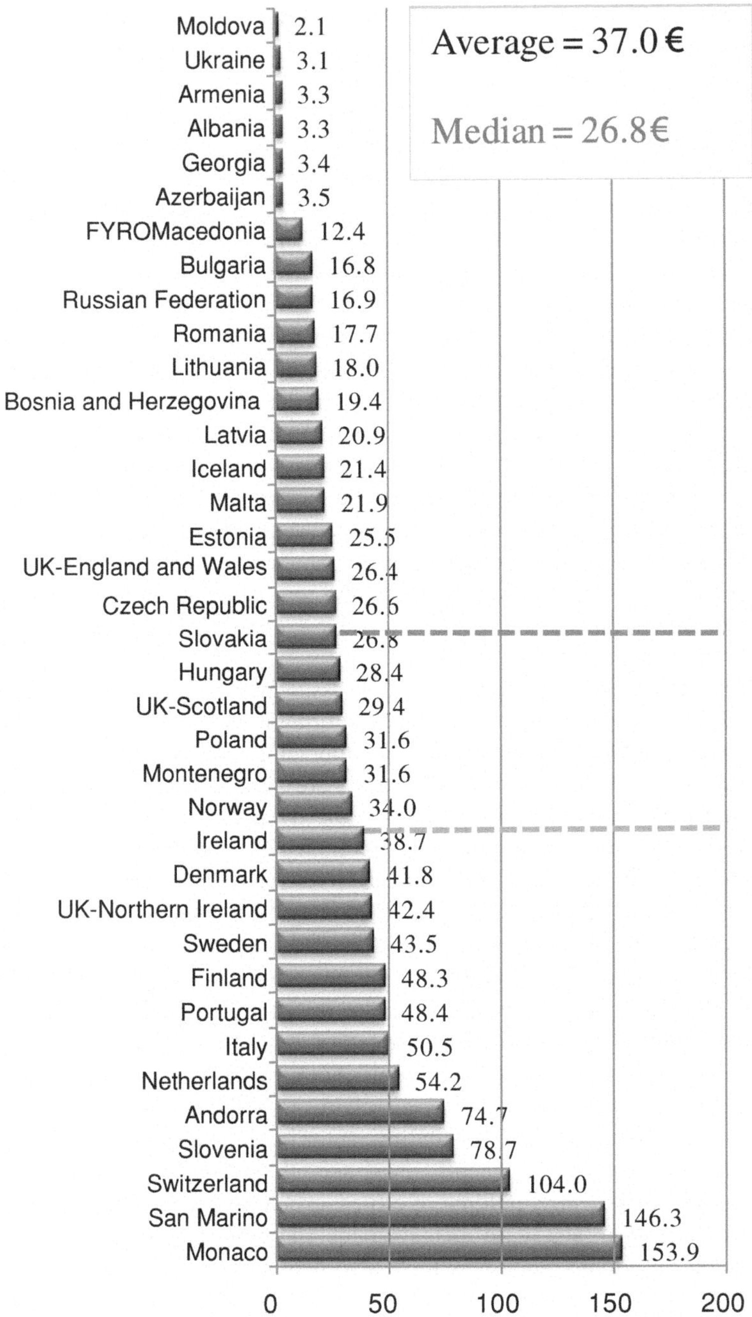

Fig. 9.2 Annual public budget allocated to all courts per inhabitant[34]

[34] Reproduced from EJS 2010, 21 (Figure 2.4).

better planning and optimisation of available resources. If the 'poor' judiciaries of Europe continue to lag behind, being bound by the old, customary procedural practices, the gap between them and the civil justice systems using new, innovative models and methods in civil procedure will become greater and greater.

Fortunately (or not), the investments in new technologies are in fact a smaller part of the judicial budgets. The average spending on IT in Europe is about three per cent of the overall court budget, and even those countries that invest a lot do not spend on this account over ten per cent. On average, the biggest share of the European court budgets goes to salaries (in particular judges' salaries) which make up seventy per cent of the total expenses. Except in England and in Ireland, the salaries in all other European countries make up over fifty per cent of the judicial budget (in some, e.g. in Greece, salaries make up 96 per cent of the court budget).[35] Therefore, the lack of investment in IT may not be so great an obstacle to overcome, and some trends towards intensifying investments in IT can already be noted even in States with more modest judicial budgets.

On the other hand, the different court budgets can also be an indicator of the different numbers of judges and of the differences in their salaries, which can also be relevant for the harmonisation processes. These issues will be discussed in the next section (see Sect. 9.2.2).

9.2.2 *Judges*

I commented more extensively on the CEPEJ findings regarding judges in other papers.[36] Therefore, in this one I will only briefly highlight two issues imminently relevant to harmonisation prospects.

Definitions and the professional status of judges are not harmonised in Europe

In the preparatory study on the evaluation of judicial systems, it was noted that 'the meaning of what a *judge* is varies also per country.'[37] The definition given in the recommendations of the Council of Europe is more related to the function, and not to the status and particular definition of judges, insofar as it includes '*all persons exercising judicial functions*, including those dealing with *constitutional, criminal, civil, commercial and administrative law* matters.'[38]

The CEPEJ evaluation reports essentially follow the same type of definition, but make it even broader and vaguer. The starting point for collecting data about judges is the definition—allegedly derived from the European Court of Human Rights case law—according to which 'a judge is a person entrusted with giving or taking part in

---

35 EJS 2010, 25–26.

36 See Uzelac 2006, 41–72; Uzelac 2011.

37 Albers 2003, 3.

38 Recommendation No. R. (94) 12 on the independence, efficiency and the role of judges of the Council of Europe, at 1.

a judicial decision [regarding] *opposing parties* who can be either physical or moral entities, during *a trial*' (emphasis added). Although this definition would on its face encompass only those issues dealing with litigious matters, just in the next sentence a line which detaches judicial status from any substantive function is added, describing a 'judge' as a person who 'decides, according to the law and following organised proceedings, on *any issue within his/her jurisdiction*' (emphasis added).[39]

From the very start it was obvious that various types of judges had to be singled out and evaluated separately. Therefore, at the outset three different types of judges were identified in European States—*professional judges* whose 'main task is to handle cases in a court and are nominated for life (or for a long and extended period),' *substitute judges* whose 'main profession... is concentrated in another legal profession,' and *lay judges* that also participate in the judicial functions, but do not have a specific legal education.[40] However, in the first evaluation round the data that were finally collected regarded only two categories, the categories of *professional* and *non-professional judges.* The category of professional judges was described in an explanatory note of the evaluation scheme as 'those who have been trained and who are paid as such (and where their main function is to work as a judge).' To that extent, the 'professional' category was essentially identified with two elements—(legal) training and financial compensation, whereas the 'non-professionals' were designated as 'volunteers who are compensated [only] for their expenses and who give binding decisions in courts,' but also were partly confounded with lay judges.[41] To cover the practices of some countries, in the first round it was further inquired whether there was an institution of *temporary judges*[42] (reported to exist in ten countries).[43]

Already difficulties occurred at the level of data collection. In the first round (EJS 2002), the number of professional judges was reported in full time equivalent (in order to reflect the participation of part-time judges),[44] but this did not reflect well the practice of engaging temporary judges. Thus, in the later rounds, a separate query related to 'professional judges occasionally presiding over a hearing' was added. However, the data on professional judges were still of much better quality than the data on non-professional judges. The reason was, as stated, that 'in some countries, non professional judges can take the place of professional judges and are a source of flexible—and often cheap—capacity to the courts,' while 'in

[39] EJS 2008, 108.

[40] Albers 2003, 3.

[41] EJS 2008, 108.

[42] EJS 2002, 33.

[43] Denmark, England & Wales, Finland, France, Italy, Norway, Portugal, Scotland, Sweden and Switzerland. In Finland and Sweden these judges were not paid, in all other countries they were compensated on the basis of their activity.

[44] The intention to count the full time equivalents of employed judges, rather than counting 'heads,' also revealed another issue—the fact that in some countries a significant number of judges are not working in the courts for various reasons, e.g. secondment to ministries of justice. Some countries also reported that illness or maternity leave results in differences between the number of fully employed judges and those who actually work in the courts.

other systems, non professional judges are required by law to handle certain cases as lay judges; these do not provide extra capacity… [and also] may, up to some point, overlap with (the notion of) "temporary judges".'[45]

The analysis of 'professional judges sitting occasionally' was deepened in the last evaluation of the CEPEJ, which reported more extensively on this category of judges in the EJS 2010 report:

> In order to tackle a legitimate demand from their citizens for 'neighbourhood' and 'rapid' justice, some States or entities have reinforced the number of judges by bringing in judges who occasionally preside over a case. These professional judges are sometimes called 'non presiding judges' or 'deputy judges.' This option is available in particular in Common-Law States or entities to lawyers who are to become full-time judges. They are therefore experienced legal professionals who have a solid basis of legal training and who have already benefited from specific training to judicial functions.[46]

Of twelve European countries that reported the existence of 'occasional' judges, a very special case was the one of England and Wales, where occasional judges—who spend between 15 and 30 days practising as judges in court sessions—are in number four times more numerous in relation to 'permanent' professional judges. But the participation of occasional judges is also significant in the Netherlands, France, Spain and Sweden.[47]

As to 'non professional' judges, although they might also have legal training (and act occasionally as honorary, i.e. unpaid judges), most of the non-professional judges in Europe are lay judges. However, their participation in civil trials (and in other types of proceedings) occurs in multiple, mutually incomparable forms. In England, lay judges sit in colleges (panels) in magistrates courts, where they generally do not deal with civil cases (but allegedly process 95 per cent of all criminal offences). The second type of non-professional judges are the justices of the peace,[48] which, according to the CEPEJ report, 'deal principally with the treatment of civil complaints of minor importance (or minor offences).'[49] The other forms of non-professional judges, primarily concerned with non-criminal cases, are those that participate in the adjudication process in specialised courts or proceedings, such as those of labour and commercial law. Finally, there is also a practice of using lay judges as assessors in some panels, where they sit and decide together with professional judges. In a number of post-Socialist countries (Czech Republic, Estonia, Poland and Slovenia), it is still a widespread practice in a number of first instance courts, both in civil and in criminal cases (e.g. the practice of using juror-judges, *suci porotnici,* in the successor countries of the former Yugoslavia).[50]

---

[45] EJS 2002, 33.

[46] EJS 2010, 121.

[47] See EJS 2010, ibidem, Table 7.4.

[48] Yet, in some countries they may be paid on an occasional basis.

[49] EJS 2010, 122.

[50] Ibidem. The CEPEJ has not included under non-professional judges the category of jurors—citizens sitting in a jury—which also exists in some European countries.

The lack of a common definition of judges, but—even more—the varying level of use of particular types and forms of judges, may be an important impediment to the harmonisation of civil procedure at the European level. For the judicial systems composed exclusively of professional, legally trained judges who operate in a closed administrative (bureaucratic) environment, there will be a natural inclination towards detailed, precisely elaborated technical rules of civil procedure. The more a system uses lay elements (but also non-professional, temporary or occasional adjudicators), the more there will be a need for a less technical approach, and the emphasis would naturally be transposed to broad principles, legal standards, fairness and substantive justice. The harmonisation of rules, without harmonisation of the structures that apply them, may create mixtures which are disharmonious, or even adverse to the interest of justice. Thus, the differences in the professional status and in the more or less closed (or open) system of engagement of judges should be seriously taken into account before any harmonisation actions are deliberated and planned.

The social functions and tasks of judges are quite different, which is reflected in the considerable differences in the figures regarding those considered to be 'judges.'

In spite of the different approaches to the status of judges, the point which seemed to be most comparable was the one regarding professional, full-time judges. All European judiciaries are largely based on professional judges, and all of the countries that participated in the CEPEJ evaluation were able to submit figures regarding their number.

The comparison resulted in interesting findings. Given the different scope of use of temporary and lay judges, as well as some local differences, it was only to be expected that the number of judges (scaled in relation to the number of inhabitants) might diverge. However, the revealed divergences far exceeded what could have been expected and explained by such elements.[51] As shown in Table 9.1, the number of judges per 100,000 inhabitants had in 2008 a span which went from 3.3 in Ireland to 53.5 in Slovenia. Even excluding the common law countries and the Caucasus region which have from 3-7 professional judges per 100,000 inhabitants, the difference between the countries of Romanic and Germanic legal tradition is one hundred per cent (from 10 to 20 and more), while countries of a former Socialist legal tradition (plus Greece) have from 25 to 50.

These findings may have an important impact on the prospects for procedural convergence in Europe. The first challenge is to explain the differences properly. The hypotheses that were mentioned in the course of the CEPEJ work, which also resulted in a more focused collection of data in these aspects, were:

---

[51] The diplomatically correct commentary in the CEPEJ report noted that 'generally speaking, an imbalance can be noticed between Western and Eastern European States or entities, there being more judges in Eastern Europe.' The explanation that a pre-eminent role is in some systems given to lay judges could, however, not cover more than a few countries, and even then only partly. See EJS 2010, 120.

Table 9.1 Number of professional judges sitting in courts (FTE) per 100,000 inhabitants in 2008[52]

Country	Number of professional judges	Country	Number of professional judges
Slovenia	53.5	Ukraine	15.5
Croatia	42.5	Belgium	15.2
Montenegro	39.7	Iceland	14.7
Serbia	34.1	Switzerland	14.1
Greece	33.3	Netherlands	13.3
FYRO Macedonia	32.2	Moldova	12.9
Czech Republic	29.2	Cyprus	12.5
Hungary	28.9	Albania	12.3
Bulgaria	28.3	Sweden	11.3
Poland	25.9	Norway	11.3
Slovakia	25.7	Spain	10.7
Russian Federation	24.2	Italy	10.2
Lithuania	22.5	Turkey	10.1
Bosnia and Herzegovina	22.3	France	9.1
Latvia	20.8	Denmark	6.9
Austria	19.9	Armenia	6.8
Romania	19.2	Georgia	6.4
Portugal	18	Azerbaijan	5.7
Estonia	17.7	UK-England and Wales	3.5
Finland	17.4	Ireland	3.3

Table 9.2 Number of incoming first instance litigious civil/commercial cases per 100,000 inhabitants in 2008[53]

Finland—183	Austria—1,325	France—2,728
Norway—340	Slovenia—1,541	Croatia—3,163
UK (England)—549	Turkey—1,562	Spain—3,579
Sweden—559	Hungary—1,888	Italy—4,768
Denmark—1,090	Poland—1,959	Belgium—6,198
Switzerland—1,133	Serbia—2,610	Russian Federation—7,157

- that in some countries the courts receive a much greater number of litigious cases than in other countries;
- that judges in some countries deal with a number of extra-judicial activities, and have a broad jurisdiction which includes involvement in resolving a number of non-litigious cases, not assigned to judges in other countries.

The data gathered would apparently support both submissions, at least at first sight. As to the number of incoming litigious civil and commercial cases per 100,000 inhabitants, here is only a sample of the results for 2008 (Table 9.2).

[52] Data taken from EJS 2010, 117–118, sorted from highest to lowest figures; the smallest States (Andorra, Lichtenstein, Monaco, San Marino and Luxembourg) are excluded for reasons of incomparability.

[53] EJS 2010, sorted data from Figure 9.5, 143.

Table 9.3 Number of incoming first instance non-litigious civil/commercial cases per 100,000 inhabitants in 2008[55]

Switzerland—71	Spain—485	Serbia—2,512
Denmark—92	Turkey—704	Finland—5,067
France—159	Czech Republic—1,027	Poland—5,143
Norway—254	Slovenia—1,580	Croatia—5,193
Sweden—230	Italy—2,132	Netherlands—5,776
Russian Federation—323	Romania—2,543	Austria—9,921

In an *ad hoc* attempt to explain these findings, the CEPEJ report stated that '*citizens seem to be more prone to go to court to solve disputes…* in the Central and Eastern Europe[an] States…, South-Eastern European States… and the countries of the South of Europe… than in the countries of the North of Europe and the States of the Caucasus.'[54]

The inquiry into the number of non-litigious cases resulted in the following findings (Table 9.3):

The differences among countries in the number of non-litigious cases, according to the CEPEJ report, 'can be explained in particular by the existence or non-existence, within the courts, of land and commercial registers.'[56] The suggested conclusion was that 'the court workload is heavily influenced by non-litigious cases in some States,' while 'in other States … litigious cases constitute the main work of the first instance courts… [where] the part of activity which is directly assigned to the judges—solving a dispute—is much higher.'[57]

A deeper analysis of both explanations for the varying level of 'judicialisation' of European justice systems may however lead to different conclusions. The suggestion that in some European countries 'citizens are more prone to go to court to solve disputes' is not supported by any serious collateral evidence, at least not if 'being prone' is defined as a cultural or societal inclination towards court litigation, irrespective of its forms, results and costs. Some studies indicate that extra-judicial methods of dispute settlement, such as conciliation, are broadly used in some cultures of the Far East (e.g. China and Japan). However, in spite of some anecdotes about the increased local eagerness to sue and litigate every dispute in life, the possible differences between various peoples in Europe are certainly not so great as to legitimise a ratio of 1 to 40 in the number of incoming civil suits reported in the neighbouring countries of Finland and the Russian Federation. People go to court to resolve disputes not because they *like to* but because they *have to*. One of the reasons for the lower number of litigious court cases may be the difficulties in the access to courts arising from high costs

[54] EJS 2010, 144. The authors swiftly added a disclaimer, asserting that the CEPEJ report 'is not the place for a sociological analysis.'

[55] EJS 2010, sorted data from Figure 9.6, 144.

[56] EJS 2010, 145.

[57] Ibidem.

and the cumbersome proceedings of getting to justice. But, while costs may still play a certain role, it is very difficult to state that countries with the lowest number of litigious cases (Finland, Norway, England and Sweden) have inaccessible civil justice systems; at least, according to the CEPEJ survey, all these countries are among those that have proportionally the largest share of their total court budget allocated to legal aid.[58] In fact, exactly these countries are among the leaders, and they offer models for other States in the formation of their legal aid policies. At the opposite end of the spectrum, it is also symptomatic that citizens flock to courts most in the countries where one would expect the least likelihood of quick decisions of high quality. Namely, some of the States having the largest reported number of litigious court cases are those that suffer from systemic problems regarding the effectiveness of legal protection (Italy, Croatia and the Russian Federation).

Viewed from this perspective, the large number of incoming litigious cases can be an indication of problems in the civil justice systems, rather than an indication of their accessibility and user-friendliness. But, the differences in the reported number of litigious cases can also be an important indicator of divergences in the understanding of what has to be counted as a proper 'litigious matter' which deserves to be resolved in a court of law. One problem may already occur with the understanding of a 'dispute,' as not all of the matters that are statistically counted as litigious may really concern a serious disagreement, difference or dispute.[59] In particular, the proceedings of collecting (uncontested) debt should in a number of jurisdictions be commenced by the formal raising of the claim in judicial proceedings—often regarded as 'litigious,' even if no objection to the claim was raised—which naturally causes a manifold rise in the number of 'litigations.' Another aspect may regard the definition and number of 'petty' cases. Irrespective of the 'harmonised' European cross-border threshold of small claims as claims not exceeding '€2,000 at the time when the claim form is received by the court,'[60] the CEPEJ survey reveals that the monetary value of a small claim in the national law of the European States again has almost a one-to-one hundred ratio.[61]

When it comes to non-litigious cases, the statement that a large number of such cases in the court statistics involve considerable activity and engagement of judges should also be subject to questioning. If the highest number of non-litigious cases

[58] Cf. EJS 2010, at 3.2, 52, Table 3.3.

[59] One of such obvious examples from the law of successor countries of the former Yugoslavia concerns 'litigious' divorce proceedings, since even the divorce proceedings initiated by the mutual agreement of the spouses are counted as 'litigation' (*parnica*). See, e.g., Croatian Family law (*Obiteljski zakon*), Official Gazette 116/03, Art. 280(2).

[60] See European Small Claims Procedure, Regulation No. 861/2007 establishing a European Small Claims Procedure, OJ 2007, L 199/1, Art. 2(1).

[61] See *supra* n. 26 and the text above it.

relate to proceedings concerned with land or company registers, or the cases of issuing payment orders in uncontested matters (if those cases are classified as non-litigious), they can clearly be handled mainly by other court personnel, or even by automated IT systems, requiring very little or no input of judicial work. The examples that might confirm this assumption are those of Finland or the Netherlands, which have a high number of reported non-litigious cases and a low number of judges per capita; another example is Austria, which has the absolutely highest reported number of non-litigious cases (almost twice as many as the first country ranked next), with the largest share of semi-automated payment orders, enforcement cases and land registry cases, all not requiring a substantive input of judicial work.[62]

In short, the analysis of figures cannot result in unequivocal statements without an in-depth study of the causes for the considerable differences from country to country. But, it is safe to reach a preliminary general conclusion regarding the meaning of the differences. There are sufficient indications that the profile of what is considered to be 'judicial work'—the social functions and tasks of judges—is quite different in different European countries. While some countries treat judges as decision-makers who provide high-quality service in important and difficult legal disputes, others treat them as a qualified but universally applicable work force for handling a number of legal matters, with the emphasis on the mass-processing of a high number of cases, not necessarily litigious and/or important cases.

These differences in the understanding of the social function(s) of judges and the divergences in their typical tasks are an important challenge to the harmonisation of civil procedure in Europe. In the different national environments, there will even be different perceptions regarding what should be the target of procedural harmonisation. For example, for judges in South-eastern European countries, the main challenges today—and in fact the main potential 'harmonisation issues'—in civil proceedings are related to payment orders, enforcement proceedings or judicial registers, all the issues that for a number of Northern justice systems are not at all interesting for judges, partly also because they are not seen as a social function of the courts at all. On the other hand, the judges trained within an environment where the indication of judicial success is the judges' 'productivity'—the processing of a set number of cases (several hundreds or even thousands a year)—are not likely to follow the passion for sophisticated methods of judicial case management, adjusted to the needs of the individual case. They will even less understand the urge to achieve excellence in legal arguments, to profile legal constructions and policies that will be used as precedents for future cases, or to master the techniques of handling complex, multi-party cases (let alone mentioning the futuristic concepts of class actions or group litigation). The visions of Judge Hercules[63] (who may have some European relatives in the North and in the

[62] Cf. Austrian Report for the Evaluation Scheme 2010 (available at http://www.coe.int/cepej; (last consulted in May 2011), 16–17.

[63] For the metaphor of Judge Hercules (an ideal, immensely wise judge fit to decide the most difficult cases) see Dworkin 1975, 1057–1109; see also Dworkin 1986.

West) and the Weberian Judge F. Bureaucrat[64] (best described in Merryman's vision of Western European judges)[65] have very thin common ground. Consequently, there is also a very small common basis upon which one could build harmonised rules of civil procedure, and it may be even smaller for the building of a common judge-made case law.[66] The starting point of the problems may already be the borders of the regulation of civil procedure: for some, the main problems might be in the attempts to reach a peaceful conclusion of the dispute before the case reaches the court, thus filtering all cases that should never land in courts; for others, the story would only begin when cases reach the court, and would concentrate around achieving the appropriate throughput and output while engaging the least effort, time and resources.

Ultimately, the differences in social functions which are reflected in the lower or higher level of 'judicialisation' (in the sense of *density* of judicial posts in the society) invoke some pragmatic opposition to harmonisation processes. Every harmonisation has its winners and losers, depending on the course of the harmonisation. For an oversized Southern European judiciary, a harmonisation based on the filtration of cases, pre-trial techniques of dispute settlement, effectiveness and substantive justice could result in a massive loss of jobs (or at least of its own *ratio vivendi*); for the slim, but effective Northern European judicial corps, the increase in formalisation, the extension of jurisdiction to 'non-judicial tasks' and the focus on bureaucratic efficiency would mean a loss of dignity and social esteem. Thus, professional resistance to any far-reaching project of harmonisation would seem to be almost inevitable.

9.2.3 Lawyers

The mosaic of actors and services for providing justice in civil cases would be incomplete without lawyers. It is therefore worth inquiring into the findings of the CEPEJ evaluation rounds related to lawyers, trying to assess their impact on the harmonisation of civil procedure.

The CEPEJ started from the definition of lawyers contained in the recommendations of the Council of Europe, where a lawyer is defined as 'a person qualified and authorised according to the national law to plead and act on behalf of

---

[64] F. is for Faceless. On the concept of the 'bureaucratic' judiciary see Uzelac 1993, 515–550.

[65] Cf., e.g., Merryman's anthological description of civil law judges as 'a kind of expert clerk' and 'a civil servant who performs important but essentially uncreative functions.' Merryman 1985, 36–37.

[66] This leads us to suspect the appropriateness of the otherwise tempting suggestion that setting minimum standards of protection and leaving the harmonisation to judge-made law is a good and flexible way to proceed. But see Eliantonio 2009, available at http://www.ejcl.org/133/art133-4.pdf (last consulted in May 2011).

his or her clients, to engage in the practice of law, to appear before the courts or advise and represent his or her clients in legal matters.'[67]

The collection of data regarding lawyers revealed divergences similar (if not greater) to those spotted regarding judges. Albeit a uniform definition of lawyers was used, the CEPEJ was soon faced with the fact that in various nations different categories of lawyers are used. In the later evaluation round, with a special reference to English division of barristers and solicitors (the latter, as a rule, not being authorised to represent clients in courts), data was collected separately for 'proper' lawyers and for legal advisors. The need for separate categories was, however, not limited only to common law countries. In Scandinavian countries and in Malta, the national reporters pointed out that registration as a lawyer with a bar association is not necessary to undertake the activities of a lawyer, as there are 'no formal requirements or licensing for practising law… or for appearing before courts.'[68] In most other countries, certain elements of lawyers' monopolies to court representation or legal advice were established, but the forms and the extent of such monopolies were rather different. These differences can only be partly illustrated by the fact that, according to the 2010 report, 17 countries (37.8 per cent) provided a monopoly of representation in civil cases, 14 countries (31.1 per cent) in administrative cases, 36 countries (80 per cent) in criminal cases for defendants, and 22 countries (48.9 per cent) in criminal cases for victims. In each of these categories, a number of fine shades may further be distinguished, as—according to comments of the reporters—in many countries different forms of monopoly are provided depending on the type of court, the value of the claim or the legal matters involved. Further comments noted that monopoly does or does not apply to the parties themselves if they wish to appear in court on their own behalf (e.g. in Switzerland), or that permission to appear and to represent before the Supreme Court may depend on a special permission of the court (e.g. in Norway).[69] Equally colourful is the regulation of organisational structures of the legal profession, with bar associations regulating the legal profession at the national, regional or local levels.[70] Another element which should be given sufficient attention in the context of the harmonisation of civil proceedings is the method of charging and calculating lawyers' fees, where CEPEJ also diagnosed a colourful mix

[67] Recommendation Rec. (2000) 21 of the Council of Europe on the freedom of exercise of the profession of lawyer.

[68] Comments of the Swedish national reporter, EJS 2010, 238.

[69] See EJS 2010, 245–246. We are sticking here to cursory comments of the national reporters—it is certain that a more detailed and studious comparison of procedural regimes would reveal many other differences.

[70] See EJS 2010, 243–244.

Table 9.4 Number of lawyers per 100,000 inhabitants in 2008[72]

Country	Number of lawyers	Country	Number of lawyers
Greece	350.6	Croatia	84.7
Italy	332.1	Montenegro	83.0
Spain	266.5	Romania	81.7
Portugal	260.2	Czech Republic	80.6
Malta	217.6	France	75.8
Germany (data 2006)	168.0	Poland	71.6
Belgium	155.9	Slovenia	57.7
Bulgaria	151.8	Estonia	49.6
Albania	126.2	Sweden	49.4
Switzerland	123.3	Latvia	48.4
Norway	122.6	Lithuania	47.3
Hungary	98.1	Ireland	45.7
Denmark	95.8	Russian Federation	43.9
Netherlands	94.8	Moldova	36.4
Macedonia	92.9	Finland	34.4
Slovakia	88.9	Bosnia & Herzegovina	32.3
Turkey	88.8	Armenia	24.4
Austria	86.7	Azerbaijan	9.0

of strict statutory regulation, binding or recommended tariffs of professional organisations and freely negotiated fee agreements.[71]

The numeric indicators regarding lawyers resulted again in interesting comparisons. Just as in the case of judges, considerable variations in the level of 'lawyerisation' have been clearly established—see Table 9.4.

Exploring the full background and meaning of these figures would deserve a separate series of studies. Superficial comparisons may drive us to various conclusions, some of them logical and some rather puzzling. So, for instance, it may be concluded that there is a positive relationship between the number of lawyers in

[71] EJS 2010, 246–247. For 2008, 14 States (30 per cent) indicated that lawyers' fees are regulated by law, 10 States (21.7 per cent) reported various types of regulation by bar association(s) (orientation standards, codes of conduct, indicative guidelines, local suggested draft agreements, binding regulation), and 37 States (78.7 per cent) asserted the possibility of freely negotiated agreements. Due to different standards for different types of cases (e.g. for criminal cases, legal aid cases, et cetera) these self-assessments should be considered with care because there might be important differences even within the categories of States that provided the same answers.

[72] Data taken from EJS 2010, 239, Figure 12.2. The smallest States (Andorra, Lichtenstein, Monaco, San Marino and Luxembourg) are excluded for reasons of incomparability. Also excluded are the data for the UK, where the discrepancy between the number of lawyers (barristers) and legal advisors (solicitors) is very significant (UK-Scotland—5.4 without and 203.6 with legal advisors; UK-Northern Ireland—35.1 without and 173.8 with legal advisors; UK-England & Wales—282.3 with legal advisors, about ten times less without them).

a country and the number of incoming civil litigious cases,[73] what corresponds to a commonsensical supposition (the more litigation, the more lawyers, and vice versa). A very low number of lawyers in some countries, such as Azerbaijan, Armenia or Moldova, may be an indication of still underdeveloped legal infrastructure in these countries that are in the process of strengthening the rule of law. But, on the other hand, the highest number of lawyers per capita (over 300) is recorded in Greece and Italy, the countries that also can hardly be regarded as the champions in the effective protection of legal rights. In fact, another similarity with the numerical analysis of the judicial profession comes to surface: a larger number of lawyers does not necessarily mean better, more effective, affordable and accessible civil justice.

In any case, it is certain that the varying organisational structures, different status and number of lawyers need to be seriously considered in any plans to harmonise civil procedure in Europe. The rules of civil procedure are applied by legal professions that are independent and self-regulated, and the lawyers are a crucial element in this chain. The way in which these rules are applied in practice depends to a great extent on the willingness, perceptions and interests of these legal professionals, and their highly autonomous and protected status make them partly immune from the efforts aimed at forcing them to change their routines and practices. The reforms of civil justice systems in South-eastern Europe often proved that innovative changes in procedural legislation failed because of opposition from legal professionals, who safely and with no consequences ignored the novelties (or their purpose). The impact of harmonisation on the market in legal services may be an important hurdle to reforms that aim to prevent litigation, accelerate judicial proceedings and simplify the proceedings, as such reforms could be perceived (often rightly) as an element that may mean the loss of business (or the need to undergo a demanding process of changing habits and *modus operandi*). These considerations do not play only in the 'over-lawyerised' countries, but also across Europe, especially since it was established that, on average, the number of lawyers in Europe grew at a median rate of seven and one-half per cent at the annual level.[74]

9.3 Roads to Harmonisation: Harmonisation of Structures v Harmonisation of Results

The purpose of this paper was to show the organisational challenges and difficulties encountered in the process of harmonisation of civil procedure in Europe. The analysis based on the evaluation of European judiciaries conducted by the

[73] I am grateful to Pim Albers for pointing to this conclusion and for submitting illustrations which support it.

[74] Average annual variation between 2004 and 2008, see EJS 2010, 241 (Figure 12.4).

European Commission for the Efficiency of Justice has demonstrated that all such efforts need to take very seriously the huge structural differences among the European civil justice systems. But, the intention of this analysis was not to argue that harmonisation is impossible or undesirable. On the contrary, like the internationalisation and Europeanization of many other fields of progress, harmonisation in the field of civil procedure is also a desirable goal. The question is only how to proceed with the harmonisation of civil procedure in the right way. I would suggest that, in addition to the mainstream efforts, there are two ways which should be explored.

As demonstrated in the previous Chapter, the harmonisation of the rules of civil procedure, which was up to now the focus of attention, needs to be supplemented by actions that will take into account the different structures that are needed to implement harmonised laws and rules of civil procedure. The harmonisation of legal norms regulating civil procedure will not harmonise civil procedure, unless further steps are undertaken. One straightforward conclusion from the already presented arguments may be the need to *harmonise procedural structures*, i.e. to diminish gradually the very considerable differences among justice systems. Considering just the numerical indicators, it has been shown that the extremes found on the territory of Europe are very far apart, often in a ratio of one-to-one hundred (or more).[75] These extremes are not tolerable, and if any serious harmonisation is planned, they need to be abolished.

Indeed, the CEPEJ evaluation rounds, covering so far the period between 2002 and 2008, show that, in certain fields, the harmonisation of structures may be traced. At least when it comes to the least developed justice systems of Europe, those that had the lowest figures in respect to their judicial infrastructures, it is clear that the extremes are being softened: the court budgets are being increased, the number of judges and lawyers is growing, and so is also their revenue and remuneration. The latest CEPEJ report contains a survey of comprehensive judicial reforms planned in a number of countries.[76] It may be early to predict their outcome, but the already established trends are on average going in the direction of convergence (in spite of some opposite examples).

The publication of the CEPEJ reports has by itself boosted some structural reforms. They were noted in particular as reforms regarding the organisation of the network of courts (the 'judicial map') in some countries. This trend was noted in the last CEPEJ evaluation round,[77] but has in particular been going on in South-eastern Europe, where, *inter alia,* the reorganisation of the court network was stimulated by the European Commission and various twinning missions as a part of the adjustment of the legal system necessary in the context of EU accession

[75] An example of differences that are far above a one-to-one hundred ratio may be the amount available for legal aid in different European countries, which ranges from €7 to €3,742 per case. EJS 2010, 289.

[76] EJS 2010, Chapter 16, 279–287.

[77] EJS 2010, 289.

negotiations. In some successor countries of the former Yugoslavia, a significant effort was made to 'rationalise,' i.e. to reduce the number of courts, which was evaluated as excessive in light of the replies from the CEPEJ scheme.[78] The results were not always the same, but at least the trend of reducing the extremely high figures was initiated, which may be taken as a form of harmonisation.

Over time, the trend of harmonising procedural structures will certainly advance. It seems that, to a certain extent, such an intention may be compatible with the CEPEJ policies of assisting the national justice systems by proposing concrete ways of improving their functioning. However, the harmonisation of procedural structures may be a very long process, and it is very questionable what its scope and effect could be. It may be a viable task to evaluate the efficiency of the court system and propose a reduction or increase in the number of courts, although some practical difficulties may affect this process (e.g. local concerns, the political situation, et cetera). But, when it comes to a potential for harmonising the legal professions, prospects for significant changes are much gloomier. In particular, a significant reduction in the number of lawyers or judges is hardly imaginable, no matter how much scientific research may prove its desirability. Changing working habits, self-understanding of inherited roles, and the traditional methods of work can be possible only if many preconditions are met. But, more importantly, for a far-reaching structural transformation a social consensus is needed, as well as the awareness of the necessity for change (and its precise direction). The critical mass may be reached in some countries that are otherwise undergoing a dynamic process of social change (which is why a number of them are labelled as 'transition' countries). Significant structural changes may be quite likely there (yet, their success is not guaranteed). But, the structural differences are great even among the circle of States that understand themselves as well-established, well-functioning democracies with functioning justice systems. The need for reforms, including the need to harmonise certain forms and structures, may exist there as well, but it is not likely that public awareness about this need is sufficient to motivate deep structural transformations, only for the sake of 'harmonisation.' In the end, one should ask whether the costs and efforts of such a transformation do pay off if the system is already producing satisfactory results.

Another direction of procedural harmonisation should therefore have precedence. When the heads of the European Union requested 'better compatibility and more convergence between the legal systems of Member States,'[79] this formula was designated to denote the need of the European citizens to be awarded the same or comparable standards of legal protection in the joint 'area of justice.' The procedural convergence need not necessarily be either the convergence of

[78] A survey of such efforts in Croatia, Bosnia and Herzegovina, Serbia, Slovenia, Macedonia, Kosovo and Montenegro was presented recently at the Regional Conference 'Reorganisation of Court Network in Montenegro' held in Budva on 15–17 November 2010.

[79] Tampere milestones, cit *supra* n. 5.

procedural rules, or the convergence of procedural structures—it can also be achieved as the *convergence (harmonisation) of results of the national justice systems.*

The results, of course, can be defined in a different way. But, the proper perspective that would correspond to the intention of the Tampere milestones, echoing at the same time the jurisprudence of the European Court of Human Rights regarding Article 6(1) of the ECHR, would be the perspective of the *end users of the justice system.* The product of civil justice is (or should be) the *effective protection of users' rights.* The protection of the rights of the users of the justice system can be effective only if it is *fair,* and if it is concretely and effectively delivered in *optimum and foreseeable* (or at least *reasonable*) *time.*

Could the results of civil justice be effectively monitored and compared across European countries? Is it possible to harmonise the speed and the essential content of legal protection in different European jurisdictions, no matter what their procedural and structural differences are? The CEPEJ has also undertaken valuable work in two related fields, trying to set the standards for the *quality* of justice,[80] and for the *timeframes* within which justice is delivered.[81] One should, however, admit that the results of the work in these two fields have not yet produced sufficiently reliable criteria for comparisons and evaluation, but rather have pointed to the existing deficiencies in the national justice systems. The developed checklists for the national justice systems, such as the Time Management Checklist,[82] have revealed that most European countries do not possess sufficient ability to monitor all relevant aspects of the duration of judicial proceedings. Some of the tools that are in the process of development, such as the common user satisfaction surveys,[83] are just about to be tested on a broader scale across the European countries.[84] The collection of data in this respect has started, but the first data gathered is far more fragmentary and incomplete than the data collected

[80] On the concept of the quality of the courts and the Judiciary and the work of the CEPEJ Working Group on Quality, see Albers 2009, 57–74.

[81] The CEPEJ has worked since its creation on the issues related to the timeframes of proceedings, first within the Task Force for Judicial Timeframes (TF-DEL), and then, since 2007, within the work of the Centre for Judicial Time Management (SATURN Centre—Study and Analysis of Judicial Time Use Research Network). See in more detail at http://www.coe.int/cepej (last consulted in May 2011).

[82] CEPEJ, Time Management Checklist, Checklist of indicators for the analysis of the length of proceedings in the justice system, adopted by the CEPEJ at its 6th plenary meeting (7–9 December 2005), document CEPEJ (2005) 12 REV.

[83] Cf. CEPEJ Handbook for conducting satisfaction surveys aimed at court users in Council of Europe Member States, adopted by CEPEJ at its 15th plenary meeting (Strasbourg, 9–10 September 2010), CEPEJ 2010, 1.

[84] The latest development in this respect concerns the collaboration of CEPEJ and the Lisbon Network (set up in 1995 within the Council of Europe and consisting of different judicial training bodies in Europe). The Lisbon network will be entrusted with the testing of the CEPEJ satisfaction surveys for court users. It remains to be seen how adequate the bodies competent for judicial training will be in fulfilling this task.

regarding the structural elements of the justice systems.[85] This may be an indication that many contemporary justice systems in Europe are still much more self-centred than user-oriented. They possess good insights into their budgets, staff and organisational structures, case-loads and backlogs, but not in those elements which are important from the users' perspective. These elements are, for example, foreseeable timeframes, clear procedural calendars, transparent time and case management, easily accessible information about the available options in the pursuit of individual and collective rights, user-friendly procedures, clearly defined fee and costs arrangements and fair legal aid systems for those who cannot afford the full costs of legal protection. The fact that several European jurisdictions are in these aspects more advanced than others only underlines the differences and enhances the need for harmonisation.

Let us return to the initial question of this paper. Is the harmonisation of civil procedure a noble, but elusive goal? In the light of the arguments presented here, it may be concluded that it is a difficult goal. With a lot of effort, it may be reached, but the proper way of trying to reach it should commence with the idea of equalising the expectations and positions of users *vis-à-vis* the justice system. Differences in this respect in Europe are not only huge, they are also not sufficiently diagnosed and monitored. The extremes, such as the established human rights violations regarding fairness and length of proceedings, are only symptoms and tentative indications. It is certain that in the current state of affairs neither in Greater Europe nor in the EU can citizens approach courts and authorities in other States with the expectation of receiving the same standards of legal protection, both regarding its fairness and its effectiveness. But, after developing and implementing instruments that are adequate for making objective comparisons across the lines of national civil procedures, the roads to harmonisation will be open, and their direction will be manifest. The harmonisation of results of civil procedure may inevitably imply some harmonisation of procedural structures, at least where it is diagnosed that underdeveloped—or disproportionately oversized—procedural structures clearly have a negative impact on the effectiveness of legal protection. Certainly, reforms adjusted to the needs and realities of every jurisdiction should be introduced in order to fine-tune the system and improve its results, thereby tending to reach the perhaps unreachable ideal of an optimally harmonised European justice. But, where different procedural structures turn out to be equally effective, fair, transparent and user-friendly, the pluralism of procedural forms may even be considered as desirable, just as harmony may be better achieved by polyphonic voices than by voices chanting in unison.

---

[85] The fact that the data regarding the timeframes of proceedings are incomplete was consistently noted in all EJS reports, including the latest edition, where the readers were warned again 'considering the limited number of responding States… to interpret the data… with care.' EJS 2010, 167.

References

Albers P (2003) Evaluating judicial systems: a balance between the variety and generalisation, document CEPEJ 12

Albers P (2009) Quality assessment of courts and the judiciary: from judicial quality to court excellence. In: Uzelac A, van Rhee CH (eds) Access to justice and the judiciary: towards New European standards of affordability, quality and efficiency of civil adjudication. Intersentia, Antwerp, pp 57–74

Betetto N (2010) Implementation of European civil procedural regulations. In: Uzelac A, Van Rhee CH (eds) Enforcement and enforceability. Intersentia, Antwerp, pp 103–110

CEPEJ (2005) European judicial systems: facts and figures. Council of Europe, Strasbourg

CEPEJ (2008) European judicial systems. Edition 2008 (data 2006). Efficiency and quality of justice (CEPEJ Studies No. 11). Council of Europe Publishing, Strasbourg

CEPEJ (2010) European judicial systems. Edition 2010 (data 2008). Efficiency and quality of justice (CEPEJ Studies No. 12). Council of Europe Publishing, Strasbourg

Domej T (2009) Efficiency in the relationship between the judge and the parties: a perspective on the future Swiss Code of Civil Procedure. In: Uzelac A, Van Rhee CH (eds) Access to justice and the judiciary. Towards new European standards of affordability, quality and efficiency of civil adjudication. Intersentia, Antwerp, pp 75–88

Dworkin R (1975) Hard cases. Harv Law Rev 88:1057–1109

Dworkin R (1986) Law's Empire. Harvard University Press, Cambridge

Eliantonio M (2009) The future of national procedural law in Europe: Harmonisation vs. judge-made standards in the field of administrative justice, vol 13.3. Electr J Comp Law. Available at www.ejcl.org/133/art133-4.pdf. (Accessed May 2011)

Freudenthal M (2010) Attitudes of European Union Member States towards the harmonisation of civil procedure. In: UzelacA Van, Rhee CH (eds) Enforcement and Enforceability. Intersentia, Antwerp, pp 3–16

Kramer XE (2010) Enhancing enforcement in the European Union. The European order for payment procedure and its implementation in the Member States, particularly in Germany, the Netherlands, and England. In: Uzelac A, Van Rhee CH (eds) Enforcement and Enforceability. Intersentia, Antwerp, pp 17–36

Merryman JH (1985) The civil law tradition. An introduction to the legal systems of Western Europe and Latin America. Stanford University Press, Stanford

Rechberger W, Klicka T (eds) (2002) Procedural law on the threshold of a new millennium. CLC, Vienna

Storme M (ed) (1994) Rapprochement du droit judiciaire de l'Union européenne/Approximation of judiciary law in the European Union. Nijhoff, Dordrecht

Triva S, Dika M (2004) Građansko parnično procesno pravo. Narodne Novine, Zagreb

Trocker N (2005) Mauro Cappeletti. In: Storme M, Carpi F (eds) In Honorem Mauro Capeletti. Tribute to an international procedural lawyer. Kluwer, The Hague, pp 13–36

Trocker N, Varano V (eds) (2005) The reforms of civil procedure in comparative perspective. In: Giappichelli G (ed) Torino

Uzelac A (1993) Evropsko sudstvo: između birokratske organizacije i korporativne svijesti. Zbornik Pravnog fakulteta u Zagrebu 43:5515–550

Uzelac A (2006) Kann die Effizienz der Justiz gemessen werden?—Versuch eines Vergleichs der europäischen Justizsysteme. In: Gottwald P (ed) Effektivität des Rechtsschutzes vor staatlichen und privaten Gerichten. Gieseking, Bielefeld, pp 41–72

Uzelac A (2011) Efficiency of European justice systems. The strength and weaknesses of the CEPEJ evaluations. Int J Proced Law 1:106–146

Van Rhee CH (ed) (2005) European traditions in civil procedure (Ius Commune Europaeum 54). Intersentia, Antwerp

Chapter 10
Harmonisation in a Global Context: The ALI/UNIDROIT Principles

Michele Taruffo

Abstract This chapter stresses the growing problem of transnational disputes due to commercial globalisation, and the difficulties arising from the application of the rule of the procedural *lex fori*. A procedural unification of national systems being impossible for various reasons, the only viable solution would be the harmonisation of such systems, at least when transnational litigation is involved. Harmonisation is a matter of degree, and the main issue is to determine what could be harmonised. The ALI/UNIDROIT Principles could be taken as a sort of 'model law' providing standards and rules for the harmonisation of national procedures. They are specific and general enough to represent a model for the harmonisation of the most important structural and functional elements of procedural systems.

Contents

Professor of Law, University of Pavia (Italy).

M. Taruffo (✉)
University of Pavia, Pavia, Italy
e-mail: michelino.taruffo@unipv.it

X. E. Kramer and C. H. van Rhee (eds.), *Civil Litigation in a Globalising World*,
DOI: 10.1007/978-90-6704-817-0_10,

10.1 Introduction

As is well known, the most important facet of the complex phenomenon that is usually labelled as 'globalisation' deals with the tendency of economics, commerce and finance to cover the whole area of the globe. Among the wide variety of problems arising from such a tendency is the increase in cross-border litigation, that is, the growing number of cases involving parties that belong—to use a non-technical word—to different jurisdictions. Transnational disputes are now very common, but the procedural regulations existing in the various national legal systems are not adequate to deal efficiently with such a peculiar kind of litigation.

Just to mention a few of the problems, there are at least two main issues that are still unresolved and that represent serious hurdles in the management of transnational disputes. The first of these problems deals with the choice of the court having jurisdiction in the specific disputes: in Europe there are special rules guiding this choice, but in the rest of the world it is open to a variety of even conflicting solutions, especially after the failure of The Hague conference that attempted to establish common patterns aimed at simplifying the choice of jurisdiction. The second problem derives from the traditional principle of the 'procedural *lex fori*,' according to which any national court applies its own domestic procedural rules even when it has to decide a transnational dispute. While international practice has *de facto* created some relatively common standards for the choice of jurisdiction, the problem of managing from abroad litigation that takes place in substantially different and possibly too 'distant' procedural systems, in which courts follow their own domestic rules, still remains unsolved.

Dealing with such a problem one has to consider that there is a wide variety of procedural systems that are basically different, not only in the structure of the proceeding and in the details of the procedural regulations, but even at the level of the fundamental guarantees of civil justice. Within Europe there are several models of civil proceedings that can be reduced to a homogeneous model of *civil law* only by setting aside England and not considering the important differences still existing among the Franco-Italian, the Austro-German, and the Spanish models and all the variations that such basic models have produced all around Europe, and in the so-called civil law countries of Latin America. Outside Europe, moreover, the landscape is even more complicated for a number of reasons: the fundamental guarantees of the administration of justice (such as the independence and impartiality of the judiciary, the due process of law and the right to be heard) are not always actually ensured, or they are ensured in different ways and to varying degrees. The procedural models may be different (also because after the English reforms of 1999 it is extremely difficult to think of a single *common law* model of civil procedure), especially if one takes into consideration the peculiar features of many 'mixed' systems, such as those of Japan and Israel, and the rapidly evolving procedural regulations in important countries like the People's Republic of China.

In this complex situation, and taking into account the frequency and the practical importance of transnational litigation, a first intellectual temptation could be to imagine a sort of unification of all the procedural regulations into a single and uniform procedural code that should be applied by any court in any country, especially when dealing with transnational disputes (but perhaps even when dealing with domestic disputes). This was the leading idea of a group of European scholars that attempted to draft a text aimed at providing a basis for the unification of at least some aspects of the procedural regulations existing in European countries.[1] However, notwithstanding the theoretical interest of such a project, it was doomed to failure. The main reason is that a procedural code is not a mere set of more or less complex rules of thumb, but above all is a 'cultural product,' the form, structure and contents of which are the product of historical, political, institutional, ethical and economic developments. This is also true within the borders of Europe and is the main reason why a unification of procedural regulations into a single and uniform code of civil procedure appears to be an impossible enterprise. *A fortiori* this is true if one considers the global dimension that civil and commercial litigation have, since many cultural factors have led the various procedural systems into very different paths: thinking of a uniform code of civil procedure that should be applied in each jurisdiction of the world is clearly pure fantasy, if not an illusion. Moreover, one could say that even if such unification were possible (which it clearly is not), it would not be beneficial and useful: the attempt to force every court of every country to apply the same code of civil procedure would be culturally and politically unacceptable.

Furthermore, one might think that although procedure is essential for the enforcement of substantive rules, this does not imply that 'the same procedure' is required in order to have a consistent application of such rules in different national jurisdictions. For instance, the same rules concerning a specific contract that are used in different national contexts may or may not be interpreted and applied in the same way independently of the kind of procedural rules that are applied by different national courts. In this sense, harmonising the substantive rules, and even harmonising their interpretation, is a specific problem that is not directly connected with the kind of procedure that is used in order to apply such rules. Different interpretations of the same rules may be given, as it actually happens, within the same national jurisdictions and—on the opposite side—the same interpretation may be adopted by different national jurisdictions. In a sense, therefore, procedural differences could be considered as not necessarily relevant in the perspective of harmonising substantive rules and their actual interpretation.

The diversity of procedural devices may be relevant from a different standpoint: actually, procedures are more or less slow and inefficient in various countries. For instance, statistics show that Italy is by far the most inefficient European country in the protection and in the enforcement of civil rights, and that it has one of the most inefficient systems in the world due to the abnormal and exceedingly long delays

[1] See Storme 1994.

both in the declaratory and in the enforcement phases of the proceeding. It means that litigating a case in Italy, or seeking enforcement of a foreign judgment in Italy, is a very long and ineffective enterprise. Once again, however, this does not mean that Italian civil procedure should necessarily be made identical to any other European or non-European procedural system. Actually, it means that the Italian system is badly in need of a deep and complete reform, which could or could not be inspired by other models existing in Europe or outside Europe. It cannot be denied that in figuring out such a reform the examples offered by other procedural systems may be extremely useful, although transplants between different systems are often dangerous. However, the task of transforming the Italian procedural machinery into an efficient system for the protection of rights is not equivalent to adopting 'another' procedural system, supposedly common to other countries or even to all the other countries.

A further argument is that no national procedural system can be considered as a sort of homogeneous whole, based upon a single procedural model. Actually, all the systems include an 'ordinary' or 'general' type of proceeding that is normally applied in whatever kind of case, unless special provisions require that, in particular disputes concerning specific matters, some different and 'special' proceedings should be applied. It is hardly a novelty: at least as far back as the fourteenth century the European Romano-canonical system of procedure was based on the distinction between the ordinary 'formal' procedure and the theoretically exceptional—but practically largely prevailing—'summary' procedure; such a distinction was still present in most of the procedural codes of the nineteenth century. On the other hand, all modern procedural systems have to deal with pressures to provide special proceedings for particular matters or particular kinds of disputes, mainly when the 'ordinary' proceeding is long and inefficient. Therefore, everywhere there is a trend to articulate the procedural system with the aim of meeting different and varying requests originating from specific areas of the administration of civil justice. The various procedural systems react in different ways to such pressures: the domain of special proceedings has become the most important factor of variety and difference among the procedural systems.

10.2 The Impossible Unification and a Possible Harmonisation of Procedural Systems

If all the above-mentioned aspects of the situation concerning the systems of civil procedure are taken into account, it is easy to understand that the issue of a possible unification of the regulation of civil proceedings is a very complex and puzzling one. In order to deal with such an issue in a reasonable way, however, a distinction has to be made between 'unification' and 'harmonisation' of procedural systems. Unifying the several systems of civil procedure would require setting aside all the existing differences and adopting one common regulation that should be used in all the national systems and applied by all domestic courts. On the contrary, harmonising the existing regulations would be much less difficult and would imply focusing on some common features that should be present in all the national systems or on some common points of reference that should be taken into account while shaping these systems.

If a real unification of procedural regulations is impossible, unnecessary and undesirable, a harmonisation of procedural regulations may be possible, useful and desirable. Actually, one may reasonably believe that the differences existing among the various national systems of civil procedure, and even within some national systems, are too many and too deep, and that significant advantages could derive from a substantial reduction of these differences. If the European and extra-European landscape of procedures were to some extent simplified and clarified—one might say—judicial resolution of transnational disputes would become easier, less complicated, less expensive and much more efficient. Such considerations are very obvious and may be shared by anyone involved in the administration of civil justice. However, after having said that a fair degree of harmonisation among the national systems of civil procedure would be desirable, the problem arises of determining 'which' harmonisation and 'what' could and should be conceived and possibly implemented.

Harmonisation is clearly a matter of degree. Moreover, since we are thinking of extremely complex sets of rules, and the idea of unification is discarded, the other side of the coin is to decide which rules, or which procedural devices, should be harmonised. Finally, a further problem would concern the technique that should be used to implement such a harmonisation.

Thinking of a possible harmonisation of the current procedural systems in terms of degree, the two extremes of the scale could be immediately set aside. The top extreme would include a narrow set of extremely general principles, such as: independence of the judiciary, fair trial, right to be heard, reasonable delay and effective protection of rights. Such principles are very important but have become so obvious and so 'common sense' that they should be assumed as valid in each modern system of civil litigation. They may not be effectively implemented—and actually they are not—in every procedural system all around the world, but they are recognised without difficulty in any system of procedure. They are also expressly stated by several national constitutions and in Article 6 of the European Convention on Human Rights as well as in other international conventions. It does not mean that these principles are stated and interpreted in the same ways in every country, and some uncertainties may arise about which principles should be included and which may not be included in this short list. However, roughly speaking it may be said that there is a general agreement about a group of principles concerning the fundamental guarantees of the administration of justice in civil matters. At this level of generality, therefore, there is no problem for a future harmonisation: to a large extent, actually, such principles are already harmonised. A further problem may be one of building up a general consensus about which principles deserve to be included in the list, and also of fostering a uniform or at least a consistent interpretation of these principles by the various national courts (mainly at the level of constitutional review, but also in the application of procedural guarantees in ordinary jurisdictions). However, it may be said that a 'substantial' convergence, if not a complete harmonisation, already exists at the level of the fundamental guarantees of civil litigation.

At the bottom extreme of procedural regulations we find a broad and chaotic array of very specific and detailed rules concerning a number of procedural devices regulating the peculiar features of judicial practice in each national system. It is well known that all the procedural codes include several hundreds of rules, many of which include a number of subsections. Moreover, a huge number of additional technical norms are necessary for the functioning of the procedural machinery. Perhaps the harmonisation of some of these rules (for instance: how to serve the notice of complaint) may be useful, but when we think of harmonising procedural systems we cannot realistically believe that it should concern all the hundreds of technical rules regulating the functioning of the proceedings in all the jurisdictions involved. In other terms: at this level the problem of harmonisation cannot be raised in general terms, although harmonising 'some' technical mechanisms could be useful.

Between these two extremes of procedural regulations there is a broad intermediate area in which several degrees can be distinguished by taking into consideration differences and similarities concerning the subject matter, the importance, the form and the structure of procedural provisions. Somewhere in this area there is a level at which a possible and fruitful harmonisation might be achieved. Setting aside both extremely general and abstract principles and the analytically detailed provisions, one might think of a set of principles and rules that could be conceived with the aim of representing a reference point for different and perhaps more specific, particular regulations. It is the level where the so-called *Model Laws*, as for instance those drafted by the United Nations Commission on International Trade Law (UNCITRAL), can be placed. It is also the level to which sets of procedural rules actually in force, such as the American *Federal Rules of Civil Procedure* or the *Federal Rules of Evidence*, may belong. These sets of rules are specific enough not to be confused with abstract principles, but general enough not to include excessively detailed regulations of procedural devices. This is just the level at which a substantial harmonisation of procedural regulations may be imagined.

10.3 The ALI/UNIDROIT Text

An interesting example of procedural harmonisation at the intermediate level defined above is the set of principles and rules that were drafted and published by the *American Law Institute* (ALI) and by the *Institut international pour l'unification du droit privé* (UNIDROIT).[2] This text includes 31 Principles and 36 Rules;

[2] See ALI/UNIDROIT 2006.

each Principle and each Rule includes several subsections. The Principles are stated in rather general terms and cover a rather long and detailed list of procedural problems such as jurisdiction, the procedural equality of the parties, due notice, provisional and protective measures, the structure of the proceeding, the obligations of the parties and of the lawyers, the direction of the proceeding, evidence, the presentation of evidence, the roles of the parties and of the court, decision, settlement, enforcement, appeals and the recognition of judgments.

The Rules are somewhat more specific and detailed, although they are also stated in rather general terms, and provide an example of how the Principles could be implemented. The Rules deal with various topics including jurisdiction, joinder and venue, the composition of the court, the contents of the pleadings, the role and powers of the court, the law of evidence and disclosure and the presentation of evidence, the final hearing and decision-making, appeals and the enforcement of judgments. If taken together,[3] the Principles and Rules represent a consistent set of provisions that are much less general than abstract principles and much less detailed than a procedural code; however, they cover a rather broad number of procedural topics and for each of these topics they provide a model of regulation

It has to be underlined that the Principles and the Rules were not initially conceived and were not proposed as a model for the procedural regulation of domestic disputes. Actually, their declared purpose is narrower and more modest: the inspiring idea was of drafting a set of procedural rules that could be applied by national courts while trying and deciding transnational commercial disputes.[4] As a rule, and as mentioned above, domestic procedures are also applied by national courts when they deal with transnational disputes, and this is exactly the point that triggered the beginning of the ALI/UNIDROIT project: the variety of domestic procedures applied by national courts to transnational commercial disputes is provoking an incredible number of problems due to the practical impossibility of controlling proceedings occurring everywhere, and under different procedural systems, in the world of the globalised economy. Ideally, then, the Principles and Rules could be applied by *any national court all around the world* when a transnational commercial dispute has to be decided. To the extent that it may happen, the proceedings and the decisions concerning transnational commercial disputes could follow the same procedural pattern, on the basis of the application of the same standards. Of course the Principles and Rules should be connected and combined with the existing domestic procedures, since such procedures should remain applicable to all the subject matters not directly regulated by the Principles and Rules. However, they could create an interesting degree of uniformity in the

[3] The project initially sponsored by the *American Law Institute* was aimed at drafting a group of Rules, with Geoffrey C. Hazard and Michele Taruffo serving as co-reporters. When UNIDROIT joined the project, the project shifted to a drafting of Principles, which finally were approved by both of the sponsoring institutions. The Rules are then—so to say—a work product that may be referred only to the *American Law Institute*. However, the two texts are the outcomes of the same project and may be read as a homogeneous system of provisions.

[4] See Hazard 2006, xlvii.

proceedings concerning transnational disputes, since they could be able to overcome, at least to some extent, the diversity of national procedures. In such a sense, the adoption of the Principles and Rules (by means of international conventions or by adoption by national lawgivers) could be a powerful factor of harmonisation in the treatment of transnational disputes by different national jurisdictions.

Although the ALI/UNIDROIT Principles and Rules were drafted with specific and explicit reference to transnational commercial disputes, it seems clear that they might also be read and used beyond the original intent of their drafters. Actually, just by setting aside a few provisions specifically concerning the transnational and commercial character of the disputes to which they refer, most of the Principles and Rules may be read as a sort of *Model Law*, i.e. as a set of rules that could also be used as a frame of reference for procedural provisions concerning domestic disputes. Provisions concerning pleadings, provisional measures, settlements, the presentation of evidence, the role of the court in managing the proceeding, the form and contents of judgments, appeals, enforcement, and so forth, could be easily taken as 'models' for domestic regulations concerning several relevant aspects of civil litigation. Of course each national lawgiver could conceive more specific and detailed regulations of these topics, but different particular regulations could be 'harmonised' just by the fact of being partially different variations based upon the same *Leitmotiv*.

For instance, Principle 16.1 ensures the free access by any party to any relevant information and Principle 16.2 provides that the court should order the disclosure of any relevant evidence not disclosed voluntarily. National lawgivers could specify with much more detailed rules, in their domestic procedural codes, how these principles should be enacted and enforced, but such codes would be 'harmonised' by being referred, on this topic, to the same basic standards. Again: Rule 12.1 adopts the so-called 'fact pleading model' by requiring that the statement of claim 'must state the facts on which the claim is based' and 'describe the evidence to support those statements.' Any national code may specify such a rule by means of more precise norms, for instance by determining the consequences of the lack of specification of the facts and of the evidence, but national regulations would be 'harmonised' by the fact of adopting the same 'fact pleading' system.

The examples of this 'use' of the Principles and Rules could be in the dozens, but the fundamental idea seems to be rather clear. They represent, as previously stated, a consistent set of provisions covering the most important aspects of civil proceedings. This set is articulated but is not exceedingly detailed, and is stated in rather general but not vague and abstract terms. Moreover, it is internally consistent, in the sense that the drafters had a basic procedural model in mind: such a basic model emerges very clearly, for instance, from Principles 9 (Structure of the proceeding), 10 (Party initiative and scope of the proceeding), 14 (Court responsibility for direction of the proceeding), 16 (Access to information and evidence), 19 (Oral and written presentations), 22 (Responsibility for determinations of fact and law), 23 (Decision and reasoned explanation), 29 (Effective enforcement) and from many of the Rules.

If one imagines that some procedural codes are reformed by making reference to this set of provisions, the possible outcome would be a group of national codes, each including a lot of detailed and specific rules but all being based upon a sort of 'common core' that would be determined by the set of provisions that were used as 'models' in drafting the various domestic rules. Since the Principles and the Rules cover a rather wide range of procedural topics, this 'common core' could represent a powerful factor of harmonisation of national procedural codes.

10.4 Problems of Harmonisation

The ALI/UNIDROIT Principles and Rules have been drafted following the principal idea of imagining a set of procedural rules that could eventually be applied all around the world, wherever a transnational commercial dispute has to be tried and decided. Actually, the final text is the outcome of a complex scientific enterprise that lasted several years with the cooperation of dozens of experts from a variety of countries, including several European countries but also China, Japan, Brazil, Argentina, and the United States among others. The experience of drafting several versions of the text, and discussing them in a number of meetings in various countries and with many experts, has been extremely significant[5]: on the one hand, each participant offered the results of his or her own specific experience from the perspective of his or her own legal and general culture; on the other hand, however, it was relatively easy to find a common language and to understand each other, overcoming the differences determined by one's own origins. Cultural differences were present and relevant at every step of the discussions and of the re-drafting, but such differences did not prevent the participants from finding a widely shared conceptual and cultural basis: such a basis allowed a fruitful effort realistically oriented to the aim of designing a set of principles and rules that could be generally approved. This did not mean setting aside cultural differences. Rather, it meant that cultural differences were not perceived as impossible hurdles in the attempt to imagine viable solutions for a number of relevant procedural problems. The ALI/UNIDROIT text received positive reception in several countries as a possible point of reference for reforms of national procedural systems. In this perspective one could infer that this text could well be used as a model in order to achieve a significant degree of harmonisation of the various procedural regulations existing in many countries. There are good reasons to believe this, mainly considering that the text has a fair degree of generality/specificity, and thus it could allow a reasonable amount of harmonisation without imposing an impossible uniformity on such diverse regulations.

---

[5] About the way in which the project was performed, see Introduction, in ALI/UNIDROIT 2006, 3, 12.

However, some further problems should be taken into due consideration. Some ALI/UNIDROIT principles are commonly acknowledged, and upon these principles it would be possible to reach a general agreement and—therefore—a rather high degree of harmonisation. For instance, Principle 1.1 says that 'the court and the judges should have judicial independence … including freedom from improper internal and external influence,' and Principle 1.3 says that 'the court should be impartial.' There is no doubt that the principles of independence and impartiality of the court are generally acknowledged by all systems. In a similar way, all systems acknowledge the principle of the procedural equality of parties (stated in Principle 3.1), the principles of due notice and right to be heard (stated in Principles 5.1, 5.3 and 5.4), the principle that a proceeding may be started only by a party and not *ex officio* (stated in Principle 10.1), the principle of good faith (stated in Principle 11.1) and several other principles that are included in the ALI/UNIDROIT Principles.

The same may be said about several Rules that are also included in the ALI/UNIDROIT text. However, a general agreement upon these principles and rules may be easily reached provided they are taken in a very general form, but the agreement may be very difficult to reach if they are taken literally in the specific terms in which they are stated in the ALI/UNIDROIT text. Actually, in order to use this text as a model law for procedural reforms, several national systems should introduce relevant changes in their own current procedural regulations. Taking again the example of the principles of independence and impartiality of courts and judges: the other statements included in Principle 1 are detailed enough to require a specific implementation that may not be easy in some systems. In a similar way, the other statements included in Principle 3 are also specific enough to require significant adaptations in several existing systems. The same may be said about the other statements included in Principle 5, in Principle 10 and in Principle 11. So far, however, the problem may be one of enacting specific uniform rules according to the model provided by the ALI/UNIDROIT text, but on the basis of a general consensus on the fundamental core of those principles.

But in this text there are some Principles that in order to be implemented would require structural changes at least in some of the existing procedural systems. Two examples may illustrate this point adequately. The first example is Principle 13, in which the so-called '*amicus curiae* brief' is admitted. Here the problem is that the '*amicus curiae* brief' is well known in common law jurisdictions, and particularly in the United States, but it is not allowed in most civil law jurisdictions. Introducing the 'brief' would certainly lead to a significant improvement in many procedural systems, but it would probably raise a lot of objections and difficulties. The second example is even more important and is offered by a group of statements included in the ten subsections of Principle 9 concerning the structure of the proceeding. The structure of the proceeding that is defined by Principle 9 corresponds to a specific and clear model of proceeding based upon three phases: a pleading phase, an interim phase and a final phase. In particular, subsections 9.3.1 to 9.3.6 include a rather detailed regulation on the interim phase of the proceeding. Here the problem is that while such a procedural model corresponds rather well to the structure of some proceedings existing in Europe, as for instance in Germany and in Spain, the structure of other systems—in Europe and elsewhere—is not based upon the same general model. Adopting the ALI/UNIDROIT Principles would mean, for such systems, not only introducing adaptations of their specific provisions but also adopting a different system of litigation. Similar remarks could be made about several other Principles that cannot be taken into specific consideration here.

A fortiori, such remarks may be made about most of the Rules included in the ALI/UNIDROIT text. The Rules are more specific than the Principles, and to adopt many of them would require relevant structural changes in the current regulation of civil proceedings in several countries. A significant example is offered by the Rules concerning the role of the court in the presentation of evidence (Rule 28.3.1) or the technique for the examination of witnesses (Rule 29.4). Other examples are offered by Rule 22 with its ten subsections concerning evidence, by Rule 21 concerning the disclosure of evidence and by the eleven subsections of Rule 18 about case management.

10.5 An Open Conclusion

Some conclusions may be drawn from the above remarks. A point that should be clear enough is that a complete unification of procedural regulations on a worldwide level would be impossible, unnecessary and—at any rate—culturally undesirable. Another clear point, however, is that a significant degree of harmonisation among such procedural regulations may be possible, useful and culturally acceptable. A third point is that this kind of harmonisation could possibly be achieved at an 'intermediate' degree, that is, by adopting—in each national system—provisions that should be similar enough to reduce the differences at least to some extent, but general and flexible enough to allow each national system to maintain a relevant amount of its own specific peculiarities. In this perspective a tension may emerge between the trends that are in favour of harmonising the various systems of litigation and the cultural and historical factors that determined the characters of each national system and still explain the current existence of different models of litigation, as well as of different specific procedural provisions.

In such a situation, the ALI/UNIDROIT text could probably be used as a viable and acceptable frame of reference for changes that could be introduced into all the existing procedural systems with the aim of achieving a relevant degree of harmonisation, still leaving enough room for national peculiarities and for specific procedural rules. Actually, this text seems to be at the right level of generality/specificity that makes a partial harmonisation possible without requiring a complete unification and covers a number of relevant procedural issues, although it is far from providing the basis for the drafting of a full-fledged Code of Civil Procedure. Moreover, such a text sounds substantially acceptable in several areas of the world, notwithstanding the different legal, political and general cultures existing in some of these areas.

Referring to the ALI/UNIDROIT Principles and Rules may be a good starting point (*rectius*: the only starting point available so far) for a harmonisation of the systems of civil litigation, but they cannot be taken as a sort of ready-made panacea for all the problems concerning the administration of justice in Europe and all around the world. After all, they were not originally conceived and drafted as a model law to be used for the reform of domestic systems of procedure, but only as a set of rules possibly applicable in transnational commercial litigation.

At least three groups of problems would arise in the perspective of using the ALI/UNIDROIT text as a frame of reference for a harmonisation of national systems of procedure:

1. The text does not deal with the plurality and the fragmentation of 'special' proceedings existing in several systems. Therefore, the text may well be used for the harmonisation of different national 'ordinary' proceedings. It could also be used as a reference for an 'internal' harmonisation of particular systems, that is, with the aim of reducing the number and the variety of special proceedings. However, this is a further issue that involves policy choices about whether such a variety should or should not be maintained. It seems clear that the harmonisation of several national systems could be achieved at a higher level if those systems were based on one general procedural model with just a few exceptions;
2. Even when accepted as a basis of harmonisation, the ALI/UNIDROIT provisions should be 'translated' and inserted into the much broader sets of procedural norms represented by the codes of civil procedure existing in each specific country. This may require an extremely complicated and sophisticated work of transcultural adaptation of the same basic set of provisions to different systems of procedural rules, and a no less difficult and sophisticated work of making different sets of provisions globally consistent with each other;
3. However, the problem is not only one of adapting the existing procedural regulations by 'transplanting' into them a group of widely accepted provisions. The problem is also that the ALI/UNIDROIT text includes a model of proceedings in a set of Principles and Rules that does not coincide with any already existing procedural system. Some of these provisions may be considered similar to some provisions existing in some systems, while others may be similar to provisions existing in another system, and many provisions do not correspond to any provision already existing in any system. This means that a national lawgiver may be inclined to accept only the parts of the text that sound more familiar in his or her own culture and tradition, but will be inclined to reject the parts that are, or sound, strange and 'foreign' if compared with the domestic regulation. Such reactions would lead to a misunderstanding and to a substantial opposition to any attempt to achieve even a partial harmonisation of the existing forms of civil litigation.

Actually, this is the core of the problem: harmonising the systems of litigation is not going to be a matter of adjusting details; it is going to be a matter of deep changes and structural reforms in many of the current national systems. Probably the moment has come and the way is open for such an undertaking, but it will probably be a long and difficult enterprise.

References

ALI/UNIDROIT (2006) Principles of transnational civil procedure. Cambridge University Press, Cambridge

Hazard G (2006) A Drafter's reflections on the principles of transnational civil procedure. In ALI/UNIDROIT. Principles of transnational civil procedure. Cambridge University Press, Cambridge

Storme M (ed) (1994) Rapprochement du droit judiciaire de l'Union européenne/Approximation of judiciary law in the European Union. Martinus Nijhoff, Dordrecht

Part III
National Approaches to Globalisation and Harmonisation

Chapter 11
United States: Harmonisation and Voluntarism. The Role of Elites in Creating an Influential National Model, the Federal Rules of Civil Procedure

Paul R. Dubinsky

Abstract The starting place for any discussion of civil procedure in the United States is the Federal Rules of Civil Procedure ('FRCP'), rules first enacted in 1938 and made applicable solely to federal courts. Even though the adoption of these rules by state courts and state legislatures has never been mandatory, nonetheless the FRCP have to a great extent served as a highly influential model impacting the development of procedural law in all 50 states. Why is this so? Why did voluntary processes succeed in bringing about the harmonisation of procedural law in the U.S.? In part the answer is that the movement that produced the FRCP was not primarily an effort to bring about harmonisation; it was as much an effort at reform. In part the answer is that from the perspective of greater access to justice and greater likelihood of justice on the merits, the FRCP were an improvement over existing state law and practice. But neither of these two explanations is a complete answer. This chapter focuses on the powerful role of emerging elites that stood much to gain from the creation of a federal law of civil procedure and from its dissemination to state systems throughout the country. Three groups in particular gained much in stature: elite law schools, the emerging class of law firms seeking to practice law on a multistate basis, and federal judges. Based on the American experience, the insight potentially useful in evaluating other harmonisation movements, especially in the EU, is that harmonisation is most likely to go forward when determined and resourceful interest groups can identify clear gains to themselves from such a process.

Associate Professor of Law and Director of Graduate Studies, Wayne State University.

P. R. Dubinsky (✉)
Wayne State University, Detroit, MI, USA
e-mail: pauldubinsky@wayne.edu

X. E. Kramer and C. H. van Rhee (eds.), *Civil Litigation in a Globalising World*,
DOI: 10.1007/978-90-6704-817-0_11,

Contents

11.1 Introduction

The judicial system in the United States consists of two main components: the federal courts and the courts of the component states of the Union. The former, created by act of Congress in 1789,[1] possess limited jurisdiction and conduct their business with funds from the federal treasury.[2] The latter are creatures of state law, funded by state treasuries, and possessed of jurisdiction that is general. In the complex interaction between these court systems over a period of more than two centuries, one date stands out. That date is 1938. In that year the Federal Rules of Civil Procedure (FRCP) entered into force.[3] Before 1938, there was great variation in the procedural law applied by courts across the country. That variation reflected major differences in the histories, economies, geographies, and demographics of the many states that joined the Union at different times and for different reasons. The immediate impact of the FRCP was to bring uniformity to procedural law in

[1] The establishment of the lower federal courts (courts inferior to the U.S. Supreme Court) was accomplished by the Judiciary Act of 1789. Since then, Congress from time to time has altered the structure of the federal judiciary and created new, specialised federal courts, such as the U.S. Tax Court, which was created by statute in 1942.

[2] The jurisdiction of federal courts over cases and litigants is limited in the sense that these courts can adjudicate matters only when Congress has authorised them to do so and, further, only when that congressional action is consistent with the jurisdictional limitations in Article III of the Federal Constitution.

[3] The year 1938 is also the date of the U.S. Supreme Court's landmark decision in *Erie Railroad v. Tomkins*, 304 U.S. 64 (1938). *Erie* held that in cases arising under state common law but adjudicated in federal court, the court must apply the substantive law of the state in which it is geographically located. For federal courts sitting in such cases, *Erie* combines with the FRCP to create a regime in which there is uniformity in the application of procedural law but often major differences in the substantive result reached in one federal court as opposed to another.

one set of American courts, the federal courts. Since 1938, every federal district court in the U.S. has been required as a matter of federal law to apply the same basic set of rules in adjudicating civil actions.[4] The impact of the FRCP, however, has not been confined to this one set of tribunals. Soon after 1938, the influence of the FRCP spread beyond the federal judiciary. One state-court system after another adopted substantial parts of the new federal regime. By the 1950s, one could refer with accuracy on the international stage to an 'American approach' to civil justice[5]—a collection of practices, values, and assumptions common to all courts in the United States (federal and state), with minor differences in detail.

The goals of this Chapter are, first, to explain how the U.S. procedural landscape went from disorder to one basic approach in a matter of a few decades. Next it takes up some related questions: Why did harmonisation come about? How was this transformation engineered in the midst of a legal and political culture that always has been suspicious of federal meddling with state institutions, especially state courts? How was so significant a set of changes brought about in so many state court systems, even in the absence of federal legislation mandating this result?

It turns out that these questions do not convincingly lend themselves to one answer. The movement that began in the early 1900s and resulted in the FRCP was propelled forward by more than one engine. To be sure, many lawyers at the time understood the project as an exercise in harmonisation. But for others, it was primarily an effort at procedural reform,[6] and for still others, the main goal was elevating the stature and effectiveness of federal courts by freeing them from subservience to state procedural law. A large literature exists on each of these perspectives on the federal rules project. The present work will not re-plough familiar ground. The focus here is limited to the role that specific interest groups played in the transformation in American procedural law from the 1920s to the 1950s. Of particular interest are the motivations that led these interest groups to support this endeavour and the benefits that accrued to them as a result. Finally, the main point is to distil from this inquiry insights that may be useful in predicting

---

[4] The most recent two decades, however, has witnessed a proliferation of 'local rules' promulgated by the courts of specific federal districts. These rules do not void or qualify the FRCP. Typically they add detail and specificity. For example, a local rule might require that the parties engage in mediation before proceeding to trial, even though the FRCP contain no such requirement. Most importantly, for present purposes, local rules differ substantially from one federal district to another. See Carrington 1996.

[5] The U.S. became a member of the Hague Conference on Private International Law in 1964 even though that organisation came into existence much earlier, in 1893. See http://www.hcch.net/index_en.php?act=states.details&sid=76 (last consulted at 5 June 2011). The relatively late date of U.S. entry into the organisation is explained in large part by the common understanding in the U.S. until the World War II era that the federal government might lack authority to compel changes in state law with respect to civil procedure and conflict of laws. See Dubinsky 2008, 301, 309–17. Some regard U.S. participation in international treaty making as a means of overcoming these constitutional and political constraints. See Clermont 1999.

[6] See, e.g., Mitchell 1949; Rosenberg 1989, 2197–98; Weinstein 1989.

which coalitions and which harmonisation efforts in other societies are likely to succeed.

Three groups of lawyers in particular were at the centre of what might be called the civil procedure revolution in the United States. These groups were: elite university-affiliated law schools and the scholars on their faculties; America's emerging class of national law firms in search of lucrative opportunities to manage litigation on a nationwide basis, and judges on the federal bench, who in applying the new FRCP had opportunities to write seminal opinions on procedural law.

Although it is always risky business to study the experiences of one society for the purpose of making recommendations regarding another, the Chapter concludes with some insights into the enterprise of global procedural harmonisation based on the American experience. These insights relate to a subject often overlooked in the existing literature—the relationship between harmonisation, legal education, and the maturation of the American legal profession during a formative period.

11.2 Harmonisation and Voluntarism

Voluntary adoption of model instruments has been the dominant mechanism for the harmonisation of procedural law in the U.S. Few in number are the instruments of federal law (statutes, treaties, regulations) that operate directly on state courts and bring about uniformity or harmonisation by compulsion. The absence of compulsory instruments at the federal level is a product of constitutional tradition[7] and political pragmatism; among the quickest ways to losing political power in the United States is to advocate an expanded role for federal authority at the expense of state and local governance.[8]

In the absence of federal legislation that is binding on state court systems, harmonisation in the field of civil procedure moves forward by a different means: the promulgation of an influential federal model followed by voluntary adoption of

[7] By longstanding constitutional understanding, each of the component states of the U.S. possesses a core of sovereignty that is highly resistant to the effects of federal lawmaking.

[8] Of course, the extent to which this conventional wisdom has proven true varies from one historical period to another. Two exceptions in particular warrant mention. Acting pursuant to the treaty power, the federal government ratified the Hague Service Convention and the Hague Evidence Convention. Both treaties have some impact on procedural practice in state courts, though the impact has been minimised by case law suggesting that litigants in U.S. courts—state or federal—rarely are required to make use of those treaties. See *Société Nationale Industrielle Aérospatiale v. US District Court*, 482 U.S. 522 (1987) (rejecting interpretation of Hague Evidence Convention requiring 'first resort' to the treaty by U.S. litigants seeking access to evidence located outside the U.S.); *Volkswagenwerk AG v. Schlunk*, 486 U.S. 694 (1988) (holding that Hague Service Convention is not the exclusive method of service of process on a foreign corporation with a wholly-owned subsidiary located in the U.S.).

substantial parts of that model by the country's component states.[9] Admittedly, such an engine can yield unpredictable results; only rarely are state authorities under an obligation to act in sync with sister states or with the federal judiciary in civil procedure.[10] Despite the foregoing, there exists today much similarity in the rules of civil procedure throughout the United States. A civil jury trial in state court in Iowa is much like one in federal court in Florida. Joinder of parties and consolidation of claims is common in all judicial systems in the U.S. The right of litigants to pursue pre-trial discovery of documents and testimony (even from non-parties) is extensive everywhere in the U.S., at least when compared to evidence gathering in other countries. The approach to the financing of litigation—contingency fee agreements, presumptions against shifting attorneys' fees, very little public funding—varies only marginally as one moves from one state to another. Thus the State-to-State and State-Federal similarity in procedure that took hold after 1938 is quite substantial.

Before examining in detail the forces that have brought about this similarity, it is worthwhile to pause briefly to appreciate the magnitude of the harmonisation that has been was accomplished. The United States is a large and diverse country. Geography and history vary tremendously from region to region and from State to State. In sparsely populated Montana, simply travelling to court can mean traversing long distances in harsh weather conditions. In Rhode Island, no part of the state is further than 100 kilometres from any other part. The economy of Delaware is dominated by being the place of incorporation of many of America's largest corporations. The economy of Hawaii is dominated by tourism. The economy of California is extraordinarily diverse. Before entering the Union, many states had common-law legal systems that could be traced to Great Britain. For other States, the British influence was modest. Some States were once independent republics. Others entered the Union as conquered territories. The ethnic and racial mix of the population in Florida bears little resemblance to that in Alaska. The copyright and trademark litigation that is common in California is rare in South Dakota.[11]

---

[9] By comparison, there is no well-developed federal model for choice-of-law rules. The resulting absence has led to a kind of 'anarchy.' See Symeonides 1997, 1248. A look today at state and federal statutory and case law in the area of choice of law reveals much disagreement from one jurisdiction to another and much unpredictability within individual jurisdictions. See Symeonides 2006 (describing the intellectual movement that uprooted the traditional foundations of conflict of laws in the U.S. and ushered in several different policy-based, multi-factored approaches).

[10] This statement comes with some important caveats. The federal constitution imposes some minimum standards in terms of the process owed to litigants. These constitutional minimum standards trump inconsistent state law. See US Const, Amend. 14 (no 'State [shall] deprive any person of life, liberty, or property, without due process of law; nor deny to any person within its jurisdiction the equal protection of the laws'). In a few situations, the Federal Constitution requires that state courts must defer to one another or cooperate with one another. See, e.g., US Const, Article IV, s. 1 ('Full faith and credit shall be given in each state to the public acts, records, and judicial proceedings of every other state').

[11] There are large differences from one region of the U.S. to another in terms of the industries that predominate. The nature of civil disputes in different regions of the country can be quite

The proportion of foreign litigants appearing in court in New York greatly exceeds that in Kansas.

Pointing out such differences serves to make intelligible something that foreign observers may find elusive: The extraordinary thing about civil procedure in the United States is not that there are differences in procedural law from one state system to another. The extraordinary thing is that there is so much Federal-State and State-to-State similarity. The extent of harmonisation that has taken place is so large that a lawyer from Massachusetts can relocate to Utah and, within a short period of time, be adept at representing clients in Utah courts. It will not be difficult for such a person to master the relatively minor differences between the procedural rules in Utah and those in Massachusetts or those in the federal system. There will be little if any subtle disadvantage or discrimination against the transplanted attorney by virtue of dialect, education, or legal culture.

For similar reasons, the in-house legal department of a Delaware corporation is fully able to supervise the company's litigation on a nationwide basis. It can do so by retaining a number of regional or local law firms that will appear in court and sign pleadings under the coordination of the client's legal department. In the case of companies that repeatedly find themselves in litigation, for example insurance companies, it is not unusual for the in-house legal department to do a large portion of the drafting and legal research required by a given case. Typically, over time, the company will have filed dispositive motions and discovery requests in many cases. A set of discovery documents used in a case in North Carolina can be revised in a minor way and then used in a different case that is pending in Nevada. Minor differences in procedural laws of these two jurisdictions likely will not pose an obstacle to doing much of the work of litigation through a centralised process that promotes cost-saving and consistency in the legal positions taken by the client nationwide. In many cases, the role played by local counsel is quite minor.[12] In contrast, the role of large multistate law firms can be quite large, at least for clients that choose to have small internal legal departments and rely on one or more large law firms to coordinate litigation across the country.[13]

(Footnote 11 continued)
different in terms of the demands made on judicial resources, the importance of preliminary relief, the relative importance of common-law development as opposed to statutes, and so forth. It is difficult to think of another country with so varied and regionalised an economy, one yielding such large differences in the types and volume of litigation before local courts in different parts of the country.

[12] This would not be true in the small percentage of cases that proceed to jury trial. Only a small proportion of lawyers in the U.S. have extensive experience in conducting civil jury trials, and the ability to perform well in a jury trial in federal court in Chicago does not necessarily translate to the ability to win a jury trial in state court in rural Arkansas. For the small percentage of high value cases that go to juries for resolution, the skills and judgment of the local lawyer selected to try the case are invaluable. Few lawyers with such a mix of skills and experience are found in the in-house legal department of a major corporation.

[13] State-to-State differences in procedural law sometimes, however, can be pronounced and outcome determinative. For example, states differ from one another and from the federal system

11.3 Model Creation

Because compulsory processes play very little role in the harmonisation of procedural law in the U.S., it pays to be clear at the outset about what is meant by voluntary pathways to harmonisation. Specifically, voluntary harmonisation as practiced in the U.S. usually consists of four distinct processes: model-creation, competition, voluntary adoption, and experimentation.

Model-creation: This refers to the process of investing substantial resources and research in creating a set of procedural rules of limited application. That is, the legal act bringing the model rules into being imposes those rules in a limited number of forums or with respect to a limited number of cases. Lack of constitutional authority or political will prevents the legislature from mandating application of the rules across the board.

Competition: The component States in the U.S. compete with one another as forums for dispute resolution. One engine of this competition is concurrent jurisdiction—instances in which more than one court possesses authority to adjudicate the same or substantially the same matter. Under these circumstances, litigants have a choice of forum and can be expected to exercise that choice to their advantage.[14] If there is a widespread perception that procedural rules in Michigan, for example, are antiquated or unpredictably idiosyncratic, then litigants, especially repeat litigants, may seek to avoid Michigan state courts.[15] Indeed, their aversion to Michigan procedure may result in avoiding Michigan in other ways: steering clear of Michigan's substantive law, avoiding transactions connected to Michigan, including those that would result in capital investment in Michigan or job creation in Michigan.[16]

(Footnote 13 continued)
in terms of the ease or difficulty of obtaining class certification, a prerequisite to proceeding with group litigation. But such differences rarely are so pronounced or unexpected as to present a barrier to a large organization's ability to monitor and coordinate litigation on a nationwide basis for purposes of consistency and cost efficiency.

14 This extensive choice of forum results from the expansive U.S. approach to adjudicative jurisdiction. A defendant may be sued in the State of its incorporation or the State where it maintains its principal place of business or in any state with which it maintains 'continuous and systematic contacts' or in any state for which there exists 'minimum contacts' among the defendant, the forum, and the acts or omissions giving rise to the claim. Thus concurrent jurisdiction among multiple courts typically exists to a greater extent in the US than in other countries. Concurrent jurisdiction also results from the existence of two largely parallel court systems existing within every state: the state court system and the federal courts located within the same state. It is often the case that the parties can bring their case to either the state courts of Alabama, for example, or the federal courts located in Alabama.

15 They might seek to do so, for example, through choice-of-forum clauses, *forum non conveniens* motions, or arbitration agreements.

16 Of course, attracting litigation has its ups and downs. Suits with little connection to Michigan can take an unjustified toll on the state's budget or cause delays for all cases in the system. On the other hand, litigation can be regarded as a revenue-generating activity. The New York legislature came to the latter conclusion when it adopted a statute directing New York courts not to apply the

Voluntary adoption: Competition can accentuate the influence of a model law. Absent competition, a court or legislature re-examining the State's procedural laws might regard the main inquiry to be whether the model is an improvement over existing law and whether the proposed model is superior to the alternatives. In the presence of competition, however, a decision maker will broaden the inquiry: will the state suffer disadvantage if its courts are out of step with those of other states or with those of the federal government?

Experimentation: By adopting a model, a State does not commit itself to march lockstep with other states indefinitely. In a federal system operating under a 'laboratories-of- democracy' culture,[17] grassroots reform is always nipping at the heels of uniformity. Changes in technology can render established procedures anachronistic. A political community's expectations of its justice system may change.[18] States may respond to these changes differently. The threat of competition may curb a particular community's inclination to depart from the status quo, but then again it may not. Instead, experimentation may lead to the creation of a new model that, through competition, may lead to a new harmonized equilibrium.[19]

From the 1920s to the 1950s, the combination of these processes produced substantial harmonisation of the law of civil procedure across the U.S. Despite subsequent periods of experimentation, a substantial degree of unity has held. At the beginning of this period, States differed markedly from one another. In terms of pleadings, for instance, state laws varied from rigid common-law pleading, to code pleading,[20] to something resembling notice pleading.[21] States also differed from one another in their treatment of claims sounding in equity, with some having merged law and equity and some having maintained a separation of law and equity. In terms of pre-trial practice, some state systems had broadened

(Footnote 16 continued)
doctrine of *forum non conveniens* to dismiss high-dollar litigation filed in New York pursuit to New York choice-of-forum and choice-of–law clauses. See New York Gen. Oblig. Law section 5-1402.

[17] The phrase belongs to Justice Louis Brandeis. See *New State Ice Co. v Liebmann*, 285 US 262, 311 (1932) (Brandeis, J., dissenting). The phrase has been quoted countless times and has come to stand for the proposition that one strength of federal systems is that reform and change can proceed in a bottom-up rather than a top-down manner.

[18] See Dubinsky 2004, 1152, 1171–74 (examining the growth in expectations in the 1990s that litigation in US courts could have a positive impact on the protection of human rights in other countries); Chayes 1976, 1281 (demonstrating a major shift in expectations in the US regarding the remedial powers of courts and the elaboration of public values through civil litigation).

[19] Consider, for instance, those state court systems in the US that were in the vanguard of phasing out paper and ushering in electronic storage and transmission; e.g., electronic filing, electronic signatures on pleadings, electronic discovery. Those states broke with the communal status quo but in doing so became attractive to certain categories of litigants.

[20] See Subrin 1988, 327–38 (describing the key features of the Field codes introduced in the latter half of the 19th century).

[21] See Oakley and Coon 1986, 1367.

pre-trial access to information beyond what was typical of common law courts in England. In other States, litigation was still geared toward resolution by jury trial, with significant potential for surprise evidence at trial. More generally, these detailed variations were a reflection of a wider divide, a divide between procedural systems that leaned toward procedural justice and those that leaned in the direction of affording litigants a resolution on the merits. The former tended to include many procedural traps for the unwary, rigidity in the application of rules, and avenues for a skilful lawyer to prevail over a less skilful one. The latter tended to incorporate the influence of populism, a desire for simplicity, and what some might label an inclination toward rough justice.[22]

11.4 From the Conformity Act to the Federal Rules of Civil Procedure

The differences in state procedural laws described above yielded two types of variation. The first was a variation from one state court system to another. The second was a difference in procedure from one federal court to another. The latter consequence resulted from an 1872 federal statute, the Conformity Act,[23] which until 1938 mandated that federal trial courts follow the procedural rules in effect in state courts in the state in which the federal court was located. So, for example, prior to the entry into force of the FRCP, a federal district court located in Montana looked to the Montana Code of Civil Procedure for rules on pleading. It also turned for guidance to the case law of the Montana state courts on how to interpret the state rules. What it did not routinely consult were cases decided by federal courts in other parts of the country. Although these were sister courts when it came to interpreting federal statutes, the rulings of such courts on procedural law were of little value because, under the Conformity Act, other federal courts applied a different set of procedural rules.[24] Under these circumstances, it was not unusual for two cases very similar on the facts to turn out differently based on differences

[22] See Subrin 1988, 311, 319 ('The American nineteenth-century codification movement was rooted in part in lay dissatisfaction with the complexity and technicality of law and antagonism to the legal profession.').

[23] This result was dictated by the Conformity Act of 1872, 17 Stat. 196 (1872), under which the 'pleadings, and forms and modes of proceeding' in federal district court were to conform to those 'existing at the time in like causes in the courts of record of the State within which such circuit or district courts' are located. This result did not apply to actions in equity or admiralty nor did the 'modes of proceeding' encompass state rules of evidence.

[24] An important exception was admiralty cases. Federal courts applied the federal procedural law governing actions in admiralty and maritime law. For reasons beyond the scope of the present work, admiralty and maritime matters are singled out in the Constitution, and disputes in these areas have always been regarded as implicating uniquely federal interests in ways that other civil matters do not.

in procedural law applied by two different federal courts, even if the claim arose under the same substantive federal law.

The impact of this absence of a federal code of civil procedure at this time was visible not only in case reports. Also impacted was the organization of the American legal profession. In the era of the Conformity Act, it was all but impossible for an individual lawyer to appear before courts in more than one state.[25] The risk of losing a case through ignorance of an idiosyncratic rule in an unfamiliar forum was substantial. It was even rare for a partnership of lawyers to expand across state boundaries. The size of law firms was small. Not until the 20th century were individual law firms regularly retained to handle a large percentage of the legal work of one of America's large corporations.[26]

Efforts were launched at the end of the 19th century to bring some unity to procedural law across the country. These efforts took two forms. The first involved reforming existing state procedural laws and harmonizing differences among them. The second project was creating a single set of rules applicable in all federal courts. The latter proved to be the route to success.

11.5 The FRCP and Interest Groups

Enactment of the FRCP and the spread of its influence on state courts owed much to the persistent efforts of three groups of lawyers: attorneys at law firms at the vanguard of multistate legal practice, law professors at a small group of university-affiliated law schools on the verge of elevating those institutions above the rest, and judges on the federal bench. Each group had much to gain from replacing a chaotic patchwork of state approaches with a more unified national framework.

11.5.1 The Transformation of American Legal Education and the Emergence of Elite Law Schools

During the period in which civil procedure was being transformed from a series of local and idiosyncratic practices to a field of law in the contemporary sense, a second transformation was also under way. This second transformation concerned key aspects of legal education: the content of what a future lawyer needs to study,

---

[25] Partly this was due to restrictive bar admission rules. Some of that restrictiveness may have been justified because differences in law and practice from one state court system to another were large.

[26] See Earle 1963, 155–85 (describing the growth of Shearman and Sterling in the 1910s); Swaine 1946 (summarizing law firm's early work for U.S. Steel Corp., International Harvester, Pennsylvania Railroad and other industrial giants).

the setting in which teaching takes place, and the relationship between law teaching and other activities, such as legal scholarship and law reform.

When serious proposals were first floated to address the chaotic state of civil procedure in the United States, it was apparent to some in legal academia that opportunities would be forthcoming for civil procedure scholars to participate in the process. Some individuals and institutions were better positioned to take advantage of this opportunity than were others. Those best positioned were scholars at university-affiliated law schools that already had begun the process of thinking of law and the legal profession in national terms. As early as the turn of the 20th century, a few law schools had embarked on this process by attracting students from all parts of the country, by teaching a curriculum centred on national trends[27] and emerging areas of federal law, and by encouraging faculty members to pursue scholarship of national significance.

11.5.2 The Emergence of an Educational Hierarchy

The most familiar aspects of contemporary legal education in the U.S. have been in place for approximately 50 years.[28] These include the expectation that the faculty will be made up predominantly of scholars and not practitioners, that the curriculum will be taught with reference to national trends rather than local law, and that the method of instruction will be analytical and not purely descriptive. Another familiar aspect of contemporary legal education is stratification. Some institutions are regarded as more prestigious and influential than others. A disproportionate share of the most influential scholarship is produced by the faculties of a relatively small number of elite law schools.[29] The graduates of these same schools go on to fill an extraordinarily disproportionate share of the available law teaching positions across the country. These same law schools also tend to be well off financially, and they enjoy great success in attracting bright students from all parts of the country. After graduation, these individuals claim a disproportionate share of the country's best legal jobs.

[27] For example, by instructing students on developments in contract law in state courts across the country rather than by focusing only on cases decided in the local jurisdiction.

[28] This is not to say that legal education has been static. Among the more important developments since the 1950s: movement away from strict Socratic teaching, widespread adoption of some form of clinical education, internationalization of the curriculum, proliferation of co-curricular activities, and receptivity to interdisciplinary work.

[29] See Shapiro 2009.

11.6 Legal Education a Century Ago

The landscape of legal education was quite different in the 19th century. There was no clear hierarchy and little uniformity. Some institutions of higher education were well known, but even these had faculties too small to exert substantial impact on the law or on American society. Referring to the period before Christopher Columbus Langdell initiated a new method of instruction that transformed the law school classroom, Oliver Wendell Holmes, Jr. described his education at Harvard Law School in the 1860s as essentially a waste of time.[30]

In the late 1800s it was not clear that the future of legal education in the United States lay with private university-affiliated law schools. These institutions faced competition. Many judges and prominent lawyers had entered the profession through apprenticeship.[31] Others had attended some courses informally only to move on without earning a degree.[32] By the turn of the century, additional paths to a legal career opened up. Independent law schools increased in number to fill the country's need for more lawyers and to offer a path into the profession for those without a college degree.[33] State-supported universities offered a state-specific legal education under a faculty of former practitioners less concerned with scholarship than with teaching, administration, and the activities of the state and local bars.[34]

---

[30] Holmes 1870, 177 ('So long as the possession of a degree signified nothing except a residence for a certain period in Cambridge or Boston, it was without value. The lapse of time insured its acquisition. Just as a certain number of dinners entitled a man in England to a call to the bar, so a certain number of months in Cambridge entitled him to the degree of Bachelor of Laws.'). Though the foregoing was from a note that was unsigned at the time of publication, it was later identified as being authored by Holmes. See White 1993, 197–198.

[31] See Chroust 1965, 173–76; White 1976 (among the highly influential judges of the late 19th century who learned the law by serving as apprentices were Thomas Cooley and John Marshall Harlan I).

[32] Roscoe Pound belongs in this category. Pound studied for one year at Harvard Law School before returning to Nebraska and sitting for the bar. After some years in private practice, Pound returned to Harvard, became dean and one of the most influential public intellectuals of his day. See Tidmarsh 2006, 513.

[33] In contrast, in 1875 Harvard began requiring as a condition of admission that applicants possess either an undergraduate degree or command of Latin. See Urofsky 2009, 26–27. Independent law schools typically drew their primarily part-time faculty mainly from the local bar. Their library collections were small, practical, and local in focus.

[34] One measure of the fluidity of entry into the legal profession in the 19th and early 20th centuries can be gathered from the biographies of justices of the United States Supreme Court. In the year 1911, among the justices were one who had studied law in his father's law office, two who had started law school but had not completed their studies, and six who had attended six different law schools, some of which were affiliated with universities and some of which were not. Just one, Charles Evans Hughes, had devoted part of his career, two years, to academia. By comparison, all nine of today's Supreme Court justices attended either Harvard Law School or Yale Law School. Among the justices are four (Breyer, Ginsburg, Kagan, and Scalia) who spent a substantial part of their careers as law professors.

So, in the early decades of the 20th century, a thin tier of law schools (Chicago, Columbia, Harvard, Michigan, Minnesota, Pennsylvania, Virginia, Yale) found themselves in an influential position in American legal education,[35] but hardly a secure one. They were becoming national and scholarly in their orientation. They were relatively free of parochial demands by state legislatures. They were succeeding in attracting talented students from far away. Not until the 1930s and 1940s, however, did these law schools move from being influential to being dominant. Not until then did they shift from operating with many constraints and facing competition from alternative pathways to the bar, to being in a position to set the agenda for legal education in the United States. Their faculty and graduates were an important part of the Progressive Era and, later, at the centre of the legal developments of the New Deal. One factor contributing to this change in status—critical for purposes of the present paper—was growth in the volume, variety, and complexity of national law[36] in the early decades of the 20th century.[37] A prime example of federal-law-creation that enhanced the status of these already leading law schools was the project to create a national set of procedural rules.

Even before the drafting process began, the project received support from the upper echelons of academia. In an address at the American Bar Association Convention of 1906, Roscoe Pound of Harvard called for a turn away from the existing formalism and gamesmanship in civil procedure.[38] William Howard Taft of Yale urged the ABA to come out in support of a national procedural law. He also supported a central role for the ABA in accrediting law schools, a position that would exclude some of the independent law schools in particular.[39] When the time

---

[35] Robert Swaine, in his three-volume history of Cravath, Swaine & Moore, summarised the firm's hiring policies in the decades preceding and following the turn of the century: 'The firm has taken most of its associates from the law schools of Harvard, Yale, and Columbia, although in the decade preceding World War II, when the number of men taken into the office greatly increased, there was a conscious effort to take at least one man a year from other law schools of high repute, such as Pennsylvania, Cornell, Virginia, Michigan, and Chicago.' See Swaine 1948. Swaine states that when these guidelines were put in place in the late 19th century, they 'were regarded as somewhat eccentric' but that they became 'commonplace' among Wall Street law firms by the 1940s. *Id.* at 3.

[36] By 'national law' I mean not only federal law but also codifications like the Uniform Commercial Code and laws that were the product of national harmonisation efforts, like the various Restatements of private law subjects.

[37] Until then, relatively little of American law was federal. All but a small portion of contemporary federal statutory law and regulations dates from the New Deal and later.

[38] See Pound 1964, 273 (text of the address that Pound delivered in 1906). John Henry Wigmore said of Pound's speech that it 'struck the spark that kindled the white flame of high endeavour, now spreading through the entire legal profession.' Wigmore 1937, 1568.

[39] Another national organisation, the Association of American Law Schools (AALS), founded in 1900, also took as one of its mandates standardizing the content and format of legal education, a task that in practice involved marginalizing apprenticeship. The first president of AALS was James Bradley Thayer of Harvard. In the organization's early years, the AALS presidency was held by individuals from a very small circle of university-affiliated law schools: Columbia, Harvard, Iowa, Michigan, Wisconsin, and Yale. All of these institutions had a stake in

arrived to begin concentrated work on what would become the FRCP, four spots on the advisory committee were assigned to academic participants. What was needed from such participants was knowledge of a number of state systems, a substantial time commitment, the ability to work on the project without remuneration, access to extensive library collections, and the wherewithal to travel extensively to public meetings at which the draft rules would be vetted. Familiarity with British procedure and access to the assistance of bright and unpaid law students or graduate fellows were also desirable.

Few law schools in the early 1900s were in a position to support the efforts of faculty members wanting to participate in such an endeavour. Four law schools, however, were in such a position: from Yale came Charles Clark, the principal draftsman of the FRCP. The University of Michigan contributed Edson Sunderland. Armistead Dobie was on the faculty of the University of Virginia, and Wilbur Cherry came from the University of Minnesota. Each of these individuals worked strenuously and over an extended period of time, first in advocating in favour of the need for a uniform set of federal procedural rules, then in drafting and defending the rules prior to their enactment, and then in producing scholarly work interpreting the rules after they had become law and maintaining that state court systems should follow the federal lead. No doubt each of these men held a genuine conviction that the federal court system and the country would be better off as a result of harmonisation and reform. There is also no doubt that the careers of each of these law professors benefitted enormously from their work on the FRCP. Their law schools benefitted also.

After joining the federal rules project in the 1920s, Charles Clark became dean of Yale Law School in 1929. His position as the principal draftsman of the Rules and one of their main defenders greatly elevated his status. Previously, he had been an important scholar. By the 1940s, he was essentially the dean of American civil procedure. He served as president of the Association of American Law Schools (AALS) in 1933[40] and became a judge on what was at that time the nation's second most important federal court. As a judge, Clark wrote seminal opinions interpreting and applying the FRCP. He continued to serve on the advisory committee, and he continued to speak and write in support of the rules.[41] Clark also continued to teach at Yale, and his junior colleague, William Moore, became

(Footnote 39 continued)
marginalising apprenticeship and other non-university paths to legal education. See Association of American Law Schools Archives, available at http://www.library.illinois.edu/archives/aals/; 'What is AALS?' available at http://www.aals.org/about.php (last consulted in July 2011) ('At the time the AALS was created, many lawyers entered the legal profession without a law school education. From the beginnings to this day, the AALS has worked to improve the quality of legal education.').

[40] See AALS, Academic Freedom and Academic Duty vi, *available at* http://www.aals.org/am2012/2012program.pdf (last consulted in July 2011).

[41] See e.g., Clark 1947 (advocating 'notice pleading' and referring to the 'complete reform of civil practice in the courts of the United States and of several of the states).

the next great Yale scholar in civil procedure,[42] a tradition at Yale that continues to the present.[43]

Like Clark, Armistead Dobie became dean of a leading law school, the University of Virginia, during his service on the federal rules advisory committee. Dobie brought Harvard's case method from New England to the South in the 1920s, and his nationally well-received scholarship in federal civil procedure[44] played an important role in elevating the University of Virginia from a regionally important law school to a nationally important one.[45] Like Clark, Dobie then moved from academia to the federal bench, where he served as a judge on the U.S. Court of Appeals for the Fourth Circuit.

From his work on the FRCP, Edson Sunderland became a central academic figure in transforming the procedural system in the state of Michigan along the lines of the new federal regime.[46] From the FRCP, he moved on to serve as a reporter for the influential American Law Institute's Restatement of the Law of Judgments. Like Clark, Sunderland authored an important text on code pleading used in law schools nationwide. Like Clark and Dobie, he served as President of AALS.[47]

Wilbur Cherry was the fourth civil procedure professor on the advisory committee. Like Clark, Dobie, and Sunderland, Cherry also became president of AALS.[48] After enactment of the FRCP, Cherry went on to spend the lion's share of his professional life writing about the federal law of civil procedure.

The careers of other supporters of the FRCP took off as well. Roscoe Pound's ABA speech earned him a national reputation.[49] Soon thereafter he became president of AALS,[50] the dean of Harvard Law School, a personification of legal academia, and one of the most influential public intellectuals of his generation.[51] William Howard Taft became President of the United States and then Chief Justice of the U.S. Supreme Court.

The key point in all this is that the movement to create an American law created the opportunity for a group of law schools to become a national elite, and those law

---

42 *Moore's Federal Practice,* now in its third edition and consisting of 33 volumes, is an essential civil procedure treatise found in every law school library.

43 Subsequent Yale scholars in civil procedure include Geoffrey Hazard and Owen Fiss.

44 See, e.g., Dobie 1939, 261; Dobie 1944, 513; Dobie 1945, 784.

45 See Bryson 1979, 197–202.

46 See Honigman 1959, 13 ('More than any other individual, Professor Edson R. Sunderland has had a tremendous impact upon the Michigan law of procedure.').

47 He served in 1930. See Academic Freedom and Academic Duty, supra. Sunderland also authored an important history of the ABA.

48 He did so in 1939. See Academic Freedom and Academic Duty, supra.

49 According to a Harvard colleague, Pound's 'national' reputation as a reformer in the field of civil procedure was established as a result of that speech. See Scott 1965, 1568.

50 He served in that capacity in 1911.

51 See Tidmarsh 2006, 513. Pound's scholarly work remains among the most cited of any American law professor. See Shapiro 2000, 409.

schools seized that opportunity. It is not that the Yale Law School of the 1880s was an unimportant place. Influential scholarship and people had come from Yale in the 19th century, but the Yale Law School of the 1930s was a far more important place. Faculty scholarship and graduates of Yale were at the centre of the New Deal. Individual faculty members had seen the benefits of a national legal culture, but their enthusiasm for national law was also motivated by the opportunities afforded to the individuals and the institutions that were at the vanguard of the transformation taking place. Thus the relationship between the two trajectories—the movement from local to national law and the movement from egalitarianism to elitism in legal education—was not merely one of correlation. The growth in national law contributed to the stratification of American legal education, and the prospect of stratification contributed to key academic support for the creation of national law.

11.7 Multistate Law Firms

Until the 20th century, law practice in the United States was the preserve of solo practitioners and small law firms.[52] Civil litigation centred on pleadings and trials and not, as today, on pre-trial discovery and dispositive motions. The local character of legal culture—the importance of local bar associations and local standards of law practice—fit into a wider ocean of localism characteristic of 19th century America.[53] The obstacles to one individual or even one law firm appearing in the courts of more than one county, much less more than one state, were formidable. For a lawyer representing an out-of-state company in Virginia, mastery of the ins and outs of Virginia's procedural law was critical. Some of that procedural law was not readily available in libraries in other states. Just as important from a client's perspective was knowledge of the personalities on the local bench, the customs that were not written down in law books and, of course, the kind of rhetoric that would persuade a local jury. Each of these was likely to be at least as important as a detailed knowledge of the substantive law governing a case. In short, straying outside one's region or even outside one's state in connection with law practice was unusual.[54]

These powerful forces tipping the scales in favour of localism changed in the aftermath of the Gilded Age[55] and the increase in interstate business and personal wealth generated during that time period. For the company with much interstate

[52] See Menkel-Meadow 1994, 621.

[53] See Hulsebosch 2002, 1049 (variation in state procedures and juries rendered American private law an unusual quilt that frustrated commercial expectations).

[54] Cf. Ely and Bodenhamer 1986, 539 (arguing that regionalism was important in shaping southern law before 1900).

[55] The period from the end of the Civil War to the turn of the 20th century saw a tremendous increase in industrial and agricultural production and the accumulation of vast personal fortunes

business, it became desirable to have a law firm in Manhattan, Chicago, or San Francisco and to centralise the management of all the company's litigation, without regard to state boundaries.

Localism had its benefits, at least for some. Members of the local bar enjoyed a monopoly in practicing in local courts and a considerable home-field advantage in federal courts. Even in those rare instances in which a lawyer from another vicinity could appear in a case in rural Virginia for instance,[56] he did so at his client's peril. Certainly this was so in terms of presenting a case to a jury, which was drawn from a local jury pool,[57] but it also was true of pre-trial practice. A seasoned attorney who had appeared in state courts for years knew the ins and outs of the state procedural code. That lawyer not only knew the procedural code and the case law but also the manner in which judges in a particular locale were inclined to interpret procedural laws—whether, for instance, they were likely to apply procedural rules strictly or, rather, were disinclined to allow technicalities to get in the way of justice on the merits. Indeed, for more than a few of the country's great 19th-century lawyers the path to the national stage was laid through years of local practice.[58]

Localism, however, was not good for everyone. Large commercial and financial interests disliked the unpredictability of local procedure and local justice. So did the emerging group of expanding law firms based in major cities and aspiring to represent the country's industrial companies on a nationwide basis. An attorney from a firm in Philadelphia might have had fancy educational credentials and a wealth of legal knowledge, but he could easily stumble into procedural traps for the unwary in another state. A local lawyer in Virginia was more familiar with common law pleading than a lawyer from a Wall Street firm and also far more likely to know what to expect from a local judge with respect to pleading, admissibility of evidence, the appropriate scope of cross examination, the form of jury instructions, and so forth. In other words, at a time when the country lacked national rules of procedure and a truly national culture, a member of the local bar enjoyed considerable autonomy and sources of remuneration. Both were eyed with envy by lawyers in New York. The latter were becoming prosperous by

(Footnote 55 continued)
by such individuals as Andrew Carnegie, Andrew Mellon, J.P. Morgan, and John D. Rockefeller through industries such as banking, petroleum, and railroads.

56 Liberal practices regarding *pro hac vice* admission (permitting a lawyer not a member of the local bar to appear in a single case) did not become common until after World War II. See Marks 2009, 1135, 1136.

57 Juries in federal cases are drawn from a geographically larger jury pool.

58 Daniel Webster's political career was launched in substantial part from his highly successful law practice in Portsmouth, New Hampshire in the early decades of the 19th century. The foundation of Abraham Lincoln's political career was in winning friends and admirers in the many rural parts of Illinois where he rode circuit. In 1855, Lincoln, who was self-taught, said the following about the future of law practice in Illinois: '[T]hese college-trained men, who have devoted their whole lives to study, are coming west, don't you see? And they study their cases as we never do.' See Stephenson 1926, 118.

representing the nation's leading railroads, banks, and industrial giants on non-litigation matters but realised that they could become wealthier still by playing a larger role in defending litigation on a nationwide basis. Doing so required a change in their relationship with local counsel. Rather than play a minor role in interfacing with local counsel in Kentucky on behalf of a Connecticut insurance company, the company's principal outside counsel in New York wanted local counsel to be relegated to a minor role, at least in the pre-trial stage. From the former's point of view, the ideal result would be for the lawyers in Kentucky to do little more than file the papers drafted in lower Manhattan.

With the turn of the century, localism receded in much of the country. Contributing factors included large-scale immigration,[59] widespread circulation of print media,[60] and the emergence of a national popular culture.[61] In the world of lawyers and judges, localism was also undercut by the wide dissemination of state statutory law and case reports.[62]

With the growth in interstate and inter-regional business, the differences among state procedural law came to be seen less as a natural part of the landscape and more as an impediment to the ambitions of people of commerce and the lawyers seeking to represent them with respect to their growing interstate operations. These new interstate opportunities for lawyers are crucial to understanding one important constituency that supported the harmonisation of civil procedure and the resulting stratification of the American bar caused in part by this development.[63]

The law firms that served as principal advisors to major banks, railroads, and insurance companies could become much more affluent than other lawyers. The ticket to financial success was in becoming the principal legal advisor to sizeable clients with interstate operations and nationwide ambition—Standard Oil,

---

[59] After the depression of the 1890s, immigration increased markedly. Kraut 1982. From 1860 to 1880, about 2.5 million Europeans immigrated to the United States. In the 1880s, the number jumped to 5.25 million. Another 16 million immigrants entered during the next quarter century, with 1.25 million in 1908 alone. *Id*; see also US Bureau of the Census, US Dep't of Commerce, Statistical Abstract of the United States, 10 Table 5 (118th ed. 1998), available at http://www.census.gov/prod/www/abs/statab.html; US Bureau of the Census, Historical Statistics of the United States: Colonial Times to 1970, Part I, 105–09 (Series C 89–119) (1975), available at http://www.census.gov/prod/www/abs/statab.html (last consulted August 2011).

[60] Dryer 2008, 541 (in the early twentieth century, the price of newspapers dropped considerably, and news became a commodity widely consumed by the general American public); see also Berger 1951; Roberts 1977.

[61] Among the major contributors to that national culture were radio, motion pictures, sports, and widely-distributed consumer products. See Pendergrast 1993; May 1983; Friedman 2004, 319, 323–24.

[62] In 1879, the West Publishing Company began to publish volumes containing state-court opinions from around the United States.

[63] See Auerbach 1976, 23. Auerbach argues that at the turn of the century, precursors to the modern corporate law firms arose to accommodate powerful commercial interests. These firms, Auerbach maintains, were 'edging to the pinnacle of professional aspiration and power' during this period and, together with corporate directors, formed a symbiotic elite which consolidated institutional control for their mutual benefit. *Id*. at 22.

J.P. Morgan, Penn Central Railroad—companies that, along with the men who ran them, generated an expanding need for legal services in many areas of law, such as corporate law, antitrust, and litigation. Great financial reward was to be had for law firms able to become indispensable to these clients. There was just one catch: in the absence of a significant body of national law, the wealth had to be shared with local lawyers around the country serving as local counsel to these emerging powerhouse law firms in Manhattan, Chicago and elsewhere. A brilliant lawyer in Philadelphia could not take full control over all litigation for an interstate railroad if cases in different states were substantially different from one another.[64] The principal law firm for a major bank could not even handle all debt collection work.[65] It was no accident that many of the individuals who led harmonisation efforts in the early 20th century were from prestigious big-city law firms. They had so much to gain. A uniform set of federal procedural rules served not only the interests of their clients, it also served their personal interests. The shift from localism to national standards in both procedural law and substantive areas of law was one factor that boosted the profitability of large law firms and catapulted some of their lawyers to positions of national prominence.[66]

In short, it was clear from early proposals for a project to create a federal procedural law that such a set of rules would create winners and losers in the American bar. The winners would be lawyers in comparatively large firms serving large corporate clients with significant interstate operations. Some of the FRCP's most important supporters were elite lawyers fitting this description. The losers were likely to be the many lawyers whose only attraction from the viewpoint of the country's powerful business enterprises was their mastery of an arcane and local legal regime. With the doors to federal court truly open after 1938,[67] that mastery was considerably less valuable.

---

[64] See *Report of the Committee on Uniformity of Procedure and Comparative Law*, 19 A.B.A. REP. 411, 419 (1896).

[65] In terms of judgment collection, it was not until the 1930s that the Full Faith and Credit Clause of the US Constitution was interpreted as imposing a nearly ironclad obligation on state courts to recognise the civil judgments of courts from other states. See *Baldwin v Iowa State Traveling Men's Ass'n*, 283 US 522 (1931) (rejecting jurisdictional challenge to enforcement of sister-state judgment) ('Public policy dictates that there be an end of litigation; that those who have contested an issue shall be bound by the result of the contest; and that matters once tried shall be considered forever settled as between the parties.'). Before then, a judgment debtor could avail itself of many exceptions and procedural delay tactics to make the collection task of a judgment creditor difficult.

[66] Large American law firms first emerged in New York City. See Wald 2008, 1803, 1806. Initially, these law firms recruited young men who had attended elite colleges and elite law schools—Harvard, Yale, or Columbia. Swaine 1948, 748 (stating that 85 per cent of Cravath partners graduated from Harvard, Columbia, or Yale law schools as of 1948).

[67] Open in the sense of applying a transparent and nationally applicable set of procedural rules and generating a case law that was widely disseminated and analysed.

11.8 The American Experience and Europe Today

What does the American experience mean for others? Of course this is a quintessential comparative-law question, and like most questions in that discipline, the answer is likely to be that some facets of the experience in Society A are informative with respect to the problems of Society B, but some aspects of Society A's experience are unique to Society A. This contribution will conclude by making some general observations in this regard with specific attention to harmonisation in Europe.

With the benefit of hindsight, it is clear to most observers, including this one, that the harmonisation of procedural law that took place in the United States from the 1920s to the 1950s was a welcome development. Among the effects of harmonisation was a strengthening of the national economy and the initiation of reforms that made legal systems across the country more equitable. Another enormously useful result was the elevation in the stature of the federal bench. By the 1950s, that elevation in stature would prove essential as American society looked to the federal courts to resolve seemingly intractable political and social issues that no other institution seemed capable of tackling.[68]

Hopefully what is clear from what has been said earlier in this Chapter, however, is that harmonisation of procedural law in the US did not come about solely because it was a good idea. In law, as in most areas of human endeavour, there are many good ideas that never happen because those ideas lack a constellation of individuals and interest groups committed to making them happen. The proposal to create a uniform set of procedural rules for federal courts in the United States made it onto the national agenda because specific individuals (e.g., Pound, Taft), specific organisations (e.g., the ABA), and specific economic interests (e.g., large-scale American business) put it on the agenda. From there, the project proceeded through the drafting and vetting phase because specific people on the advisory committee (e.g., Clark, Sunderland) laboured long and hard in what they saw as the national interest and in what surely turned out to be in their own interest and the interests of the elite university law schools of which they were a part. Once enacted at the federal level, the FRCP then exerted a powerful influence on state procedural law throughout the US for more than a generation. It did so in part because federal judges were now in command of an important new body of law, because their written opinions in this area were more widely circulated than those of state judges, because federal judges were in possession of more resources to write careful procedural-law opinions than were state judges, and because the new

[68] See, e.g. *Brown v Board of Education of Topeka*, Kansas, 347 US 483 (1954) (racial desegregation of public schools); *Roe v Wade*, 410 US 113 (1973) (limitations on the power of state governments to legislate in ways that interfere with personal privacy and reproductive freedom); *Zorach v Clauson*, 343 US 306 (1952) (the nexus between religion and state-funded schools).

field of federal procedure presented an opportunity for individual judges on the federal bench to establish a national reputation for themselves.

Is the situation in Europe today at all similar to that in the US several generations ago? Is there a comparable set of interest groups? Are similar incentives in place? The answer to these questions would seem to be at least a qualified yes.

To even the casual observer of legal education in the EU over the last two decades, a striking development has been the Europeanization of legal education. Not only has the teaching of EU law affected universities everywhere, so also have exchange programs for faculty and students. A generation ago, a faculty member at a university in the UK could rest on being an expert in the British law of civil procedure and private international law. Increasingly, that is becoming no longer tenable. It is rare to read the work of a British scholar in these fields without seeing frequent references to EU-wide legislation and case law and references to approaches in continental Europe. A generation ago, some of the most highly regarded universities in Europe played a minor role in fostering European integration. That is not true today. European legal academia today is experiencing at least a variation on what beset legal academia in the US during a crucial period in the early 1900s: Universities compete with one another as never before for prolific faculty members and for students. Universities at the vanguard of European integration in fields such as civil procedure have much to gain in terms of EU funding and in terms of placing their graduates in prestigious positions in the EU Commission and in EU-wide law firms and industry. As one surveys the landscape of scholars passionately devoted to EU-wide codification projects, it is hard not to conclude that many stand to reap much in career advancement from the acceleration of the EU enterprise. In other words, just as an academic elite was critical to the harmonisation of procedural law in the US, so an academic elite in Europe could be critical to the transformation of procedural law in Europe.

The same appears to be true of the legal profession. The past two decades have witnessed a large volume of cross-border mergers and acquisitions among law firms. Not long ago, small law firms in Germany were overwhelmingly the norm, and a non-national's admission to the bar was one of the four freedoms that was more theoretical than real. In the last two decades, however, there has been an acceleration in the development of large, trans-European law firms capable of servicing the needs of their clients in many European countries. This is most clearly so in the areas of European competition law, banking law, pharmaceuticals, and transportation. It is not yet fully true of litigation. Although some firms based in Europe have the capacity to participate in or monitor litigation in more than one EU country, major differences among procedural regimes still pose an obstacle to the kind of centralization of litigation management that long has been typical in the U.S. For this reason, some of Europe's larger law firms stand to gain much from a series of harmonisation measures in civil procedure that would enable them to fill this need of their clients.

As for judges, there are differences, of course, between judges in the EU and federal judges in the United States. Most obviously, the numbers are drastically different. By virtue of executive federalism, most of EU law is enforced by

Member State authorities, and most actions that require some interpretation of EU law are initiated in the courts of EU Member States. The parties to such actions must comply with the procedural law of the national legal system in which they find themselves, subject to the ECJ's formula that national procedural law must not discriminate on the basis of nationality or residence and must not make it impossible in practice to attain a remedy for the violation of rights conferred by the EU treaties or EU legislation.[69] In practical terms, this means that given the current structure of the EU judicial system, there is less opportunity for judges on the EU level to play the leading rule in authoring opinions interpreting a new body of EU law in the realm of procedure. A second consideration is that opinions of the ECJ and the Court of First Instance are unsigned.

Neither of these obstacles is insuperable. The courts of the EU, and individual judges, have in the past been instrumental in bringing about harmonisation in other areas of EU law, such as EU constitutional law and the application of the Brussels and Rome Conventions.

References

Auerbach JS (1976) Unequal justice: lawyers and social change in modern America. Oxford University Press, Oxford

Berger M (1951) The story of the New York Times 1851–1951. Simon and Schuster, New York

Bryson WH (ed) (1979) Legal education in Virginia: a biographical approach. University Press of Virginia, Charlottesville

Carrington PD (1996) A new confederacy? Disunionism in the federal courts. Duke Law J 45:929–999

Chayes A (1976) The role of the judge in public law litigation. Harvard Law Rev 89:1281–1316

Chroust AH (1965) The rise of the legal profession in America. University of Oklahoma Press, Norman

Clark CE (1947) Handbook of the law of code pleading. West Publishing, St. Paul

Clermont KM (1999) Jurisdictional salvation and the Hague treaty. Cornell Law Rev 85:89–132

Dobie AM (1939) The federal rules of civil procedure. Virgina Law Rev 25:261–315

Dobie AM (1944) The revision of the federal rules of civil procedure. Virginia Law Rev 30:513–530

Dobie AM (1945) Additional suggested changes in the federal rules of civil procedure. Virginia Law Rev 31:784–797

Dryer TD (2008) All the news that's fit to print: the New York Times, yellow journalism, and the criminal trial 1898–1902. Nevada Law Rev 8:541–569

Dubinsky PR (2004) Justice for the collective: the limits of the human rights class action. Mich Law Rev 102:1152–1174

Dubinsky PR (2008) Is transnational litigation a distinct field? The persistence of exceptionalism in American Procedural Law. Stanford Law Rev 44:301–317

[69] See in particular ECJ 9 March 1978, Case C-106/77, ECR 629 *(Administration delle Finanze dello Stato v. Simmenthal Spa*) and ECJ 19 June 1990, Case C-213/89, ECR I-2433 (*Regina v. Secretary of State for Transport, Ex Parte Factortame, Ltd. and Others*), see generally Dubinsky 1994, 325–336.

Dubinsky PR (1994) The essential function of federal courts: the European Union and the United States compared. Am J Comp Law 42:295–346
Earle WK (1963) Mr. Shearman and Mr. Sterling and how they grew: being annals of their law firms. Yale University Press, New Haven
Ely JW Jr, Bodenhamer DJ (1986) Regionalism and American legal history: the Southern experience. Vanderbilt Law Rev 39:539–567
Friedman LM (2004) The one-way mirror: law, privacy, and the media. Wash Univ Law Q 82:319–342
Holmes OW (1870) Harvard University, Law School, Am Law Rev 5:177
Honigman JL (1959) Edson R. Sunderland's role in Michigan procedure. Mich Law Rev 58:13–40
Hulsebosch DJ (2002) Writs of rights: "navigability" and the transformation of the common law in the nineteenth century. Cardozo Law Rev 23:1049–1105
Kraut A (1982) The huddled masses: the immigrant in American Society, 1880–1921. Harlan Davidson, Arlington Heights
Marks M (2009) Ethics in the multijurisdictional practice of admiralty lawyers. Fordham Int Law J 32:1135–1153
May L (1983) Screening out the past: the birth of mass culture and the motion picture industry. University of Chicago Press, Chicago
Menkel-Meadow C (1994) Culture clash in the quality of life in the law: changes in the economics, diversification and organization of lawyering. Case West Reserve Law Rev 44:621–663
Mitchell WD (1949) The federal rules of civil procedure, in David Dudley field, Centenary Essays, New York University Law School, pp 73–78
Oakley JB, Coon AF (1986) The federal rules in state courts: a survey of state court systems of civil procedure. Wash Law Rev 61:1367–1434
Pendergrast M (1993) For God, country and coca-cola: the unauthorized history of the great American soft drink and the company that makes it. Scribner's, New York
Pound R (1906) The causes of popular dissatisfaction with the administrations of justice, 29 A.B.A. Rep. 395 (1906), reprinted in 35 F.R.D. 241, 273–291
Report of the Committee on Uniformity of Procedure and Comparative Law (1896), 19 A.B.A. Rep., 411–419
Roberts CM (1977) The Washington Post, The first 100 years. Houghton Mifflin, Boston
Rosenberg M (1989) Federal rules of civil procedure in action: assessing their impact. University Pennsylvania Law Rev 137:2197–2212
Scott AW (1965) Pound's influence on civil procedure. Harv Law Rev 78:1568–1577
Shapiro FR (2009) The most-cited legal scholars. J Legal Stud 29:409–426
Subrin SN (1988) David Dudley field and the field code: a historical analysis of an earlier procedural vision. Law Hist Rev 6:311–338
Swaine RT (1948) The Cravath firm and its predecessors: 1819–1947. Ad Press, New York
Symeonides SC (1997) The judicial acceptance of the second conflicts restatement: a mixed blessing. Md Law Rev 56:1248–1279
Symeonides SC (2006) The American choice-of-law revolution: past, present and future, vol 4. The Hague Academy of International Law Monographs, Martinus Nijhoff Publishers, Boston
Tidmarsh J (2006) Pound's century and ours. Notre Dame Law Rev 81:513–539
Urofsky M (2009) Louis D. Brandeis: a life. Pantheon, New York
Wald E (2008) The rise and fall of the WASP and Jewish law firms. Stanford Law Rev 60:1803–1867
Weinstein JB (1989) After fifty years of the federal rules of civil procedure: are the barriers to justice being raised? University Pennsylvania Law Rev 137:1901–1941
White GE (1976) The American judicial tradition: profiles of leading American judges. Oxford University Press, New York
White GE (1993) Justice Oliver Wendell Holmes: law and the inner self. Oxford University Press, Oxford
Wigmore JH (1937) Roscoe Pound's St. Paul address of 1906. J Am Judic Soc 20:943–967

Chapter 12
Switzerland: Between Cosmopolitanism and Parochialism in Civil Litigation

Tanja Domej

Abstract On 1 January 2011, the new Swiss Code of Civil Procedure entered into force, replacing the twenty-six cantonal codes of civil procedure. One of the main incentives for unifying civil procedure was the perception that divergent rules were inhibiting the efficient administration of justice. Despite Switzerland's close economic and cultural ties with other countries the focus was, however, almost exclusively on finding compromises between different cantonal models. Meanwhile, comparatively little attention was directed to international developments in the field of civil procedure. Nevertheless, international models have had an important impact on Swiss civil procedure. One of the most influential has been the Lugano Convention on Jurisdiction and the Enforcement of Judgments in Civil and Commercial Matters. It not only created uniform rules applicable in all contracting States regarding jurisdiction and enforcement in cases with an international element but also influenced legislation and case law in purely domestic cases. The Swiss legislature and Swiss case law often voluntarily follow European developments even in cases where they are contrary to Switzerland's original political intentions. The development of the European area of freedom, security and justice has, however, advanced far beyond the matters originally contained in the Brussels Convention and now in the Brussels I Regulation. Switzerland has not been partaking in this development. Even as regards jurisdiction and recognition and enforcement of foreign judgments, Switzerland risks losing contact with the impending reforms on the EU level. As opposed to the situation in several other areas of law, 'autonomous implementation' (*autonomer Nachvollzug*), i.e. the

Professor of Civil Procedure, Enforcement and Insolvency Law, Private Law.

T. Domej (✉)
University of Zurich, Zurich, Switzerland
e-mail: tanja.domej@rwi.uzh.ch

X. E. Kramer and C. H. van Rhee (eds.), *Civil Litigation in a Globalising World*,
DOI: 10.1007/978-90-6704-817-0_12,

enactment of national provisions mirroring EU law, is not considered, in general, to be an option in the field of civil procedure.

Contents

12.1 The Swiss Legislature's Attitude Towards Harmonisation of Civil Procedure

On 1 January 2011, the new Swiss Code of Civil Procedure (*Schweizerische Zivilprozessordnung/Code de procédure civile/Codice di diritto processuale civile svizzero*)[1] entered into force, replacing the twenty-six cantonal codes of civil procedure.[2] Thus, for the first time in history, there is now a unified law of civil procedure in Switzerland—after a series of failed attempts over the course of the twentieth century to achieve this.[3]

The report accompanying the government draft of the new code pointed out that divergent rules were creating artificial dividing lines cutting across regions with a common economy, language and culture. This, the report stated, was inhibiting the efficient administration of justice in these regions and creating adverse economic effects.[4] Thus, one of the main incentives for unifying civil procedure was the wish to remove such obstacles.

Switzerland has close economic and cultural ties with other countries, especially with neighbouring European States and with the European Union as a whole.

[1] SR 272.

[2] Meanwhile, the Federal Act on Federal Civil Procedure (*Bundesgesetz über den Bundeszivilprozess*, SR 273) which applies in cases where the Bundesgericht (Federal Court), i.e. the Swiss supreme court, decides at first instance, was not abrogated. This Act's scope of application, however, has been narrowed down very much in recent reforms.

[3] See Domej 2006, 241 with further references.

[4] Botschaft 2006, 7228 et seq.

One might, therefore, expect that a legislature that saw harmonisation of civil procedure as an instrument to facilitate economic and cultural exchange would also think deeply about international harmonisation. But this was not much the case in the legislative process that led to the new Swiss code. Apparently, only the borders between the cantons, not those with other countries, were considered to be *artificial* dividing lines. In the eyes of the authors of the code, harmonisation of civil procedure meant harmonisation of the different cantonal models. Meanwhile, comparatively little attention was directed to international developments in the field of civil procedure.

Especially in the earlier stages of the drafting process, there was a certain reluctance to deal with international developments. At least, one might get such an impression from reading the explanatory report accompanying a preliminary draft[5] that was drawn up by a group of experts in 2003. In the introductory passages of that report, the relations between Switzerland and the EU were, indeed, mentioned as a relevant factor in the legislative process—but, rather curiously, only with regard to the mobility of the legal profession:

> Another argument [i.e. in favour of harmonisation of Swiss civil procedure] is the free movement of lawyers, be it in the Swiss single market, be it within the framework of the bilateral treaties with the EU. One might probably consider it as a factual discrimination if in Switzerland, as opposed to the situation in the other EU Member States, there is no single national law of civil procedure, but, besides the rules of procedure of the Federal Court, 26 cantonal laws of civil procedure—a situation that is downright prohibitive for the cross-border practice of law.[6]

Undoubtedly, the international mobility of lawyers is an important issue; but certainly it is not the only one worth considering in respect of Switzerland's positioning towards what might once become a real single European area of justice.

As already pointed out, however, international harmonisation was not a top priority for the group of experts. The explanatory report stated:

> The future Swiss Code of Civil Procedure should continue the Swiss legal tradition, that is, the accepted foundations and principles that are expressed in the cantonal codes of civil procedure. Innovations that were developed in foreign legal systems can only be taken into consideration if they are suitable for implementation in the Swiss legal system and if such implementation would bring about a real improvement.[7]

Later, the report goes on to list some foreign developments that the group of experts viewed with scepticism or at least with reserve, especially class actions and 'so-called mediation.'[8] As regards mediation, however, the legislature was somewhat more open-minded than the group of experts, perhaps because mediation was considered as a possible instrument for reducing the burden on courts and

---

[5] Expertenkommission 2003a.

[6] Expertenkommission 2003b, 5 et seq. All translations are my own.

[7] Expertenkommission 2003b, 10.

[8] Expertenkommission 2003b, 15.

thus for making the system of civil procedure more efficient; and history teaches that increasing the efficiency of civil procedure is a goal of any legislature in the field of civil procedure.[9] A 'foreign innovation' the group of experts considered suitable for implementation in Switzerland was the enforceable authentic instrument.[10] I will come back to that later on.[11]

What the group of experts failed to see (or at least to write down) was that not only spectacular 'innovations' come from abroad, but that one might also learn from one's neighbours and their experiences in more down-to-earth issues of civil procedure. It is hardly surprising that among the most controversial topics in the legislative process were the position of the judge, the role of the parties in giving evidence and the admissibility of late allegations. All of these have been much discussed internationally in recent years, but the group of experts failed to take notice of this international debate—or if it did take notice of it, it did not share its thoughts about the international developments in these fields with the public.

Considering the rather conservative attitudes that predominated in the group of experts, it is certainly not surprising that the 'Anglo-American class action' (as it was called in the report) was not deemed to be compatible with the Swiss system of civil procedure.[12] And perhaps the attempt to introduce controversial 'innovations' from abroad would really have endangered a project that was considered risky enough as it was. One reason why such a strong emphasis was placed on the 'cantonal traditions' was that there were apprehensions in the legislative process that the attempt to unify civil procedure would fail, as so many had before, and that such a failure might especially be caused by the reluctance of the cantons to give up their venerated procedural traditions.[13] Therefore, the sceptical attitude towards foreign 'innovations' displayed by the group of experts in the explanatory report might be a political message designed to obviate such potential opposition. Legal history shows that statements of this sort do not always tell the whole truth about all the factors really influencing the content of legislative proposals. Nevertheless, one can safely say that systematic and intense analysis of foreign models obviously did not take place in the preparation of the draft by the group of experts.

The preliminary draft drawn up by the group of experts served as the basis for a public consultation. Subsequently, a government draft[14] was drawn up on the basis of the preliminary draft, taking into account some of the results of the consultation.[15] In the consultation, some—though not many—criticised the lack of comparative

[9] See, in this context, Oberhammer 2004a, 217 et seq.

[10] Expertenkommission 2003b, 15.

[11] See 12.3.2 below.

[12] For a more balanced discussion of instruments of collective redress, see, e.g. Romy 1997; Gordon-Vrba 2007.

[13] See Domej 2006, 241 et seq.

[14] *Schweizerische Zivilprozessordnung*—Entwurf 2006.

[15] The results are compiled in Bundesamt für Justiz 2004.

research in the preparation of the preliminary draft.[16] Perhaps it was a reaction to such criticism that the report accompanying the government draft refers to international developments somewhat more extensively.[17] But in this phase of the legislative process it was too late for real in-depth research. It is no wonder, therefore, that the passages on international trends in civil procedure and on how such trends are reflected in the government draft are on a rather superficial level. In my view, they mainly serve aesthetic and rhetorical purposes.

12.2 The Lugano Convention as a Driving Force for Harmonisation of Civil Procedure

I have drawn a picture that makes important actors of the Swiss legislative process appear somewhat narrow-minded or even nationalist. Nevertheless, international models have had a very important impact on Swiss civil procedure in recent years. One of the most influential has been the Lugano Convention on Jurisdiction and the Enforcement of Judgments in Civil and Commercial Matters. The Convention did not only create uniform rules applicable in all contracting States regarding jurisdiction and enforcement in cases with an international element. Probably in most contracting States it also influenced legislation and case law in purely domestic cases (as well as in international cases outside the scope of application of the Convention). It certainly did so in Switzerland, and experiences from abroad show that the Lugano Convention (as well as the Brussels Convention and later the Brussels I Regulation) has been one of the most important driving forces of procedural harmonisation in Europe (besides Article 6 para 1 of the European Convention on Human Rights, which is also of considerable importance as a source of common procedural standards).[18]

Especially, many of the provisions of the Swiss Act on jurisdiction in domestic cases (*Gerichtsstandsgesetz*) that entered into force in 2001[19] were modelled after those of the Lugano Convention.[20] These provisions are now included (with some

[16] See, especially, the statement by the University of Zurich, Bundesamt für Justiz 2004, 76; Oberhammer 2004b, 1038 et seq.

[17] Botschaft 2006, 7248 et seq.

[18] In particular, the case law of the European Court of Human Rights is also taken into account by the Swiss Federal Court when interpreting the domestic rules on the right to a fair trial, especially Art. 29 of the Swiss Federal Constitution, see BGE 133 I 100, 103. On Art. 6 para 1 of the European Convention on Human Rights as a driving force of procedural harmonisation, see also the contribution by Andrews (Chap. 2) in the present Vol.

[19] Amtliche Sammlung 2000, 2355.

[20] Botschaft 1998, 2834 et seq.

modifications) in the Swiss Code of Civil Procedure.[21] The case law of the Swiss Federal Court (*Bundesgericht*) has also been strongly influenced by the Lugano Convention and by the case law of the European Court of Justice relating to the Brussels Convention and the Brussels I Regulation. Often, such case law is followed not only when applying the Lugano Convention but also when interpreting functionally equivalent provisions of national law.[22]

One example of this is the case law on *lis pendens* in domestic cases: contrary to its earlier case law, here the Federal Court followed the case law of the European Court of Justice according to which an action for negative declaration bars a subsequent action for performance.[23] Another example where the case law of the ECJ influenced the Swiss Federal Court is the interpretation of the provisions of Swiss national law on jurisdiction in cases involving multiple defendants.[24] The Federal Court is clearly of the opinion that there is an interest, at least in the field of jurisdiction and *lis pendens*, to create as much harmony as possible between domestic cases, Lugano cases and international cases not within the Convention's scope of application (except, of course, in cases where the Swiss legislature deliberately chose a solution different to the one chosen by the authors of the Lugano Convention).[25]

This development continues. Several provisions of the new Swiss Code of Civil Procedure on jurisdiction and on *lis pendens* were modelled after provisions of the Lugano Convention or influenced by them. It is, for instance, worth noting that the new Swiss Code of Civil Procedure contains a rule conferring jurisdiction on the court at the place of performance in cases concerning contractual matters (Article 31 *Zivilprozessordnung*). Only a few years ago, such a provision would have been considered as contrary to established principles of Swiss civil procedure

[21] The *Gerichtsstandsgesetz* was abrogated by the *Zivilprozessordnung*, see Annex 1 to the *Zivilprozessordnung*, point I. The rules on jurisdiction in domestic cases are now contained in Arts. 9 et seq *Zivilprozessordnung*, while jurisdiction in international cases outside the scope of application of bi- or multilateral treaties is still subject to the provisions of the *Bundesgesetz über das Internationale Privatrecht* (Act on Private International Law) SR 291.

[22] See Domej 2008b, marginal No. 39; Walther 2002, 128 et seq; Walter 2007, 268 et seq.

[23] BGE 128 III 284, 287 et seq. See, however, also BGE 123 III 414, 430; 131 III 319, 325 et seq where the *Bundesgericht* decided that in such cases, the prerequisites of national law for a *Feststellungsinteresse* (legal interest to seek a declaratory judgment) have to be fulfilled, and that the mere interest to secure a favourable forum does not suffice in this regard. According to a recent judgment of the *Bundesgericht*, this also applies to cases within the scope of application of the Lugano Convention (BGE 136 III 523).

[24] See BGE 129 III 80, 84 et seq; 134 III 27, 31 et seq; 134 III 80, 84.

[25] See, e.g. BGE 129 III 80, 87.

(at least in cases involving a Swiss defendant). Under the Lugano Convention 1988, Switzerland originally even made a reservation according to which foreign judgments could not be recognised and enforced in Switzerland if the jurisdiction of the court had been based only on Article 5 No. 1 of the Convention (see Article Ia, Protocol 1 of the Lugano Convention 1988).[26] The reservation ceased to have effect on 31 December 1999.[27] But the forum at the place of performance was still considered as problematic, and the *Gerichtsstandsgesetz* did not provide for such a forum (though the original draft of the Act did).[28] In the negotiations on the reform of the Brussels and Lugano Conventions, Switzerland originally even pleaded for the total abolition of Article 5 No. 1.[29] But in the end, the forum at the place of performance has now also made its way into the rules on jurisdiction in domestic cases.[30] This and other examples demonstrate that the Swiss legislature and Swiss case law sometimes voluntarily follow European developments even in cases where they are contrary to Switzerland's original political intentions.

Thus, on the whole, there is a rather strong tendency in Switzerland to try to harmonise rules contained in conventions to which Switzerland is a party and national law that applies outside such conventions' scope of application. There can be two main reasons for this 'internal harmonisation,' as one might call it, i.e. harmonisation between different sets of rules that are all in force in Switzerland but apply to different types of cases. There can be the impression that the rules contained in the convention work well—and that they are acceptable as models because Switzerland has partaken of their negotiation (or has at least taken a sovereign decision to become a contracting State of the convention). But even if the rules in themselves or in the way that they are applied under the convention are not considered to be fully satisfactory, there can still be an inducement to harmonise national law with them as it may be considered as inefficient if divergent rules apply within the convention's scope of application and outside it.

---

[26] See, in this context, Botschaft 1990, 267.

[27] According to the prevailing opinion, the reservation ceased to have effect also with regard to judgments given before 2000; see BGE 126 III 540; Knoepfler 1996, 537 et seq; Kren Kostkiewicz 1999, 243 et seq; Domej 2008a, marginal No. 3 et seq; contra: Markus 1999, 63 et seq.

[28] See Botschaft 1998, 2858 et seq.

[29] See Botschaft 2009, 1788.

[30] Note, however, that Art. 31 *Zivilprozessordnung* differs from Art. 5 No. 1 Lugano Convention in that it confers jurisdiction on the court for the place of performance of the characteristic obligation irrespective of the type of contract. This solution had also been proposed (unsuccessfully) by the Swiss delegation in the negotiations on the reform of the Brussels and Lugano Conventions, see Botschaft 2009, 1789.

12.3 The Wish to Avoid 'Self-Discrimination' as an Argument in Favour of Harmonising Civil Procedure

12.3.1 Introduction

Besides the reasons mentioned above,[31] a popular argument for adapting Swiss law to certain foreign models has been the wish to avoid 'self-discrimination,'[32] meaning, especially, that Swiss creditors should also be able to profit from instruments of debt enforcement that are at the disposal of foreign creditors (or of creditors importing judgments or authentic instruments from other contracting States of the Lugano Convention into Switzerland). This was also the reason given for several amendments in the field of enforcement law which were introduced by the legislation implementing the 2007 revised Lugano Convention in Switzerland[33] and—directly or indirectly—influenced by the Lugano Convention.

12.3.2 Enforceable Authentic Instruments

One of the most widely discussed innovations in the new Swiss Code of Civil Procedure is the enforceable authentic instrument. Under the Lugano Convention (Article 50 of the 1988 and Article 57 of the 2007 Lugano Convention), authentic instruments, if they are enforceable in the State of origin, can be declared enforceable in all other contracting States as well—regardless of whether the law of the State of enforcement also provides for such enforceable authentic instruments. Therefore, for example, enforceable notarial deeds from Germany or Austria have to be declared enforceable in Switzerland. They have to be treated like judgments. In the procedure for the enforcement of money claims, an authentic instrument that is enforceable in its State of origin is a title for a so-called *definitive Rechtsöffnung*.[34] This means that a debtor can prevent execution only if he or she can produce documentary evidence that the claim has been paid or deferred, or that the limitation period has expired (and also, according to the prevailing opinion, that the claim does not exist at all).

---

[31] See 12.2.

[32] See, e.g. Botschaft 1998, 2835; Botschaft 2006, 7268; Botschaft 2009, 1821.

[33] *Bundesbeschluss über die Genehmigung und die Umsetzung des Übereinkommens über die gerichtliche Zuständigkeit und die Anerkennung und Vollstreckung von Entscheidungen in Zivil- und Handelssachen* (Federal Enactment on the Approval and Implementation of the Convention on Jurisdiction and the Recognition and Enforcement of Judgments in Civil and Commercial Matters), Amtliche Sammlung 2010, 5601.

[34] BGE 137 III 87; Staehelin 2005, 207; Visinoni-Meyer 2005, 429 et seq; Naegeli 2008, marginal No. 49 with further references.

Traditionally, Swiss law did not provide for such enforceable authentic instruments. Under Swiss law, an authentic instrument used to be only a title for so-called *provisorische Rechtsöffnung* (Article 82 *Schuldbetreibungs- und Konkursgesetz*).[35] It did not give the creditor any more rights than any ordinary document containing an acceptance of the claim (for example, a written contract naming the sum owed by the debtor).[36] The *provisorische Rechtsöffnung* is a special summary procedure that is embedded in the procedure for the enforcement of money claims. To put it simply, it enables creditors possessed of certain types of documentary evidence to obtain an enforceable title in a summary procedure if the debtor cannot show that very probably the claim is not good. If the application for a *provisorische Rechtsöffnung* is granted, the debtor may, within twenty days, bring an action for negative declaration called *Aberkennungsklage* (Article 83 para 2 *Schuldbetreibungs- und Konkursgesetz*). While such an action is pending, only provisional enforcement is possible (Article 83 para 1 *Schuldbetreibungs- und Konkursgesetz*). In the case of a *definitive Rechtsöffnung* (Article 80 *Schuldbetreibungs- und Konkursgesetz*), meanwhile, the creditor can proceed to definite enforcement in any case, and the debtor is only able to bring an action for negative declaration that does not automatically carry with it a stay of execution (Article 85a *Schuldbetreibungs- und Konkursgesetz*). Therefore, a creditor who had a Swiss authentic instrument used to be in a weaker position than a creditor with a foreign authentic instrument enforceable in the State of origin. This was one of the main reasons given for including the new provisions on enforceable authentic instruments in the Swiss Code of Civil Procedure.[37]

The Swiss Code of Civil Procedure now contains provisions on enforceable authentic instruments (Articles 345 et seq *Zivilprozessordnung*). Enforceable authentic instruments concerning money claims are now titles for *definitive Rechtsöffnung* (see Article 347 *Zivilprozessordnung* and the amended Article 80, para 2, No. 1 *bis Schuldbetreibungs- und Konkursgesetz*). These rules aim to put a creditor with a Swiss authentic instrument in the same position as one with an authentic instrument from another Lugano State where the instrument is directly enforceable. Besides that, they were also meant to have another effect: as long as authentic instruments were not directly enforceable in Switzerland, Swiss notaries were not able to draw up authentic instruments that are enforceable abroad under the Lugano Convention. The new rules on authentic instruments contained in the *Zivilprozessordnung* and in the *Schuldbetreibungs- und Konkursgesetz* were supposed to change this.[38] The notaries of some cantons are export-oriented and frequently notarise documents for foreign parties—which can be attractive for these parties because the Swiss fees are generally cheaper than those of German notaries. Being able to draw up enforceable authentic instruments might create another competitive advantage for Swiss notaries. It is open to doubt, however,

[35] Act on Debt Enforcement and Insolvency, SR 281.1.

[36] Oberhammer 2005, 248 et seq; Naegeli 2008, marginal No. 32 with further references.

[37] Even the group of experts saw a 'real need' for this, see Expertenkommission 2003b, 15.

[38] See, e.g. Kofmel Ehrenzeller 2010, marginal No. 1.

whether the new rules really comply with the prerequisite contained in Article 57 Lugano Convention 2007 (Article 50 Lugano Convention 1988) that the document must be 'enforceable' in the State of origin, as Article 349 para 1 *Zivilprozess-ordnung* and Article 82 para 2 *Schuldbetreibungs- und Konkursgesetz* give the debtor the possibility to raise substantive objections against the obligation to perform in the enforcement procedure itself if he or she has ready proof for the grounds of objection.[39]

12.3.3 Provisional Measures

Another example of an innovation that was at least partly motivated by the idea that self-discrimination should be avoided are the new rules on protective measures securing the enforcement of already existing titles that were introduced by the legislation implementing the 2007 Lugano Convention.

Traditionally, Swiss law was rather reluctant in granting such measures. Especially, the *Arrest*, that is, the attachment of assets to secure a money claim, used to be available only if the debtor was domiciled abroad or in certain cases where there was typically a really manifest danger that the claim would not be satisfied (if the debtor had no fixed domicile at all or if he or she was planning to escape or to dissipate his or her property, or if the creditor had unsuccessfully tried to enforce the claim before; see Article 271 *Schuldbetreibungs- und Konkursgesetz* in its wording before the reform). Meanwhile, the mere fact that the creditor had an enforceable title was not grounds for granting protective measures against a debtor domiciled in Switzerland.

Under Article 39 of the 1988 and Article 47 of the 2007 Lugano Convention, on the other hand, a creditor whose application for a declaration of enforceability has been granted at first instance is entitled to apply for protective measures. Such measures must be granted without any further prerequisites, especially regardless of whether there is a risk that the claim will otherwise not be satisfied.[40] And, of course, in Switzerland, the restrictions that the debtor must be a foreigner or that there must be one of the other specified grounds for granting an *Arrest* were not applicable in this context.[41]

Thus, if the debtor was domiciled in Switzerland, a creditor with an enforceable title from another contracting State used to be in a stronger position than a creditor with a Swiss title. This has now changed. Under the amended Article 272

---

[39] Oberhammer 2011b, marginal No. 24.

[40] Staehelin 2008, marginal No. 5.

[41] Note also, in this context, that opinions differed widely in Swiss case law and literature as to which measures under domestic law were best suited as provisional measures under Art. 39 para 2 Lugano Convention 1988 with regard to money judgments (see, e.g. Staehelin 2008, marginal Nos. 16 et seq with further references). This controversy is now obsolete, as the federal legislature has meanwhile decided in favour of the *Arrest* (see Botschaft 2009, 1821).

Schuldbetreibungs- und Konkursgesetz, the *Arrest* is available to any creditor with an enforceable title regardless of whether the title falls within the scope of the Lugano Convention. With regard to non-money judgments, Article 340 *Zivilprozessordnung* authorises the enforcement court to order protective measures. Again, the idea that self-discrimination should be prevented was one of the key arguments in favour of the introduction of these new rules into Swiss civil procedure.[42]

12.4 The European Area of Justice and Switzerland

All in all, the Lugano Convention has strongly influenced the recent development of Swiss civil procedure—even in purely domestic cases. This is not a phenomenon limited to Switzerland. Conventions can be a very powerful tool to achieve international harmony or at least approximation of national laws of civil procedure. Even where such conventions have a limited scope of application and only apply in cross-border cases (or even only in the relations between the contracting States), there is still a chance that in the long run national law outside the scope of application is also harmonised. Especially, the Lugano and Brussels regimes have probably contributed more to the knowledge in European States about each other's procedural systems and even to the approximation of national laws of civil procedure than any other instrument or project has done so far.

The development of the European area of freedom, security and justice has advanced far beyond the matters originally contained in the Brussels Convention and now in the Brussels I Regulation. Switzerland has not been partaking in this further development. Even as regards jurisdiction and recognition and enforcement of foreign judgments, Switzerland risks losing contact with the impending reforms on the EU level. After years of negotiations, the new Lugano Convention has re-established the parallelism between the Lugano and the Brussels I regimes. The reform envisaged for the Brussels I Regulation,[43] however, may soon once more disrupt that parallelism. Furthermore, the other European instruments in the field of civil procedure (besides the Brussels I Regulation) have not been extended to the EU-Switzerland relations at all, and there appears to be little hope that this will substantially change in the foreseeable future. If one regards these EU instruments as cornerstones of a European civil procedure, then 'Europe' is not a geographical or a cultural area but the European Union, and it is doubtful if at all and in what way countries like Switzerland will be able or even willing to become a part of the emerging 'single judicial area.'[44]

---

[42] See Botschaft 2009, 1821.

[43] European Commission 2010.

[44] See also Domej 2010, 409 et seq.

In some other areas of law, Switzerland has enacted national provisions mirroring European law. This is especially the case in those areas of law that are considered to be of primary importance for cross-border trade. This phenomenon is referred to as 'autonomous implementation' of EU law (*autonomer Nachvollzug*).[45] In the field of civil procedure, however, such autonomous implementation is not, in general, considered to be an option. There might even be a tendency towards a restrictive handling of international cooperation in matters where Switzerland does not partake of an internationalised regime. The concepts of 'sovereignty' and 'territoriality' in law enforcement are, it seems, increasingly cherished by Swiss courts and also in parts of Swiss doctrine in certain areas of civil procedure where there is no international cooperation on the basis of conventions.

One example is the field of international insolvency law and of civil proceedings connected with insolvency proceedings. In recent years, the case law of the Federal Court has gradually brought about more and more restrictions as regards the rights of foreign liquidators to act in Switzerland. Switzerland does not recognise the universal effect of main insolvency proceedings opened abroad in the sense that assets in Switzerland would be directly available for the foreign insolvency proceedings. Instead, if a decision opening insolvency proceedings abroad is recognised in Switzerland, territorial insolvency proceedings have to take place in Switzerland, and only their net profit (after privileged Swiss creditors have been fully paid) is handed over to the liquidator in the main insolvency proceedings (see Articles 166 et seq *Bundesgesetz über das Internationale Privatrecht*). This procedure even has to take place if there are no privileged Swiss creditors, and especially in the (not infrequent) cases where there is only a Swiss bank account and no other connecting factor in Switzerland at all. It might even be considered as a criminal offence if the liquidator simply contacts a Swiss bank and demands that the balance of a Swiss bank account be paid to him or her.[46]

Moreover, the Federal Court is not very enthusiastic at the moment about cross-border cooperation in cases where an insolvent party domiciled in Switzerland is in any way involved—even if the foreign proceedings are ordinary civil proceedings. This attitude even gave rise to a dispute (meanwhile discontinued) between Belgium and Switzerland before the International Court of Justice[47]: the Federal Court decided that Swiss proceedings on a *Kollokationsklage* (i.e. an action concerning a creditor's right to participate in the distribution of the proceeds)

---

[45] In this context, see, e.g. Bieri 2007, 708 et seq; Piaget 2006, 727 et seq.

[46] See, in this context, BGE 134 III 366 = Praxis 97 (2008) Nr. 144; 135 III 40; 135 III 666; Oberhammer 2009, 431 et seq; Oberhammer 2011a, 327 et seq; Jaques 2006, 19 et seq; Lorandi 2008, 560 et seq; Neuroni Naef and Naef 2008, 1396 et seq; Gehri and Kostkiewicz 2009, 204 et seq.

[47] International Court of Justice Case of *Belgium v Switzerland*, Jurisdiction and Enforcement of Judgments in Civil Matters, General List No. 145. Belgium discontinued the proceedings in March 2011; see http://www.icj-cij.org/docket/index.php?p1=3&p2=1&code=besu&case=145 (last consulted 22 August 2011).

cannot on any account be staid on the basis that proceedings on the creditor's claim are pending abroad. The Court took the position that the Swiss courts are exclusively competent to decide about the right to participate in insolvency proceedings and that results of foreign proceedings cannot be taken into account in such matters, apparently not even as regards the existence of the claim under substantive law.[48]

12.5 Conclusion

International harmonisation of civil procedure does not seem to be a goal of primary importance in the eyes of the Swiss legislature today. There might be a certain tendency to consider civil procedure as a field where an emotional need for preserving 'local legal culture' and national sovereignty might be satisfied without incurring great economic risks. Against this background, the most promising way of harmonising civil procedure (or certain aspects of it) seems to be by way of international conventions. Such conventions often turn out to be important for the development of civil procedure even outside their proper area of application. Meanwhile, there seems to be some reluctance to take foreign national law or non-binding sets of principles or rules as models for Swiss legislation in this field. Therefore, the chances for informal international harmonisation of civil procedure (at least as a conscious process) appear to be limited at the moment from a Swiss point of view.

References

Bieri L (2007) L'application du droit suisse reprenant de manière autonome des directives communautaires, Aktuelle Juristische Praxis 6:708–716

Botschaft (1990) Botschaft betreffend das Lugano-Übereinkommen über die gerichtliche Zuständigkeit und die Vollstreckung gerichtlicher Entscheidungen in Zivil- und Handelssachen. Bundesblatt II, 265

Botschaft (1998) Botschaft zum Bundesgesetz über den Gerichtsstand in Zivilsachen. Bundesblatt, 2829

Botschaft (2006) Botschaft zur Schweizerischen Zivilprozessordnung. Bundesblatt, 7221

Botschaft (2009) Botschaft zum Bundesbeschluss über die Genehmigung und die Umsetzung des revidierten Übereinkommens von Lugano über die gerichtliche Zuständigkeit, die Anerkennung und die Vollstreckung gerichtlicher Entscheidungen in Zivil- und Handelssachen. Bundesblatt, 1777

Bundesamt für Justiz (2004) Vorentwurf für ein Bundesgesetz über die Schweizerische Zivilprozessordnung (ZPO)—Zusammenstellung der Vernehmlassungen. http://www.ejpd.admin.ch/content/dam/data/staat_buerger/gesetzgebung/zivilprozessrecht/ve-ber.pdf (Accessed 22 Aug 2011)

[48] BGE 135 III 127; see also BGE 135 III 386.

Domej T (2006) Die künftige schweizerische Zivilprozessordnung—Struktur und Charakteristika des Verfahrens. Zeitschrift für Zivilprozess International 11:239–269

Domej T (2008a) Commentary on Article Ia, Protocol 1 of the Lugano Convention 1988. In: Dasser F, Oberhammer P (eds) Kommentar zum Lugano-Übereinkommen. Stämpfli, Berne, pp 833–837

Domej T (2008b) Commentary on the preamble of protocol 2 of the Lugano convention 1988. In: Dasser F, Oberhammer P (eds) Kommentar zum Lugano-Übereinkommen. Stämpfli, Berne, pp 873–897

Domej T (2010) Das EU-Zivilprozessrecht und die Schweiz: parallel oder aneinander vorbei? In: Busch et al (eds) Europäische Methodik. Jahrbuch Junger Zivilrechtswissenschaftler 2009, Boorberg, Stuttgart, pp 405–432

European Commission (2010) Proposal for a regulation of the European Parliament and the Council on jurisdiction and the recognition and enforcement of judgments in civil and commercial matters (recast), COM (2010) 748 final

Expertenkommission (2003a) Schweizerische Zivilprozessordnung: Vorentwurf der Expertenkommission. http://www.bj.admin.ch/content/dam/data/staat_buerger/gesetzgebung/zivilprozessrecht/entw-zpo-d.pdf. (Accessed 22 Aug 2011)

Expertenkommission (2003b) Schweizerische Zivilprozessordnung: Bericht zum Vorentwurf. http://www.ejpd.admin.ch/content/dam/data/staat_buerger/gesetzgebung/zivilprozessrecht/vn-ber-d.pdf. (Accessed 22 Aug 2011)

Gehri M, Kostkiewicz G (2009) Anerkennung ausländischer Insolvenzentscheide in der Schweiz—ein neuer réduit national? Schweizerische Zeitschrift für internationales und europäisches Recht 2:193–222

Gordon-Vrba L (2007) Vielparteienprozesse. Schulthess, Zurich

Jaques C (2006) La reconnaissance et les effets en Suisse d'une faillite ouverte à l'étranger, Commissione ticinese per la formazione permanente dei giuristi, Lugano

Knoepfler F (1996) La Convention de Lugano au soir du 31 décembre 1999. In: Zen-Ruffinen P et al (eds) De la constitution. Études en l'honneur de Jean-François Aubert. Helbing Lichtenhahn, Basle, pp 531–541

Kofmel Ehrenzeller S (2010) Commentary on Article 347 Zivilprozessordnung. In: Oberhammer P (ed) Kurzkommentar Schweizerische Zivilprozessordnung. Helbing Lichtenhahn, Basle, pp 1241–1246

Kren Kostkiewicz J (1999) Vorbehalt von Art. 1a des Protokolls Nr. 1 zum Lugano-Übereinkommen—quo vadis? Schweizerische Juristen-Zeitung 95:237–244

Lorandi F (2008) Handlungsspielraum ausländischer Insolvenzmassen in der Schweiz. Aktuelle Juristische Praxis 5:560–567

Markus A (1999) Der schweizerische Vorbehalt nach Protokoll Nr. 1 Lugano-Übereinkommen: Vollstreckungsaufschub oder Vollstreckungshindernis? 135 Zeitschrift des Bernischen Juristenvereins, pp 57–74

Naegeli G (2008) Commentary on Article 50 Lugano Convention 1988. In: Dasser F, Oberhammer P (eds) Kommentar zum Lugano-Übereinkommen. Stämpfli, Berne, pp 705–727

Neuroni Naef E, Naef F (2008) Droit suisse de la faillite internationale: la faillite d'un systeme? Aktuelle Juristische Praxis 11:1396–1412

Oberhammer P (2004a) Speeding up civil litigation in Austria: past and present instruments. In: Van Rhee CH (ed) The law's delay. Essays on undue delay in civil litigation. Intersentia, Antwerp, pp 217–232

Oberhammer P (2004b) Zivilprozessgesetzgebung: content follows method. In: Honsell H et al (eds) Privatrecht und Methode, Festschrift für Ernst A. Kramer. Helbing & Lichtenhahn, Basel, pp 1025–1050

Oberhammer P (2005) Die vollstreckbare öffentliche Urkunde im Vorentwurf einer eidgenössischen ZPO. In: Riemer et al (ed) Schweizerisches und internationales Zwangsvollstreckungsrecht. Festschrift für Karl Spühler. Schulthess, Zurich, pp 247–263

Oberhammer P (2009) Remarks on Bundesgericht 23.9.2008, 5A_222/2008=BGE 135 III 40, Schweizerische Zeitschrift für Zivilprozess- und Zwangsvollstreckungsrecht 2008/2009, pp 430–438

Oberhammer P (2011a) Jäger des verlorenen Schatzes: Deutsche Insolvenzverwalter in der Schweiz. In: Kern BR, Lilie H (eds) Jurisprudenz zwischen Medizin und Kultur. Festschrift für Gerfried Fischer. Peter Lang, Frankfurt, pp 327–348

Oberhammer P (2011b) Commentary on Article 57 Brussels I regulation. In: Stein, Jonas, Kommentar zur Zivilprozessordnung. Mohr Siebeck, Tübingen (forthcoming)

Piaget E (2006) L'influence de la jurisprudence communautaire sur l'interprétation des lois suisses relatives à la proprieté intellectuelle: argument contraignant ou simple aide à l'interprétation? Zeitschrift für Immaterialgüter-, Informations- und Wettbewerbsrecht, pp 727–739

Romy I (1997) Litiges de masse: des class actions aux solutions suisses dans les cas des pollutions et les toxiques. Editions Universitaires, Fribourg

Schweizerische Zivilprozessordnung—Entwurf (2006) Bundesblatt 7413

Staehelin D (2005) Die vollstreckbare öffentliche Urkunde—eine Ausländerin vor der Einbürgerung. In: Jametti, Greiner et al (eds) Rechtssetzung und Rechtsdurchsetzung. Festschrift für Franz Kellerhals. Stämpfli, Berne, pp 205–216

Staehelin D (2008) Commentary on article 39 Lugano Convention 1988. In: Dasser F, Oberhammer P (eds) Kommentar zum Lugano-Übereinkommen. Stämpfli, Berne, pp 644–657

Visinoni-Meyer C (2005) Die Vollstreckung einer öffentlichen Urkunde gemäss Art. 50 LugÜ in der Schweiz: Definitiver oder provisorischer Rechtsöffnungstitel? In: Riemer et al (ed) Schweizerisches und internationales Zwangsvollstreckungsrecht. Festschrift für Karl Spühler. Schulthess, Zurich, pp 419–431

Walter HP (2007) Das rechtsvergleichende Element—Zur Auslegung vereinheitlichten, harmonisierten und rezipierten Rechts, 126 Zeitschrift für Schweizerisches Recht, vol I, pp 259–277

Walther F (2002) Die Auslegung des schweizerischen Zivilprozessrechts, insbesondere des Bundesgesetzes über den Gerichtsstand in Zivilsachen. Stämpfli, Bern

Chapter 13
Globalisation and Scottish Law

Peter Beaton

Abstract Scotland is a mixed jurisdiction and the development of its legal system has been open to broader global influences and hence is open and liberal in its approach to international legal relations. This can provide an exceptionally good opportunity for Scottish jurists to contribute to the development of global international law projects. The Chapter supports these propositions by reflecting on some selected areas in which Scottish law has shown itself capable of being influenced by and in turn influencing other systems. Scotland had a tradition of openness to the civil law world, notably in France and the Netherlands, and had developed a set of rules of direct jurisdiction based on residence as the prime connecting factor. This openness was also demonstrated in the reception into the internal law of Scotland of the rules of the Brussels Convention as the basis for the rules on the competence of the Scottish courts. Also as regards recognition and enforcement the Scottish practice was to be rather liberal in enabling orders of foreign courts to be enforced. No requirement for reciprocity or an international convention was made nor did Scottish courts seek to impose their own jurisdictional criteria but rather took a global view as regards the competence of the courts of the requesting legal system. Scotland was also an early recipient of international arbitration law by applying the UNCITRAL model law in its domestic system and

The author is currently a consultant in European Civil and Private International Law and has worked closely with the Hague Conference on Private International Law; from 1991 to 2003 he held the post of head of the Civil Justice and International Division in the Scottish Justice Department and from 2004 to 2007 was a Special National Expert in the Civil Law Unit of DG JLS of the European Commission.This Chapter is dedicated to the memory of Professor A.E. Anton who died on 6 June 2011 and whose work on Private International Law made an important scholastic contribution to the subject not only in Scotland but globally.

P. Beaton (✉)
The Hague, The Netherlands
e-mail: petermurdochbeaton@yahoo.co.uk

X. E. Kramer and C. H. van Rhee (eds.), *Civil Litigation in a Globalising World*,
DOI: 10.1007/978-90-6704-817-0_13,

this strengthened an already lively tradition of supporting arbitration as a method of dispute resolution. The support which the Scottish system gave to party autonomy in general and also as regards arbitration reflects very much the modern global approach in international commercial law. The Scottish doctrine of *Forum non Conveniens* since received by many jurisdictions also supports a liberal open approach to the competence of the courts and would tend to minimise the effects of a strict adherence to *lis pendens*. Finally Scottish jurists have frequently played an important role in the world of Private International Law as for example their involvement in the work of the Hague Conference on Private International Law has shown. That has also demonstrated that Scottish law can be seen to be a bridge between the major law systems of the world.

Contents

13.1 Introduction

It is reasonably well known that the Scottish legal system counts among the relatively few which have been described as 'mixed.' In the case of Scotland, like South Africa, Quebec and to a degree Louisiana, this describes a situation whereby the Roman/Civilian origins of Scottish Law are to be found in the influence and writings of European continental jurists and legal theorists whilst later the resultant civilian basis of the law became overlaid to an extent by other traditions and influences notably from the English legal system.[1]

What may be less well known is that when the Scottish parliament was reconstituted in 1999, the founding legislation made it clear that among the competences of that parliament, and so of the Scottish Executive or Government

[1] As to mixed legal systems in general see, inter alia, Smits 2001 and Du Plessis 2006.

which is answerable to it, is the power to legislate on all matters of Scots Private Law including Private International Law.[2]

That being the case and given the development in recent years of a global approach to law, notably commercial and private international law, there is now, it is argued, an exceptionally good opportunity for Scottish jurists to continue to take part in and contribute fully to the formulation of new global international law projects given also that there are distinct features of the Scottish legal system which indicate that it is relatively open to interaction with other laws and legal systems.[3] This Chapter attempts to illustrate this proposition with a number of examples.

13.2 Jurisdiction Issues

Assumption of jurisdictional competence by Scottish Courts has been based on direct rules from as far back as can be described.[4] By the end of the sixteenth century at the latest it was clear that in general the Scottish courts did not take

---

[2] Scotland Act 1998, 1998 c. 46; see section 126 (4); the basic proposition set out in the founding statute is that the Scottish parliament is omnicompetent save as respects matters defined in the Scotland Act as 'reserved' to the UK parliament in London which are listed in Schedule 5 to the Act. The Scottish parliament took an early opportunity to exercise its powers as regards matters of Private International Law in the Adults with Incapacity (Scotland) Act 2000, 2000 ASP 4; section 85 and Schedule Three contain provisions regarding jurisdiction and Private International Law relating to vulnerable adults which derive from and relate to the Hague Convention on the International Protection of Adults of 1999 thus enabling the UK to ratify that Convention for Scotland only in 2003. This was the first ratification of the Convention and the first time since 1707 that a global International Convention had been ratified for Scotland. The Convention came into force as regards France, Germany and Scotland on 1 January 2009 and as regards Switzerland on 1 July 2009 and Finland on 1 March 2011. It will come into force as regards Estonia on 1 November 2011. It has been signed by a further eight States, all of which are Member States of the EU, including the Netherlands which signed the Convention in January 2000 as the first State to do so.

[3] As regards Scottish Law as a mixed Legal System see inter alia Smith 1962, 46 and 72; Reid and Carey-Millar 2005; and Zweigert and Kotz 1998, 202, 'In the fourteenth and fifteenth centuries Scots lawyers went to the Universities of Orleans, Avignon and Louvain for their education and to Leyden, Utrecht and Groningen after Scotland turned to Calvinism. Thus Scotland had a true reception of Roman Law; at the same time, in contrast to the Common Law which developed an insular self-sufficiency, Scots Law acquired a cosmopolitan and 'international' character, with a very distinctive combination of indigenous customary law (especially the feudal land law), Scots statutes, Roman Law, and the teachings of natural law'; and, with particular respect to the Law of Contract, MacQueen 2000.

[4] See generally, on Private International Law in Scotland, Anton 1967, and on jurisdiction at 91 et seq.

jurisdiction merely on the basis of presence of the defender but there had to be further connection between the forum and either the defender or the subject matter of the litigation.[5] The idea of an objective connecting factor was thus present from relatively early on in Scottish law and practice and the competence of the Scottish Courts was never based on purely procedural considerations.[6]

Whilst the defender's residence was and remains the key basic connecting factor, though as regards personal jurisdiction in certain personal actions domicile was sometimes preferred,[7] special rules were created for particular causes. Also Scottish law knew the doctrine of the assumption of jurisdiction through the presence of moveable property on Scots territory through the arrestment *ad fundandam jurisdictionem*, which remains valid today except as regards litigations subject to the rules of the Brussels I Regulation and Lugano Convention regimes.[8]

One particular feature of the Scottish system reinforces the principle of the suitability of the forum for the cause which is the basis of the general jurisdiction rules. This is the idea that a court should also consider whether it or another court is the more suitable to hear the case based on considerations of justice. This idea known alternatively as the principle of *forum non conveniens* or sometimes *forum conveniens* was applied by the Scottish Courts[9] particularly when jurisdiction was assumed on the basis of arrestment of moveable property to found jurisdiction, though generally the courts would examine the situation wherever a court elsewhere was competent.[10] In cases of arrestment to found jurisdiction the somewhat

---

[5] The Scottish courts have also tended to accept competence based on the effectiveness of execution of an order within the territory; see Anton 1967, 92 and *Fraser v Fraser & Hibbert* (1870) 8 M. 400 per Ld President Inglis at p. 405.

[6] The Scottish Courts did not accept competence due to the mere presence of the defender, but required residence within the territory of the court for a period of forty days unlike the courts in England where jurisdiction could be created by service on a defender present within the territory of the courts; this is also the case in the USA where the jurisdiction thereby created, known colloquially as 'the tag' jurisdiction, is rather widely used.

[7] For example in actions on personal status and other family law matters.

[8] According to Anton 1967, 160, n. 30 and cases cited therein, the rule on arrestment to found jurisdiction was borrowed from Dutch commentators. It founds competence alone as regards the subject matter of the action in connection with which it is used and not general jurisdiction against the defender. See also Anton and Beaumont 1990, 188–193.

[9] The Scottish Courts had and still have the practice of considering of their own motion whether a case is not within their competence if it is within the privative jurisdiction of another court. See Anton 1967, p. 93.

[10] See, generally as regards Forum non Conveniens, Brand and Jablonski 2007.

exorbitant effects of the use of this procedure were quite frequently tempered by the court through the acceptance of a plea as to *forum non conveniens*.[11] These rules and practices indicate a tendency for the Scottish Courts to be open to broader ideas when considering issues of jurisdictional competence. This was taken further in the process of adapting the internal jurisdiction rules when the Brussels Convention was incorporated into Scottish Law after the UK joined the European Community.

The accession to the Brussels Convention which accompanied membership of the EEC changed the basis of the Scottish rules of jurisdictional competence.[12] The impending UK membership of the EEC required consideration to be given to the arrangements for jurisdiction as between the UK and the other Member States but the opportunity was taken to review the rules as between the three UK law districts.[13] This led to the Brussels Convention rules being adopted in the main as a part of UK internal law for this purpose, albeit with some modifications. *Forum non conveniens*, which had not been accepted for incorporation into the Brussels Convention during the negotiations for the accession of the UK and Ireland, was retained nevertheless within the intra-UK jurisdictional regime.[14]

---

[11] Among the many Scottish cases on the use of Forum non Conveniens where jurisdiction is founded on arrestment of moveable's perhaps the most succinct expression of the balancing nature of the doctrine is to be found in *Societe de Gaz de France v Armateurs Francais*, 1926 S.C. (HL) 13 where, at p. 22, the following passage appears: 'The object… is to find that forum which is more suitable for the ends of justice and is preferable because pursuit of the litigation in that forum is more likely to secure those ends'; the court, per Lord Dunedin at 18, also approved a statement by Lord Kinnear in the earlier Scottish case of *Sim v Robinow*, (1892) 19 R, p. 665 where the following appears at p. 668: '… the plea [of Forum non Conveniens] can never be sustained unless the court is satisfied that there is some other tribunal, having competent jurisdiction, in which the case may be tried more suitably for the interests of all the parties and for the ends of justice.'

[12] Preparation for accession to the Brussels Convention by the UK took the form of the establishment of two committees composed of experts in Private International Law who were invited to consider what internal arrangements should be made in legislation and procedure. The advice which these committees gave was then incorporated in UK legislation in the form of the Civil Jurisdiction and Judgments Act 1982, 1982, c. 27. See also Convention of 9 October 1978 on the accession of Denmark, Ireland and the United Kingdom to the Brussels Convention, OJ [1978], L 304, 30 October 1978.

[13] Of the three law districts in the United Kingdom—England and Wales, Northern Ireland and Scotland—the Scottish is the only one which has a legislature dedicated to law-making for that law district; at present legislation of a primary nature for the other two law districts can only be passed in the UK parliament in London. Each law district has its own judicial structure and hierarchy. The juridical structure of the UK was the subject of a number of comments by Professor Peter Schlosser in his report to the Accession Convention; see OJ [1978], C 59/71, 5 March 1979.

[14] See Civil Jurisdiction and Judgments Act, 1982, Part II and Schedule 4, notably section 49 as regards the retention of Forum non Conveniens in non EU situations; it is noteworthy that the 1982 Act enables both decisions of the European Court of Justice on the interpretation of the Brussels Convention and Regulation and the Explanatory Reports by Paul Jenard to the original Convention and of Peter Schlosser to the Accession Convention to be referred to by the courts in the UK in interpreting the provisions of Schedule 4; see section 16(3).

Scotland went rather further than any other part of the EC by deploying the Brussels Convention jurisdiction rules as the basis of its internal law for distribution of competence among the territorial courts in Scotland.[15] In doing so the decision was taken to retain certain grounds of jurisdiction which had been outlawed as exorbitant in the Convention, including arrestment to found jurisdiction,[16] and also *forum non conveniens.*[17]

Another area in which Scottish ideas on jurisdiction were open to broader and global influence arose in relation to prorogation of jurisdiction and arbitration. The Scottish Courts had always considered party autonomy to be important. A choice of court conferred competence on the chosen forum to the exclusion of other possible competent fora except when the court chosen was not competent *ratione materiae* to hear the type of case concerned or when the subject matter of the case had nothing to do with Scotland when the principles of connection which lay behind the Scottish doctrine of *forum non conveniens* would be exercised.

The Scottish courts in turn would accept prorogation of a court outside the country and in this respect they anticipated the rules on prorogation which later appeared in the Brussels Convention.[18] Also, as regards arbitration, any such a restriction as applied to prorogation of jurisdiction of courts was even less likely. The Scottish Courts took and continue to take the view that an agreement to go to arbitration was effective to disapply any competence of the courts to try the merits of the subject matter of the arbitration and this also applies if the arbitration clause or contract provides for arbitration outside Scotland.[19] The characteristic expression of this principle was made in the following terms—'If the parties have contracted to arbitrate to arbitration they must go.'[20]

This support for party autonomy can be seen as reflective of a principle which is now in the ascendant generally and which can be found not only as regards jurisdiction rules but also in relation to applicable law and is therefore an

---

[15] See 1982 Act, Part III and Schedule 8.

[16] Except for cases subject to the Brussels Convention/Regulation and the Lugano Convention; see 1982 Act, Schedule 8, para 2 (h) (i).

[17] See 1982 Act, section 22(1); in Scotland the pleas of Forum non Conveniens and Lis Alibi Pendens were not mutually exclusive as is the case in law systems elsewhere and were frequently pled together in case of parallel actions thereby giving a degree of discretion and flexibility to the courts. This is subject to the general duty on the courts to consider their own competence and to decline ex proprio motu to judge a case where another court has exclusive competence—Schedule 8 para 8—or where they have no competence which would be compatible with the jurisdiction rules of schedule 8—see para 9.

[18] The current situation is to be found in Schedule 8, para 6. Any jurisdiction conferred by prorogation is exclusive.

[19] See Anton 1967, 235–237 and *Hamlyn & Co v Talisker Distillery*, [1894] 21 R p. 204 and (HL) p. 21; this rule does not entirely exclude the competence of the courts which can still enforce a decree arbitral or pronounce on the cause once resort to arbitration has taken place; the court will sist the case to await the outcome of the arbitration; see Hamlyn (HL) at p. 25 per Lord Watson.

[20] See *Sanderson & Son v Armour & co* 1922 S.C. (HL) p. 117 per Lord Dunedin at p. 126.

expression of the freedom of contract which is entrenched in modern global international commerce. There are of course issues about this, notably where contracts of a formal nature with standard terms and conditions are sought to be enforced and it is not clear whether, or which of, the standard terms were agreed.[21] But increasingly the choice of the parties is favoured as a matter of policy to give clarity to the rule and, it is argued, enhanced certainty to the parties themselves.[22]

Whilst this all tends to confirm the fact that the basis of much modern international commercial practice as regards jurisdiction is the freedom to select a forum of choice, that also applies even as regards a court with which the issues at dispute have no obvious connection. In this regard it might be considered a pity that the doctrine of *forum non conveniens* has generally been excluded from the internal EU jurisdiction regimes[23] since this might have had the effect of acting as a counterbalance to certain of the results of the strict adherence to the rules of jurisdiction and the application of a *lis pendens* rule which has been shown, perhaps unanticipated, to work against party autonomy not only as regards prorogation of the jurisdiction of the courts but also arbitration.[24]

It may be that this issue will be somewhat eased for the broader global situation once the Hague Choice of Court Convention[25] enters into force and has achieved substantial support, in particular if the EU Member States fulfil their declared intention that the EU ratify the Convention.[26] That Convention contains a provision which makes it clear that the jurisdiction of the chosen court should prevail, except in a limited number of exceptional circumstances, and any court not chosen has to decline to act in any case brought before it.[27] Its application globally as well

---

[21] 'Battle of the Forms' refers to the situation where in a particular contract both or several parties have sought to apply different terms expressed in standard forms and the resulting dispute turns on which of the forms are to be applied and thus what the actual contract was. This can also arise in relation to standard terms for dispute resolution such as prorogation of courts or resort to arbitration. For a recent discussion of the problem of the Battle of the Forms in the context of Scottish and South African Law see Forte 2006.

[22] See, for example, the preamble to Regulation No. 593/2008 on the law Applicable to Contractual Obligations (Rome I), OJ 2008, L 177/6, notably recitals Nos. (11), (12) and (16) and recital (14) in the Preamble to the Brussels I Regulation; see also the Preamble to the Hague Choice of Court Convention.

[23] An exception of a limited nature can be found in Art. 15 of the Brussels IIbis Regulation.

[24] A number of decisions of the European Court of Justice have emphasised that the effect of the *Lis Pendens* rule in the Brussels Convention/Brussels I Regulation tends to undermine party autonomy in choice of court and agreement to arbitrate by insisting that this has to be interpreted so as to override resort to a chosen court or to arbitration; one of the latest examples is Case C-185/07 Allianz SpA, formerly *Riunione Adriatica di Sicurtà SpA and Generali Assicurazioni Generali SpA v West Tankers Inc.*, 10 February 2009 (agreement to arbitrate held not to prevent resort to litigation).

[25] Convention of 30 June 2005 on Choice of Court Agreements.

[26] See Council Decision of 26 February 2009 (2009/397/EC)—OJ L 133, 29/05/2009, p. 3; on the relationship between the Choice of Court Convention and the Brussels I Regulation see Pertegas 2010.

[27] See Art. 6. The European Community signed the Convention on 1 April 2009.

as within the EU, if that should happen, could enable a more open approach and a more considered application of *lis pendens* in a way which gives greater support to party autonomy and at the same time does not destroy the principles of connectivity on which jurisdictional competence should be based.[28]

Even though there is still limited knowledge of and application of *forum non conveniens* in many legal systems it would be salutary if in due course the example set by the agreed text on the matter which was negotiated as a part of the ill-fated world-wide judgments project at the Hague might find its way into global acceptance as a way of balancing the need for certainty and order on the one hand and justice on the other as has been typified in the Scottish experience.[29]

13.3 Recognition and Enforcement

Just as with jurisdiction, the Scottish courts traditionally had a rather open position as regards recognition and enforcement of the orders of non Scottish Courts. In general they were prepared to give effect to such an order provided that it was clear that the court which issued it had jurisdictional competence of an international nature.

What was sufficient to constitute competence would be a matter for the Scottish court to decide but generally if it could be shown that the court seized had derived jurisdiction from the residence of the defender, prorogation, the actual or threatened commission of a delict on the territory of the court or, in an action in rem, the subject of the action within the territory of the court then the Scottish Court would generally allow the procedure for recognition and give effect to the order.[30] The Scottish Courts did not impose their own jurisdiction rules as a preliminary condition nor did they require reciprocity, far less a bilateral or multilateral agreement.[31]

---

[28] The proposal from the European Commission for a revised text of the Brussels I Regulation contains ideas for mitigating the effects of the *Lis Pendens* rule and for favouring the jurisdiction of a chosen court as well as the choice of arbitration for dispute resolution; see COM(2010) 748/3, 14/12/2010 notably recast Art. 29.

[29] See Preliminary Draft Convention adopted on 30 October 1999, notably Art. 21 and 22; the text can be found on the web site of the Hague Conference in Preliminary Document No. 11 of August 2000 among the preliminary documents to the Choice of Court Convention.

[30] The Court of Session has a specific procedure for giving effect to orders of courts and other judicial or quasi-judicial deliverances known as Decree Conform which is rather similar to the procedures for exequatur to be found in legal systems on the mainland of Europe, though it is not required to give effect to orders of the Scottish courts internally.

[31] See Anton 1967, 572 et seq; see also the remarks of Lord McLaren in *Waygood & co v Bennie* (1885) 12 R, 651 at p. 655: 'For the purposes of the present case I have thought it not irrelevant to consider what would be the limits of jurisdiction of this court in cognate matters. But I am far from saying that we are to apply the rules and practice of the Scottish courts in such matters as an absolute test of the regularity of the procedure of the English Courts in the assertion of their jurisdiction'.

These rules were varied by statute as regards recognition and enforcement of the orders of Courts in the other law districts of the UK and the opportunity was taken by the incorporation of the Brussels Convention to set up a simple process of registration of orders for enforcement in cross-border cases within the UK.[32] This obviated the necessity of raising a separate action of decree conform in the Court of Session for conversion of an incoming order from another UK law district into a Scottish Decree. This had been anticipated to a limited extent in arrangements for recognition and enforcement of orders for Courts in countries of the British Commonwealth and some other foreign territories, but these statutes had tended to emphasise reciprocity as a condition of recognition which reflected rather the English than the Scottish background thereof.[33]

13.4 Authentic Instruments

Another aspect of the Scottish system which enables it to be more open to a global approach is the way in which enforcement can take place of obligations contained in documents creating voluntary obligations without the need to approach a court to seek and an order for the purpose. The existence of procedures for registering agreements and other documents which create obligations, whether unilateral, bilateral or multilateral, gives great flexibility in general but also as regards contracts where there is an international element.[34] So a multi party contract where the parties are from different countries could be registered in the appropriate Scottish Register for execution and it, or an extract there from or certificate related thereto, can be used directly to effect procedures for enforcement.[35]

Whilst this technique is not shared with the other law districts of the UK, nor with other countries in the English law diaspora, it is common to many systems on the mainland of Europe and it is an advantage for the Scottish system given the inclusion of authentic instruments in the recognition and enforcement process in Brussels I, the Lugano Convention and other EU instruments.[36] The open, even

[32] See 1982 Act, *supra* cit. at n. 14, Sections 18 and 19 and schedules 6 and 7.

[33] See Administration of Justice act 1920 (10 &11 Geo 5, c 81) Part II and the Foreign Judgments (Reciprocal Enforcement) Act 1933 (23 & 24 Geo 5, c 13).

[34] Authentic instruments are not known generally in the legal systems of England and the English legal diaspora, a fact noted by Professor Schlosser in his report to the Accession Convention; see Schlosser 1979, para 226.

[35] Documents can be registered for execution in the Books of Council and Session or the Sheriff Court Books.

[36] See, for example, Art. 57 of the Brussels I Regulation, Art. 46 of Regulation No 2201/2003 concerning jurisdiction and the recognition and enforcement of judgments in matrimonial matters and the matters of parental responsibility, OJ 2003, L 338/1 (Brussels II bis) and Art. 48 of Regulation No 4/2009 on jurisdiction, applicable law, recognition and enforcement of decisions and cooperation in matters relating to maintenance obligations, OJ 2009, L 7/1, as well as Art. 57 of the new Lugano Convention.

global, approach thereby reflected indicates a continuing tendency for Scottish legal interests to be aware of the need for inter reaction with the wider legal community.

13.5 Arbitration

Arbitration is another area where Scottish law has shown itself to be open to global influence and interaction. As noted earlier, the right of parties to choose dispute resolution by voluntary arbitration was recognised from early on in Scotland. Many contracts were drawn up incorporating arbitration clauses both where the parties and the subject matter were in the country as well as where there was an international element. This was protected by the courts by ensuring that parties could not agree to arbitrate and the next minute turn round and effectively repudiate such agreement by seeking to litigate on the disputed issues on which they had agreed to go to arbitration.[37]

Scotland was the first part of the UK to incorporate the UNCITRAL Model Law on International Commercial Arbitration into its domestic legal structure.[38] This was done partly because of the wish of Scottish arbiters to attract arbitration business to Scotland, which otherwise was being dealt with elsewhere, but also as a matter of principle as a way of taking arbitration forward in an international context given the leading role which this form of dispute resolution plays, notably, in international commercial disputes. That incorporation law has now been succeeded by a comprehensive Arbitration statute which contains the essence of the UNCITRAL rules as well as enabling changes to be made to the statute itself and to the Arbitration code which accompanies it whenever changes are effected to the UNCITRAL Model Law.[39]

13.6 The Interaction Between Scottish Lawyers and Continental Jurists

Scottish lawyers and jurists have for many centuries interacted with colleagues in other parts of the world and that continues to this date. In the period of the formative years of the law and right up till the late eighteenth century Scottish law

[37] An example of what can happen in the situation where an agreement to refer a dispute to arbitration is subsequently disavowed by one of the parties is seen in the case of 'West Tankers' referred to *supra* at n. 24.

[38] See Law Reform (Miscellaneous Provisions)(Scotland) Act 1990, 1990, c. 40, section 66 and Schedule 7.

[39] Arbitration (Scotland) Act 2010, 2010 asp 1.

students and jurists were to be found on the mainland of Europe, first in France and later in the Netherlands where they trained and acquired a knowledge not only of the substantive civilian law of these countries but also of the procedural and other practices of the lawyers and courts.[40]

This enabled Scottish lawyers to achieve a rather open global view of the relationship between the Scottish system and other legal systems in Europe at a time when these systems were themselves the most developed in the world. It was therefore quite natural that Viscount Stair, the author of the first comprehensive work treating the Law of Scotland, should have taken refuge in the Netherlands from the political and religious turbulence in his own country and continued his studies there under the auspices of the University of Leiden in the footsteps of many earlier Scottish lawyers and law students.[41]

In the modern era Scottish lawyers have also been active globally as can be seen in the contacts between Scottish legal academics with their counterparts not only in the other mixed jurisdictions notably South Africa but also, for example, in Germany and the Netherlands. To some extent also the proximity to and influence of the English legal system has not had a totally deleterious effect on Scottish global legal links since it has allowed Scottish jurists and judges to participate in International legal arrangements through the network of the British Commonwealth and Anglo-American legal systems.

Individually Scottish and Scotland-based jurists have also had a relatively major role in certain negotiations of international instruments both at the Hague Conference[42] and also within the UK delegations at EU negotiations and at the Hague Conference.[43] Scottish academics and legal policy officials have been seen

---

[40] See again Smith 1962, xvii et seq and 46 et seq.

[41] See Stair 1681; Viscount Stair lived in Leiden from 1682 to 1689; his *Institutions of the Law of Scotland*, published in 1681, were modelled on the Institutes of Justinian.

[42] In recent times two Hague Conventions were negotiated under the Chairmanship of Scottish jurists, namely the 1980 Hague Child Abduction Convention, the concluding negotiations for which were chaired by Professor Anton, and the 1999 Convention on the Protection of Adults, the negotiations for which were concluded under the chairmanship of Professor Eric Clive.

[43] Present in many negotiations of Hague Conventions and EU instruments in Private International Law has been Professor Paul Beaumont, Professor of European and Private International Law of the University of Aberdeen; also, during the negotiations on the Brussels IIbis Regulation, the UK delegation contained and was greatly assisted by Peter McEleavey, now Professor of International Family Law at the University of Dundee. Furthermore, historically, officials of the Scottish Justice Department were members of the UK delegation at negotiations on key instruments including the review of the Brussels and Lugano Conventions, the Brussels IIbis Regulation, the Hague Choice of Court, Protection of Children and Protection of Adults Conventions; the momentum in this regard appears to have lessened in recent years, somewhat ironically given the re-establishment of the Scottish parliament in 1999.

to an extent which might not have been expected given the relatively minor influence of Scottish interests in other areas of UK international activity.[44]

Finally it should be noted that two of the four first UK judges at the European Court of Justice were Scottish lawyers.[45]

13.7 Conclusions

Despite its relatively small size the Scottish legal system has contributed to the global legal world to a degree which is disproportionate as well as surprising considering the pervasive influence of its southern neighbour and it continues to do so though perhaps more now in conjunction with rather than in opposition to or competition with that neighbour. Reception of doctrines from other legal systems is a strength of the Scottish system especially where, as it sometimes is the case, notably where the work derives from the Scottish Law Commission, this follows extensive comparative research.[46]

The fact that the Scottish system contains elements of the two great western European legal traditions in its mixed nature is of assistance in this regard and there are countless examples of the influence which it has had on the other system. There is now an opportunity for the Scottish system more than ever to offer itself as a bridge between these traditions at a time when global legal development has become ever more expressed in international instruments and within the EU the move for harmonising Private International Law to considering harmonised or even unified substantive law is gathering ground.[47]

That Scottish legal academics have been conspicuously involved in the work leading up to and preparing for this process is characteristic of the capacities and strengths of the Scottish system and it is to be hoped that other representatives of the Scottish legal system, as well political as legal, will see their way to

[44] Both Professor Eric Clive and Professor Hector MacQueen of the University of Edinburgh have been active in the various projects for development of European Private and Contract Law, the former being one of the joint editors of the draft Common Frame of Reference and the latter a member, inter alia, of the Ole Lando group.

[45] Lord Mackenzie Stuart was a member of the court from 1973 to 1988 and was its President from 1984 to 1988, and Sir David Edward was a member from 1992 to 2004 having been appointed as a member of the court of first instance in 1989.

[46] See, on this point, Smits 2008, para 6.

[47] Amongst the many commentators who have argued that Scots Law as a mixed system has much to offer in the construction of common legal norms are Henri Levy Ullman who went rather far in this respect by pronouncing that; 'Scots law as it stands gives us a picture of what will be, some day … the law of the civilised nations, namely, a combination between the Anglo-Saxon system and the continental system'; see Lévy-Ullman 1925, 390; Du Plessis 1998, 339 and Whitty 1996, 457.

contributing to this process and bringing to it the particular insights which are available from that part of Europe.[48]

References

Anton AE (1967) Private international law. A treatise from the standpoint of Scots law, Scottish Universities Law Institute. W. Green & Son, Edinburgh

Anton AE, Beaumont PR (1990) Private international law. A treatise from the standpoint of Scots law, Scottish Universities Law Institute. W. Green & Son, Edinburgh

Brand RA, Jablonski SR (2007) Forum non Conveniens. History, global practice, and future under the Hague convention on choice of court agreements, CILE studies, vol 3. Oxford University Press, Oxford

Du Plessis J (1998) The promises and pitfalls of mixed legal systems: the South African and Scottish experiences. Stellenbosch Law Rev 9:338–350

Du Plessis J (2006) Comparative law and the study of mixed legal systems. In: Reimann M, Zimmermann R (eds) The Oxford handbook of comparative law. Oxford University Press, Oxford

Forte A (2006) The battle of the forms. In: MacQueen, Zimmermann (eds) European contract law: scots and South African perspectives. Edinburgh University Press, Edinburgh Studies in Law, pp 98–122

Lévy-Ullman H (1925) The law of Scotland. Juridical Rev 37:370–391

MacQueen HL (2000) Scots law and the road to the new Ius Commune. Elect J Comp Law. http://www.ejcl.org/ (accessed June 2011)

Pertegas M (2010) The Brussels I regulation and the Hague convention on choice of court agreements. ERA-Forum 11(1):19–27

Reid E, Carey-Millar D (eds) (2005) A mixed legal system in transition: TB smith and the progress of Scots law. Edinburgh University Press, Edinburgh

Schlosser P (1979) Report on the convention on the association of the kingdom of Denmark, Ireland and the United Kingdom of Great Britain and Northern Ireland to the convention on jurisdiction and the enforcement of judgments in civil and commercial matters and to the protocol on its interpretation by the Court of Justice, Official Journal, C 59/71

Smith TB (1962) Studies critical and comparative. W. Green & Son, Edinburgh

Smits JM (ed) (2001) The contribution of mixed legal systems to European private law. Intersentia, Antwerp

Smits JM (2008) Mixed jurisdictions: lessons for European harmonisation? Electron J Comp Law 12.1. http://www.ecjl.org/121/art121-23.pdf

Stair V (1681) Viscount stair. Institutions of the law of Scotland, Edinburgh

Whitty NR (1996) The civilian tradition and debates on Scots Law. Tydskrif vir die Suid-Afrikaanse Reg, pp 227–239 and 442–457

Zweigert K, Kotz H (1998) Introduction to comparative law, 3rd edn. Clarendon Press, Oxford

[48] For a recent commentary on the theme of Mixed Jurisdictions and European harmonisation see Smits 2008.

Chapter 14
A Dutch Perspective on Civil Litigation and its Harmonisation

Paulien van der Grinten

Abstract This chapter addresses the challenges of the globalisation of civil litigation from a Dutch perspective. It is submitted that for national governments it is inevitable to deliberate on harmonisation. Countries face similar problems and challenges in national civil justice and in the increasing number of cross-border disputes. If governments do not think about harmonisation, others will, in particular the European Commission. National legislators respond in different ways to European intervention depending on whether or not they already have a solution for the specific problem, are working on a solution at that moment or have recently done so. Simultaneous legislative activities create specific challenges, such as in the area of collective redress where both the national legislator and the EU are active at the moment. When faced with the choice between a sectoral approach or a general approach, the Dutch legislator usually prefers a general approach. Furthermore, the Dutch approach to cutting the costs and burden of litigation for citizens and for governments and mass claims are addressed, for which harmonisation at the European level may be considered. In a globalising world the interaction between national and international activity is not just a choice, it is a fact of life. Governments should find their own strategy and vision to deal with it.

Coordinating legal advisor, Ministry of Security and Justice, the Netherlands.

P. van der Grinten (✉)
Ministry of Security and Justice, Hague, The Netherlands
e-mail: p.van.der.grinten@minvenj.nl

X. E. Kramer and C. H. van Rhee (eds.), *Civil Litigation in a Globalising World*,
DOI: 10.1007/978-90-6704-817-0_14,

Contents

14.1 Introduction

This contribution focuses on a Dutch government's perspective on the challenges of the globalisation of civil litigation. As my personal responsibilities in the past years have concentrated on national and European aspects of civil litigation, the European element will also be a focus. I shall discuss why thinking about harmonisation of civil litigation is inevitable for any European government and what strategies governments can develop to deal with activity in this field from 'Brussels.' Two specific challenges—cutting the costs and burden of civil litigation for citizens and for governments and dealing with mass claims—will be discussed separately.

14.2 Why Thinking About Harmonisation is Inevitable

National laws on civil procedure tend to be closely linked to national culture and history—although certain groups of systems can be identified.[1] Therefore, they vary immensely and harmonisation is difficult. This should not stop us from thinking about the relation between our national rules on civil procedure and the rest of the world. On the contrary, in this era an active government strategy on the interaction between national and international activity is inevitable for numerous reasons, of which I mention only three.

1) *Same problems in national civil justice and same challenges*
The problems we face in our national civil justice systems are rather similar for all of us. Cutting the costs and burden of litigation for citizens and for governments, the need for an efficient way to obtain an enforceable title in cases of unpaid debts,

[1] See, inter alia, Gottwald 2005, 23–35; Storme 1994, 87–99.

the increasing number of mass claims which require collective solutions and the insufficient rates of actual enforcement of judgments are just a few of the common challenges for courts and for governments in all countries. To this we can add the effects of the financial crisis which have forced all European governments to make huge cuts in their budgets for the coming years. Budgets for courts and litigation will not be exempt from this in most States.[2] We can and must learn from each other's solutions and practices in order to best address these challenges.

2) *Increasing number of cross-border disputes*
Moreover, an increasingly globalised world brings with it an increasing number of cross-border disputes. And these cross-border disputes tend to involve a higher number of people, that is, more mass claims. Clearly, in cross-border disputes the need for internationally agreed rules comes more naturally. The powers of national courts stop at the national border unless agreed otherwise at an international level. For this type of international agreement mutual trust is normally required together with a certain level of harmonisation of the national civil procedural rules for international cases. States will only accept a foreign court's decision within its territory if certain crucial requirements of civil procedure have been met. Common rules on respect for the defendant's rights in the procedure leading to the judgment is an example of this.[3] This is at the core of the judicial cooperation within the European Union and its idea of mutual trust. The same idea can be found in the work within the Hague Conference on Private International Law ever since the Conference came into existence.

3) *If we do not think about harmonisation as Member States, others (i.e. the European Commission) will*
Every Member State of the European Union is part of a multilayered system of powers, politics and levels of initiatives in which each player has to play its own role. In civil matters, including civil litigation, the European Commission has the exclusive right of initiative for new proposals. The European Commission is therefore a key player that has to maintain this key position by coming up with relevant proposals and by being indispensable to the functioning of the Union. This means that the European Commission has an interest in trying to be ahead of the Member States in the issues they take on board and in creating a link with the single internal market. Once a problem has been solved by Member States at a national level, there is much less need for European intervention. Therefore, it is in

[2] In the Netherlands, these budget cuts have led to far-reaching proposals and a draft bill to make court fees more cost-effective, at least at an overall level, resulting in court fees sometimes ten times as high as before. The proposals have been criticised by many as regards their effects on access to justice in the Netherlands. Whether the bill will be adopted by the Dutch Parliament remains to be seen. Whatever happens to the bill, it clearly stresses the need for more efficient means for citizens to solve their legal problems.

[3] Cf. Art. 6 of the European Convention on Human Rights whose rule on fair trial has led to a much greater awareness of this rule as a fundamental right of each party involved in civil litigation.

the interest of the European Commission to create and maintain a need for supranational, European action rather than national action in order to meet the subsidiarity requirement. This need for European action can be found both where cross-border issues are involved and where certain Member States completely lack efficient rules and European intervention is said to be necessary in order to create a so-called level playing field. These general principles also apply to civil procedural law.

Therefore, any smart government ought to take a huge interest in the possible interaction between European and national measures.

14.3 European Activity in Civil Procedural Law and How to Deal with it

14.3.1 European Activity

Over the last ten years we have seen increased activity on the part of the European Union in the field of civil procedural law. This increased activity can be seen in three different areas.

The first area is the classic area of international cooperation. A very successful example of a European instrument facilitating cross-border dispute resolution by uniform rules on international jurisdiction and recognition and enforcement, whilst at the same time harmonising certain rules of civil procedure regarding the defendant's safeguards, is, of course, Regulation Brussels I of the European Union (No. 44/2001). At a global level the Hague Convention on the Service of Documents could serve as an example.[4] Other European examples would be Regulation 1348/2000 on the Service of Documents and its successor, Regulation 1393/2007.[5]

The second area is the area of specific European civil procedures for certain specific types of cases, such as the Regulations on a European Payment Order Procedure (No. 1896/2006) and a European Small Claims Procedure (No. 361/2007).[6] On grounds of restrictions to the powers of the European legislator under Article 65 of the Treaty establishing the European Community (now replaced by Article 81 of the Treaty on the Functioning of the European Union), these are limited to cross-border cases only. The Directive on certain aspects of mediation in

---

[4] Hague Convention of 15 November 1965 on the Service Abroad of Judicial and Extrajudicial Documents in Civil or Commercial Matters, see http://www.hcch.net/index_en.php?act=conventions.text&cid=17 (last consulted in June 2011).

[5] Regulation No. 1348/2000 on the service in the Member States of judicial and extrajudicial documents in civil or commercial matters, OJ 2000, L 160 as replaced by Regulation No. 1393/2007 on the service in the Member States of judicial and extrajudicial documents in civil or commercial matters (service of documents), OJ 2007, L 324, and repealing Regulation No. 1348/2000, OJ 2007, L 324.

[6] Regulation No. 1896/2006 creating a European order for payment procedure, OJ 2006, L 399 and Regulation No. 861/2007 establishing a European Small Claims Procedure, OJ 2007, L 199.

civil and commercial matters (No. 2008/52) does not belong to that area completely, but does force the harmonisation of certain elements of the national civil procedural laws of the Member States.[7] However, the scope of that Directive is also limited to cross-border mediations. It will therefore only have a limited impact on the national laws on civil procedure.[8] Forthcoming are the projects meant to improve the enforcement of judgments in civil matters: the attachment of bank accounts and the transparency of the debtor's assets.[9] Even if these last two will be limited to cross-border cases, they will probably be far more problematic than the ones previously mentioned. I will discuss this in more detail when discussing unsatisfactory enforcement rates as one of our common challenges.

The third area of increased harmonising activity is the enforcement of the existing acquis. Examples of this last area are the Directive on the Enforcement of Intellectual Property Rights and the forthcoming projects in the field of collective redress in competition law and consumer law.[10] The reason for this increased activity is that in the European Union the harmonisation of the substantive laws in those fields has to a wide extent been completed. But that harmonisation has not resulted in a perfect internal market. The effects of those harmonised substantive laws on the European internal market have been unsatisfactory. A further harmonisation—not of the substantive laws, but—of the rules regarding the enforcement thereof, aims to improve the functioning of the internal market in specific fields. All the instruments and projects in these second and third areas exist because the European Commission or the European legislator has identified them as problematic or as an obstacle to the proper functioning of the internal market.

A fourth area is announced in the Stockholm Action Plan of the European Commission as published on 20 April 2010.[11] It concerns the outright harmonisation of aspects of civil procedural law. The Commission intends to publish a green paper on minimum standards for civil procedures in 2013.

---

[7] Directive (EC) 2008/52 on certain aspects of mediation in civil and commercial matters, OJ 2008, L 136.

[8] However, most Member States have chosen to transpose the Directive also for internal cases.

[9] See COM (2011) 445 final, Proposal for a Regulation of the European Parliament and of the Council creating a European Account Preservation Order to facilitate cross border debt recovery in civil and commercial matters which is a follow-up from the Green Paper on improving the efficiency of the enforcement of judgments in the European Union: the attachment of bank accounts, COM (2006) 618 (final). See also the Green Paper on the effective enforcement of judgments in the European Union: the transparency of debtors' assets, COM (2008) 128 (final).

[10] Directive 2004/48/EC of the European Parliament and of the Council of 29 April 2004 on the enforcement of intellectual property rights, OJ 2004, L 157 and its corrigendum in OJ 2004, L 195; White Paper on damages actions for breach of the EC antitrust rules, COM (2008) 165 (final) and Green Paper on consumer collective redress, COM (2008) 794 (final).

[11] Delivering an area of freedom, security and justice to Europe's citizens—Action Plan Implementing the Stockholm Programme, COM (2010) 171 (final).

14.3.2 How Governments Deal with this European Activity

How do national governments deal with this European activity in the field of civil procedural law? What strategies on harmonisation do we have? Roughly speaking, three types of strategies can be distinguished.

1) *When they already have a well-established national solution*
Sometimes these governments have had to come up with solutions for a problem long before the European Union started to address the problem in the context of the internal market. For example, the German *Mahnverfahren* had been in place for ages when the European Commission launched its Green Paper on a European Payment Order.[12] Where this is the situation and where European action is nevertheless required (the subsidiarity requirement has been met), national systems may serve as a model for European solutions based on a 'best practices' approach. And after adoption, the national procedure and the European procedure may merge.

2) *When they do not have a specific solution*
Sometimes, on the contrary, a government has not implemented any specific rules addressing the problem. In such a situation, things become slightly more complicated for a national government. Here, the same European Payment Order Procedure may be used as an example, but now in relation to the Netherlands.[13] The Dutch Code of Civil Procedure does not contain a specific procedure for debt collection. We had nothing against a European Payment Order as such and were in favour of a fast procedure for cross-border debt collection. But the way in which internal claims for debt collection are conducted in practice by the Dutch courts in ordinary civil proceedings will normally be quicker and for the courts less costly than the specific European Payment Order Procedure. For those reasons the Dutch government has implemented the European Payment Order in a strict way, limited to cross-border cases without extending its scope to internal cases. Should it turn out that the European Payment Order is a huge success, we may reconsider an extension of the scope.[14] The harmonisation of national law on civil procedure would then be the effect of such an extension of scope.

3) *When they have recently or are still working on a solution*
A third possibility is when 'Europe' and national governments are working on solutions for problems simultaneously. In my view, this is an even more difficult

---

[12] Green Paper on a European order for payment procedure and on measures to simplify and speed up small claims litigation, COM (2002) 746 (final) resulting in Regulation (EC) 1896/2006 creating a European order for payment procedure, OJ 2006, L 399.

[13] See Kramer and Sujecki 2007, 1–8. See specifically on the implementation of the European order for payment procedure, Van der Grinten 2010, 109–128.

[14] In view of the government's plans on more cost-effective court fees, the Dutch Parliament has already asked for a payment order procedure for internal cases.

scenario. An example of simultaneous work at a global, a European and a national level would be the work done on collective redress. Nearly all Member States have recently worked on or are currently working on either specific or general collective redress mechanisms, each of the States in very different ways. For some years now the European Commission has been working on collective redress in competition law and consumer law. At first this was based on a sectoral approach with different solutions for competition law and consumer law, depending on the Directorate General within the European Commission responsible for either competition law or consumer law. This sectoral approach was different from the one taken in at least some Member States, such as the Netherlands. Vast opposition has led the Commission to a change in strategy. The proposal for an instrument on competition law was never launched. The plans for collective redress for consumers are now the shared responsibility of three Commissioners: Justice, Competition, and Health and Consumers (Sanco). Thereafter, the Commission announced a single approach for both competition law and consumer law enforcement. To prove its good intentions the Commission started a public consultation on a 'coherent approach' to collective redress within the European Union.[15] It is not at all clear what direction will be taken by the Commission.[16] These rules are meant to apply at a global level.

Here we face a real challenge. On the one hand, this is, at least for Europe, a relatively new area of law and best practices have yet to be established. Any European initiative trying to create a European collective mechanism or trying to harmonise the very recent national mechanisms would threaten to kill those national initiatives. On the other hand, the problem of mass claims is acute. Questions which arise are: who comes first, the national legislators or the European Union? Are there any issues which are inherently transnational and which cannot be solved at the national level but which require European or even global coordination, such as the question regarding jurisdiction in mass claims?

This is where law meets politics. In a Union with 27 Member States there will always be Member States that need the European legislator to force them to take action. Other Member States that are further ahead in their national development in the area of collective redress—like the Netherlands—will want to safeguard their successful national initiatives, initiatives which may not be seen by others as a suitable solution for them. So far the Dutch government's strategy has been to explain and promote its—rather unique—mechanism to other Member States and to the European Commission. Where we see opportunities for European intervention, e.g. in coordinating transnational mass claims, we try to convince those

[15] Towards a coherent European approach to collective redress, SEC (2011) 173 (final).

[16] At the same time the International Law Association (ILA) adopted a resolution on international collective redress during its sessions in Rio de Janeiro in 2008: Paris-Rio guidelines on best practices for transnational group actions, prepared by the ILA committee on international civil litigation and the interests of the public, to be downloaded from their website, www.ila-hq.org (last consulted in June 2011).

responsible to focus on these opportunities rather than coming up with a separate European mechanism for collective redress.

4) *When faced with the choice between a sectoral or specific approach versus a general approach*

A further strategy required from governments, regardless of the three situations mentioned above, is the choice for a sectoral or specific approach rather than a general approach, or vice versa. Examples of a sectoral approach where one could also imagine a general approach are mostly found in the third area of the Commission's activities: new rules on the enforcement of the existing acquis. The policy of the Dutch Ministry of Security and Justice is that a general approach is preferable to a sectoral approach as is clear from the Dutch response to several green papers in the area of civil procedure and collective redress. A general approach prevents fragmentation of the law. The confusion and lack of clarity caused by this fragmentation threatens *de facto* the access to justice for citizens whilst intending the opposite. On the Enforcement of Intellectual Property Rights the Dutch did not manage to stop the Directive from being adopted. However, as explained above, as regards the European Commission's sectoral activities in the area of collective redress we and others have been more effective.

The choice for either a specific instrument or a general approach is the choice for a '28th regime' or minimum standards. Different arguments can be used in favour of either option. For the United Kingdom the choice is simple. As long as the scope of a European instrument is limited to a separate regime for cross-border cases, they can accept such an instrument regardless of how many trimmings such an instrument will get.[17] For them, the prime concern is to ensure that their own national civil procedural law remains unaffected. In the past, the Dutch approach was in general that harmonisation is to be preferred. Harmonisation seems to fit in better with a system of codified law. A separate European regime leads—just as a sectoral approach—to fragmentation and to the existence of different legal systems side by side. This is considered to be undesirable.

Applied to the example of the forthcoming proposal for a European attachment of bank accounts, a special European regime is potentially boundless and disproportionate. In order to create a uniform regime for the European Union, provisions on the ranking of the attachment and on the attachment of joint accounts might have to be included. But at least under Dutch law those provisions are not even part of our civil procedural law. They are at the heart of our substantive law on joint ownership and ranking of debts in general.

However, the harmonisation of attachment of bank accounts may be problematic, too. Where national laws on civil procedure, like the Dutch Code of Civil Procedure, have a general scheme for protective attachments against a third party, the harmonisation of the rules on the attachment of bank accounts alone would seem problematic. Such a European harmonised system for the attachment of bank

[17] See also Van der Grinten 2009.

accounts would interfere with the Dutch scheme for protective attachments against a third party as a whole. However, the consequences for those other types of attachment against a third party will not have been taken into account in the realisation of this European instrument. Moreover, a harmonised European regulation for the attachment of bank accounts threatens to override qualitatively better national rules in this respect.

Thus, governments should carefully choose their strategy in these matters. The Dutch strategy in this specific example of the attachment of bank accounts has been to suggest alternatives and to explain the importance of keeping the attachment itself local, regardless of who gave the order or permission to attach.

14.4 Common Challenges and How to Deal with Them

In this last part of my contribution I want to discuss, from a Dutch government's perspective, some of the challenges in civil procedural law which all of us face. I will focus on two of them but many others could be given. The two challenges are: (1) cutting the costs and burden of litigation for citizens and for governments and (2) mass claims.

14.4.1 Cutting the Costs and Burden of Civil Litigation for Citizens and for Governments

The costs of civil litigation are considered to be the ultimate obstacle for parties to embark upon court proceedings. The financial crisis has forced us to make budgetary cuts in our civil justice system in the amount of hundreds of millions of euros. The Dutch government has decided that the court fees will be increased substantially in order to cover these hundreds of millions, partly by a raise in incoming fees and partly by a drop in the number of cases.[18] At the same time the government wants to present an Innovation Agenda that should lead to better and more efficient court proceedings and to better alternatives for going to court.[19] Thinking about this innovation as very preliminary thoughts, I personally see a threefold approach which the government could take.

Firstly, we want to improve substantive laws to provide clear and simple rules which prevent legal disputes. Examples could be stricter and more predictable statutory standards for child maintenance, termination of employment contracts

[18] See the draft bill which is available on the government's website http://www.rijksoverheid.nl/documenten-en-publicaties/regelingen/2011/04/04/wetsvoorstel-invoering-van-kostendekkende-griffierechten.html (last consulted 1 July 2011) and e.g. *Kamerstukken* 31753, Nos. 27 and 36.

[19] See *Kamerstukken* 31753, No. 27.

and damages. Another example would be to provide that any method sufficient for entering into a contract will do for its termination. For example, if sending a text message by SMS is the way a consumer can obtain a certain SMS service, then sending a text message by SMS—rather than a registered letter as often required under the standard terms of the contract—is a sufficient means to terminate this service. A successful example of existing legislation is the Dutch Statute on Electricity (*Elektriciteitswet*) together with the Dutch Grid Code. These include a provision that puts an obligation on the provider to compensate consumers for a fixed amount for a power failure of more than four hours. Each commercial party in the Dutch energy market is bound by the Grid Code, which is part of the party's licence. For the liability of employers we consider the introduction of an insurance-based system rather than a civil liability system.

Secondly, only those cases in which court intervention can be effective should be brought before the court. This should save expenses for the government and for parties that can choose an alternative route to solve their legal problems. To achieve this goal, the use of ADR schemes like our Consumer Claims Tribunals and mediation could be stimulated also financially by using different legal aid fees if an alternative could have been used. Moreover, parties should be stimulated financially to use our Legal Desk as their intermediary before going to a lawyer and asking for legal aid. The use of specialised lawyers in family law should be stimulated. In this way we can filter those cases where non-specialised lawyers start unnecessary or even vexatious proceedings either because they lack sufficient knowledge of the law or because they do not care and only want to get their legal aid money.

A completely different measure with the same goal has been the introduction in July 2010 of the 'partial dispute' procedure in personal injury cases. This procedure will help the parties to resolve their dispute out of court. Either party can ask the court to intervene on one or more specific issues which are an obstacle to resolving their dispute out of court (e.g. on liability, or on medical data). The court only intervenes if its intervention can positively affect the out-of-court resolution of the dispute as a whole. To ensure access for the victim, all the costs of the partial dispute procedure will be borne by the person held liable (his or her insurer) and can be claimed in full should proceedings on the dispute as a whole follow. Moreover, to help the parties in a personal injury case to resolve their dispute, a self-regulatory Code of Conduct exists with rules on a transparent and harmonious compensation scheme.

Thirdly, cases should be dealt with efficiently and speedily. This means that where appropriate, cases should be dealt with in one instance only. This may seem a rather radical measure to propose. However, it offers a high level of predictability for the parties in assessing their risk of starting litigation and it brings their dispute to a close much sooner. In order to be able to have evidence-based proposals in this area, an empirical study will be carried out in 2011 and 2012 on the types of cases in which and the reasons why an appeal is lodged. A condition for a one-instance-only approach is, of course, a high-quality first instance court. Improvements can be made in the Dutch rules and Dutch practice on the taking of evidence and by the introduction of a wizard-based electronic simple claims procedure.

Interestingly enough, the European Commission has put the Regulation on the taking of evidence in its Stockholm Action Plan in order to 'if necessary come up with minimum standards for the taking of evidence.'[20] A more European approach to the sort of information which parties should be able to receive from each other and from third parties could have added value and prevent expensive forum shopping.

14.4.2 Mass Claims Which Require Collective Solutions

In this section, the Dutch approach to mass claims will be discussed separately. Dealing with mass claims in an efficient way can prevent numerous individual claims concerning the same legal dispute from being brought before the court. In that respect, they fit perfectly well in an approach to create a civil justice system where court intervention is focused and efficient.

The Dutch collective redress mechanism is laid down in the Dutch Collective Settlement Act of 2005.[21] It is based on court approval of a collective settlement between the party that is held responsible for the damage and representative organisations on behalf of the injured parties. The Dutch Collective Settlement Act is rather successful. It has led to higher amounts paid to injured parties than anywhere else in Europe (far over a billion euros). It is also a mechanism which has proved to work in cross-border mass claims.[22]

The Dutch system on collective redress does not stop at the Dutch Collective Settlement Act. Dutch civil procedural law has a collective action in which liability can be established but in which no compensation can be claimed collectively. The bundling of individual mass claims in one procedure is also allowed. We are currently looking at measures to promote ways to efficiently deal with mass claims. A bill is pending in Parliament to introduce the possibility for a court to pose a preliminary question to the Dutch Supreme Court if the answer to that question is relevant to a number of cases.[23] Thus, the early intervention of the Dutch Supreme Court can help to resolve many other similar individual cases at an

[20] See no. 9, 22–23.

[21] Dutch Collective Settlement Act of 23 June 2005 (*Wet collectieve afwikkeling massaschade*, 'WCAM'), Staatsblad 2005, 340.

[22] See the research report commissioned by the Ministry of Security and Justice 'The Dutch Collective Settlements Act and Private International Law, Aspecten van Internationaal Privaatrecht in de WCAM' prepared by Erasmus School of Law (Van Lith, supervised by De Ly and Kramer), available at http://bit.ly/kqHTRP (or www.wodc.nl), also published as Van Lith 2011; Van Boom and Arons 2010, 857–883.

[23] Bill submitted to Parliament in 2010, introducing the possibility for courts to ask preliminary questions to the Dutch Supreme Court ('Wijziging van het Wetboek van Burgerlijke Rechtsvordering en de Wet op de rechterlijke organisatie in verband met de invoering van de mogelijkheid tot het stellen van prejudiciële vragen aan de civiele kamer van de Hoge Raad (Wet prejudiciële vragen aan de Hoge Raad)'), *Kamerstukken* 32 612, Nos 2 and 3.

early stage whether by the lower courts or even out of court. Another measure included in a draft bill to improve our Collective Settlement Act is the possibility for either of the parties involved to ask the court for a prehearing to see what would be needed to facilitate a settlement. In this prehearing the court could, for example, identify points of law which will have to be addressed—either in court proceedings or out of court—before parties will be ready to come to an agreement. Yet another measure considered is to allow collective legal aid both in legal aid schemes and under legal aid insurance policies. This would entail the possibility for the insurer to deal with a mass claim of many individual insureds on a collective basis, e.g. by hiring a lawyer to start a collective action rather than all those individual procedures for individual claims. At the same time we look for ways to put some limits to the rather open system of mass representation by way of *ad hoc* associations. This is a more recent challenge which we face in a civil justice landscape where claims and especially mass claims have become a real market.

In order for the Dutch system on collective redress to work even more effectively we see some room for intervention by the European Union. For example, the European Court of Justice (ECJ) has ruled in a decision on legal aid insurance that any insured person has the right to choose his or her own lawyer under the Directive on legal expenses insurance.[24] In order to work complementarily at a national and European level, it would be very helpful if at a European level we would accept an exception to this rule for the purpose of the efficient handling of mass claims.

Moreover, in cross-border cases and in order to have better coordination at least within the European Union we would need supplementary rules at a European level. These rules do not relate to a European collective redress mechanism or to minimum standards for a national collective redress mechanism. All we need for the time being are rules for international jurisdiction in collective redress of mass claims and rules and clarifications on the meaning of *lis pendens* in mass claims. For example, could or should the Dutch procedure to get approval of a collective settlement of mass claims for the purpose of *lis pendens* count as a procedure concerning the right to compensation of the injured parties? Even if the Dutch court accepts jurisdiction in an international mass claim, that Dutch court cannot stop an individual injured party from starting a procedure in another Member State regarding the same event which caused the mass claim. European rules could solve this. The International Law Association rules on transnational collective procedures could be used as a source of inspiration.

At a later stage when national practices in internal and international cases have been better established a further harmonisation of collective redress could be considered. Of course, we try to promote our model as a pragmatic approach to collective redress which could work for Europe, too. But if a majority would fail to

---

[24] ECJ 10 September 2009, Case C-199/08, ECR I-8295 (*Dr. Erhard Eschig v UNIQA Sachversicherung AG*); Directive 87/344/EEC of 22/06/1987 on the coordination of laws, regulations and administrative provisions relating to legal expenses insurance, OJ 1987, L 185/79.

see the benefits of the Dutch solution to the problem of mass claims, then what? In my view we ought to think twice before we adopt a supranational European collective redress mechanism. Supposedly, the aim of any European project in the field of collective redress is to enhance the enforcement of mass claims and compensation to victims in those cases in Europe. If these mass claims are cross-border, some coordinating provisions seem necessary, but otherwise national mechanisms may address the need for mass compensation in a perfectly acceptable and successful manner. Only if and to the extent that a State does not have any mechanism for efficiently dealing with mass claims, we may, at least within the European Union, want to stimulate them to create some sort of mechanism. As long as such a mechanism is effective, should we care what it looks like? Should we bother whether it is an opt-in or an opt-out mechanism, or a settlement-based scheme? Having harmonised rules should not be an aim in and of itself. A national mechanism like the Dutch Collective Settlement Act providing for successful collective redress to injured parties should not have to be amended just for the sake of European harmonisation.

Moreover, in as far as the aim is enforcement of the rules violated by the person held liable, we should first discuss whether private law mechanisms can and do indeed serve that purpose.

14.5 Where to Go: Civil Justice in Europe

In this contribution I have not dealt with the legal basis for judicial cooperation in Europe. In practice this may give rise to endless discussions and it may prevent us from getting results where we want them. At the same time, I have seen previous examples where the legal basis for a European measure was at best doubtful. When everybody involved wants a measure badly, there will not even be a blocking minority to stop the measure from being adopted just because of a missing legal basis.

I think in the globalising world in which we live the interaction between national and international activity is not just a choice. It is a fact of life. What governments can do with this fact of life is that they should find their own strategy and vision to deal with it. What issues are best dealt with at the international/ European level? In what manner should the issue be dealt with at that level? What can best be left to national law? For example, we consider the exclusion of appeal in Dutch civil procedural law based on an analysis of the types of cases in Dutch appeal proceedings in which the case in appeal is not about a second chance or a revision of the first court's decision but rather about the fact that one of the parties is still angry that his or her partner has left him or her.

References

Gottwald P (2005) Comparative civil procedure, Ritsumeikan Law Rev, 22:23–35

Kramer XE, Sujecki B (2007) Fundamentele herbezinning op de betalingsbevelprocedure. Invoering van een betalingsbevelprocedure in het licht van het Eindrapport Fundamentele herbezinning en de Europese betalingsbevelprocedure, Tijdschrift voor Civiele Rechtspleging, 1–8. English abstract http://repub.eur.nl/res/pub/10830/(PDF version) (Accessed July 2011)

Storme M (1994) Procedural consequences of a common private law for Europe. In: Hartkamp A et al (eds) Towards a European civil code, 1st edn. Ars Aequi Libri, Nijmegen

Van Boom WH, Arons T (2010) Beyond tulips and cheese: exporting mass securities claim settlements from the Netherlands. Eur Bus Law Rev 21(6):857–883

Van der Grinten PMM (2009) Challenges for the creation of a European law of civil procedure, http://ssrn.com/abstract=1392006 (Accessed July 2011)

Van der Grinten PMM (2010) De inbedding van de Europese betalingsbevelprocedure in het Nederlandse burgerlijk procesrecht: een leerzaam proces. In: Polak MV (ed) Inbedding van Europese procesrechtelijke normen in de Nederlandse rechtsorde. Ars Aequi Libri, Nijmegen, pp 109–128

Van Lith H (2011) The Dutch collective settlements act and private international law. Aspecten van Internationaal Privaatrecht in de WCAM. Maklu, Antwerp

Chapter 15
The German Approach to the Globalisation and Harmonisation of Civil Procedure: Balancing National Particularities and International Open-Mindedness

Stefan Huber

Abstract Germany participates actively in the competition between the different judicial systems. The German Bar Association, the German Judges Association and the German Notaries Association have even published a brochure entitled *Law—Made in Germany* with a view to informing about the advantages of the German judicial system and German law. This initiative has launched an important reform process in Germany. A bill now before Parliament proposes to establish special court chambers for transnational commercial disputes where the entire proceedings, from the statement of claim up to the judgment, shall be conducted in English. The reform process, however, concentrates on the rules which govern the proceedings in German courts. The situation is different for the classical area of international civil procedure. Here, Germany still gives much importance to the idea of state sovereignty in the administration of cross-border judicial assistance, and the German way of recognising and enforcing foreign judgments from non-EU Member States reflects an ambivalent mixture of an open-minded point of departure on the one hand, and an accentuation of national interests and concepts on the other. Against this background the present paper comes to the conclusion that the modernisation of German civil procedure should be based on four aspects: first, concentration on the parties' interests rather than on the idea of state sovereignty; second, recognition of party autonomy in respect of procedural rules; third, specialisation of judges who are capable of conducting the entire proceedings in English; and, fourth, adoption of special procedural rules for transnational cases.

S. Huber (✉)
Institute for Comparative Law, Conflict of Laws and International Business Law, Heidelberg University, Heidelberg, Germany
e-mail: huber@ipr.uni-heidelberg.de

X. E. Kramer and C. H. van Rhee (eds.), *Civil Litigation in a Globalising World*,
DOI: 10.1007/978-90-6704-817-0_15,

Contents

15.1 Introduction

The transnational character of a dispute leads to certain problems which do not occur in purely national cases. These problems must be the starting point of an analysis of the German approach to the globalisation of civil procedure. Three different categories of typical procedural problems in transnational litigation shall be considered for the present purposes: (1) the classical category concerns the situation where a procedural act needs to be performed outside the territory of the forum state; (2) the second category comprises all the problems that arise from the foreign nationality or seat of at least one of the parties; (3) finally, problems occur in connection with court proceedings that take or have already taken place in a foreign State.[1]

The way in which the German legislator, German judges, solicitors and other professionals have addressed these problems so far characterises the *status quo* of the German approach to the globalisation and harmonisation of civil procedure (Sect. 15.2 below). The most significant particularity of the German approach to the globalisation of civil procedure, however, is a current reform project which intends to establish special chambers for transnational commercial disputes with English as the court language (Sect. 15.3 below).

---

[1] There is a fourth category comprising all the problems which result from applying rules of foreign law to the substantive matter in dispute. As those problems are closely connected with the conflict of laws rules, they will not be dealt with in the present paper. See for an in-depth analysis of all the questions related to this category Esplugues et al. 2011 and Hübner (forthcoming).

15.2 German Reactions to the Specific Challenges of Transnational Litigation

15.2.1 Cooperation with Foreign Authorities: Efficient and Reluctant at the Same Time

The classical solution to the classical problem that a procedural act needs to be performed outside the territory of the forum state is cooperation with foreign authorities. The service of documents and the taking of evidence abroad are two areas where such cooperation is well established.

A long time before the European legislator created two specific instruments in this area,[2] the Hague Conference on Private International Law adopted the Convention on Civil Procedure,[3] the Convention on the Service of Documents[4] and the Convention on the Taking of Evidence Abroad.[5] As to the last two Conventions, Germany was among the first signatories,[6] and, at least in the area of transnational service of documents, German authorities execute foreign requests for judicial assistance swiftly.[7] But this is only one side of the coin.

---

[2] Council Regulation (EC) No 1206/2001 of 28 May 2001 on cooperation between the courts of the Member States in the taking of evidence in civil or commercial matters, OJ L 174, 27 June 2001, 1–24; Council Regulation (EC) No 1348/2000 of 29 May 2000 on the service in the Member States of judicial and extrajudicial documents in civil or commercial matters, OJ L 160, 30 June 2000, 37–52; this regulation has been replaced by Regulation (EC) No 1393/2007 of the European Parliament and of the Council of 13 November 2007 on the service in the Member States of judicial and extrajudicial documents in civil or commercial matters (service of documents), and repealing Council Regulation (EC) No 1348/2000, OJ L 324, 10 December 2007, 79–120.

[3] Convention of 1 March 1954 on civil procedure; the text and the status of this convention can be consulted at http://www.hcch.net/index_en.php?act=conventions.text&cid=33 (last consulted in May 2011).

[4] Convention of 15 November 1965 on the Service Abroad of Judicial and Extrajudicial Documents in Civil or Commercial Matters; the text and the status of this convention can be consulted at http://www.hcch.net/index_en.php?act=conventions.text&cid=17 (last consulted in May 2011).

[5] Convention of 18 March 1970 on the Taking of Evidence Abroad in Civil or Commercial Matters; the text and the status of this convention can be consulted at http://www.hcch.net/index_en.php?act=conventions.text&cid=82 (last consulted in May 2011).

[6] Cf., the status tables at http://www.hcch.net/index_en.php?act=conventions.status&cid=17 and at http://www.hcch.net/index_en.php?act=conventions.status&cid=82 (last consulted in May 2011).

[7] Cf., the German response to the 2008 service questionnaire, which can be consulted at http://hcch.e-vision.nl/upload/wop/2008germany14.pdf (last consulted in May 2011). This document shows that approximately 90 per cent of the requests for service received in 2007 were executed within 2 months and approximately another 9 per cent within 4 months. This is much faster than the average processing time under the Service Convention; cf., the summary of responses to the service questionnaire, 17, which can be consulted at http://hcch.e-vision.nl/upload/wop/2008pd14e.pdf (last consulted in May 2011). The results under the Evidence Convention do not reflect the same degree of efficiency; cf., the German response to the 2008 evidence questionnaire, which can be consulted at http://hcch.e-vision.nl/upload/wop/2008germany20.pdf (last consulted in May 2011); here the German processing time seems to be the average time under the

On the other side of the coin are the many objecting declarations and reservations which Germany has made with respect to these Conventions. Well known is the objection against the execution of letters of request which are issued for the purpose of obtaining pre-trial discovery of documents as known in common law countries. However, this reservation has been made by the vast majority of the Contracting States (40 out of 52).[8] For our purposes, the following reservations are more interesting: in derogation from Article 4(2) of the Evidence Convention, Germany does not accept letters of request in the English or French language although the majority of the non-English- and non-French-speaking Contracting States has agreed to do so (23 out of 44).[9] Furthermore, Germany has objected against the taking of evidence by diplomatic officers or consular agents if German nationals are involved and thus belongs to a minority of 14 out of 52 Contracting States.[10]

As to the Service Convention, Germany has declared its opposition to the direct transnational service of documents by postal channels—once again in contrast to the majority of the Contracting States (35 out of 62).[11] And finally, Germany has restricted direct service through diplomatic or consular agents of another State to nationals of that State; 28 out of 62 Contracting States have decided differently.[12]

Even within the limited area of the European Union Germany had excluded the possibility for private persons who are involved in foreign proceedings to effect service of documents directly through German officials under the first EC Service Regulation,[13] although such a possibility exists for certain documents in purely national cases.[14]

(Footnote 7 continued)
Evidence Convention; cf., the summary of responses to the evidence questionnaire, 17, which can be consulted at http://hcch.e-vision.nl/upload/wop/2008pd12e.pdf (last consulted in May 2011).

[8] Cf., the status table of the Evidence Convention at http://www.hcch.net/index_en.php?act=conventions.status&cid=82 (last consulted in May 2011).

[9] Cf., the status table of the Evidence Convention at http://www.hcch.net/index_en.php?act=conventions.status&cid=82 (last consulted in May 2011).

[10] Cf., the status table of the Evidence Convention at http://www.hcch.net/index_en.php?act=conventions.status&cid=82 (last consulted in May 2011).

[11] Cf., the status table of the Service Convention at http://www.hcch.net/index_en.php?act=conventions.status&cid=17 (last consulted in May 2011).

[12] Cf., the status table of the Service Convention at http://www.hcch.net/index_en.php?act=conventions.status&cid=17 (last consulted in May 2011).

[13] Cf., former Article 1071 of the German Code of Civil Procedure which was abolished in 2008. This Article deviated from Article 15 of the Council Regulation (EC) No 1348/2000 of 29 May 2000 on the service in the Member States of judicial and extrajudicial documents in civil or commercial matters. Certainly, the new EC Regulation on the service of documents (1393/2007), which has replaced the first Service Regulation, no longer gives the Member States the right to declare such a reservation. Cf., Article 15 of the new regulation.

[14] Cf., for example, Article 191 et seq, 922(2) and 936 of the German Code of Civil Procedure for the case of provisional measures.

These examples illustrate the important role which respect for state sovereignty plays for Germany in the area of judicial assistance for civil proceedings in foreign courts. Voices that plead for a different concept of judicial assistance, at least at the European level, are fortunately getting louder and louder.[15] The interests of the parties, not the sovereignty of States, should be in the centre of any legal analysis in the context of judicial assistance for civil proceedings. But the German administrative instructions concerning judicial assistance with foreign States (*Rechtshilfeordnung für Zivilsachen*, hereafter ZRHO)[16] still adhere to the traditional concept. They contain, for example, a rule forbidding German authorities to examine witnesses in a foreign State by postal channels without the judicial assistance of that State.[17]

All this shows that Germany gives much importance to respect for the sovereignty of other States as well as its own. Germany still takes the idea of state sovereignty as a cornerstone during its negotiations in the area of judicial assistance. As a consequence, it is also reluctant in the implementation of international optional instruments. It is therefore not surprising that Germany is not among those Contracting States where foreign commissioners who are authorised to take evidence under the Hague Convention can apply for assistance to obtain evidence by compulsion.[18]

15.2.2 Interests of the Foreign Party

The second category of problems comprises all the difficulties which arise from the foreign nationality or seat of at least one of the parties. The foreign party will be confronted with a couple of problems that a German party does not encounter.

15.2.2.1 The Language Problem

First of all, the foreign party has to cope with the language problem. The German Courts Constitution Act[19] provides that court proceedings are to be conducted in German (Article 184). Certainly, the foreign party has the right to an interpreter at the trial stage. But dependence on the services of an interpreter is a considerable disadvantage. In addition, it is very costly.

---

[15] Cf., for example, Hess 2010, § 3 para 62 et seq; Stadler 2002, 1281, 1285.

[16] Rechtshilfeordnung für Zivilsachen (ZRHO); available at http://www.datenbanken.justiz.nrw.de/pls/jmi/ir_start (last consulted in May 2011).

[17] Article 39 ZRHO.

[18] Cf., the status table of the Evidence Convention at http://www.hcch.net/index_en.php?act=conventions.status&cid=82 (last consulted in May 2011).

[19] *Gerichtsverfassungsgesetz*; an English translation is available at http://bundesrecht.juris.de/englisch_gvg/index.html (last consulted in May 2011).

For these reasons, certain chambers of some German courts have introduced the English language at the trial stage. This is possible under Article 185(2) of the German Courts Constitution Act. If all parties agree on English as the trial language, the trial will be conducted in English. The precursors of this approach were, not surprisingly if one considers the predominance of merchant and maritime traditions, the courts in Hamburg. Other courts followed, and since 2010 there are even special chambers at the regional courts (*Landgerichte*) of Bonn, Cologne and Aachen as well as at the Court of Appeal (*Oberlandesgericht*) in Cologne where in transnational cases parties can apply for the trial to be conducted in English.[20]

In reaction to this German pilot project the French Commercial Court of Paris staffed one of its chambers with judges who understand English, Spanish or German. The idea is to allow the parties to present documentary evidence in one of these languages. The judges may even permit the parties to plead in those languages. However, the judgment has to be issued in French.[21]

The rule in the German Courts Constitution Act which permits the use of foreign languages in German courts is also limited to the oral stage of the proceedings.[22] Parties can present their case, including any evidence, in a foreign language; but the statements of claim and defence are to be submitted in German and the judgment has to be written in German.[23]

This might change in the near future. On 7 May 2010 the Federal Council (*Bundesrat*)—one of the Chambers of Parliament—adopted a bill which seeks to establish special court chambers for transnational commercial disputes where the proceedings can be conducted entirely in English—from the stage of the claim up to the judgment.[24] It is not yet clear whether this draft will become a statute. The President of the German Federal Supreme Court, Klaus Tolksdorf, criticised the

---

[20] The trial is conducted in English only if all parties to the case file such a request; cf., the court business allocation plans (*Geschäftsverteilungspläne*) of the mentioned courts at: http://www.lg-bonn.nrw.de/10_wir_ueber_uns/120_GVP/index.php (Bonn); http://www.lg-koeln.nrw.de/wir_ueber_uns/index.php (Cologne); http://www.lg-aachen.nrw.de/wir_ueber_uns/index.php (Aachen); http://www.olg-koeln.nrw.de/001_wir_ueber_uns/geschaeftsverteilung/index.php (Court of Appeal in Cologne) (last consulted in May 2011). See for a general explanation of this pilot project the press release of the Court of Appeal in Cologne published on 15 January 2010 at http://www.olg-koeln.nrw.de/presse/archiv/archiv_2010/004_01-13-15_handout_gerichtssprache englisch_vita.pdf (last consulted in May 2011). Armbrüster 2011a, 102 expresses doubts whether the present version of Article 185(2) of the German Courts Constitution Act provides a sufficient legal basis for this pilot project.

[21] Bulletin du Barreau de Paris, 6 December 2010, n° 41, at http://www.lebulletin.fr/le-conseil-41/2554-creation-dune-chambre-internationale-au-tribunal-de-commerce-de-paris.html (last consulted in May 2011).

[22] The wording of Article 185(2) of the German Courts Constitution Act is very clear; cf., Bundesgerichtshof (German Federal Supreme Court) 14 July 1981, *Neue Juristische Wochenschrift* 1982, 532, 533.

[23] Bundesgerichtshof 14 July 1981, *Neue Juristische Wochenschrift* 1982, 532, 533; Hoppe 2010, 373–374.

[24] Entwurf eines Gesetzes zur Einführung von Kammern für internationale Handelssachen, BR-Drs. 42/10.

idea of using English in German courts. He expressed doubts about the language skills of German judges which, if not sufficient, might even lead to wrong decisions.[25]

The proponents of the project argue that German courts might lose their importance in the area of international trade because foreign parties would fear that the use of German as the court language might be a serious disadvantage.[26] Therefore, international contracts would frequently contain choice of court clauses in favour of courts in English-speaking countries. Accordingly, the parties would choose English law for their business relationships.[27] The idea on which the bill is based is to make the choice of a German forum and of German law more attractive. Furthermore, the use of the English language in civil proceedings is intended to avoid a clash of two languages—the language of the contract from which the dispute arises and the language of the proceedings aimed at settling the dispute.[28] Such a clash generates high translation costs, in particular for documentary evidence,[29] and may also cause misunderstandings and lead to wrong decisions (for a more detailed analysis of this project, see *infra* Sect. 15.3).

15.2.2.2 Protection Against Unexpected National Particularities

It is not only the German language which constitutes an obstacle for the foreign party. National particularities of German civil procedure might create further difficulties. Two examples shall be discussed: firstly, the German answer to the parties' need of documents which are in the control of the opponent, and, secondly, German default judgments.

The German way of document production

German civil procedure is well known for its traditionally restrictive approach to document production. Until 2001 the German Code of Civil Procedure did not know a purely procedural general duty to produce documents which support another party's case.[30] The underlying principle was *nemo tenetur se ipsum prodere*,[31] which means nobody is obliged to assist in proving a case against himself.

---

[25] Cf., the summary of Tolksdorf's speech, which he held at the New Year's Reception of the Supreme Court in February 2010, available at http://www.unternehmer.de/bgh-prasident-sieht-probleme-bei-englisch-als-gerichtssprache-32621 (last consulted in May 2011).

[26] Cf., the preparatory works of the draft law, BR-Drs. 42/10, 7 Mai 2010, 6; Müller-Piepenkötter 2010, 2–3.

[27] Cf., the preparatory works of the draft law, BR-Drs. 42/10, 7 Mai 2010, 7; Prütting 2010, 113.

[28] Cf., the preparatory works of the draft law, BR-Drs. 42/10, 7 Mai 2010, 7.

[29] Kreindler and Rust 2007, 1278, para 16; for the possibility to rely on documents in a foreign language cf., Armbrüster 2011b, 812, 813.

[30] Huber 2008, 106 et seq, 159.

[31] Huber 2008, 107, 158 et seq.

This does not, however, mean that a party had no possibility to claim the production of documents. It is true that there was no general procedural duty. But the procedural law referred to the substantive law, which provides for numerous obligations to produce documents.[32] Those obligations, however, always concern very specific situations.[33] Thus, it could be quite difficult to find out whether a party to civil proceedings was under a duty to produce documents or not. This concept was confusing, unjust and in contrast with the international principle of access to information and evidence now expressed in Principle 16 of the ALI/ UNIDROIT Principles of Transnational Civil Procedure.[34]

The important reform of the German Code of Civil Procedure in 2001 rectified the traditional concept of document production, which had already been softened to a certain degree by the German Federal Supreme Court.[35] It gave the judge the power to oblige the parties to produce certain documents even if there is no obligation under substantive law.[36] In this context the judge generally disposes of a wide range of discretion; only under very specific circumstances does the judge have the duty to issue a production order.[37]

This new procedural authority of the German judge is a considerable step towards the international standard.[38] It is nevertheless regrettable that the German legislator did not replace the traditional system by a completely new one, which would be based on a purely procedural obligation to produce documents. Instead of doing so, the legislator added just one new element whose exact scope is not yet clear.[39] However, at least it is clear that the principle of *nemo tenetur se ipsum*

---

[32] Cf., Articles 422 and 429 of the German Code of Civil Procedure (*Zivilprozessordnung*); for an in-depth analysis of these provisions cf., Huber 2008, 117 et seq, 159.

[33] Huber 2008, 203 et seq.

[34] Huber 2008, 392 et seq; the ALI/UNIDROIT Principles of Transnational Civil Procedure can be consulted at http://www.unidroit.org/english/principles/main.htm (last consulted in May 2011); see also a special issue of the Uniform Law Review/Revue de Droit Uniforme (2004 No. 4) with contributions by Brinkmann, Einstein/Phipps, Glenn, Karrer, Kerameus, Nhlapo, Scarpinella Bueno; for the French reaction to this project see Ferrand 2004.

[35] Cf., for example, Bundesgerichtshof 20 January 1961, *Neue Juristische Wochenschrift* (*NJW*) 1961, 826, 828; Bundesgerichtshof 12 November 1991, *Neue Juristische Wochenschrift* (*NJW*) 1992, 1817–1819; Bundesgerichtshof 24 June 2004, *Kommunikation und Recht* 2004, 443; Bundesgerichtshof 26 November 1968, *BGHZ* 51, 91; Bundesgerichtshof 27 April 2004, *Neue Juristische Wochenschrift* (*NJW*) 2004, 2011; Bundesgerichtshof 5 July 1973, *BGHZ* 61, 118 (121); Bundesgerichtshof 27 September 1957, *Versicherungsrecht* 1958, 107; Bundesgerichtshof 7 June 1971, *BGHZ* 74, 256; for an analysis of this evolution cf., Huber 2008, 126 et seq, 160 et seq.

[36] Huber 2008, 166 et seq, 213 et seq.

[37] Huber 2008, 296, 297.

[38] For an analysis of the international standard cf., Huber 2008, 357 et seq.

[39] Huber 2008, 215 et seq and 296 et seq; cf., Bundesgerichtshof 26 October 2006, *Neue Juristische Wochenschrift* (*NJW*) 2007, 155, where the Court still referred to traditional principles; for an analysis of this decision cf., Huber 2008, 168, n. 354.

prodere has been overcome in the area of civil procedure,[40] and the lower courts use their new power in many situations.[41] But there is still too much room for uncertainty, which is a problem in civil litigation in general, and in particular for a foreign party who is not familiar with the German traditional principles and their evolution.

German default judgments

The example of document production cannot, however, be generalised. In order to guarantee the equitable and swift solution of transnational disputes, traditional rules are not necessarily to be abolished for the only reason that they deviate from the international standard. Certain traditional rules might even be more appropriate for transnational commercial litigation than the international standard. For example, the German Code of Civil Procedure provides that a default judgment, which is entered against a defendant who, without justification, fails to appear, is exclusively based on the factual allegations of the claimant (Article 331). A German judge does not analyse whether the claim is reasonably supported by evidence.[42]

This is a clear deviation from the international standard established in Principle 15 of the ALI/UNIDROIT Principles of Transnational Civil Procedure. Nevertheless, parties of transnational transactions might prefer the German solution. If parties that enter into a contract were asked which dispute resolution mechanism they would like to choose, they would probably opt for a system which guarantees the swift and efficient issuing of a judgment in a situation where the contractual partner fails to fulfil his contractual obligations and does not cooperate any more in any way, neither in negotiations nor in court proceedings. In such a situation, any question of evidence is an obstacle that creates a risk of delay and uncertainty. Certainly, a protection mechanism against unjustified default judgments, which might be issued due to the fraudulent behaviour of one party, is necessary. But firstly, such protection is guaranteed by appropriate notification rules and by the court's obligation to set aside the default judgment and to reopen the proceedings if an application for the setting aside is made within the time limit provided for in Article 339 of the German Code of Civil Procedure. Apart from the time limit, such an application does not depend on any conditions. Secondly, the risk of unjustified judgments due to the fraudulent behaviour of one side will rarely be the focus of the parties' interests when they conclude a contract, at least if there is a minimum basis of mutual trust. Against this background, the German default judgment rule might find approval in the area of international trade.

---

[40] Huber 2008, 167, 168.

[41] Cf., for example, Oberlandesgericht (Court of Appeal) Hamm 13 September 2006, 8 U 84/05 Juris; for further cases and their analysis cf., Huber 2008, 167.

[42] Rosenberg et al. 2010, 588.

15.2.2.3 Conclusion

This leads to the following conclusion: on the one hand, Germany has recognised the necessity to enhance the suitability of the German court system and German civil procedure for transnational commercial disputes. As already mentioned, the German Bar Association, the German Judges Association and the German Notaries Association have even published a brochure with the title *Law—Made in Germany*[43] designed to advertise the advantages of the German judicial system and German law. This is a reaction to the brochure *England and Wales: The jurisdiction of choice*, which was published by the Law Society of England and Wales and which praises the advantages of English law, the English judicial system and London as the place of arbitration for transnational disputes.[44]

On the other hand, Germany is still engaged in an on-going, difficult process of overcoming certain traditional principles which are inappropriate for transnational disputes. However, it is not desirable that this process throws all traditional rules which deviate from the international standard overboard, as some of them might even be perceived as a competitive edge over other systems.[45]

15.2.3 Effects of Foreign Judgments

The third category of problems that may arise in the context of transnational civil litigation concerns the effects of proceedings that are or have been conducted in a foreign State. Within this category the rules on recognition and enforcement of foreign judgments shall illustrate the characteristics of the German approach to the globalisation of civil litigation. The national rules are influenced by international treaties and superseded by European law except for judgments which have been rendered outside the European Union in a State that has not entered into any convention on the recognition of judgments with Germany, as for example the United States. In such a situation the German Code of Civil Procedure applies and implements a general principle of recognition of foreign judgments. This general principle is, however, limited by five exceptions. Besides internationally well-established exceptions, such as the public policy exception,[46] there are three exceptions which seem to be more doubtful.

---

[43] This brochure can be consulted at http://www.lawmadeingermany.de/ (last consulted in May 2011); in this context, cf., von Westphalen 2010, 241.

[44] The brochure can be consulted at http://www.lawsociety.org.uk/documents/downloads/jurisdiction_of_choice_brochure.pdf (last consulted in May 2011).

[45] See for an analysis of the competition between different judicial systems the contribution of Van Rhee (Chap. 3 of the present volume); Kötz 2010, 1, 5 et seq.

[46] But compare the on-going steps by the European Commission to remove or reduce the scope of the public policy exception in instruments of European Union law dealing with the recognition of foreign judgments; cf., for example, the proposal for a [new] regulation of the European

15.2.3.1 The Reciprocity Exception

A foreign judgment will not be recognised in Germany if the foreign State does not recognise German judgments of the same nature.[47] The idea behind this exception is clear: foreign States shall be put under pressure to cooperate in the area of cross-border enforcement. It must be noticed, however, that this strategy has failed—at least up to now.[48] In addition, the negative consequences of this exception are manifest. It can be very difficult for a party to prove that the reciprocity condition is fulfilled.[49] Uncertainty and unnecessary difficulties arise. For this reason, many authors have been arguing for a long time to abolish the reciprocity exception[50]—unfortunately up to now in vain.

15.2.3.2 Strict Priority of German Judgments in Case of Irreconcilable Decisions

A second highly criticised exception concerns the conflict between two irreconcilable decisions. A foreign judgment will not be recognised in Germany if it is irreconcilable with a German judgment.[51] The chronological order of the judgments does not matter. This leads to a strict priority of German judgments over foreign judgments even in cases where the German court has violated its own rules of *lis pendens*.[52] This solution is not convincing, but it is still in accordance with the European standard: the European regulation on jurisdiction and the recognition and enforcement of judgments in civil and commercial matters provides the same rule[53]; and the proposal for a reform of this regulation, which the European

(Footnote 46 continued)
Parliament and of the Council on jurisdiction and the recognition and enforcement of judgments in civil and commercial matters, COM (2010) 748 final.

47 Cf., Article 328(1) No. 5 of the German Code of Civil Procedure; for an analysis of this provision cf., for example, Huber 2009, 735, 830.

48 Cf., Schack 2010, paras 43, 964.

49 The German Federal Supreme Court has decided that the party who seeks the recognition of a foreign judgment has to prove the facts which show that the reciprocity condition is fulfilled; Bundesgerichtshof 29 April 1999, *BGHZ* 141, 286; for a critical analysis of this decision see Pfeiffer 1991, 734, 751 et seq.

50 Cf., for example, Schack 2010, paras 880, 969.

51 Article 328(1) No. 3 of the German Code of Civil Procedure; for an analysis of this provision cf., Huber 2009, 829.

52 Geimer 2009, para 2891.

53 Article 34 No. 2 of the Council Regulation (EC) No 44/2001 of 22 December 2000 on jurisdiction and the recognition and enforcement of judgments in civil and commercial matters, OJ L 12, 16 January 2001, 1–23; for an analysis of this provision cf., Huber 2009, 764. Some specific instruments of European civil procedure do, however, establish a solution which is based on the chronological order of the decisions; cf., for example, Article 22 of the European Small Claims Regulation.

Commission published in December 2010, upholds the strict priority of judgments of the enforcement state.[54] It would have been more convincing to give priority always to the judgment rendered in the proceeding commenced first if the court of the enforcement State has violated its *lis pendens* rules by issuing a judgment. A similar solution was recommended by the Heidelberg Report on the application of the Brussels I Regulation.[55] Appropriate *lis pendens* rules could avoid a denial of justice resulting from lengthy proceedings in a foreign state.

15.2.3.3 Review of the Jurisdiction of the Foreign Court

The review of the jurisdiction of the foreign court can also lead to unpleasant surprises. German courts execute this review on the basis of their own jurisdiction rules.[56] In other words: the German judge analyses whether the foreign judge would have had jurisdiction if he had applied the German jurisdiction rules. If the answer is negative, the recognition of the foreign judgment is excluded.

This approach establishes an unjustified threshold where the foreign ground of jurisdiction is far from being exorbitant but unknown under German procedural law. This concerns, for example, the situation of a plaintiff who wants to sue several defendants from different countries. German law of civil procedure does not allow the concentration of closely connected claims against multiple defendants, unless there is jurisdiction over each individual defendant on an independent basis; German law does not provide a solution similar to Article 6(1) of the Brussels I Regulation.[57] As such, only the foreign judgment against the main defendant will be recognised in Germany even though the concentration of the claims does not necessarily violate the interests of the defendants, enhances an efficient solution of the dispute and is standard, at least in the countries of Roman legal culture.[58]

In addition, the German way of reviewing the foreign court's jurisdiction does not even achieve its objective of protecting the defendant against exorbitant *fora*. This objective is undermined by the existence of exorbitant *fora* within the German system itself, for example jurisdiction based on the mere presence of the defendant's assets.[59] The German Federal Supreme Court has expressly left open

[54] Articles 43 and 48 of the Proposal for a [new] regulation of the European Parliament and of the Council on jurisdiction and the recognition and enforcement of judgments in civil and commercial matters, COM (2010) 748 final.

[55] Hess et al. 2007, paras 564, 565, available at: http://ec.europa.eu/civiljustice/news/docs/study_application_brussels_1_en.pdf (last consulted in May 2011).

[56] Cf., Article 328(1) No. 1 of the German Code of Civil Procedure; for an analysis of this provision cf., Huber 2009, 827.

[57] Gottwald 2007, 194, para 393.

[58] Jenard 1979, commentary on Article 6(1).

[59] Cf., Article 23 of the German Code of Civil Procedure and the analysis of this provision by Roth 2003 and Vollkommer 2010, commentary on Article 23.

the question whether this ground of jurisdiction is limited by a minimum contact requirement in the context of recognition and enforcement of foreign judgments.[60]

All this makes clear that a general minimum contacts test would be the more convincing solution. A change for the better might result from a reform of the Brussels I Regulation. In its reform proposal, published in December 2010, the European Commission suggests extending the scope of application of this instrument to defendants who are not domiciled within the EU.[61] This would mean that the Brussels I Regulation would leave no room for the application of national jurisdiction rules in the area of transnational commercial litigation. Under such circumstances, German courts which have to decide on the recognition of a foreign judgment from a non-EU Member State might review the jurisdiction of the foreign court on the basis of the Brussels I Regulation. Whether the results of such an approach are appropriate would certainly depend on the grounds of jurisdiction provided for in the new Brussels I Regulation.

15.2.3.4 National Particularities in Applying European Instruments

At the EU level the recognition and enforcement of foreign judgments in civil and commercial matters is governed by the Brussels I Regulation. This instrument should be applied in a uniform manner throughout the Union. If there are doubts as to the interpretation of its provisions, national courts of last instance are obliged to refer the question for a preliminary ruling to the European Court of Justice. It is regrettable that the German Federal Supreme Court did not do so when considering whether a creditor who has obtained a judgment in his favour in one Member State of the European Union is entitled to apply for a declaration of enforceability under the Brussels I Regulation in another Member State, although he has already got a certification of the original title as a European Enforcement Order[62] in the Member State of origin.[63] The German Federal Supreme Court decided this question itself—against the creditor.

The Court based its decision on the argument that the creditor would have no legitimate interest to initiate enforceability proceedings because the European Enforcement Order would constitute a title which is directly enforceable in Germany.[64] At first glance, this might seem convincing. A closer look, however,

---

[60] Bundesgerichtshof 29 April 1999, *BGHZ* 141, 286.

[61] Article 4 of the Proposal for a [new] regulation of the European Parliament and of the Council on jurisdiction and the recognition and enforcement of judgments in civil and commercial matters, COM (2010) 748 final.

[62] Regulation (EC) No. 805/2004 of the European Parliament and of the Council of 21 April 2004 creating a European Enforcement Order for uncontested claims, OJ L 143, 30 April 2004, 15–39.

[63] Bundesgerichtshof 4 February 2010, *Praxis des Internationalen Privat- und Verfahrensrechts* (*IPRax*) 2011, 81.

[64] Bundesgerichtshof, *supra* n. 63, at para 10.

shows that the German Court decided on the question of the relationship between two European instruments by reference to a German principle, the so-called *Rechtsschutzbedürfnis*, which means that a person who wants to initiate court proceedings needs a 'legitimate interest' to do so.[65] A similar requirement might exist at the EU level. Nevertheless, it is not for the national courts but for the European Court of Justice to ascertain whether such a general threshold to remedies under European procedural law does or does not exist.

In addition, the German Federal Supreme Court has overlooked that a declaration of enforceability under the Brussels I Regulation creates more legal certainty for the creditor than the enforcement on the basis of a European Enforcement Order certificate. This results from Article 10 of the Enforcement Order Regulation which entitles the debtor to require the withdrawal of the European Enforcement Order certificate if it was clearly wrongly granted. Certainly, Article 1081 of the German Code of Civil Procedure provides for a time limit of one or two months[66] for such an application, which starts to run when the certificate is served. This brings the application for a withdrawal of the Enforcement Order certificate issued in Germany in line with the time limit for an appeal against a declaration of enforceability under Article 43(5) of the Brussels I Regulation. But firstly, the two situations are not comparable, and it is doubtful whether the national rules of civil procedure can set a short time limit, which is not provided in Article 10 of the Enforcement Order Regulation; and secondly, many EU Member States do not set any time limit in this context.[67] This leads to the question whether the relation between two European instruments can depend on the national rules which implement those instruments.

All this makes clear that it is more convincing to give a creditor the right to proceed with the enforcement of his title under both the Enforcement Order Regulation and the Brussels I regime. The problem of coexisting enforcement titles can be solved at the enforcement stage. In any event, the German Federal Supreme Court should have referred this question to the European Court of Justice.

In summation, the German way of recognising and enforcing foreign judgments is characterised by an ambivalent mixture of an open-minded point of departure on the one hand, and an accentuation of national interests and concepts on the other.

---

[65] Cf., the critique from Pfeiffer 2010, No. 303291; Mansel et al. 2011, 1, 21, 22; other authors support the reasoning of the German Federal Supreme Court; cf., for example, Bittmann 2011, 55.

[66] This depends on whether the certificate was to be served abroad or in Germany.

[67] Cf., the information about the implementation of Article 10 in the Member States at http://ec.europa.eu/justice_home/judicialatlascivil/html/rc_eeo_communications_en.htm (last consulted in May 2011); see, for example, for France Cuniberti et al. 2011, para 236.

15.3 Future Perspectives

In the context of transnational litigation, a current project of law reform is the subject of severe discussions: the already mentioned draft law on establishing special chambers for transnational commercial cases with English as the court language (cf., *supra* Sect. 15.2.2.1).

15.3.1 Special Chambers for Transnational Cases

The idea of special chambers for transnational cases has many advantages, irrespective of the language problem. It allows the judges to develop the special qualifications which are needed for good case management in transnational matters. Such a specialisation is clearly indispensable if the German legislator should adopt an additional set of special rules for transnational litigation (see *infra* Sect. 15.3.3); but it is already desirable in the present situation: judges who are not familiar with the complex questions of conflict of laws tend to look for dubious ways to apply German law even in cases where this is not convincing.[68] Furthermore, the specific handling of transnational judicial assistance and the application of international conventions require a certain degree of specialisation in order to guarantee a swift and efficient procedure.

Some special chambers for transnational cases have already been established at certain courts[69]; these examples could be the model for a nationwide system. There is clearly no need for a special chamber at each and every court. It is more efficient to concentrate the venue for transnational cases at certain courts.[70] The idea of local proximity, which is generally an argument for a decentralised court system, is not a convincing counter-argument in the case of transnational commercial matters.

15.3.2 English as Optional Court Language

The use of the English language in German courts is of particular interest for disputes about transactions where the whole documentation and correspondence has taken place in English. As English has become the *lingua franca* in

---

[68] Cf., Kegel and Schurig 2004, 143.

[69] For example at the Court of Appeal in Stuttgart; this special chamber not only decides on commercial cases but also on other civil cases in a transnational context; in contrast to the special chambers for transnational commercial cases at the courts in Aachen, Bonn and Cologne, the trial is, however, conducted in German.

[70] Cf., Prütting 2010, 113, 115; Calliess and Hoffmann 2009, 1, 4.

international trade, this concerns not only business relationships with companies from English-speaking countries but also transactions between business partners from two or more non-English-speaking countries.

The existence of special chambers for transnational cases could guarantee sufficient language skills on all sides for conducting the entire proceedings in English, from the statement of claim up to the judgment. In this context it is interesting to notice that chambers for commercial matters at German first instance courts are composed of one professional and two non-professional judges, who are businessmen and work only part-time as a judge. It is obvious that businessmen who carry out their main activity in a transnational context and communicate regularly in the English language are the perfect candidates for English-speaking chambers.

15.3.2.1 No Conflict with the Principle of Public Proceedings

Still, the question has been raised whether the use of the English language in German courts would conflict with the principle of public proceedings.[71] Such a conflict can only arise if the principle of public proceedings requires more than physical accessibility to the courtroom. Four different levels are to be distinguished: first, the German Courts Constitution Act provides that court hearings are to be public (Article 169); second, the German Constitution (*Grundgesetz*) does not expressly require the public character of court hearings, but the German Constitutional Court considers the idea of a public hearing as an essential element of the right to a fair trial, which is guaranteed by Articles 20(3) and 28(1) of the German Constitution, and of the principle of democracy, which is laid down in Article 20(1) of the Constitution[72]; third, Article 47(2) of the Charter of Fundamental Rights of the European Union establishes the right to a public hearing and to a public pronouncement of the judgment[73]; and fourth, Article 6(1) of the European Convention on Human Rights provides for the same rights.[74] The latter is quite similar to Article 14 of the International Covenant on Civil and Political Rights, which the United Nations General Assembly adopted on 16 December 1966.[75]

[71] Cf., Handschell 2010a, 103 and idem 2010b, 395, 397; Piekenbrock 2010, No. 5, editorial.

[72] Bundesverfassungsgericht (German Constitutional Court) 24 January 2001, *BVerfGE* 103, 44, 63.

[73] Although the second aspect is not explicitly mentioned in Article 47(2), it is comprehended by the procedural guarantee of Article 47; see Eser 2011, para 35; Grabenwarter 2009, 369.

[74] ECHR 17 January 2008, No. 14810/02, *Ryakib Biryukov v Russia*.

[75] The document can be consulted at http://www2.ohchr.org/english/law/ccpr.htm (last consulted in May 2011).

All these provisions pursue a double objective: protecting the parties against judicial arbitrariness and strengthening the public confidence in the judicial system.[76] They do not, however, confer on citizens who are not party to the proceedings an individual right to attend a specific hearing,[77] let alone a right to proceedings being conducted in a manner which guarantees the understanding of the proceedings by outsiders. Rather, they establish a subjective right exclusively for the parties, although it is true that this subjective right is of public interest. Consequently, the European Court of Human Rights has decided that the parties can waive their right to a public hearing if such a waiver does not conflict with an important public interest.[78]

So if the use of English in German courts should limit the public character of the hearing, the parties' choice to have English as the court language constitutes a waiver in this respect. Such a waiver is also effective: since a significant part of the German population is able to understand English,[79] and the media are able to overcome any difficulties resulting from the use of English in German courts, proceedings which are entirely conducted in English are not secret proceedings. All participants in the proceedings have to be aware of the fact that their procedural behaviour might be observed. The objective of the principle of public proceedings is complied with.[80] Under such circumstances no public interest can be identified which would render the parties' waiver ineffective.

[76] For the German Courts Constitution Act see Handschell 2010b, 395, 397; Schreiber 1995, para 4; for the German constitutional law see Bundesverfassungsgericht, *supra* n. 72, 63; for the Charter of Fundamental Rights of the European Union see Eser 2011, 35; for the European Convention on Human Rights see Frowein and Peukert 2009, commentary on Article 6, para 187; Loucaides 2008, 219; Sudre 2011, para 215; Guinchard et al. 2011, para 411.

[77] For Article 169 of the German Courts Constitution Act see Schreiber 1995, para 3; for the principle of public proceedings under the German Constitution cf., Bundesverfassungsgericht (German Constitutional Court), *supra* n. 72, 64; for Article 6(1) of the European Convention on Human Rights see Frowein and Peukert 2009, commentary on Article 6, para 4; generally cf., Ewer 2010, 1323, 1325 et seq; cf., Renucci 2007, 283, 434, who characterises the principle of public proceedings as *droit particulier du justiciable*; *contra* for Article 47(2) of the Charter of Fundamental Rights of the European Union Blanke 2007, para 16.

Such a right follows, however, from the fundamental right to receive information; cf., *infra* at the end of 15.3.2.1.

[78] ECHR 23 June 1981, No. 6878/75, 7238/75, *Le Compte, van Leuven and de Meyere v Belgium*, para 59; ECHR 21 February 1990, No. 11855/85, *Hakansson and Sturesson v Sweden*, para 67; in this second case, the Court held that even a tacit waiver is to be given effect; European Commission of Human Rights, 3 December 1990, No. 13366/87; even those authors who, under Article 6(1) of the European Convention on Human Rights or under Article 47(2) of the Charter of Fundamental Rights, try to construe a right of every citizen to attend court hearings submit this right to the outer circumstances and to a waiver of the parties; see for example Blanke 2007, commentary on Article 47, para 16.

[79] Cf., preparatory works of the draft law, BR-Drs. 42/10, 26 April 2010, 12, where the drafters refer to an analysis carried out by the Allensbach Institute for Public Opinion Research.

[80] Cf., Remmert 2010, 1579, 1582, 1583.

This line of reasoning also applies to Article 47(2) of the Charter of Fundamental Rights of the European Union, because this provision is modelled after Article 6(1) of the European Convention on Human Rights, and Article 52(3) of the Charter refers expressly to the meaning of corresponding rights in the Human Rights Convention.[81]

The situation is different under the German Constitution and under Article 169 of the German Courts Constitution Act. Here, the public aspect of the principle of public proceedings is considered to be of such great importance that the parties cannot waive their right to public proceedings.[82] It is doubtful whether this is convincing in commercial matters. But even if one accepts this position, the use of the English language in German courts is possible. Article 169 of the German Courts Constitution Act is only a rule of statutory law which the legislator can easily modify; and the German Constitution leaves much flexibility to the German legislator on how to regulate the public access to court proceedings. The legislator has the power to limit the public character of court proceedings in the interest of the parties and the efficient functioning of the judicial system.[83] Against this background, a provision permitting civil proceedings to be conducted in English would not constitute a violation of the constitutional principle of democracy and the constitutional right to a fair trial, which are the constitutional foundation of the principle of public proceedings.

It must certainly not be overlooked that the right to receive information, which is guaranteed by Article 5(1) of the German Constitution, Article 11(1) of the Charter of Fundamental Rights of the European Union, Article 10(1) of the European Convention on Human Rights and Article 19(2) of the International Covenant on Civil and Political Rights, grants every citizen the right to follow court proceedings.[84] However, firstly, the right to receive information grants access to the information exclusively in its original language; and secondly, even if the use of the English language should constitute an interference with the right to receive information, the interference would be justified because the right to receive

[81] Cf., the explanations relating to the Charter of Fundamental Rights, OJ C 303, 14 December 2007, 17, 30; Voet van Vormizeele 2009, para 2.

[82] Kissel and Mayer 2010, commentary on Article 169, paras 19, 58; Prütting 2010, 113; Stürner 2001, 699–700.

[83] Bundesverfassungsgericht (German Constitutional Court), *supra* n. 72, 64; Kloepfer 2005, para 63.

[84] For the German Constitution see Bröhmer 2002, 229, 235, 241; more reluctant: Bundesverfassungsgericht (German Constitutional Court), *supra* n. 72, 59 et seq; for the European Convention on Human Rights see the decision of the European Commission of Human Rights, 3 December 1990, No. 13366/87; this line of reasoning also applies under the Charter of Fundamental Rights; cf., Article 52(3) of this Charter.

information can be limited in the interest of the parties to the proceedings and the efficient functioning of the judicial system.[85]

15.3.2.2 Protection of Third Parties

If proceedings are conducted in English, the rules concerning third-party notice and voluntary intervention of third parties will certainly have to be adapted. A third party, who has either the right or the obligation to participate in the proceedings, cannot be obliged to use the English language—at least if he is not sufficiently proficient in English. In such a case, the proceedings would have to be conducted in German, which would undermine the parties' choice of the English language. This problem calls for special rules for third-party intervention in proceedings conducted in English.

The draft law proposes to give the third party the right to refuse acceptance of the third-party notice if the document is written in English. If the third party exercises this right, the party who has issued the third-party notice can either refrain from the third-party notice or provide the third party with a German translation.[86] If the third party decides to participate in the proceedings, he has a right to an interpreter and the tribunal can even decide that the proceedings are to be continued in German.[87] This last solution would also apply in cases where a voluntary intervener has a legitimate interest in participating.

This solution protects the third party quite effectively, but it undermines the parties' choice of the English language to an unnecessary degree. It seems more convincing to distinguish between a third-party notice and a voluntary intervention.

As a third-party notice is in the interest of one of the parties to the proceedings, it would be preferable to let the parties choose between a very high degree of certainty of having English as the court language at the price of the exclusion of third-party notices if the third party is not willing to accept English as the court language and keeping the unlimited right to issue a third-party notice at the price of a lower degree of certainty of having English as the court language. If a contract contains a clause providing for the proceedings to be conducted in English and

---

[85] For the German Constitution cf., Bundesverfassungsgericht (German Constitutional Court), *supra* n. 72, 61 et seq where the Court analysed whether public access to court proceedings can be restricted; in that decision the Court even denied any interference with the rights guaranteed by Article 5(1) of the German Constitution; Bröhmer 2002, 241; for the European Convention on Human Rights see the decision of the European Commission of Human Rights, 3 December 1990, No. 13366/87; this line of reasoning also applies under the Charter of Fundamental Rights; cf., Article 52(3) of this Charter.

[86] Cf., Article 2 of the draft law which proposes a modification of Article 73 of the German Code of Civil Procedure.

[87] Cf., Article 1(5) of the draft law which proposes a modification of Article 184 of the German Courts Constitution Act.

excluding third-party notices, such a clause should be respected. Consequently, one party—usually the defendant—could not deviate from this clause and issue a third-party notice with the aim of switching the language button and thereby slowing down the proceedings. Alternatively, the parties to a contract could agree on a clause which obliges the party that wishes to issue a third-party notice, with the consequence that the proceedings will be conducted in German, to bear the costs of changing the language, irrespective of the outcome of the proceedings.

Even if one should consider that German civil procedural law already gives room for party autonomy in this respect, it would be helpful to make this clear by a statutory rule. A further question is whether the exclusion of a third-party notice is in conformity with Article 65 of the Brussels I Regulation, which refers to the German instrument of third-party notice. As the European Court of Justice gives party autonomy under Article 23 priority over the jurisdiction rule of Article 6(2),[88] which has been modified for Germany by Article 65, the answer should at least be positive if the exclusion of third-party notices is based on the parties' consent.

The case of voluntary interveners, who have a legitimate interest in participating in the proceedings, is certainly different. The parties cannot deprive third persons of their right to participate if those third persons are affected by the outcome of the proceedings. This is the case if the final decision is binding even in their regard. Under very specific circumstances German law provides for such an effect, especially in certain types of family and company matters.[89] There are only two alternatives *de lege ferenda*: either the third party has no right to participate if he is not willing to accept proceedings conducted in English, but then the final decision cannot have binding effect on him; or, where the efficient administration of justice requires such a binding effect, the third party must have the right to participate and use German—at least if he does not have an adequate command of English. In this respect the German draft law needs to be developed further.

15.3.2.3 English Proceedings in Two Instances

It is doubtful whether it will be realistic to conduct civil proceedings in English in three instances up to the German Federal Supreme Court.[90] The bill provides for the possibility to organise proceedings before the German Federal Supreme Court in English.[91] This is not, however, mandatory. The use of the English language is

---

[88] Cf., ECJ 14 December 1976, case 24/76, *Rüwa Polstereimaschinen GmbH*, ECR 1976, 1831; ECJ 9 November 1978, case 23/78, *Nikolaus Meeth v Glacetal*, ECR 1978, 2133; these decisions concern the Brussels Convention, the predecessor of the Brussels I Regulation; but they are still to be taken into account; for the Brussels I Regulation, see Hess 2010, 291, para 88; Muir Watt 2007, commentary on Article 6, para 38; Fentiman 2010, paras 9, 87.

[89] Cf., the enumeration by Vollkommer 2010, commentary on Article 66, para 11 et seq.

[90] Cf., the critique of Tolksdorf 2010, *supra* Sect. 15.2.2.1.

[91] Article 1(5)(b) of the draft law.

at the discretion of the Supreme Court. This creates a source of uncertainty for the parties.

The solution might once again be party autonomy. The parties can exclude their right to a third instance, i.e. the German Federal Supreme Court.[92] They are well advised to do so in their contract if they want to ensure the use of the English language for the entire proceedings. At the level of the regional courts and the appellate courts the existence of special chambers, which are able to conduct proceedings in the English language, seems realistic and sufficient. Alternatively, the parties could agree that the party that seeks to continue the proceedings in the third instance has to bear the costs of changing the language, irrespective of the outcome of the proceedings.

15.3.2.4 German Version for the Enforcement

The German enforcement authorities will certainly need a German version of the operative provisions of the judgment.[93] It is clear that only one version can be the authentic one. In this respect German law could profit from the experience with EU instruments for cross-border enforcement.

15.3.3 Special Rules for Transnational Cases

All the foregoing makes clear that there is a need for special rules for transnational commercial litigation in addition to those which the German Code of Civil Procedure contains already.[94] This observation is not meant to be a plea for a completely new set of procedural rules. It is rather preferable and more realistic to apply the general rules of civil procedure and to modify or amend them for specific questions in the context of transnational commercial litigation. Additional rules should at least be adopted for establishing special chambers for transnational disputes, for permitting the use of English and for regulating third-party notices as well as voluntary interventions.

This leads to another problem: the elimination of the clash between the language of the business relationship and the court language must not be replaced by a clash between the court language and the language of the applicable law. Consequently, an English version of all procedural rules, including the general rules of civil procedure, is indispensable. There is already an English translation of the German Courts Constitution Act, which can be downloaded from the website

---

[92] Wagner 1998, 527 et seq, 541, 553, 554.

[93] The draft law provides for such a translation in Article 1(5)(b); cf., Prütting 2010, 113, 115.

[94] Cf., for example, Articles 274(3)(2) and 339(2).

of the German Ministry of Justice[95]; but unfortunately, there is no official English version of the German Code of Civil Procedure. It is desirable that the German Ministry of Justice accelerate the implementation of its translation programme for German statutes. In addition, one might think about an official commentary to the special rules of transnational civil procedure in order to facilitate their application.

As far as the substantive law is concerned, there is an English translation of the German Civil Code. Other important statutes still need to be translated. A current European project might also contribute to avoiding a clash between the language of the business relationship and the language of the applicable law: the European Commission has published a Green Paper on policy options for progress towards a European contract law.[96] In this Paper one of the proposals submitted is to work out a regulation which would set up an optional instrument of European Contract Law. The English version of such an instrument would have official character, it would be of transnational nature, and all national courts of the EU should be familiar with its application. As such, it could be an interesting option for contracting parties to choose such a set of rules as the law governing their contractual relationship.

15.3.4 Model Clause Combining Choice of Jurisdiction, Venue, Language and Law

The special procedural rules of transnational litigation should come into play if a case is heard by one of the special chambers for transnational litigation. As there will be only one special chamber within one tribunal, the parties can indirectly choose a special chamber by designating the corresponding tribunal in their contract. The German legislator should elaborate a model clause which the parties can use in order to make such a choice. In addition, the model clause should provide for the choice of the English language, the limitation of the proceedings to two instances and a stipulation for the handling of third-party notices. A choice of law model clause would complete the package. It would be for the parties to select only certain elements of this package in order to frame a dispute resolution mechanism which is appropriate for their purposes.

In accordance with the costs-by-cause principle one might certainly think about higher court fees for proceedings which are conducted entirely in the English language.

[95] See http://www.gesetze-im-internet.de/englisch_gvg/index.html (last consulted in May 2011).

[96] Green Paper from the Commission on policy options for progress towards a European Contract Law for consumers and businesses, 1 July 2010, COM(2010) 348 final.

15.4 Final Conclusions

Germany is on the way to modernising its procedural rules for transnational civil litigation. The following aspects should be the cornerstones in this reform process: first, concentration on the parties' interests rather than on the idea of state sovereignty; second, recognition of party autonomy in respect of procedural rules; third, specialisation of judges who are capable of conducting the entire proceedings in English; and, fourth, adoption of special procedural rules for transnational cases. A reform that will develop these elements further would be an important step forward, such as the reform of the German arbitration law in 1998 was, and contribute to making the German judicial system more suitable for the resolution of transnational disputes. This certainly does not mean that improving the procedural law would be sufficient. There are several aspects of German substantive law which also have to be brought in line with the needs of international trade, first and foremost the rules on general terms and conditions. Both reforms, a reform of the judicial system and a reform of the substantive law, have to go hand in hand.

References

Armbrüster C (2011a) Englischsprachige Zivilprozesse vor deutschen Gerichten? Zeitschrift für Rechtspolitik 44(4):102–104

Armbrüster C (2011b) Fremdsprachen in Gerichtsverfahren. Neue Juristische Wochenschrift 64(12):812–818

Bittmann DC (2011) Das Verhältnis der EuVTVO zur EuGVO, Praxis des Internationalen Privat- und Verfahrensrechts (IPRax), pp 55–57

Blanke H (2007) Commentary on Article 47 of the Charter of fundamental rights of the European Union. In: Calliess C, Ruffert M (eds) Das Ver-fassungsrecht der Europäischen Union mit Grundrechtecharta, 3rd edn. Beck, Munich

Brinkmann M (2004) The synthesis of common and civil law standard of proof formulae in the ALI/UNIDROIT principles of transnational civil procedure. Unif Law Rev/Revue de Droit Uniforme, 875–891

Bröhmer J (2002) Transparenz als Verfassungsprinzip. Mohr Siebeck, Tübingen

Calliess G-P, Hoffmann H (2009) Effektive Justizleistungen für den globalen Handel. Zeitschrift für Rechtspolitik, 1–4

Cuniberti G, Normand C, Cornette F (2011) Droit international de l'exécution—Recouvrement des créances civiles et commerciales. L.G.D.J., Paris

Einstein CR, Phipps A (2004) The principles and rules of transnational civil procedure and their application to New South Wales. Unif Law Rev/Revue de Droit Uniforme, 815–828

Eser A (2011) Commentary on Article 47 of the Charter of fundamental rights of the European Union. In: Meyer J (ed) Charta der Grundrechte der Europäischen Union. Nomos, Baden-Baden

Esplugues C, Iglesias J-L, Palao G (2011) Application of foreign law. Sellier, Munich

Ewer W (2010) Das Öffentlichkeitsprinzip—ein Hindernis für die Zulassung von Englisch als konsensual-optionaler Gerichtssprache? Neue Juristische Wochenschrift 63:1323–1326

Fentiman R (2010) International commercial litigation. Oxford University Press, Oxford

Ferrand F (2004) La procédure civile mondiale modélisée. Editions Juridiques et Techniques, Paris

Frowein J, Peukert W (2009) Europäische Menschenrechtskonvention, 3rd edn. Engel, Kehl
Geimer R (2009) Internationales Zivilprozessrecht, 6th edn. Beck, Munich
Glenn P (2004) The ALI/UNIDROIT principles of transnational civil procedure as global standards for adjudication? Unif Law Rev/Revue de Droit Uniforme, 829–845
Gottwald P (2007) Internationales Zivilprozessrecht, 6th edn. Otto Schmidt, Cologne
Grabenwarter C (2009) Europäische Menschenrechtskonvention, 4th edn. Beck, Munich
Guinchard S et al (2011) Droit processuel—Droits fondamentaux du procès, 6th edn. Dalloz, Paris
Handschell T (2010a) Englisch als Gerichtssprache? Zeitschrift für Rechtspolitik 43(3):103–104
Handschell T (2010b) Die Vereinbarkeit von Englisch als Gerichtssprache mit dem Grundgesetz und europäischem Recht. Deutsche Richterzeitung 88(12):395–399
Hess B (2010) Europäisches Zivilprozessrecht. C.F. Müller, Heidelberg
Hess B, Pfeiffer T, Schlosser P (2007) Report on the application of regulation Brussels I in the member states. C.F. Müller, Heidelberg
Hoppe C (2010) Englisch als Verfahrenssprache—Möglichkeiten de lege lata und de lege ferenda, Praxis des Internationalen Privat- und Verfahrensrechts (IPRax), pp 373–377
Huber S (2008) Entwicklung transnationaler Modellregeln für Zivilverfahren. Mohr Siebeck, Tübingen
Huber S (2009) Vollstreckung ausländischer Entscheidungen in Deutschland. In: Dierck, Morvilius, Vollkommer (eds) Handbuch des Zwangsvollstreckungsrechts. Beck, Munich, pp 735–830
Hübner R Grundlagen und europäische Perspektiven der Ermittlung ausländischen Rechts im gerichtlichen Verfahren (forthcoming)
Jenard P (1979) Report on the convention on jurisdiction and the enforcement of judgments in civil and commercial matters. Off J Eur Union C 59/1
Karrer PA (2004) Internationalization of civil procedure—beyond the IBA rules of evidence. Unif Law Rev/Revue de Droit Uniforme, pp 893–897
Kegel G, Schurig K (2004) Internationales Privatrecht, 9th edn. Beck, Munich
Kerameus KD (2004) Scope of application of the ALI/UNIDROIT principles of transnational civil procedure, Unif Law Rev/Revue de Droit Uniforme, 847–857
Kissel OR, Mayer H (2010) Gerichtsverfassungsgesetz—Kommentar, 6th edn. Beck, Munich
Kloepfer M (2005) Verfassungsrechtlicher Schutz der freien Bildung der öffentlichen Meinung. In: Isensee J, Kirchhof P (eds) Handbuch des Staatsrechts, vol III, part 5, 3rd edn., C.F. Müller, Heidelberg
Kötz H (2010) Deutsches Recht und Common Law im Wettbewerb. Anwaltsblatt, pp 1–7
Kreindler R, Rust O (2007) Wahl zwischen ordentlichen Gerichtsverfahren und Schiedsverfahren. In: Büchting H, Heussen B (eds) Beck'sches Rechtsanwaltshandbuch, 9th edn. Beck, Munich, pp 1275–1291
Loucaides LG (2008) The European convention on human rights: collected essays. Martinus Nijhoff Publishers, Leiden
Mansel H-P, Thorn K, Wagner R (2011) Europäisches Kollisionsrecht 2010: Verstärkte Zusammenarbeit als Motor der Vereinheitlichung? Praxis des Internationalen Privat- und Verfahrensrechts (IPRax), pp 1–31
Muir Watt H (2007) Commentary on Article 6 of the Brussels I regulation. In: Magnus U, Mankowski P (eds) Brussels I regulation. Sellier, Munich
Müller-Piepenkötter R (2010) Englisch als Gerichtssprache. Deutsche Richterzeitung 88(1):2–8
Nhlapo RT (2004) ALI/UNIDROIT principles of transnational civil procedure—keynote by the chairman of the joint ALI/UNIDROIT study group. Unif Law Rev/Revue de Droit Uniforme, 811–813
Pfeiffer T (1991) Kooperative Reziprozität, Rabels Zeitschrift für ausländisches und internationales Privatrecht, 734–768
Pfeiffer T (2010) BGH: Verhältnis zwischen der Vollstreckbarkeit nach der EuVTVO und nach der Brüssel I-VO, Fachdienst Zivilrecht—LMK, No. 303291

Piekenbrock A (2010) Englisch als Gerichtssprache in Deutschland, Europäisches Wirtschafts- und Steuerrecht, pp 160–161

Prütting H (2010) In Englisch vor deutschen Gerichten verhandeln? Anwaltsblatt, pp 113–115

Remmert A (2010) Englisch als Gerichtssprache: Nothing ventured, nothing gained, Zeitschrift für Wirtschaftsrecht, pp 1579–1583

Renucci JF (2007) Traité de droit européen des droits de l'homme. L.G.D.J., Paris

Rosenberg L, Schwab KH, Gottwald P (2010) Zivilprozessrecht, 17th edn. Beck, Munich

Roth H (2003) Commentary on Article 23 of the German code of civil procedure. In: Stein J (eds) Kommentar zur Zivilprozessordnung, vol I, 22nd edn. Mohr Siebeck, Tübingen

Scarpinella Bueno C (2004) Principles and rules of transnational civil procedure and Brazilian civil procedure compared: a first assessment. Unif Law Rev/Revue de Droit Uniforme, 859–874

Schack H (2010) Internationales Zivilverfahrensrecht, 5th edn. Beck, Munich

Schreiber K (1995) Commentary on Article 169 of the German Courts Constitution Act. In: Wieczorek S (eds) Zivilprozessordnung und Nebengesetze—Großkommentar, vol V, 3rd ed, Walter de Gruyter, Berlin

Stadler A (2002) Grenzüberschreitende Beweisaufnahmen in der Europäischen Union—die Zukunft der Rechtshilfe in Beweissachen. In: Schütze (ed) Einheit und Vielfalt des Rechts—Festschrift für Reinhold Geimer zum 65. Geburtstag, Beck, Munich, pp 1281–1306

Stürner R (2001) Gerichtsöffentlichkeit und Medienöffentlichkeit in der Informationsgesellschaft, Juristenzeitung, pp 699–703

Sudre F (2011) Droit européen et international, 10th edn. Presses Universitaires de France, Paris

Voet van Vormizeele P (2009) Commentary on Article 47 of the Charter of Fundamental Rights of the European Union. In: Schwarze J, Becker U, Hatje A, Schoo J (eds) EU-Kommentar, 2nd edn. Nomos, Baden-Baden

Vollkommer M (2010) Commentary on Articles 23 and 66 of the German Code of Civil Procedure. In: Zöller, Zivilprozessordnung, 28th edn. Otto Schmidt, Cologne

Wagner G (1998) Prozessverträge. Mohr Siebeck, Tübingen

von Westphalen FG (2010) Englisch statt Deutsch, Zeitschrift für Vertragsgestaltung, Schuld- und Haftungsrecht, p 241

Chapter 16
Convergence of Civil Procedure Systems in Europe: Comments from a Belgian Perspective

Benoît Allemeersch and Els Vandensande

Abstract This chapter looks into how a country like Belgium deals with civil justice in a globalised world and the ensuing need for more convergence. For the sake of this analysis, much attention is paid to a clear delineation of the object of study and a detailed description of the various methods to induce convergence. It is pointed out that the current euphoria around procedural harmonisation is not always justified: many harmonisation efforts encounter great difficulties to being implemented into the national systems. The Belgian example illustrates how regional harmonisation and the reception of foreign law are also viable options in striving towards more convergence. The authors raise the question as to why the Benelux—the economic union between Belgium, the Netherlands and Luxembourg—could not become a laboratory for pan-European initiatives in the field of civil justice.

Contents

Beniot Allemeersch—Professor of procedural law, Catholic University of Leuven.
Els VandenSande—Junior researcher, Catholic University of Leuven.

B. Allemeersch (✉) · E. Vandensande
Catholic University of Leuven, Leuven, Belgium
e-mail: benoit.allemeersch@law.kuleuven.be

E. Vandensande
e-mail: els.vandensande@student.kuleuven.be

X. E. Kramer and C. H. van Rhee (eds.), *Civil Litigation in a Globalising World*, DOI: 10.1007/978-90-6704-817-0_16,

16.1 Introduction

The globalisation of civil and commercial litigation and the development towards further harmonisation of civil justice is for most countries an impetus to civil justice reform and will perhaps even force some to redesign their legal systems. This is all the more so in Europe, where the trend towards more convergence is well on its way. The challenges that States face in coping with this evolution may prove greater for some than for others. Much will depend on circumstances such as the constraints imposed by a constitution, the socio-political situation, the organisation of the State and its legislative process, the size of its population and the available budget, as well as the quality of the justice system, its structures and its personnel. It is not the intention of the authors of this chapter to make an inventory of all relevant factors that influence a State's ability to deal with the issues of globalisation and harmonisation, nor to examine their impact. We will not list the Member States that may face more difficulty either, if that would even be possible. Instead, we wish to explore this issue through a case study of Belgium. We will look into how a country like Belgium deals with civil justice in a globalised world and the ensuing need for more convergence. Drawing on these findings, we will come to the conclusion that regional harmonisation and the reception of foreign law are valuable alternatives for a uniform European civil procedure code, at least for the immediate future.

We will begin with a short analysis of the different terms used in the discussion, followed by an overview of the current state of affairs in Europe. We will then make some comments on the obstacles for the European convergence effort and subsequently put the focus on Belgium.

16.2 What are We Talking About?

The discussion about globalisation, convergence, harmonisation, approximation and unification of procedural law often results in confusion. This is largely due to an inaccurate delineation of the object of discussion. Different authors often talk about different things when discussing this subject. To avoid misunderstanding, we will first engage in an analysis of these concepts.

Globalisation is a container term which refers to two major trends: the increasing global connectivity and the increasing global consciousness.[1] The term globalisation is often used in an economic context, where it stands for the increased integration of the markets and frequently takes on a rather negative connotation, partly due to the critical analysis made by so-called 'anti-globalists.' Globalisation is more than just an economic development, though; it has an impact on all aspects of society, including the way society deals with disputes. Civil justice is more and more confronted with transnational conflicts, and justice policy is increasingly becoming a subject of transnational or supranational discussion. In addition, there is increased 'jurisdictional competition' with States promoting their local civil justice system to attract international investors or disputes.[2]

Convergence ('rapprochement') is the act of bringing national legal systems closer together so as to make differences smaller or even to eliminate them altogether. This can be done to various degrees. Convergence through *unification* entails that existing rules are entirely replaced by common rules, either in one single legal text that is accepted by each and every State involved or by multiple texts that are identical in content. There exists a number of instruments that may help to realise this goal, such as model laws, codifications and the reception of foreign law. *Harmonisation* and *approximation* are considered to be synonyms. *Harmonisation* is defined by Dembour as 'the legal mechanism by which national legislations are aligned so as to eliminate or at least attenuate the inconvenience arising from their disparities.'[3] Boodman speaks of harmonisation as 'a process in which diverse elements are combined or adapted to each other so as to form a coherent whole while retaining their individuality.'[4] Harmonisation is most often understood to be a less drastic means of realising convergence. In the literature on the methods of convergence, it is often said that unification implies *l'uniformité*, while harmonisation is about *l'affinité*.[5]

In the context of the European project, the effort towards more convergence has been characterised both as unification as well as harmonisation or approximation. In the Treaty of Rome the term 'approximation' was used,[6] but the preparatory documents occasionally spoke about 'unification' of laws.[7] The use of the latter term was, however, not entirely appropriate. Convergence has always been seen as

[1] Robertson and White 2007, 64.

[2] Zekoll 2006, 1336 and 1341.

[3] Dembour 1996, 1.

[4] Boodman 1991, 702.

[5] Trompenaars 1989, 9–10, para 13 (quoting Malintoppi 1968).

[6] Arts. 100–102 of the Treaty Establishing the European Economic Community.

[7] See, e.g., in respect of tax law: Comité intergouvernemental créé par la conférence de Messine, Rapport des chefs de délégation aux ministres des affaires étrangères ('Spaak Report'), Brussels, 1956, at 64.

a means to avoid distortions in the European common market, which was thought to benefit from a complete level playing field, but it was quite clear from the beginning that Europe was not aiming for absolute uniformity. Rather, it sought a special form of convergence that would leave room for some divergence and variation in the legislation of the different Member States.[8]

16.3 Convergence Initiatives with Relevance to European Civil Justice

The objective to bring national systems of civil procedure closer together has been shared by many. Still, the number of projects that have been undertaken to achieve this goal has remained fairly limited. The approach has also varied. In what follows, we will briefly describe past and on-going convergence initiatives that are most relevant to European civil justice. Given the number of initiatives, we will need to categorise. Kerameus distinguishes two levels of procedural convergence, depending on whether they aim to improve the quality of justice (the 'ideal' level) or aim to eliminate disparities between different legal systems (the 'practical' level).[9] This distinction is not always easy to make, though, as many initiatives have mentioned both of these elements as an objective. For the sake of our analysis, we will make a distinction on the basis of the nature of the actor who is taking charge of the harmonisation effort, as well as the nature of its product. This leads us to distinguish four categories.

16.3.1 First Category: Convergence on a National Level at the Initiative of the Individual States

In the first category, we have the States. Each State can bring about convergence on its own simply through the reception of foreign law. Indeed, when States find inspiration abroad for their civil justice reforms, this leads to convergence just as well, albeit without international coordination. The reception of foreign law may occur when States solve specific problems through detailed adjustments of their procedural rules. Solutions already tested in a foreign jurisdiction are an attractive solution. A more 'principles-driven' form of foreign law reception often occurs when a fundamental reform of civil procedure is imminent. In the last decade, a number of Member States in the European Union have revised their civil procedure and while doing so their legislature often was, in one way or another, inspired by solutions from abroad.[10] This development follows a similar development in

---

[8] Dembour 1996, 29; Boodman 1991, 699.

[9] Kerameus 1995, 401.

[10] E.g. Germany: Zekoll 2006, 1338.

scholarly research. After a period of hesitation, academic writing in procedural law has for several years now joined the globalisation trend by engaging more and more in comparative research.[11]

16.3.2 Second Category: Informal Initiatives on an International Level

This category encompasses the initiatives taken on an international level and originating from an informal cooperation, most often working groups of legal academics. In Europe, the most telling example is the Storme Commission. In 1987 a group of academics formed a working group called 'The Commission for a European Judicial Code' under the chairmanship of Marcel Storme. The initial goal was to prepare a complete European model Code of Civil Procedure. The final report of the commission, issued in 1994, was more modest in its approach.[12] It had become a draft proposal for a Directive on the approximation of laws and rules of the Member States concerning certain aspects of the procedure for civil litigation. Although some chapters dealt with specific aspects in great detail, most of the text contained only basic principles of a unified civil procedure. The report was hailed by some as a valuable contribution to the harmonisation debate. Other, more critical commentators on the report observed that the effort of finding common ground had not always resulted in an improvement in quality.[13] The text was submitted to the European Commission, which seemed to ignore it. Many years later, however, sporadic reference to the report was made by the Commission.[14]

16.3.3 Third Category: Initiatives in the Context of Intergovernmental Cooperation

The third category relates to the attempts at convergence that are the result of what we could call an institutional effort by intergovernmental organisations which have as a mission, to one extent or the other, the harmonisation of civil justice but do not have the power to issue on their own motion binding instruments. As an example of such an intergovernmental organisation, we mention UNIDROIT, which has a long-standing track record in unification. In respect of convergence of national

[11] Zekoll 2006, 1328; Van Rhee and Verkerk 2006. See also Chase et al 2007; Gidi 2006, 502 et seq.

[12] Storme 1994.

[13] Juenger 1997, 932–933.

[14] Green Paper on a European Order for Payment Procedure and on Measures to simplify and speed up Small Claims Litigation, COM (2002) 746 def., 12.

civil justice systems, it has joined the American Law Institute in a project aimed at formulating uniform principles and rules for the procedural treatment of transnational disputes of a civil and commercial nature. This has led to the publication of the renowned Principles of Transnational Civil Procedure and the Rules of Transnational Civil Procedure.[15] The use of the term 'transnational' makes it abundantly clear that this is a convergence effort concentrated on cross-border disputes. However, the focus on principles for transnational disputes has not restrained the authors from formulating from the outset of their text the ambition to be influential on a much greater scale: *These Principles may be equally appropriate for the resolution of most other kinds of civil disputes and may be the basis for future initiatives in reforming civil procedure.*[16] Despite this ambition, the concrete impact of the project on the current state of transnational law of procedure around the world has not yet become visible as such.[17] Its success remains to be judged.

In Europe, the work of the Council of Europe springs to mind. Its greatest achievement in the strive for convergence in civil procedure is undoubtedly the European Convention on Human Rights. This treaty has probably done more to bring civil procedure systems together than any other legal instrument in the world. In the last two decades the Council has concentrated its convergence activities on the improvement of access to justice and the efficiency of national civil justice systems.[18] In doing that, the Council of Europe functions somewhat as a think tank and an expertise centre for the civil justice reforms in its Member States. It issues non-binding recommendations, opinions and studies. At the Warsaw summit in 2005, the Member States of the Council of Europe renewed and affirmed their political commitment to the Council's project.[19] In the action plan adopted at this summit, the priorities of the Council for the following years were outlined.[20] These were the development of European standards through the advice and assistance of the European Commission for Democracy through Law (the so-called 'Venice Commission'), the promotion and further development of legal cooperation, the development of the evaluation and assistance functions of the European Commission for the Efficiency of Justice (CEPEJ) and the use of the opinions given by the Consultative Council of Judges of Europe (CCJE) to help Member States with delivering justice fairly and rapidly and developing alternative means for the settlement of disputes. These commitments make it clear that the

---

15 ALI/UNIDROIT 2004. For an introduction to the Rules and Principles, see Hazard et al. 2001. For an early critique of a preliminary draft, see Weintraub 1998 (who questions the need for transnational rules and principles, at 414–415).

16 ALI/UNIDROIT 2004, 758.

17 Chase et al 2007, 574–575.

18 Storskrubb 2009, 1.

19 Warsaw declaration, http://www.coe.int/t/dcr/summit/20050517_decl_varsovie_en.asp (last consulted in May 2011).

20 Action plan of the Council of Europe (17 May 2005), CM (2005) 80, http://www.coe.int/t/dcr/summit/20050517_plan_action_en.asp (last consulted in May 2011).

approach of the Council of Europe will be more theoretical and technical than political.

16.3.4 Fourth Category: Initiatives on a Supranational Level

The fourth category comprises the initiatives of supranational organisations. While the authors are aware that it is debatable whether the European Union constitutes a supranational, intergovernmental or hybrid form of governance, we believe it is fair to treat the EU here as being on the supranational level.

Procedural autonomy, which entails that each Member State uses its own national procedural law when applying material European law, is until today still a fundamental element of EU policy. Yet, this autonomy is not absolute. Hence, in the course of the last ten years, the European Union has proved itself to be the most influential actor in the harmonisation of procedural law systems in Europe. Its activity in this field is remarkable, not just because of the number of initiatives, but also because its harmonisation is increasingly more sophisticated. The EU has indeed begun with the creation of uniform European procedural law. In execution of the Tampere summit conclusions,[21] the intermediate measures required to enable the recognition and enforcement of judgments were abolished for small claims[22] and uncontested claims,[23] and uniform procedural rules for courts in all Member States were established. It has also issued two directives, one on legal aid and one on mediation which aim to introduce common standards for procedures in national courts. In addition, some European instruments issued on other matters also contain procedural rules.

Almost all of the before-mentioned instruments have a scope limited to cross-border disputes. Hess has correctly pointed out that the European Union is thus creating 'European Transnational Procedural Law,' a distinct type between national and international civil procedural law.[24] In practice, the influence of these instruments reaches further, though: there is a 'spill-over effect.'[25] The Mediation Directive of 2008 illustrates this. This Directive imposes minimum requirements for the legal regime of mediation in national courts. It contains, for example, an obligation to inform the general public about how to contact a mediator and to encourage the development of voluntary codes for mediators. It is difficult to see how these obligations can be fulfilled without affecting national procedures. For

---

[21] Presidency Conclusions—Tampere European Council, para 33, http://www.europarl.europa.eu/summits/tam_en.htm (last consulted in May 2011).

[22] Regulation No. 861/2007 establishing a European Small Claims Procedure, OJ 2007, L 199, 1–22.

[23] Regulation No. 1896/2006 creating a European order for payment procedure, OJ 2006, L 399, 1–32.

[24] Hess 2002, 4. See also Tell 2003, 455 (who speaks of 'harmonisation de type fédéral').

[25] Storskrubb 2009, 12.

most Member States, the consequence of this Directive will be the enactment of comprehensive legislation which governs mediation in all disputes before national courts, whether they qualify as European cross-border disputes or not. This is exactly what observers favouring further integration have in mind, as it fits perfectly with the purpose of building a European judicial culture. A common European judicial culture will strengthen the mutual trust which is key to Member States accepting the enforcement of decisions from other Member States without imposing burdensome formalities. As the European Council has put it in the Stockholm Programme of 2009, 'a certain level of approximation of laws is necessary to foster a common understanding of issues among judges…, and hence to enable the principle of mutual recognition to be applied properly, taking into account the differences between legal systems and legal traditions of Member States.'[26] We may therefore expect more activity in this respect, such as the development of minimum standards or standard rules of civil procedure.[27]

An important question is whether any new legislative instruments coming from the European Union in this respect will continue to limit their scope to cross-border disputes. The chapter on procedural harmonisation in the Stockholm Programme suggests that this will remain the case. However, it is noteworthy that the European Union has already harmonised procedural law without making a distinction between cross-border and other disputes. This has been the case in the Directive on the enforcement of intellectual property rights, which directs Member States to adapt their national procedural laws to bring their intellectual property enforcement measures and remedies up to a common standard.[28] Whether this is the starting point of a series of instruments creating truly uniform procedural law remains to be seen. The attempts to introduce some form of class action in the fields of consumer protection and competition could be the next chapter in this development, but as is commonly known, these have not yet been successful.

Finally, we should not underestimate the influence of the European Court of Justice (ECJ) on the convergence of national laws of civil procedure.[29] The considerable role played by the Court stems from the great weight given by the Court to the right to an effective remedy.[30] To assure the full application of European law, the Court has determined minimum standards for the procedural law of the Member States. Cases such as *Océano Grupo*, which touched upon the power of the Court to raise legal issues on its own motion,[31] have had a direct impact on domestic procedural theory in transnational cases and thus add to the

---

[26] Council of the European Union, The Stockholm Programme. An open and secure Europe serving and protecting citizens, OJ C 115 of 4.5.2010, 14.

[27] Council of the European Union, The Stockholm Programme. An open and secure Europe serving and protecting citizens, OJ C 115 of 4.5.2010, 15.

[28] Directive 2004/48/EC on the enforcement of intellectual property rights, OJ 2004, L 157/16, 16–25.

[29] Sala 2008, 208.

[30] Dougan 2004.

[31] ECJ 27 June 2000, Case C-240 to 244/98), ECR I-04941 *(Océano Grupo)*.

convergence of procedural law in Europe.[32] In the field of administrative justice, some have even submitted that procedural harmonisation through legislative instruments is less attractive than seeking convergence through the setting of minimum procedural standards by the ECJ.[33] We believe, however, that for civil and commercial dispute resolution the control of the ECJ would not suffice.

16.4 Challenges and Obstacles

The harmonisation of civil procedure is a difficult and controversial theme. This chapter does not have the ambition to analyse in depth such a fundamental issue. We will limit ourselves to some comments in anticipation of the case study in the following Sect. 16.5. The most important is that the debate on the harmonisation of civil justice may still not have matured entirely. There is a need for a more intense exchange of thoughts about whether we need harmonisation at all, and if so, how we should go about it.

Historically, the view that procedure is too closely linked to a nation's identity for it to adapt to a foreign model seems to have been predominant.[34] In contemporary times, however, the harmonisation of procedure is more favourably viewed, at least on a European level. Scholars such as Storme have long voiced support for a great harmonisation effort.[35] Procedural scholars do not always offer a clear justification for this point. It seems that many perceive uniform civil procedure as necessarily superior to isolated national procedure,[36] but predominant of course is the idea that a uniform procedure will contribute to market integration.[37] Some also stress the contribution a harmonised European civil justice may make to the greater ideal of a European polity.[38] More sceptical observers have questioned the need for a full-blown harmonisation.[39] Their argument is that a plurality of procedural systems is necessary because nobody knows what the ideal procedure is, and States should therefore have the opportunity to experiment and compare.[40] It is added that plurality is beneficial because it allows for jurisdictional competition, which will encourage States to continuously improve their dispute resolution

---

[32] Delicostopulos 2003, 229 et seq. See also, for a critical observations: Zekoll 2006, 1338 and 1351 et seq.

[33] Eliantonio 2009, 10.

[34] Van Rhee 2000, 598.

[35] Storme 2005, 87. See also Freudenthal 2003, 10; Van Rhee 2003, 217 et seq.

[36] See, e.g., Lowenfeld 1997, 653.

[37] Kerameus 1995, 401–402.

[38] Hartnell 2002, 130.

[39] Zuckerman 2002, 325; Juenger 1997, 933.

[40] Zuckerman 2002, 322; Andrews 2008, 281.

mechanisms.[41] This link with the enhancement of civil justice is actually also made by the proponents of harmonisation, who agree that its success will depend on its capacity to increase our civil justice system's efficiency.[42]

The discussion about the pros and cons of procedural harmonisation is extremely insightful, and the international literature has eloquently described it, even from a Law and Economics perspective.[43] In Europe, however, the debate does not seem to have opened up entirely yet. As a matter of fact, in the current state of European integration, the discussion about harmonisation should not be so much about whether we should harmonise or not, as this process has already started, but more about how we should harmonise and what the best approach is. Even the more sceptical voices do not preclude harmonisation altogether. Rather, some say we should just continue to limit this harmonisation to transnational disputes.[44] They prefer a consensus on fundamental values and doctrines to complete unification or an in-depth harmonisation.[45] Others reply that if one can find consensus about the principles, one can also give effect to them in a uniform way.[46] That is as far as the debate goes. It is clear that what Europe lacks now is a well-thought out concept on how it should approach procedural harmonisation.[47] Best placed to initiate this debate is the European Commission, which is already conducting a similar exercise in relation to the specific issue of collective actions.[48]

The proposed focus on the approach to harmonisation does not mean narrowing the debate to one about technicalities. In searching for our own model for procedural harmonisation, the reflection should also probe into our priorities, what the end result should be, whether it should be an integrated or a piecemeal harmonisation and what the scale of the effort should be. We will also need to contemplate whether we really want to invest solely in harmonisation on a European level, or whether regional or global levels are also still worth our time. In respect of the global harmonisation efforts supported by various international agencies and organisations, for instance, this point has already been made convincingly.[49]

The question as to who should be involved also merits attention. Good governance requires consultation with those who will work with the product of the harmonisation, the legal practitioners. Their input is required, as the success of a European civil justice depends on their commitment. Yet, the level of involvement of European practitioners is still not satisfactory. It seems that today, despite the

---

[41] Zuckerman 2002, 322.

[42] Hess 2010, 207–208; Storme 2005, 99.

[43] Chase et al 2007, 562 et seq. See also Visscher (Chap. 4) in the current Volume.

[44] Juenger 1997, 936.

[45] Andrews 2009, 56.

[46] Storme 2005, 96.

[47] Freudenthal 2003, 2.

[48] See the consultation on collective redress: Commission Staff Working Document. Public Consultation: Towards a Coherent European Approach to Collective Redress, SEC(2011) 173.

[49] Ferrand 2003, 430–436.

creation of a European Judicial Network in Civil and Commercial Matters as well as a European Judicial Training Network, the Council of Europe is better at involving judges and lawyers in their work on comparative civil justice than the European Union.

It is commonly accepted that national tradition is an important obstacle to a successful harmonisation of civil procedure. This is less attributable to the supposedly close link between a procedure and a nation's identity, but has everything to do with the fact that procedure is embedded in a national structure for the administration of justice and that the intricacies of such structure vary from State to State. As Damaška has brilliantly demonstrated, the organisation of a State's justice system as well as the ideological content of State authority in respect of dispute resolution are factors with a decisive influence on a nation's procedural tradition.[50] This convinced Professor Kerameus to take a pessimistic stance: 'the organizational features of the administration of justice depend so heavily on the overall structure of the respective State as to make harmonization here extremely difficult unless one thinks of global unification of whole legal systems.'[51] Kerameus may have overstated these impediments, but the fact remains that thinking through a harmonisation policy also means taking into account national traditions and State organisation. In the Stockholm Programme, the European Union reiterated its intention to take into account the different legal traditions of the Member States.[52] In the reality of daily practice some have the impression that the Union fails to live up to its commitment.

Some thought could be given to finding a more appropriate method of harmonisation in order to strike a better balance between national tradition and the strive for uniformity. We know of the tendency among the States to stand for more flexible harmonisation methods, such as benchmarking systems and exchanges of best practices. The Treaty of Lisbon already provides for 'open coordination' as an appropriate way to seek convergence in many areas.[53] Perhaps this could be a valuable option for harmonising civil justice as well. Open methods of coordination (OMC) can take several forms but always aim to harmonise law by an elaborated procedure of naming and shaming.[54] Policy goals are translated into guidelines, indicators, benchmarks and best practices, which the countries can transpose or adopt in the way they see fit. Compliance by Member States is measured. The advantage of this instrument is that each country can choose how it

[50] Damaška 1986.

[51] Kerameus 1995, 412.

[52] Council of the European Union, The Stockholm Programme. An open and secure Europe serving and protecting citizens, OJ C 115 of 4.5.2010, 11, 12 and 13.

[53] For example Art. 156 of the Treaty on the Functioning of the European Union (TFEU) (in respect of social policy) and Art. 168 lid 2 TFEU (in respect of public health) stipulate that Member States should weigh in advance their respective policies against stipulated European criteria.

[54] For an overview of the different appreciations of the OMC in the literature, see: Zeitlin and Pochet 2005, 22.

wants to realise certain goals. Some countries will particularly profit from the fact that best practices will be exchanged in a structured and accessible manner. The success of the harmonisation will be assessed using a set of parameters identified at the outset. The difficulty will be to reach an agreement about these parameters. There is a real risk for this method to result in a kind of superfluous statement of basic principles, which all countries agree on but which are too broad to measure.

Aside from national tradition, other local particularities may also play an obstructive role. From the impressive scholarly work of Oscar Chase we already know that civil procedure cannot be detached from national culture.[55] So too Kennet concludes his research on enforcement of judgments in Europe with the comment that 'the cultural dimension cannot be ignored in assessing the likely success of harmonization initiatives.'[56] In some areas, for example, there can be very powerful domestic lobby groups, such as trade unions.[57] A willingness among all the different national actors to cooperate cannot be assumed.[58] This cooperation can be and should be created by a process of explaining, demonstrating and implementing jointly.

16.5 Belgium: A Case Study

16.5.1 Reception of Foreign Law in Belgian Civil Procedure

Belgian civil procedural law has benefitted from the reception of foreign law. For instance, the introduction of the 1967 Judicial Code was preceded by an elaborate study of the reputed 'bâtonnier' Charles Van Reepinghen, working in his capacity as Royal Commissioner for the Reform of Judicial Institutions from 1956 to 1964. He delivered his conclusions to parliament in the form of a written report, the—today still authoritative—'Report of the Judicial Reform' (1967) which contains a detailed commentary on the text of the new code and included numerous references to foreign law.[59] Admittedly, such an extensive reflection on the future of Belgian civil justice on the basis of comparative analysis has not been witnessed at any time since then. Comparative analysis still occasionally finds its way into the legislative process, though, but only in the context of very specific legislative adjustments of the procedure code. For example, the changes to cost shifting rules in one of the reform acts of 2007 were inspired by scholarly research of cost shifting rules in a number of European countries.

55 Chase et al 2007; Chase 1997.

56 Kennett 2000, 306.

57 Kennett 2000, 306.

58 Kennett 2000, 309.

59 Van Reepinghen 1964, 12–14.

It is fair to say that the Belgian legislator could do much more to learn from foreign solutions and experiences. Is Belgium simply waiting for the European Union to do the work? One can only speculate about whether the harmonisation efforts on the supranational level have made national governments lose their appetite to work at convergence on their own. What we do know for certain is that the legislative process in Belgium is structurally falling short of a professional framework to enhance its foreign law capabilities. More use could be made of comparative research to prepare legislative action if a more coordinated approach were taken. As the legislative process is currently organised, the means for expert advice on civil justice—including comparative analysis—are too dispersed to guarantee excellence. To start with, a lot of preparatory work is done by the Legislation Service at the Federal Ministry of Justice, which is comprised of civil servants only and operates in a rather isolated way. The Legislation Service reports to the Minister of Justice, whose Cabinet employs its own policy researchers as well. The latter work on a temporary basis and are usually recruited amongst professionals from the legal field (lawyers, magistrates, researchers, et cetera). The Cabinet is supposed to work closely together with the Legislation Service, but that it is not always the case. The Minister's Cabinet and its policy staff sometimes prefer to work with external advisors instead, such as law professors. Alongside the government, there is of course the parliament where the larger parliamentary factions usually employ policy advisors with a shared focus on (civil) justice. However, these are usually so overburdened that they rarely have time to be involved in comparative analysis. Next, there is the Council of State ('Conseil d'Etat,' 'Raad van State'), a judicial body whose Legislative Department issues independent opinions on legislative proposals. The Council is not involved until a draft bill has been prepared. It is not involved in the thinking process preceding the drafting and it is not considered to develop policy considerations of any kind. Rather, its advice concentrates on the legal merits of the draft. Its opinions usually focus on the technical consistency of the draft bill, its conformity with hierarchically superior norms (such as the Constitution and treaties) and its compatibility with our legal system in general. There is generally little or no room for comparative reflections in these opinions. Finally, the High Council of Justice ('Hoge Raad voor de Justitie,' 'Conseil Supérieur de la Justice') also issues opinions on legislative proposals in the field of justice. This body, comprised of representatives of the magistrature as well as the civil society, is mostly known for its crucial role in the recruitment and selection of magistrates. It also has duties in respect of policy advice, organising conferences as well as issuing policy briefings and opinions on legislative proposals. The High Council is probably the advisory actor that has most affinity with the comparative method, but it lacks the budget and staff to turn the comparative analysis into a sophisticated instrument of our justice policy.

It is not likely that the deficiencies of the legislative process will be remedied any time soon, as this requires structural political reform. Meanwhile, the judiciary, which has a vested interest in the optimisation of our procedures, may perhaps fill the gap. In the last few years, Belgian magistrates' contacts with their foreign colleagues have intensified, in part with the help of European funding. Some interesting innovation has come from it. For example, in 2002, Antwerp-based judges convinced the Belgian Minister of Justice to launch an experiment with Québec-style court-annexed 'mediation by judges.'[60] And in 2010, the juvenile section of the Ghent court of appeals announced that it would introduce settlement hearings following the Dutch 'schikkingscomparitie' model.[61]

16.5.2 Intergovernmental and Supranational Harmonisation

As far as the ALI/UNIDROIT principles are concerned, these have gone largely unnoticed in Belgian legal doctrine. Most scholarly writings dedicated to harmonisation have focused on European harmonisation. The same can be said in relation to the case law of Belgian courts, which does not contain a single recorded reference to the said ALI/UNIDROIT principles. One can only conclude that no direct influence of the ALI/UNIDROIT Principles of Transnational Civil Procedure on the Belgian civil justice system can be observed, even though our Judicial Code already seems largely compatible with the Principles.

The work of the Council of Europe has proved to be slightly more influential. For example, its recommendations on mediation are known to have inspired the Belgian legislation on the subject.[62] Also, in a recent report,[63] a parliamentary commission advised the government to reflect on the public prosecutor's current role in civil proceedings taking into account the Council of Europe's recommendation on this issue.[64]

Most attention has of course gone to the harmonisation efforts of the European Union and especially to the European order for payment and the European small claims procedure. These proceedings are only applicable to cross-border disputes and now co-exist with national procedures. This entails that citizens having a cross-border claim can use the European procedure while citizens with other claims are deprived of that procedure. Some have argued that this gives rise to an unlawful discrimination.[65] Others reported on a way to circumvent the problem: a national claim can be turned into a cross-border claim by assigning it to a contracting party from another Member State. This illustrates the point made by Storskrubb that the

---

60 Allemeersch 2003, 451–455.

61 Oplinus 2010, 1370.

62 Recommendation on mediation in civil matters (Rec (2002) 10) and recommendation on family mediation (Rec(98)1E), http://www.coe.int (last consulted in May 2011).

63 Commission of Inquiry, Parliamentary Documents: House of Representatives 2008–2009, No. 52 1711/007, 70, para 1.3. Available at http://www.dekamer.be (last consulted in May 2011).

64 Recommendation of the Parliamentary Assembly on the Role of the public prosecutor's office in a democratic society governed by the rule of law (Rec 1604 (2003)).

65 E.g. Van Turnhout 2007, 338. See also Storme 2009b, 38, para 55; Storme 2010, 376. *Contra*: Storme 2009a, 27.

introduction of superior procedures for cross-border claims will inevitably create pressure to reform procedures for purely national claims as well.[66]

16.5.3 Regional Harmonisation (Benelux)

The most influential unification effort in Belgian law to date has been the Uniform Law on the Civil Coercive Fine (*astreinte*),[67] drafted and enacted in concert between the Kingdom of Belgium and the Kingdom of the Netherlands as well as the Grand Duchy of Luxembourg. This model law of eight articles still governs the civil coercive fine in all three Benelux countries.[68] It is widely seen as a solid piece of legislation[69] and has found its natural place in the legal systems of the three States concerned. Uniform interpretation is guaranteed by the Benelux Court of Justice by means of a system of preliminary ruling.[70]

The text of the uniform law was drafted by the Commission for the Study of Unification of Laws in the Benelux, incorporated by the three States in 1948 and composed of law professors and magistrates. This commission also authored a convention on the legal profession,[71] and on a number of other subjects. Although the commission that drafted the text was strictly speaking entirely independent, the project was conducted with the help and under the auspices of the so-called Benelux Economic Union. The Benelux is a form of intergovernmental cooperation between Belgium, the Netherlands and Luxembourg and was established in 1946 in the form of a customs union. As such, it was the embryonic predecessor of the customs union which later became the EU.

Since the 1980s the commission has remained inactive.[72] In the last few years, suggestions have been made to reinstate the commission, such as in 2004 by then acting President of the Belgian Chamber of Representatives Herman de Croo.[73] It seems, however, that the harmonisation of civil justice has for a long time been out of the organisation's gun sights. Nowadays, the content of the Benelux's justice policy is to be found in the Senningen Agreement,[74] which focuses mainly on issues of criminal justice and policing.

---

66 Storskrubb 2009, 12.

67 Benelux—Convention holding the Uniform Law concerning the Civil Coercive Fine, signed at The Hague on 26 November 1973.

68 The Netherlands: Art. 611a–Art. 611h of the Dutch Code of Civil Procedure. Belgium: Art. 1385 bis–Art. 1385 nonies of the Judicial Code. Luxembourg: Arts. 2059–2066 Civil Code.

69 Wouters and Vidal 2007, 555.

70 Art. 4 of the Convention. For a commentary on the system of preliminary reference to the Benelux Court of Justice, see Limpens 1977.

71 Benelux—Convention on the attorney's profession, signed at Brussels on 12 December 1968.

72 Wouters et al 2006, 111.

73 Wouters et al 2006, 111.

74 Memorandum of understanding dated 4 June 1996 concerning the cooperation in the field of policing, justice and immigration.

Recent research has suggested that the Benelux has actually outlived its original objectives and is ready for a new project.[75] Wouters and Vidal propose to transform the Benelux into a flexible project organisation focusing on limited and clearly defined policy areas where it could fulfil its role as a laboratory for future pan-European initiatives.[76] The Treaty of Lisbon offers two possibilities for the Member States to engage in a more intense cooperation. Article 350 TFEU explicitly authorised broader and more far-reaching cooperation between Belgium, the Netherlands and Luxembourg. Article 20 of the Treaty on European Union covers another type of enhanced cooperation: this article creates the possibility for Member States to use the institutions of the EU for establishing more far-reaching cooperation in the area of non-exclusive competences of the Union.

Hence, the question can be raised as to why the Benelux could not become a laboratory for pan-European initiatives in the field of civil justice. Even the most ardent supporters of a unified European civil procedure have admitted that a step-by-step approach would be prudent and that we could best start off with some kind of regional harmonisation.[77] The great success of the Uniform Law on the Civil Coercive Fine may not guarantee repeat success, but it does testify to the three countries' willingness and capacity to find common ground for a unified procedure.

16.6 Conclusion

It is sometimes perceived that in Europe, given the dominance of the European Union in respect of the convergence of laws, the role of the national actors has lost all meaning. This is far from correct. The national actors still have a contribution to make. At worst, if they have lost anything, it is their appetite for bringing about convergence on their own. In this chapter, we have studied how a smaller Member State like Belgium deals with the need for further convergence. We have concluded that both the reception of foreign law and intergovernmental cooperation on a regional level offer good prospects for the further harmonisation of civil procedure. Both will encounter less resistance and will be less tedious to be put into effect. In particular, we have made the suggestion that the Benelux countries should explore the possibility of reviving their cooperation in the field of harmonisation and putting it to work for the benefit of bringing their three civil justice systems closer together. By doing so, the 'Low Countries' could serve as a laboratory for the harmonisation of civil procedure on a European level.

---

[75] Wouters and Vidal 2007, 555.

[76] Wouters and Vidal 2007, 558.

[77] Storme 2005, 95 (who proposes focusing first on the Continental civil law systems).

References

ALI/UNIDROIT (2004) Principles of transnational civil procedure. Unif Law Rev 4:758–810

Allemeersch B (2003) Bemiddeling en verzoening in het burgerlijk proces. Proeve van een beginselenleer in een Belgisch en Europees perspectief. Tijdschrift voor Privaatrecht 40:409–500

Andrews N (2008) The modern civil process. Mohr Siebeck, Tübingen

Andrews N (2009) A modern procedural synthesis. The American Law Institute and UNIDROIT's principles and rules of transnational civil procedure. Tijdschrift voor Civiele Rechtspleging 14:52–57

Boodman M (1991) The myth of harmonization of laws. Am J Comp Law 39:699–724

Chase OG (1997) Some observations on the cultural dimension in civil procedure reform. Am J Comp Law 45:861–870

Chase OG et al (2007) Civil litigation in comparative context. West Publishing, St. Paul

Damaška M (1986) The faces of justice and state authority. Yale University Press, New Haven

Delicostopulos JS (2003) Towards European procedural primacy in national legal systems. Eur Law J 9:599–613

Dembour M-B (1996) Harmonization and the construction of Europe: variations away from a musical theme. European University Institute Department of Law, Florence

Dougan M (2004) National remedies before the court of justice. Issues of harmonisation and differentiation. Hart Publishing, Oxford

Eliantonio M (2009) The future of national procedural law in Europe: harmonisation vs. judge-made standards in the field of administrative justice. Electron J Comp Law 13(3):1–10. Available at http://www.ejcl.org/133/art133-4.pdf (Accessed May 2011)

Ferrand F (2003) La procédure civile internationale et la procédure civile transnationale: l'incidence de l'intégration économique régionale. Unif Law Rev 8:397–436

Freudenthal M (2003) The future of European civil procedure. Electron J Comp Law 7.5:1–10. Available at http://www.ejcl.org/ejcl/75/art75-6.html (Accessed May 2011)

Gidi A (2006) Teaching comparative civil procedure. J Legal Edu 56:502–509

Hartnell HE (2002) EUstitia: institutionalizing justice in the European Union. Northwest J Int Law Bus 23:65–138

Hazard GC Jr, Taruffo M, Sturner R, Gidi A (2001) Introduction to the principles and rules of transnational civil procedure. NY Univ J Int Law Politics 33:769–782

Hess B (2002) The integrating effect of European civil procedure law. Eur J Law Reform 4:3–17

Hess B (2010) Deutsches Zivilprozessrecht zwischen nationaler Eigenstandigkeit und europaischem Anpassungszwang. Ritsumeikan Law Rev 27:191–208

Juenger F (1997) Some comments on European procedural harmonization. Am J Comp Law 45:931–937

Kennett W (2000) The enforcement of judgments in Europe. Oxford University Press, Oxford

Kerameus K (1995) Procedural harmonization in Europe. Am J Comp Law 43:401–416

Limpens J (1977) L'interprétation des lois uniformes et la Cour de Justice Benelux. Unif Law Rev 5:68–81

Lowenfeld A (1997) The elements of procedure: Are they separately portable? Am J Comp Law 45:649–655

Oplinus S (2010) De schikkingscomparitie en het her-oraliseren van het civiele geding. Rechtskundig Weekblad 73:1370–1377

Robertson R, White K (2007) What is globalization? In: Ritzer G (ed) The Blackwell companion to globalization. Blackwell Publishing, Oxford, pp 54–66

Sala RM (2008) European private law without European law in civil procedure. In: Vaquer A (ed) European private law beyond the common frame of reference. Essays in honour of Reinhard Zimmerman. Europa Law Publishing, Groningen, pp 203–216

Storme M (ed) (1994) Approximation of judiciary law in the European Union/Rapprochement du Droit Judiciaire de l'Union européenne. Kluwer, Dordrecht

Storme M (2005) A single civil procedure for Europe: a cathedral builders' dream. Ritsumeikan Law Rev 22:87–100
Storme H (2009a) Uniforme Europese procedures voor versnelde afhandeling van grensoverschrijdende geschillen. Cahier du Juriste—Cahier van de Jurist 7(1):27–31
Storme ME (2009b) De verhouding tussen de Europese procesrechtelijke verhoudingen (in het bijzonder geringe vorderingen) en het interne Belgische procesrecht. Ius Actores 3:19–40
Storme ME (2010) België als no-go-zone voor schuldeisers? Tijdschrift voor Privaatrecht 47:373–382
Storskrubb E (2009) What changes will European procedural harmonisation bring? Paper presented at the IAPL conference 'the future of categories—categories of the future,' Toronto, Canada, 3–5 June 2009. Available at http://www.iapl2009.org/documents/5EvaStorskrubb.pdf (Accessed May 2011)
Tell O (2003) La construction de l'espace unique européen en matière de justice face à l'harmonisation universelle de la procédure civile: propos réalistes d'un acteur européen. Unif Law Rev 30:453–460
Trompenaars BWM (1989) Pluriforme unificatie en uniforme interpretatie. Kluwer, Deventer
Van Reepinghen C (1964) Report on the judicial reform, Preparatory documents Sentae
Van Rhee CH (2000) Civil procedure: a European Ius Commune? Eur Rev Priv Law 8:589–611
Van Rhee CH (2003) Towards a procedural Ius Commune? In: Smits J, Lubbe G (eds) Remedies in Zuid-Afrika en Europa. Intersentia, Antwerp, pp 217–232
Van Rhee CH, Verkerk R (2006) Civil procedure. In: Smits (ed) Elgar encyclopedia of comparative law. Edgar Elgar, Cheltenham, pp 120–134
Van Turnhout R (2007) Europese procedure voor geringe vorderingen. Kritische analyse vanuit Belgisch standpunt, Tijdschrift voor procesrecht en bewijsrecht/Revue de droit judiciare et de la preuve, pp 325–340
Weintraub RJ (1998) Critique of the Hazard-Taruffo transnational rules of civil procedure. Tex Int Law J 33:413–423
Wouters J, Vidal M (2007) Towards a rebirth of Benelux? Revue Belge de droit int 40:533–568
Wouters J et al (2006) De Benelux: Tijd voor een wedergeboorte? Intersentia, Antwerp
Zeitlin J, Pochet P (2005) The open method of co-ordination in action. Peter Lang, Brussels
Zekoll J (2006) Comparative civil procedure. In: Zimmermann R, Reimann M (eds) Oxford handbook of comparative law. Oxford University Press, Oxford, pp 1327–1362
Zuckerman AAS (2002) Conference on 'the ALI-UNIDROIT principles and rules of transnational civil procedure,' hosted by the British Institute of International and Comparative Law, London 24 May 2002. Civ Justice Q 20:322–325

Chapter 17
The French Approach to the Globalisation and Harmonisation of Civil Procedure

Frédérique Ferrand

Abstract The traditional approach of French academics and French courts was that civil procedure was exempt from any harmonisation as it belonged to national public policy. The current French approach to the globalisation and harmonisation of civil procedure shows that instances of the reception of certain institutions from another legal tradition do occur, so that the national legal system sometimes becomes a subtle 'blend' while still retaining its roots. Several foreign procedural techniques have been admitted into private international law, most notably the freezing order, the anti-suit injunction and estoppel. Furthermore, French courts, especially the *Cour de cassation*, have recognised some procedural institutions imported from foreign jurisdictions and sometimes make use of comparative studies in the area of civil procedure. The initial negative response to the global initiative of the ALI/UNIDROIT Principles of Transnational Civil Procedure has gradually shifted to a possible acceptance. It can be concluded that neither French lawyers nor French case law is totally reluctant to some harmonisation of civil procedure. The academic world has been used to mandatory harmonisation in the framework of European civil judicial cooperation for over ten years and is open to comparative legal studies and to some foreign institutions that could enrich French civil procedure.

Professor at University Jean Moulin Lyon 3, Honorarprofessorin at the University of Augsburg.

F. Ferrand (✉)
University Jean Moulin Lyon 3, Lyon, France
e-mail: frederique.ferrand@univ-lyon3.fr

X. E. Kramer and C. H. van Rhee (eds.), *Civil Litigation in a Globalising World*,
DOI: 10.1007/978-90-6704-817-0_17,

Contents

17.1 Introduction

For many years, French academics and French case law were convinced that civil procedure was—like the right of enforcement measures—a typically national field of law. Civil procedure was regarded as exempt from any harmonisation attempt because it was perceived as being too strongly linked with State sovereignty[1] and the national judicial culture[2] and, therefore, as belonging to national *ordre public* (public policy).[3] This view of things is, however, diminishing, especially within the framework of Europe or even of the Ibero-American countries (i.e. in geographical areas which are integrated to a greater or lesser degree).[4] Some international instruments aim at harmonising procedural issues. Nonetheless, the peculiarities of procedural laws still hold out against procedural unification or

[1] Cf. Storme 2001, 765. Justice as a public service was regarded as an expression of political authority and its institutions were imparted State duties, see Sánchez-Cordero Dávila 2006, xxxiii.

[2] See the historical background in Wijffels 2005, 25, 46 ('During the nineteenth century, French law was part of a cultural model which was more prone to influencing other systems than absorbing foreign influences') and 47, see footnote 84.

[3] See Kerameus 2003, 448.

[4] See in particular in the European Union: several instruments of civil procedure dealing with jurisdiction, recognition and enforcement (like the Brussels I and Brussels IIa Regulations) but related to the service of judicial or extrajudicial documents in civil and commercial matters, the cooperation between the courts of the Member States in the taking of evidence, to legal aid, to mediation… The most recent European instruments have even created specific European proceedings: the European payment order (Regulation No. 1896/2006 creating a European order for payment procedure, OJ 2006, L 399) and the small claims procedure (Regulation No. 891/2007 establishing a European Small Claims Procedure OJ 2007, L 199).

harmonisation attempts, at least as regards a unique model Code of Civil Procedure. The culture of the lawsuit still deeply reflects the culture of the society.

The first movement which led French courts to contribute to a certain kind of harmonisation of civil procedure was the inclusion in French case law of the requirements stated by Article 6(1)[5] of the European Convention on Human Rights (ECHR).[6] It was only in 1981 that France recognised the right to individual application (*droit de requête individuelle*)[7] before the European Court of Human Rights (ECtHR). In the 1970s, Law Faculties offered very few classes in European Human Rights. Attorneys seldom argued the human rights guaranteed by the European Convention although the French Constitution states that ratified international treaties prevail over Acts of national law, even when the latter have been enacted at a later date. Gradually, however (and increasingly since the 1990s), the European Convention on Human Rights grew in popularity and was often used as a legal ground for claims or defence. Nowadays, after a first phase during which the French *Cour de cassation* was reluctant to modify its case law on the ground of the European case law relating to Human rights,[8] we find French courts basing their decisions on principles and rules which are stated in the ECHR and also on the interpretation given to those principles and rules by the ECtHR. Therefore, the principles of effective access to justice, due process of law, the right to a judge provided by law, the adversarial nature of the proceedings in the presence of the parties involved (*principe contradictoire, rechtliches Gehör*), reasonable time to reach a decision or the right to enforcement of court decisions are usually interpreted and applied in accordance with this international legal instrument.[9] The ECtHR plays its part (where the forty-seven Member States of the Council of

---

[5] Art. 6(1) ECHR states that 'In the determination of his civil rights and obligations or of any criminal charge against him, everyone is entitled to a fair and public hearing within a reasonable time by an independent and impartial tribunal established by law. Judgement shall be pronounced publicly by the press and public may be excluded from all or part of the trial in the interest of morals, public order or national security in a democratic society, where the interests of juveniles or the protection of the private life of the parties so require, or the extent strictly necessary in the opinion of the court in special circumstances where publicity would prejudice the interests of justice'.

[6] See the interesting contribution by d' Avout 2009, 165 et seq, about fundamental rights and coordination between legal systems, '*Droits fondamentaux et coordination des ordres juridiques en droit privé*'.

[7] See Art. 34 ECHR ('The Court may receive applications from any person, non-governmental organisation or group of individuals claiming to be the victim of a violation by one of the High Contracting Parties of the rights set forth in the Convention or the Protocols thereto. The High Contracting Parties undertake not to hinder in any way the effective exercise of this right').

[8] See e.g. ECHR 4 December 1995, *Bellet v France*, Serie A, No. 333-B; JCP 1996, II, 22 648 (violation of Article 6(1) ECHR - access to court - in the application of the Law Act No. 91-1406 of 31 December 1991) and the resistance put up by the *Cour de cassation* to the European case law, Cass. civ. I 9 July 1996, RTDCiv. (1997), 146 obs. P. Jourdain; D. 1996, 610 obs. Y. Lambert-Fauvre; even the plenary assembly resisted, Cass. ass. plén. 6 June 1997, Fondation Saint-Marc, Bull. A. P. No. 8 p. 20; Guinchard 2004a, 288.

[9] Cf. Rouhette 1998, 285 et seq.

Europe are concerned) in achieving a certain harmonisation of civil proceedings based on the central notion of *fair trial* contained in Article 6(1) ECHR[10] from which the Court has drawn a triptych: firstly, effective access to court; secondly, the right to fair justice (fairness of proceedings, equality of arms, publicity, independence and impartiality of judges); and thirdly, the right to the enforcement of court decisions. Even if the European Court of Human Rights does not interfere with the details of the procedural legislation of the contracting States, it lays out requirements based on an extensive interpretation of Article 6(1) ECHR. This has sometimes led to modifications of Acts of national law regarded by the European Court as violating the principles contained in Article 6.[11] Nowadays, the European Charter of Fundamental Rights has become binding since the entry into force of the Treaty of Lisbon, Article 47 of which states guarantees very similar to those contained in Article 6(1) ECHR.

Some harmonisation, even standardisation, gradually ensues from these conventional principles which have recently (during the last few decades) 'been constitutionalised' in some jurisdictions.[12] Procedure is attracted by fundamental rights[13] and is becoming a technique to protect them, the instrument of a procedural democracy. A certain 'modelling' within globalisation (*modélisation dans la mondialisation*)[14] is occurring with the international framework of *fair trial.*[15]

In France, the tendency towards certain more restricted or sectional harmonisation is perceived (in some respects with a critical eye) as being strong due to the phenomenon of globalisation.[16] Globalisation is connected with increased mobility and makes, in civil and commercial proceedings, the requirements of efficiency, transparency, foreseeability and proportionality more important and more acute.[17] Indeed, academics themselves contribute to this harmonisation, as well as—to a

---

[10] European Convention for the Protection of Human Rights and Fundamental Freedoms of 4 November 1950.

[11] See e.g. ECHR, 30 July 1998, *Aerts v Belgium*, No. 25357/94 (criteria for awarding legal aid); 27 October 1993, *Dombo Beheer B.V. v the Netherlands*, No. 14448/88 (violation of the equality of arms and hearing of a party to the proceedings as a witness); 19 December 1997, *Helle v Finland*, No. 20772/92 (reasoning of court decisions). See also the very numerous decisions sanctioning a violation of the 'reasonable time' of the proceedings. The requirement of efficiency and speed of the proceedings (i.e. reasonable time) has contributed in many jurisdictions to the establishing of the principle of concentration and of an active role of the judge as a 'court manager' (see Storme 2008, 357: 'the dispute is in the hands of the parties. The litigation is in the hands of the judge').

[12] Guinchard 2000, 355.

[13] Guinchard 2004a, 267, 287 et seq (*l'attraction par les droits fondamentaux*).

[14] *Ibidem.*

[15] On the basis of the principle of *fair trial*, France has recognised new fundamental principles of procedure: *principe de loyauté* (principle of fairness), *principe de dialogue* (principle of dialogue) and *principe de célérité* (principle of prompt rendition of justice, cf. p. 7 of the ALI/UNIDROITt Principles of Transnational Civil Procedure), cf. Guinchard 2005, 288.

[16] See Deguchi and Storme 2008.

[17] See Storme 2001, 768.

certain extent—national or regional (especially European) case law. To give an example, French case law has adopted foreign institutions such as the *amicus curiae*[18] or *estoppel*[19] in order to give them a special function in civil proceedings.

The French approach to the globalisation and harmonisation of civil procedure shows that instances of the reception of certain institutions from one legal tradition to another do occur, so that the national legal system sometimes becomes a subtle 'blend'.[20] This does not, however, lead to the disappearance of the roots of the national legal system. French courts have admitted some foreign procedural techniques (coming from common law countries) into private international law, showing their open-mindedness in cases where a party claimed the recognition of the common law institution would constitute a violation of French international *ordre public* (Sect. 17.2). French domestic civil procedure is also (directly or indirectly) influenced by some foreign institutions and laws (Sect. 17.3). French reactions to harmonisation attempts in the field of civil procedure in a global context are more mitigated. The draft of the ALI/UNIDROIT *Rules* of Transnational Civil Procedure was first strongly criticised during an October 2000 meeting in Paris. Three years later, however, in Lyon, the atmosphere regarding the *quasi* final draft of the *Principles* (Sect. 17.4) was much more positive.

17.2 The Admission of Foreign Procedural Techniques in Private International Law

A traditional way of classifying the legal systems, where substantive law as well as civil procedure is concerned, consists in distinguishing between Common law and Civil law traditions,[21] even if this distinction does not truly take into account all the nuances and tendencies relating to procedure.[22] And even if those two

[18] See Cass. ass. plén., 31 May 1991, D. 1991, p. 417, report Y. Chartier and obs. D. Thouvenin; 29 June 2001, JCP G 2001. II. 10 569, report P. Sargos and concl. J. Sainte-Rose; Cass. ch. mixte, 23 November 2004, D. 2004. IR. 3 191; CA Paris, 16 October 1992, D. 1993, p. 172, note Y. Laurin. See also Mazeaud 1995, 109 et seq; Encinas de Munagorri 2005, 88.

[19] Dealing with arbitration, see Cass. civ. I, 3 February 2010, D. 2019, 448 and earlier already Cass. civ. I, 11 July 2006, Bull. civ. I, No. 369; D. 2006. AJ 1422, obs. X. Delpech and Cass. civ. I, 6 May 2009, D. 2009. Pan. 2966, obs. Th. Clay. In civil proceedings before State courts, the *estoppel* has been admitted only under strict conditions, see Cass. ass. plén., 27 February 2009, D. 2009. Jur. 1245, obs. D. Houtcieff; D. 2010. Pan. 169, obs. N. Fricero; JCP G 2009. II. 10 073, obs. P. Callé.

[20] Cf. Cadiet 2010, 635; Amrani-Mekki 2010, 157 et seq.

[21] Murray 2008, 326–331.

[22] Kronke 2004, 18, who speaks of *stéréotypes*.

categories of legal system are becoming in some respect closer, and indeed even share common orientations nowadays,[23] the classic, basic dichotomy remains.[24] Nonetheless, in the last few years French case law, especially with regard to the *Cour d'appel de Paris* and the *Cour de cassation*, has given important judgments recognising in France the effects of common law institutions such as freezing orders (Sect. 17.2.1), anti-suit injunctions (Sect. 17.2.2) or estoppel (Sect. 17.2.3).

17.2.1 The Freezing Order Before the French **Cour de cassation**

In private international law, court decisions from another State are neither recognised nor enforced if this would be (in European law 'manifestly'[25]) contrary to public policy in the Member State in which recognition is sought. In European law, the European Court of Justice (ECJ) restricts the scope of domestic public policy: it is to be used only in exceptional cases to deprive the court decision from another Member State of any recognition or enforcement.[26] In France, most of the

---

[23] Andrews 2008, No. 1.02, who mentions with humour that 'In fact English law is sandwiched between civil law Europe and the distinctive Common law system of the USA' and describes how English law has adapted and still has to adapt in order to offer an attractive and modern civil justice model. Cf. Stürner 2004, 9. See also Cadiet 2005, 49 et seq, 57. ('The Code is essentially a work in composition, neither adversarial nor inquisitorial; the qualifications do not suit what civil litigation fundamentally is. It is a work in composition because it must conciliate the liberal principles of French tradition which make parties the owners of the lawsuit, and the affirmation of the powers of the judge, who must—as a procedural mandate—realize his mission to achieve the fairest solution to the dispute, which is in the general interest. Justice is a public service and impartiality is not passivity.').

[24] Hazard et al. 2006, xxviii.

[25] See Art. 34.1 Regulation No. 44/2001 on jurisdiction and the recognition and enforcement of judgments in civil and commercial matters, OJ 2001, L 12.

[26] ECJ 4 February 1988, Case C-145/86, ECR I-645 *(Hoffmann v Krieg):* See also ECJ 28 March 2000, Case C-7/98, ECR I-1935 *(Krombach)*, and ECJ 11 May 2000, Case C-38/98, ECR I-2973 *(Régie nationale des usines Renault SA v Maxicar)*: 'While the Contracting States in principle remain free, by virtue of the provision in Article 27, point 1, of the Convention, to determine, according to their own conceptions, what public policy requires, the limits of that concept are a matter for interpretation of the Convention. Consequently, while it is not for the Court to define the content of the public policy of a Contracting State, it is none the less required to review the limits within which the courts of a Contracting State may have recourse to that concept for the purpose of refusing recognition to a judgment emanating from a court in another Contracting State' (Krombach decision, points 22 and 23). See also Cass. Civ. I 17 January 2006, No. 03-14-483, BICC No. 639.

foreign court orders for which recognition or enforcement are sought are not viewed as being contrary to French public policy.[27]

The French *Cour de cassation* had to decide whether a common law procedural institution (the Mareva injunction, now called freezing order) could be recognised in France and develop effects on French territory. In a decision of 30 June 2004 (*Stolzenberg*),[28] it ruled that an English Mareva injunction could be enforced in France because

> *... cette interdiction faite à la personne du débiteur de disposer en tout lieu de ses biens, dans la mesure où il s'agit de protéger les droits légitimes du créancier, ne saurait porter atteinte à un droit fondamental du débiteur, ni même indirectement, à une prérogative de souveraineté étrangère...; que n'étant donc pas contraire à l'ordre public international, elle peut être reçue dans l'ordre juridique français.*[29]

The *Cour de cassation* displayed its open-mindedness towards foreign court decisions by adding (in a European context) that the right to a fair trial guaranteed by Article 6(1) ECHR belongs to international public policy, but that

> *... le moyen tiré de la contrariété à l'ordre public ne doit être considéré que dans des cas exceptionnels où les garanties inscrites dans la législation de l'État d'origine n'ont pas suffi à protéger le défendeur d'une violation manifeste de son droit de se défendre devant le juge d'origine.*[30]

The French *Cour de cassation* also ruled that an American court decision containing a condemnation to a civil penalty based upon *contempt of court* could

---

[27] See e.g. Cass. Civ. I 28 February 1984, Gaz. Pal. 1984. 350, obs. J. Mauro; CA Douai, 7 October 1982, Gaz. Pal. 1983. 309, obs. J. Mauro; Cass. Civ. I 13 October 1992, 16 June 1993, 12 July 1994 and 18 October 1994, Rev. crit. DIP 1995, 69, obs. B. Ancel. On the other hand, French courts often decide that the necessity to give reasons (or equivalents to reasons) in a court decision is part of French international public policy, Cass. Civ. I 17 May 1978, JDI 1979. 380, obs. D. Holleaux; CA Paris 18 January 1980, Rev. crit. DIP 1981, 113, obs. D. Holleaux; Cass. Civ. I, 9 October 1991 and CA Versailles 26 September 1991, Rev. crit. DIP 1992, 516, obs. H. Gaudemet-Tallon. Also see Cass. Civ. I 8 February 2000, Bull. civ. I, No. 42; D. 2000. IR. 75; JCP 2000. IV. 1546; 22 October 2008, D. 2008, 2801. Cf. with regard to Art. 6(1) ECHR and Art. 27(1) Brussels Convention the English provision that required a *cautio judicatum solvi* from the litigant who had no domicile in the United Kingdom, Cass. Civ. I 16 March 1999, Pordéa, D. 1999, IR, 101; Muir Watt 1999, 747: the *Cour de cassation* ruled that the decision of the appellate court permitting the enforcement of an English court order condemning the French litigant to pay £20,078 of costs, although he could not have access to court since he had not paid the required *cautio judicatum solvi*, infringed the right to access to court stated in Art. 6(1) ECHR and French public policy.

[28] JCP 2004. II. 10198, concl. J. Sainte-Rose; Procédures 2005, No. 9 obs. C. Nourissat.

[29] ... the prohibition made to the debtor to dispose of his or her property wherever located, insofar as it aims at protecting the creditor's legal rights, does not infringe a fundamental right of the debtor nor indirectly a prerogative of foreign sovereignty ...; therefore, since it is not contrary to international public policy, it can be admitted into the French legal system.

[30] ... the argument based on the violation of public policy may be considered only in exceptional cases where the guarantees given by the legislation of the State of origin were not sufficient to protect the defendant from an infringement of his or her right to defend before the court of the State of origin.

be enforced in France on condition that the amount be proportionate to the value in dispute.[31] These examples show that French courts are more and more receptive to foreign (especially common law) mechanisms and procedural institutions. The same has been applied for anti-suit injunctions since the recent ruling of the *Cour de cassation* in 2009.

17.2.2 Recognition of Foreign Anti-Suit Injunctions in France

In the European context where the Brussels I Regulation—that is, Council Regulation (EC) No. 44/2001 of 22 December 2000—applies, the French *Cour de cassation* must, and does indeed, follow the solutions stated by the European Court of Justice which has ruled that issues related to the scope of the Brussels Convention (or of Council Regulation (EC) No. 44/2001 which supersedes the 1968 Brussels Convention) that are decisive for jurisdiction in an international context shall be regarded as mandatory provisions (*d'ordre public*).[32] This means that where European provisions are applicable, the courts of the Member States must apply them. To quote an example, the ECJ ruled that the Brussels Convention (now the Brussels I Regulation)

> ... precludes a court of a Contracting State from declining the jurisdiction conferred on it by Article 2 of that convention on the grounds that a court of a non-Contracting State would be a more appropriate forum for the trial of the action even if the jurisdiction of no other Contracting State is in issue or the proceedings have no connecting factors to any other Contracting State.[33]

Therefore, the *forum non conveniens* doctrine may not be used in the context of Council Regulation (EC) No. 44/2001 as it would be 'liable to undermine the predictability of the rules of jurisdiction laid down by the Brussels Convention, in particular that of Article 2, and consequently to undermine the principle of legal certainty, which is the basis of the Convention'.[34] The ECJ also refuses the use by the court of a Member State of *anti-suit injunctions* in the European context. The

---

[31] Cass. Civ. I 28 January 2009, No. 07-11.729.

[32] ECJ 19 January 1993, Case C-89/91, ECR I-139 *(Shearson Lehman Hutton Inc. v Treuhangesellschaft)*, Rec. 139. See also for France Cass. Ch. mixte 31 March 2005, two decisions, Nos. 02-41371 and 02-41372, Rev. Contrats (2005) p. 1186, obs. P. Deumier; Rev. crit. DIP (2005), p. 732, obs. H. Gaudemet-Tallon; Cass. Civ. I 3 October 2006, No. 04-19.466, Europe Nov. (2008), 20, No. 35.

[33] ECJ 1 March 2005, Case C281/02, ECR I- 1383 *(Owusu v Jackson)* Rev. crit. DIP (2005) p. 698 obs. S. Chalas, Gaz. Pal. 27–28 May 2005, 31, obs. M.-L. Niboyet. See also the later English court decision applying the *forum non conveniens* doctrine because a jurisdiction clause had been concluded, conferring jurisdiction to a third State, High Court of Justice, 10 May 2005, Rev. crit. DIP (2005), p. 722 obs. Muir Watt.

[34] See the reasons mentioned in ECJ 1 March 2005, Case C281/02, ECR I- 1383 *(Owusu v Jackson)*, point 41.

Brussels Convention precludes 'the grant of an injunction whereby a court of a Contracting State prohibits a party to proceedings pending before it from commencing or continuing legal proceedings before a court of another Contracting State, even where that party is acting in bad faith with a view to frustrating the existing proceedings'.[35] Such a prohibition has recently been repeated in the case *Allianz SpA v West Tankers*.[36] The use of an anti-suit injunction to prevent a court of a Member State, which normally has jurisdiction to resolve a dispute under Article 5(3) of Council Regulation (EC) No. 44/2001, from ruling, in accordance with Article 1(2)(d) of that Regulation (exclusion of arbitration from the scope of the Regulation), on the very applicability of the Regulation to the dispute brought before it necessarily amounts to stripping that court of the power to rule on its own jurisdiction under that Regulation. An anti-suit injunction is therefore contrary to the general principle that every court seised determines itself, under the rules applicable to it, whether it has jurisdiction to resolve the dispute before it.[37] This latest decision has been strongly criticised by some academics and arbitrators. Indeed, any party, in bad faith, could bring an action before a State court which would have jurisdiction under the Regulation, simply in order to delay the arbitration proceedings.

In 2009[38] the French *Cour de cassation* had to reach a decision in an international recognition case *(In Zone Brands)* connected with a third State (i.e. a country where Council Regulation (EC) No. 44/2001 did not apply). The contract between the American company In Zone Brands and the French company In

---

[35] ECJ 27 April 2004, Case C-159/02, ECR I-1423 *(Turner v Grovit)*, Gaz. Pal. 14–15 January 2005, obs. M.-L. Niboyet; Rev. crit. DIP (2004) p. 654, obs. H. Muir Watt.

[36] ECJ 10 February 2009, Case C-185/07, ECR I-633 *(Allianz)*, D. 2009, 981, obs. C. Kessedjian; Europe 2009, No. 176, obs. L. Idot; Rev. crit. DIP (2009) p. 373, obs. Muir Watt: 'It is incompatible with Council Regulation No. 44/2001 on jurisdiction and the recognition and enforcement of judgments in civil and commercial matters, OJ 2001, L 12, for a court of a Member State to make an order to restrain a person from commencing or continuing proceedings before the courts of another Member State on the ground that such proceedings would be contrary to an arbitration agreement.'

[37] The ECJ also asserts that in obstructing the court of another Member State in deciding, on the basis of the rules defining the material scope of that regulation, including Article 1(2)(d) thereof, whether that regulation is applicable, such an anti-suit injunction also runs counter to the trust which the Member States accord to one another's legal systems and judicial institutions and on which the system of jurisdiction under Regulation (EC) No. 44/2001 on jurisdiction and the recognition and enforcement of judgments in civil and commercial matters, OJ 2001, L 12, is based. Lastly, if, by means of an anti-suit injunction, the national court itself were prevented from examining the preliminary issue of the validity or the applicability of the arbitration agreement, a party could avoid the proceedings merely by relying on that agreement and the applicant, who considers the agreement void, inoperative or incapable of being performed, would thus be barred from access to the court and would therefore be deprived of a form of judicial protection to which he is entitled.

[38] Cass. civ. I 14 October 2009, *Société In Beverage International v In Zone Brands Inc.*, No. 08-16.369 and 08-16.549, JCP (2009) No. 505, obs. C. Legros; Rev. crit. DIP 2010, 158, obs. H. Muit Watt; RLDC May 2010, No. 3796, p. 7, obs. G. Cuniberti; Procédures Dec. 2009, No. 11, obs. C. Nourissat.

Beverage International contained a jurisdiction clause (*clause attributive de competence*) conferring jurisdiction to the courts of the US state of Georgia. The American company decided to rescind the contract. The French company brought a claim before a French court, but at the same time, the American company seised a court in Georgia, which issued an anti-suit injunction prohibiting the French party from continuing legal proceedings before the French court, and also recognised the principle of the existence of a claim by the American company, which asked for *exequatur* in France of the American order. The French party argued that an anti-suit injunction could not be recognised or enforced in France because it would be contrary to French international *ordre public* (public policy) since it would violate the sovereignty of the French State and the right of access to court of the French party,[39] resulting in an infringement of both Article 509 of the French Code of Civil Procedure and Article 6(1) ECHR.[40] Nevertheless, the French *Cour de cassation* did not agree with this line of reasoning and rescinded its former ruling.[41] It dismissed the further appeal (*pourvoi en cassation*) and ruled that

> *... n'est pas contraire à l'ordre public international l'anti-suit injunction dont, hors champ d'application de conventions ou du droit communautaire, l'objet consiste seulement, comme en l'espèce, à sanctionner la violation d'une obligation contractuelle préexistante.*[42]

The *Cour de cassation* expressly excludes the situation where an international convention or European Union law would apply.[43] In the relationship with third States, it admits that an anti-suit injunction (measure *in personam* against the

[39] See the French company's written submissions resumed in the decision made by the *Cour de cassation*: '*une telle injonction porte atteinte tant à la prérogative de souveraineté de l'État français qu'au droit d'accès au juge de la partie ayant saisi la juridiction française ou envisageant de le faire*'.

[40] See Cass. civ. 25 May 1948, Lautour, in B. Ancel and Y. Lequette, *Les grands arrêts de la jurisprudence française de droit international privé*, No. 19: the *ordre public* exception expresses *les principes de justice universelle considérés dans l'opinion française comme doués de valeur internationale absolue*.

[41] Cass. civ. I 30 June 2004, Stolzenberg, JCP 2004, II, 10198, concl. J. Sainte-Rose; Procédures 2005, No. 9 obs. C. Nourissat: in this decision, an anti-suit injunction is seen as violating the State sovereignty and affecting the jurisdiction of the court that has been seized in another State than the court issuing the anti-suit injunction.

[42] ... an anti-suit injunction is not contrary to international public policy when it only aims at sanctioning the violation of a pre-existing contractual obligation.

[43] The *Cour de cassation* follows, therefore, the European case law and limits the recognition of anti-suit injunctions to the context of international litigation in which a third State court is involved. Nonetheless, the decision shows that domestic courts are not in favour of expanding the European Area of Justice, Freedom and Security, see Muir Watt, Rev. crit. DIP (2010) p. 163 who quotes a decision given by the High Court of Justice (Queen's Bench Division, Commercial Court) of 10 May 2005, Konkola Copper Mines (effects of a jurisdiction clause conferring jurisdiction to the court of a third State and *forum non conveniens*), Rev. crit. DIP (2005) p. 722.

defendant) issued by a common law court may indeed have effects in France.[44] The reasons given in the decision of the *Cour de cassation* are based on the binding force of the contractual jurisdiction clause. The anti-suit injunction aims at protecting the jurisdiction of the chosen (American) court and at preventing procedural bad faith of one litigant. The chosen court shall have primacy over other courts to decide on its own jurisdiction and on the validity of the jurisdiction clause. This is an extremely open-minded solution for conflicting international proceedings.[45]

It should be noted that the French *Cour de cassation* had ruled as early as 2002,[46] i.e. before the European Regulation on Insolvency No. 1346/2000 came into force, that in an international insolvency proceeding, a *French* court may issue an anti-suit injunction (*injonction contre poursuite*) in order to centralise all recovery claims brought by creditors before the French court having jurisdiction.[47] Since the international jurisdiction of the French court was established, this court was allowed to issue such an injunction.[48]

17.2.3 Estoppel and International Arbitration

For French attorneys and academics,[49] estoppel is a typical common law concept with mysterious outlines.[50] Or maybe 'was' is more accurate. The reality is that estoppel is becoming part of the French legal system through its case law, sometimes directly under the name of 'estoppel', sometimes under the '*principe*

---

[44] In 2007, the *Cour de cassation*, in a very important decision (Cornelissen), overruled its former case law and stated that the legality of foreign court decisions shall be controlled in France only with regard to three conditions: the indirect jurisdiction of the foreign court (based upon the link between the dispute and the seised court), the compliance with (substantive or procedural) French international public policy and the absence of any fraud (Cass. Civ. I 20 February 2007, No. 05-14.082, D. 2007, 1115, obs. L. d'Avout and S. Bollée; Rev. crit. DIP (2007) p. 420, obs. B. Ancel and H. Muir Watt).

[45] Bermann 1990; Mc Lachlan 2009.

[46] Cass. civ. I 19 November 2002, *Banque Worms v Eépoux Brachot*, JCP 2002, II, 10 201, concl. J. Sainte-Rose, obs. S. Chaillé de Néré; D. 2003, 797, obs. I. Khairallah.

[47] A French creditor had brought a claim against the defendant before a Spanish court in order to obtain the sale of an immovable belonging to the debtor. But since an insolvency proceeding had been started in France, the French court issued an anti-suit injunction (on the ground of equality between creditors in case of insolvency proceedings) prohibiting the French creditor from continuing legal proceedings in Spain.

[48] Cuniberti 2010, No. 3796, 9, who does not think that the decision in *Banque Worms* can be seen as a general admission in France of anti-suit injunction issues by French courts.

[49] Pinsolle 1998, 905; Moréteau 1990; Béhar-Touchais 2001; Mazeaud 2006; Fauvarque-Cosson 2007a.

[50] In some civil law countries, the Latin rule *non concedit venire contra factum proprium* is in some respect the equivalent of the estoppel doctrine.

selon lequel une partie ne saurait se prévaloir de prétentions contradictoires au detriment de ses adversaires' (principle according to which a party may not invoke contradictory claims to the detriment of the opposing parties).[51] At first, the estoppel doctrine was used in international arbitration and international private law.[52] The *Cour d'appel de Paris* applied the estoppel doctrine for the first time in a decision of 17 January 2002.[53] It stated that a party invoking an arbitration clause and taking part in the arbitration proceedings without any reserve was not allowed to claim for the annulment of the arbitration award on the grounds that the arbitration court had no jurisdiction.[54]

The French *Cour de cassation* admitted the rule of estoppel (using this precise terminology, *règle de l'estoppel*) for the first time in a decision of 6 July 2005, *Golshani v Government of the Islamic Republic of Iran*[55]*:* the claimant Golshani required the annulment of an arbitration award although he had himself seised the court of arbitration. Instead of basing its reasoning on the claimant's renunciation (*renunciation*) of a proceeding before State courts, the *Cour de cassation* expressly refers to the *règle de l'estoppel*: For Mr. Golshani, who himself brought the arbitration claim before the arbitration court and participated for nine years without any reserve in the arbitration proceeding, it is 'inadmissible (*irrecevable*), by virtue of the estoppel rule, to object, through a new, contradictory argument,[56] that the arbitration court has ruled without any arbitration clause or upon a void arbitration clause'. Under French case law, the estoppel is a *fin de non recevoir* (demurrer, plea of non-admissibility).

In an international dispute connected with insolvency proceedings, the French *Cour de cassation*[57] also used the terminology estoppel and confirmed the judgment of the appellate court which held that the official liquidator of the company had deliberately avoided taking part in the arbitration proceedings in order to preserve a means of recourse against the arbitration award ('*que, dès lors que les domaines d'application respectifs de la règle de l'estoppel et du principe de la renonciation peuvent, dans certains cas, être identiques et qu'il appartient au juge*

---

[51] Sometimes, the 'principle of consistency' (*principe de cohérence*) is put forward as the French pendant to the common law estoppel, see Houtcieff 2009, No. 463.

[52] In favour of the admission of the estoppel doctrine in French law, see Muir Watt 1994, 303.

[53] CA Paris, 17 January 2002, *SA ITM Logistique International v Gavaud*, Revue de l'arbitrage (2002), 205.

[54] See also a more recent decision, CA Paris 28 February 2008, D. 2008, 1325, obs. R. Meese; RTDCom. (2008), 516, obs. E. Loquin.

[55] D. 2006, 1424, obs. E. Agostini; Revue de l'arbitrage 2005, p. 993, obs. Pinsolle; Rev. crit. DIP (2006) p. 602, obs. H. Muir Watt.

[56] Before the admission of the estoppel in France, the courts already declared inadmissible the submissions of a party which were incompatible with the party's former submissions, arguments of procedural behaviour, see Cass Com 26 June 1990, Bull. civ. IV No. 187, p. 129.

[57] Cass. Civ. I 6 May 2009, No. 08-10.281, SA Jean Lion, Bull. Civ. I, No. 86; RTDCom. 2009, 546, obs. E. Loquin; JCP 2009, II, 534, obs. G. Bolard (very critical); JCP 2009, I, 462, obs. J. Béguin; Procédures 2009, No. 236, obs. B. Rolland.

de l'annulation de faire respecter la loyauté procédurale des parties à l'arbitrage, c'est sans violer le principe de la contradiction que la cour d'appel a qualifié d'estoppel l'attitude procédurale du liquidateur'). The French Court here connects estoppel and 'procedural fairness of the parties to the arbitration proceedings'.[58] This decision has been severely criticised[59] since the official liquidator was not a party to the arbitration proceedings and could therefore not be obliged to any procedural conduct.

As recently as 3 February 2010, the *Cour de cassation*[60] quashed a judgment made by an appellate court which held that the behaviour of the French party (the Mérial company) was to be sanctioned by estoppel (the French litigant had not opposed a procedural order made by the arbitration court, but had later claimed for annulment of the order before the State court). The *Cour de cassation* held that in this case, the procedural behaviour of the Mérial company could not be seen as a '*changement de position, en droit, de nature à induire la société Klocke en erreur sur ses intentions et ne constituait donc pas un estoppel*' (change of legal argumentation which was able to mislead the Klocke company regarding the intentions of the opposing party and therefore was not an estoppel). Even if this court decision excludes the sanction of estoppel in the concrete case to be decided, it gives hints about (*a*) the conditions to be fulfilled (a contradiction, because a litigant behaved unambiguously in two opposite manners); (*b*) the sanction: the inadmissibility of the claim (or means of recourse), which deprives the party of the right to access to court; and (*c*) the fact that the *Cour de cassation* controls the application of the estoppel by the lower courts (therefore, it is not a legal notion left to the free appreciation of the lower court). Since the consequences of an estoppel are serious, the *Cour de cassation* wants to control its application in order to avoid unfairness and to guarantee legal certainty.[61] Therefore, the contradiction between the successive submissions of one party must be clear, and may not be justified by special circumstances of the case.

The estoppel must be distinguished in French case law from the *renonciation* (renunciation) and from the *acquiescement*, i.e. the act by which a party against whom a suit has been brought admits that the demand made upon him or her is well founded. While it is true that both concepts consist of the inconsistent behaviour of the party, and their scope of application can be the same as the estoppel doctrine,[62] the condition of detriment to the other party is not required.

The reference to the estoppel by French courts was first limited to private international law and to international arbitration. In a recent decision, however, the

---

[58] On the *principe de loyauté* (principle of fairness), see M.-E. Boursier, *Le principe de loyauté en droit processuel* (Dalloz 2003).

[59] Bolard 2009, II, 534.

[60] Cass. civ. I 3 February 2010, No. 08-21.288, JCP 2010, No. 626 obs. D. Houtcieff.

[61] Cf. Houtcieff 2010, 1177. See also Kleiman 2010, doctr. No. 303.

[62] Cass. Civ. I 6 May 2009, No. 08-10.281, SA Jean Lion, Bull. Civ. I, No. 86; RTDCom. (2009), 546, obs. E. Loquin; JCP 2009, II, 534, obs. G. Bolard.

Cour de cassation also admits as a principle the estoppel rule in domestic civil procedure, even if it refuses to apply it to the case.[63] This has led to controversy. Some commentators deny the usefulness of the reference to the common law concept,[64] whereas others[65] think that the import of the estoppel doctrine could—at least in international law and arbitration—be an enrichment for French proceedings. In fact, French law does not ignore the necessity for a litigant to be consistent with his or her former submissions, and in reality courts refuse to admit claims which are incompatible with former submissions.[66]

17.3 French Civil Procedure Influenced by Foreign Institutions and Law

French courts, especially the *Cour de cassation*, which is the highest court for civil and commercial matters, have recognised and admitted some procedural techniques imported from foreign jurisdictions (Sect. 17.3.1). Furthermore, the French *Cour de cassation* sometimes makes use of comparative studies, especially in civil procedure, before deciding to modify its case law (Sect. 17.3.2).

17.3.1 French Case Law

The most remarkable imports from the Common Law are seen in the practice before French courts of allowing one or several *amici curiae* to give an opinion on some issue that should not be a legal one (Sect. 17.2.1.1). Furthermore, estoppel

[63] See n. 23.

[64] Houtcieff 2010, 1177–1178: '*la transplantation de l'estoppel est inadéquate, tant elle paraît complexe et tant il existe de variantes à ce mécanisme, dont certaines sont contestées même par la doctrine anglosaxonne*'; furthermore, '*une fin de non recevoir sanctionne le comportement incohérent en droit positif français*, so that a new instrument is not needed because *l'interdiction de se contredire participe de tout système juridique*.' See also Cadiet 1996, 25 (those who describe the estoppel as a general legal principle only refer to the spirit of this institution and not to the strict conditions for its application). See also Fauvarque-Cosson 2007b, 59, '*La confiance légitime et l'estoppel*', Soc. de législation comparée: the estoppel *n'est qu'un leurre: l'estoppel est aussi impénétrable qu'un bouclier, aussi dangereusement aiguisé qu'une épée.*

[65] Muir Watt 1994, 303.

[66] E.g. Cass. civ. III 28 January 2009, No. 08-10.333, D. 2009, 2008, obs. D. Houtcieff; RDC (2009), 999, obs. D. Mazeaud: a party cannot invoke a legal position that he or she has excluded before; 7 June 1989, No. 87-14.083, Bull. Civ. III, No. 134. See also Cass. com. 7 April 2009, No. 08-11.737: the claimant '*n'est pas recevable à invoquer devant la Cour de cassation une thèse contraire à celle soutenue devant les juges du fond*'; 27 November 2007, No. 06-19.076, *Procédures* 2008, No. 18, obs. B. Rolland: the claimant 'n'est pas recevable à présenter devant la Cour de cassation un moyen contraire à ses propres écritures.' See Bolard 2004, 51.

has been broadly admitted by the *Cour de cassation* in the context of arbitration, and more restrictedly in national civil proceedings under the notion of *principe de loyauté procédurale* or *principe de cohérence* (Sect. 17.2.1.2).

17.3.1.1 The *Amicus Curiae* Before French courts[67]

The French Code of Civil Procedure makes no mention of possible submissions of an *amicus curiae* before civil courts. Nevertheless, the *Cour d'appel de Paris,* followed by the *Cour de cassation*, introduced this practice into French civil proceedings at the end of the 1980s and in the early 1990s.[68]

The person called *amicus curia* is neither an expert (*expert*) nor a witness (*témoin*) whose legal status would be contained in the Code of Civil Procedure. The *amicus curiae* is only a so-called *sachant* who brings his or her experience and/or knowledge in order to help the court in deciding a case that raises difficult legal, social or ethical issues. A former President of the *Cour de cassation*, Pierre Dray,[69] described the *amicus curiae* in the following manner:

> *... pour enrichir les débats qui se déroulent devant elle, les faire porter au niveau élevé qui doit être le leur, en raison de leur technicité ou de leur spécificité, la Cour de cassation se doit de les ouvrir aux apports de l'extérieur, dès lors que les compétences sollicitées sont incontestables, représentatives et de haute valeur morale et humaine.*

For D. Mazeaud,[70] it is a

> *personnalité dont l'autorité morale, scientifique et humaine est unanimement reconnue et qui est invitée par le juge à lui fournir des informations propres à l'éclairer sur le litige qui lui est soumis; il est une conscience, une source d'inspiration et de liberté, parce que ses informations permettront au juge de rendre sa décision en toute conscience et lucidité.*[71]

The admission of the *amicus curiae* before French civil courts is justified by the growing complexity and technical nature of law. The judge, in a pragmatic way, seeks information in order to give his or her decision more credibility. The existence of new scientific data, of new ethical issues (especially with regard to

---

[67] Laurin, JCP 92. l. 3603; Mazeaud 1995, 109 et seq.

[68] The French practice started, therefore, prior to the drafting of the ALI/Unidroit Principles of Transnational Civil Procedure that state on p. 13: 'Whenever appropriate, written submission concerning important legal issues in the proceeding and matters of background information may be received from third persons with the consent of the court, upon consultation with the parties. The court may invite such a submission. The parties should have the opportunity to submit written comment addressed to the matters contained in such a submission before it is considered by the court.' See also Comment P-13.C stating that in most civil law countries, there is no established practice of allowing the submission of *amicus curiae* briefs but that some countries like France have developed similar institutions in their case law.

[69] *Rentrée solennelle de la Cour de cassation le 6 janvier* 1989 (oral remark, not published).

[70] Mazeaud 1995, 110.

[71] Mazeaud 1995, 118.

bioethics) require the submissions of specialists, or of 'wise' persons whose experience and sometimes fame will confer more 'legitimacy' to the court decision.[72]

The fundamental point to be underlined is that the *amicus curiae* can present submissions not only on factual, but also on legal issues, which French law prohibits an expert from doing.[73] In several decisions, appellate courts and the *Cour de cassation* called on one or several *amici curiae*. This was, for example, the case when the *Cour de cassation* had to decide whether a contract between a couple and a surrogate mother, and the subsequent adoption of the child by the couple, could be valid.[74] The *Cour de cassation* decided to interview the President of the *Comité consultatif national d'éthique pour les sciences de la vie et de la santé*, Professor Jean Bernard. In 2001,[75] in a criminal case (possible manslaughter relating to a foetus in a car accident), the *Cour de cassation* required a written submission by the Academy of Medicine concerning the definition of a human being, and interviewed several key figures.

The *Cour d'appel de Paris*[76] interviewed as an *amicus curiae* Professor Montagnier, an AIDS research specialist, in order to obtain information about the AIDS virus, its evolution, and the time between contamination and occurrence of the disease. In another dispute relating to the professional specialisations of an attorney, the same court decided to hear the Chairman of the Bar in Paris[77] as an *amicus curiae*. The litigant, an attorney, tried to challenge the *amicus curiae* on the basis of possible partiality. The appellate court gave an interesting definition of the *amicus curiae*'s usefulness and status:

> *... la cour, dans sa recherche des éléments d'information et de conviction, est libre d'organiser cette recherche, suivant la démarche qu'elle souhaite et suivant des modalités qui n'ont pas à lui être dictées; que la désignation du bâtonnier Lafarge, en qualité d'amicus curiae, n'a été qu'une de ces modalités et qu'elle n'exclut pas la désignation d'autres personnalités aux mêmes fins; que la garantie d'un procès équitable au sens européen du terme est assurée au demandeur au recours, dès lors que celui-ci assistera à l'exposé de l'amicus curiae et pourra formuler toutes observations utiles, outre le droit qui lui sera, ci-après reconnu, de proposer à la cour l'audition de telle ou telle personnalité de son choix, à l'effet de compléter son information objective et 'équilibrée'. Considérant que l'amicus curiae, qui n'est ni un témoin, ni un expert, n'est pas soumis aux règles du nouveau code de procédure civile relatives à la récusation; que sa venue devant la cour, sur l'invitation que celle-ci lui adresse, et son audition ne sont soumises qu'aux seules règles tendant au respect du principe du contradictoire et au respect des droits de*

---

[72] Mazeaud 1995, 111.

[73] See Art. 238(3) French Code of Civil Procedure: *Il ne doit jamais porter d'appréciation juridique*.

[74] Cass. ass. plén., 31 May 1991, D. 1991. 417, report Y. Chartier, obs. D. Thouvenin; JCP 1991, II, 21 572 obs. F. Terré.

[75] Cass. ass. plén., 29 June 2001, JCP éd. G 2001, II, 10 569, report P. Sargos and concl. J. Sainte-Rose.

[76] CA Paris, 16 October 1992, D. 1993, 172, obs. Y. Laurin.

[77] CA Paris, 21 June and 6 July 1988, D. 1989. 341, obs. Y. Laurin.

la défense; que telle doit être, en l'occurence, la seule exigence et que, dès lors, doit être rejetée la requête à fin de 'récusation' du bâtonnier Philippe Lafarge.[78]

The court then decided that each litigant should in addition suggest the name of another (former) chairman of the Bar to inform the judges.

This practice is known to come from England and the United States of America.[79] It is also used by the European Court of Human Rights and the European Court of Justice. It is an information technique at the disposal of the judge. French case law does not seem to include it in the means of evidence, so that the provisions of the Code of Civil Procedure do not apply. The interview of an *amicus curiae* increases the oral character of the proceedings. In France, this practice is more criticised by specialists of civil law[80] than by procedural lawyers. Indeed, some see in this *ami de la cour* a kind of 'alibi'[81] used by the court as a prestigious authority behind whom the judge can hide in order to give an 'accepted' judgment. A risk of an arbitrary questioning of the legal sources as well as an infringement of the evidence rules[82] have been underlined.[83] These dangers are undeniably real. One can understand the necessity for the judge to search for information and support on issues which are so important that only the united front of law and science is able to give a convincing and lasting response.[84] The difficulty arises in cases where the *amicus curiae* might have an interest in the solution that is to be given.[85] The civil judge shall remain free[86] not to share the *amicus curiae*'s submission and to give judgment on the ground of all the elements of the case, and the parties shall have opportunity to comment on the *amicus curiae* submission (*principe du contradictoire*).[87] In France, the admission of the *amicus curiae* can be seen as one expression of the interference of the civil society, its debates and stakes in the civil proceedings.

---

78 ... the interview of the Chairman of the Bar is one of the possible modes for the court to search for information and convincing elements; the *amicus curiae* is neither a witness nor an expert and is therefore not subject to challenge. His interview by the court shall only respect the *principe contradictoire* and the defence rights.

79 Angell 1967, 1017.

80 See Mazeaud 1995, 111 et seq; F. Terré, obs. under Cass. ass. plén., 31 May 1991, JCP 1992, II, 21 752.

81 Mazeaud 1995, 112; Gobert 1992, 489, 502.

82 R. Perrot, obs. in RTDCiv. (1989) p. 138.

83 Gobert 1992, No. 17.

84 Mazeaud 1995, 116.

85 Cf. Comment P-13A of Principle 13 ALI/Unidroit Principles of Transnational Civil Procedure 2006: 'Such a brief might be from a disinterested source or a partisan one.'

86 Cf. Comment P-13B of Principle 13 ALI/Unidroit Principles of Transnational Civil Procedure 2006: 'Caution should be exercised that the mechanism of the amicus curiae submission not interfere with the court's independence.'

87 Cf. Comment P-13E of Principle 13 ALI/Unidroit Principles of Transnational Civil Procedure 2006: 'The parties must have opportunity to submit written comment addressed to the matters in the submission before it is considered by the court.' The same is contained in the last sentence of Principle 13 itself.

17.3.1.2 The Partial Recognition of *Estoppel* in French Civil Procedure

As described above,[88] French case law has admitted that the estoppel of common law origin could apply in international (and sometimes in national[89]) arbitration proceedings. This did not mean that French courts would also agree to recognise a role to this doctrine in domestic civil proceedings before State courts. An important judgment in this respect was given by the plenary assembly of the *Cour de cassation* on 27 February 2009[90] (*Sédéa électronique v Pace Europe*). The appellate court had applied the estoppel doctrine and held that the Sédéa company was not admitted to bring in two successive civil proceedings of two opposite claims (one requesting the delivery of goods and the other one requesting that the sales contract be declared void). The *Cour de cassation* quashed the appellate court decision on the legal basis of Article 122 CPC (Code of Civil Procedure)[91] which defines the *fins de non recevoir* (plea of non-admissibility) and held that '*attendu que la seule circonstance qu'une partie se contredise aux dépens d'autrui n'emporte pas nécessairement fin de non recevoir*' (the mere circumstance that a party brings contradictory submissions to another party's detriment does not necessarily lead to a plea of non-admissibility). In this case, the two claims (two disputes) were not of the same nature, not based on the same contracts nor opposing the same parties. Therefore, in this specific context, it was legally admissible for the Sédéa company to bring opposite claims against two different companies. As one can see, three criteria are given by the highest French court in civil and commercial matters: first, the nature of the contradictory claims; second, the legal basis of the claim (same contract or not); and third, the parties in the dispute. There is still controversy with regard to the question whether those three criteria shall be cumulative or not.

Several other decisions given by the *Cour de cassation* seem to admit the principle of an estoppel sanction, but refuse to apply it in the pending case.[92] In a more recent decision of 3 February 2010,[93] the *Cour de cassation* checked whether the conditions of an estoppel were fulfilled, and held that it was not the case. This decision was given in the context of an international arbitration proceeding. The

---

[88] Supra, n. 12 et seq.

[89] See CA Paris, 7 February 2008, *Société Française de Rentes et de financements Crédirenter v Cie Générale de Garantie S.A.*

[90] No. 07-19.841, D. 2010, 172, obs. N. Fricero; D. 2009, 1245, obs. D. Houtcieff; D. 2009, 723, obs. X. Delpech; JCP 2009, II, 10 073, obs. P. Callé.

[91] Art. 122 CPC states that 'a plea of non-admissibility is any ground whose purpose is to get the adversary's claim declared inadmissible, without entering into the merits of the case, for lack of a right of action, such as a not being the proper party, lack of interest, statute of limitations, fixed time-limit or res judicata'.

[92] Cass. Civ. I 20 June 2006, No. 04-19.636; Soc. 11 July 2007, No. 06-44.345; 25 September 2007, No. 06-43.155; Com. 11 December 2007, No. 06-26.093, 06-16.104, 06-16.105; 8 April 2008, No. 06-18.362.

[93] Cass. civ. I, 3 February 2010, No. 08-21.288, see supra under n. 14.

Cour de cassation required a contradiction because a litigant behaved unambiguously in two opposite manners and made it clear that the sanction consists of the inadmissibility of the claim (or means of recourse) which deprives the party of the right of access to court. In accepting to use the word 'estoppel' in some decisions now (or in defining it as the *principe de l'interdiction de se contredire au detriment d'autrui*), the French *Cour de cassation* recognises this common law principle as an element of the principle of procedural fairness (*loyauté procédurale*) which is binding on the parties.

If the French civil courts seem to be (reasonably) attracted by the estoppel doctrine, this cannot be asserted where the administrative courts are concerned. In a judgment given as recently as 1 April 2010,[94] the *Conseil d'État* (the highest administrative court) ruled that the estoppel is not applicable in taxation law. The *Conseil d'État* gives the following definition of estoppel:

> *règle générale de procédure en vertu de laquelle une partie ne pourrait, après avoir adopté une position claire ou un comportement non ambigu sur sa future conduite à l'égard de l'autre partie, modifier ultérieurement cette position ou ce comportement d'une façon qui affecte les rapports de droit entre les parties et conduise l'autre partie à modifier à son tour sa position ou son comportement, règle relevant dans certains systèmes juridiques du principe dit de l'estoppel, issu à l'origine du droit anglais.*

It denies the existence of such a principle in taxation law. This could be explained by the fact that French procedural law already has equivalent tools such as the prohibition of new submissions (*moyens nouveaux*) and the inadmissibility of a claim when the claimant has no interest to claim (*défaut d'intérêt*).

The admission of the estoppel doctrine in French civil procedure shows how French courts react to globalisation, and to a possible harmonisation of civil procedure, in this case through the acceptance of a common law institution in French civil proceedings. Nevertheless, this has led to harsh criticism based on the danger, the uselessness and the inadequacy of such a foreign technique with vague outlines. Even if the *Cour de cassation* seems to require first, a clear and non-ambiguous representation given by one litigant, second, the fact that the other party has legitimately believed in the representation and behaved consequently and third, the contradictory behaviour of the litigant as an expression of bad faith; it insists upon the fact that these conditions must be controlled by the Court itself in order to guarantee common general principles.

These examples show that French courts do not remain limited to the concepts and institutions which are traditionally rooted in their national civil procedure. They are aware of the globalisation occurring and accept to extend those institutions to proceedings taking place in France. This is a sign of the current open-mindedness that prevails.

[94] CE, avis No. 334465, 1 April 2010, SAS Marsadis.

17.3.2 The Use of Comparative Legal Studies by the French Cour de cassation

For the last ten years or so the French *Cour de cassation* has also shown an open mind towards comparative legal studies. On several issues, before giving judgment, the court has requested from Comparative Law Institutes comparative studies on certain key issues. As an example, the *Institut de droit comparé Edouard Lambert* in Lyon was requested to draft a comparative study on two important issues. The first, marriage between same-sex persons, relates more to civil law. The mayor of a French town had agreed to marry two men in order to provoke a discussion and a possible revolutionary case law that would have applied the principle of equality. The *Cour de cassation* ordered a comparative study on several legal systems and finally held that it was not its task but that of the legislator to allow same-sex partners to marry.

Also, the commissions which have been appointed by the Government to suggest possible reforms in the field of appeal (Commission *Magendie II*, 2008)[95] or with regard to the attribution of contentious matters in the different civil courts of first instance (Commission *Guinchard*, 2008)[96] have made use of comparative legal studies. For example, the German reform of 2001 of the *Berufung* (appeal) in civil matters has been presented to the Commission *Magendie II* by a German practising lawyer and by myself; also the ALI/UNIDROIT Principles of Transnational Civil Procedure have been presented to the Commission. In the framework of the Commission *Guinchard*, the German order for payment as well as the tasks of the *Rechtspfleger* have been compared with the French system. Several other legal systems have been studied in order to decide whether the Commission should promote a nonjudicial divorce proceeding before a notary public.

The second field of study was *res judicata*, an important issue in civil procedure. In 1994, the *Cour de cassation* had given a restricted scope to the *autorité de chose jugée* (*res judicata*) which prevents a party from starting again the 'same' proceedings before another court. It decided that a party was allowed to bring a new claim if the same was claimed, but on another legal ground.

In 2006, the *Cour de cassation* was contemplating enlarging the scope of *res judicata* in order to avoid new proceedings in cases where the claimant had simply not brought all possible legal grounds for his or her claim. Therefore, the Court asked the *Institut de droit comparé Edouard Lambert* to draft a comparative study. English, German, Italian and Spanish law and case law were studied in depth and

---

95 See *Célérité et qualité de la justice devant la cour d'appel*, rapport au Garde des Sceaux Ministre de la Justice 24 May 2008, doc. franc. 2008.

96 See *L'ambition raisonné d'une justice apaisée*, rapport au Garde des Sceaux Ministre de la Justice, June 2008, doc. franc. 2008.

presented in a study which can still be found on the Court's website.[97] In fact, English and Spanish law have opted for a broad scope of the *res judicata* effect, whereas German and Italian law continued to keep the same restricted one as in France until 2006. The *Cour de cassation*[98] overruled the 1994 decision and held that it is incumbent upon the claimant to present even in the proceedings relating to the first claim all possible submissions he or she considers appropriate to justify the claim. The new French case law aims at concentrating all the litigious matter in one proceeding.

Even if the French *Cour de cassation* shows its interest in other legal systems, these considerations have never been mentioned in its judgments. The reference to foreign and comparative law can only be found in the reports drafted by one of the judges (i.e. *conseiller rapporteur*) or by the public prosecutor who also takes part in civil proceedings before the *Cour de cassation* to give an opinion on the legal issues at stake. Neither in judgments nor in such reports have the ALI/UNIDROIT Principles of Transnational Civil Procedure, which are a worldwide attempt to harmonise civil procedure, ever been mentioned in France.

17.4 French Reactions to Harmonisation in a Global Context: The ALI/UNIDROIT Principles of Transnational Civil Procedure

A worldwide attempt to harmonise transnational civil procedure has been achieved in the framework of a 'joint venture' between the American Law Institute and UNIDROIT. These two institutions have adopted the *Principles of Transnational Civil Procedure*.[99] Their aim is to guarantee, where the foreign party who has to claim or to defend before the court of another State is concerned, some fundamental principles of fair justice inspired by the procedural requirements laid out by the European Court of Human Rights as well as by the *principes directeurs du procès civil* (leading principles governing civil proceedings) contained in the first

[97] See *L'étendue de l'autorité de la chose jugée en droit comparé*, Institut de droit comparé Edouard Lambert, at http://www.courdecassation.fr/IMG/File/Plen-06-07-07-0410672-rapport-definitif-anonymise-annexe-2.pdf (last consulted in May 2011).

[98] Cass. Ass. Plén. 7 July 2006, *Cesareo*, Bulletin Assemblée plénière No. 8 p. 21; D. 2006, 2135, obs. L. Weiller: '*Mais attendu qu'il incombe au demandeur de présenter dès l'instance relative à la première demande l'ensemble des moyens qu'il estime de nature à fonder celle-ci; Qu'ayant constaté que, comme la demande originaire, la demande dont elle était saisie, formée entre les mêmes parties, tendait à obtenir paiement d'une somme d'argent à titre de rémunération d'un travail prétendument effectué sans contrepartie financière, la cour d'appel en a exactement déduit que Gilbert Y... ne pouvait être admis à contester l'identité de cause des deux demandes en invoquant un fondement juridique qu'il s'était abstenu de soulever en temps utile, de sorte que la demande se heurtait à la chose précédemment jugée relativement à la même contestation.*'

[99] ALI/Unidroit Principles of Transnational Civil Procedure.

articles of the French Code of Civil Procedure. Some fundamental principles in fact do transcend the traditional opposition between Continental law systems and Common law systems. The Principles of Transnational Civil Procedure certainly establish a kind of common procedural fund based on the fairness of trial. With regard to some issues, however, they have opted for a (sometimes softened) common law approach, such as in the areas of evidence, settlement during the proceedings and the possible role of an *amicus curiae*. The Principles are *soft law* that interested States can decide to adopt, to totally or partially integrate into their national legal system. Mexico, for instance, has shown its interest in this 'model law', which has influenced its new civil procedure.

In October 2000 in Paris and then again in June 2003 in Lyon, two international conferences were devoted to the study of the ALI (and then ALI/UNIDROIT) draft of the Transnational Rules (and then Principles) of Civil Procedure. The first French reaction was mostly negative (Sect. 17.4.1), whereas the atmosphere of the second conference was considerably more open and tolerant (Sect. 17.4.2).[100]

17.4.1 A First, Mostly Negative Reaction

In October 2000 in Paris, Professor Hazard and Professor Taruffo presented the ALI draft of 17 March 2000 of the Transnational Rules of Civil Procedure (Preliminary Draft No. 2) to French lawyers (judges, barristers, university members). The purpose of the session was to debate the project openly focussing on two topics. The first was the opportunity and utility of establishing transnational rules of civil procedure and according to which methodology to set them, and the second was the analysis of the content of a possible harmonisation. Most of the French academics and barristers who expressed their views were very critical. Mayer[101] described the project as 'unworkable' (*impracticable*) and 'of limited use' (*utilité des plus restreintes*) because procedure is fundamentally linked to mentalities, and because the parties are 'less motivated by the form of procedure than the potential partiality of the judge'. The project would create two types of justice inside each respective country: a Civil law justice for internal disputes and an 'American Common law' justice for transnational litigation.

The method was also criticised by H. Muir Watt.[102] The unification of procedural rules in order to better manage transnational litigation is not appropriate and a

[100] Cadiet 2010, 635 et seq.

[101] Mayer 2001, 23 et seq.

[102] Muir Watt 2001, 39 et seq.

more pragmatic approach would be preferable.[103] The model chosen cannot be accepted since it is not neutral, but rests on the American model. It would be better to identify abnormal risks in an international dispute and to consider, case by case, the most appropriate way to resolve the situation.

Furthermore, the issue of the scope of the Rules is a key question to assess the advisability of the project: for M.-L. Niboyet,[104] the scope of the Rules should be limited to international trade litigation. Litigation should be excluded where procedural aspects and substance are linked and where specialised courts are involved. The localisation criterion governing the applicability of the Rules (usual place of residence) should be complemented by other criteria.

Many questions were also raised with regard to the 'judge' who would have to enforce the transnational rules of civil procedure.[105] Even if some contributions were more open to the ALI draft[106] and recognised the possible compatibility of several ALI Rules[107] with French civil procedure, the refusal by the French audience to accept what was seen as 'American imperialism' was clear. At the end of the conference, Professor Fouchard asked whether a *mauvais procès* had been made against the draft, i.e. whether there had been unfair criticism. He also asked whether the authors of the draft had chosen *la bonne procédure* (the appropriate process) first, in opting for Rules and not for less detailed Principles and, second, in presenting a draft of clear American inspiration with some rules which 'may shock', especially witness preparation by the lawyer. The reluctance in the French lawyers' circle was palpable.

It is difficult to know whether these predominantly critical reactions were based on the precise contents of the draft or on its origin and its clearly American inspiration. It cannot be denied that the possible ulterior motives of an expansion of the American procedural model has led to many objections. The 'joint venture' between the American Law Institute and UNIDROIT aiming at drafting Principles of Transnational Civil Procedure acceptable to many parts of the world has led to an improvement of the first draft, and to a new acceptance in France.

---

[103] '*La voie qui consiste à imposer une « règle » du jeu' universelle s'avère à la fois disproportionnée aux besoins réels du contentieux international et intrinsèquement indésirable*'; '*une voie plus modeste, mais plus acceptable, consisterait à identifier les frictions constitutives d'un risque anormal de l'internationalité du procès, afin de déterminer au cas par cas la solution la plus ajustée*' (p. 40).

[104] Niboyet 2001, 51 et seq.

[105] Gaudemet-Tallon 2001, 67 et seq.

[106] Normand 2001, 89 et seq; Cadiet 2001, 115 et seq.

[107] Cadiet 2001, 119: 'A number of provisions are consistent with the French current law or with the way French lawyers would like it to evolve. In particular, the evolution of the American and French legal systems has helped bringing them closer. The role of the judge as regards evidence has been increased by the New French Code of Civil Procedure, while the excesses in the discovery law have been reduced giving room to the judge's role.'

17.4.2 Towards a Possible Acceptance

Three years later, a very different atmosphere prevailed at the Lyon conference in June 2003.[108] Instead of Professor Taruffo, Professor Hazard was accompanied by Professor Kronke, Secretary General of UNIDROIT. The different contributions no longer dealt with the acceptability of Transnational Rules of Civil Procedure, but with the framework of the ALI/UNIDROIT draft of Principles, especially its objectives,[109] the relationship between Principles and Rules,[110] and the appreciation of the Principles by a French barrister[111] and a French judge,[112] prove that the discussions had moved a step further on the feasibility of proceedings applying the Transnational Principles. Of course, some critical issues were raised, but some Principles also received strong approval and support.[113] Even the structure of the proceedings in three phases was seen as

> *pas très éloignée, dans son architecture, tout au moins en ce qui concerne la phase introductive et la phase intermédiaire, des règles que nous connaissons relatives au contenu de l'assignation et à la tenue d'audiences préliminaires par le juge de la mise en état ou le juge rapporteur.*[114]

On the contrary, the integration of provisions of private international law into the Principles was again criticised during the Lyon conference.[115] It would have been more reasonable to omit all those issues of jurisdiction and to refer to national provisions or international conventions on jurisdiction.[116]

The second part of the conference was devoted to aspects of civil procedure. The commencement of the proceedings (*introduction de l'instance*),[117] the

---

[108] Cadiet 2010, 635 et seq.

[109] Kronke 2004, 17 et seq; Hazard et al. 2006, 23 et seq.

[110] Ferrand 2004, 27 et seq.

[111] Junillon 2004, 35 et seq.

[112] Moussa 2005, 47 et seq.

[113] See e.g. Moussa 2005, 49: approval of Principle 1 requiring independence and impartiality from the judge; p. 51: approval of all the Principles on the defendant's rights.

[114] … in its structure, at least as far as the pleading and the interim phases are concerned, not very far from the French rules relating to the content of the summons and the preliminary hearings organised by the judge who prepares the case. Moussa 2005, 52 who even adds at the end (55): '*Je ne suis pas pour autant opposé à la démarche entreprise par les promoteurs de ces Principes en dépit de mon approche méfiante de départ. Je leur souhaite, au contraire, bon courage et bon vent, convaincu que je suis de l'utilité et de la nécessité de tout ce qui peut simplifier la procédure et faciliter les échanges internationaux. Tout projet innovant et à ce point ambitieux paraît de prime abord utopique, mais est-ce une raison pour ne pas entreprendre.*'

[115] Gaudemet-Tallon 2004, 71 et seq.

[116] Gaudemet-Tallon 2004, 79.

[117] Croze 2004, 93 et seq.

respective roles of the parties and the judge,[118] evidence[119] and the financial aspects of the proceedings (costs, cost sanctions).[120] It was during this part of the conference in particular that most of the contributors expressed a positive opinion: '*le juriste français n'est nullement dépaysé lorsqu'il compare les Principes de procédure civile transnationale et les principes directeurs auxquels son propre code l'a accoutumé*'[121] (the French lawyer is not disorientated when comparing the Principles of Transnational Civil Procedure with the guiding principles of his own Code of Civil Procedure). All French guiding principles of civil procedure are contained in the ALI/UNIDROIT Principles. Professor Normand concludes that 'the project is in the end relatively flexible and balanced' (*assez souple et assez équilibré*); 'it does not present anything that could shock the French lawyer',[122] and this because the American members of the Study Group have accepted on many issues to take into account the wishes of Old Europe.
It should be noted that L. Cadiet, who took part in the first conference in Paris and in the second one in Lyon, insisted upon the positive effects of dialogue and the evolution of the new version of the draft (replacing Rules with Principles). He considered the ALI//UNIDROIT Principles as acceptable[123] and the project as feasible. His conclusion is that '*ce n'est donc pas sur le terrain de la preuve que peuvent être trouvées des raisons sérieuses de repousser les Principes de procédure civile transnationale*' (it is therefore not in the field of evidence that reasons can be found to object to the Principles of transnational civil procedure).

In his final report, S. Guinchard summarised the different contributions made during the conference and reminded the audience of the mood at the Paris conference in the year 2000: '*préventions fortes à l'égard d'un projet perçu comme la manifestation de l'impérialisme d'une grande puissance amie, comme une opération d'acculturation juridique, comme une importation à marche forcée de règles techniques auxquelles la vielle Europe [...] était viscéralement réfractaire*'.[124] He underlined the serenity of the discussions in Lyon and the calm debates where no one tried to stir up controversy. The drafting process of the new ALI/UNIDROIT draft was the right one since the ALI/UNIDROIT Study Group could guarantee a fair balance between different legal traditions.

---

[118] Normand 2004, 103 et seq.
[119] Cadiet 2004, 119 et seq.
[120] Mecarelli 2004, 139 et seq.
[121] Normand 2004, 103.
[122] Normand 2004, 114.
[123] Cadiet 2004, 134 et seq.
[124] Guinchard 2004b, 156.

17.5 Conclusion

Today it can be asserted that neither French lawyers nor French case law is totally reluctant to some harmonisation of civil procedure. The academic world has been used to mandatory harmonisation in the framework of European civil judicial cooperation for over ten years. It is open to comparative legal studies and to some foreign institutions that could enrich French civil procedure if they can be acculturated without any major difficulty. Even case law is open-minded towards common law techniques that can help to implement the fairness principle, the efficiency of justice or the right adjudication of the case by the civil judge.

References

Amrani-Mekki S (2010) Les catégories de common law et de civil law à l'épreuve de l'office du juge et des parties. In: Guinchard MS (ed) Justices et droit du procès, Du légalisme procédural à l'humanisme processuel. Dalloz, Paris, pp 157–175

Andrews N (2008) The modern civil process, Veröffentlichungen zum Verfahrensrecht, vol 50. Mohr Siebeck, Tübingen

Angell E (1967) The amicus curiae, American development of English institutions. Int Comp Law Q 16:1017–1044

Avout Ld'(2009) Droits fondamentaux et coordination des ordres juridiques en droit privé. In: Dubout E, Touzé S (eds) Les droits fondamentaux: charnières entre ordres et systèmes juridiques. Pedone, Paris, pp 159–192

Béhar-Touchais M (2001) L'interdiction de se contredire au détriment d'autrui. Economica, Paris

Bermann G (1990) The use of anti-suit injunctions in international litigation. Columbia J Transnatl Law 28:589–610

Bolard G (2004) Le moyen contraire aux précédentes écritures'. In: Buffet MJ (ed) La procédure dans tous ses états. Petites affiches, Paris, pp 51–57

Boursier ME (2003) Le principe de loyauté en droit processuel. Dalloz, Paris

Cadiet L (1996) La renonciation à se prévaloir des irrégularités de la procédure arbitrale. Revue de l'arbitrage 1:1–38

Cadiet L (2001) Quelles preuves? discovery, témoins, experts, rôle respectif des parties et du juge. In: Fouchard P (ed) Vers un proces civil universal? Les règles transnationales de procédure civile de l' American Law Institute. Panthéon-Assas, Paris, pp 115–124

Cadiet L (2004) La preuve. In: Ferrand F (ed) La procédure civile mondiale modélisée. Editions juridiques et technique, Paris, pp 119–138

Cadiet L (2005) The new French code of civil procedure. In: Van Rhee CH (ed) European traditions in civil procedure. Intersentia, Antwerp, pp 49–68

Cadiet L (2010) Avenir des catégories et catégories de l'avenir: perspectives. In: International conference Toronto 2009, Supreme Court Review—Second series, vol 49, pp 635–655

Croze H (2004) L'introduction de l'instance. In: Ferrand F (ed) La procédure civile mondiale modélisée. Editions juridiques et technique, Paris, pp 93–102

Cuniberti G (2010) La reconnaissance en France d'une injonction anti-suit américaine, Lamy Droit Civil No. 3796, pp 7–9

Deguchi M, Storme M (2008) The reception and transmission of civil procedural law in the global society. Maklu, Antwerp/Apeldoorn

Encinas de Munagorri R (2005) L'ouverture de la Cour de cassation aux amici curiae. Revue trimestrielle de droit civil 88–93

Fauvarque-Cosson B (2007a) Société de législation comparée 2007. Electron J Comp Law 11(3):349–376

Fauvarque-Cosson B (2007b) La confiance légitime et l'estoppel, vol 4. Société de Législation Comparée, Paris

Ferrand F (2004) Rapports entre Principes et Règles dans le projet ALI/UNIDROIT. In: Ferrand F (ed) La procédure civile mondiale modélisée. Editions juridiques et technique, Paris, pp 27–33

Gaudemet-Tallon H (2001) Quel juge? In: Fouchard P (ed) Vers un procès civil universel? Les règles transnationales de procédure civile de l'American Law Institute. Panthéon-Assas, Paris, pp 67–81

Gaudemet-Tallon H (2004) Les aspects de droit international privé du projet ALI/UNIDROIT. In Ferrand F (ed) La procédure civile mondiale modélisée. Editions juridiques et techniques. Paris, pp 71–83

Gobert M (1992) Réflexions sur les sources du droit et les 'principes' d'indisponibilité du corps humain et de l'état des personnes. Revue trimestrielle de droit civil 24:489–524

Guinchard S (2000) Retour sur la constitutionnalisation de la procédure civile. In: DraiLe MP (ed) In juge entre deux millénaires. Dalloz, Paris, pp 355–368

Guinchard S (2004) Touche pas à mon code. In: Buffet MJ (ed) La procédure dans tous ses états. Petites affiches, Paris, pp 267–297

Guinchard S (2004b) Rapport de synthèse. In: Ferrand F (ed) La procédure civile mondiale modélisée. Editions juridiques et technique, Paris, pp 155–168

Guinchard S (2005) Touche pas à mon code!. In: Mélanges Jean Buffet, La procédure dans tous ses états, Paris, Petites affiches, pp 269–291

Hazard G (2004) Les objectifs du projet ALI/Unidroit. In: Ferrand F (ed) La procédure civile mondiale modélisée. Editions juridiques et technique, Paris, pp 23–25

Hazard G (eds) et al (2006) Reporters preface. In ALI/Unidroit principles of transnational civil procedure. Cambridge University Press, Cambridge

Houtcieff D (2009) Essai de maïeutique juridique: la mise au jour du principe de cohérence. La Semaine Juridique Édition Générale 47:42–48

Houtcieff D (2010) Chronique de l'estoppel ordinaire en droit positif français. Semaine Juridique Édition Générale 23:1176–1178

Junillon J (2004) Le projet ALI/Unidroit, vue critique d'un praticien du droit. In: Ferrand (ed) La procédure civile mondiale modélisée. Editions juridiques et technique, Paris, pp 35–47

Kerameus KD (2003) Some reflections on procedural harmonisation reasons and scope. Unif Law Rev 1(2):443–451

Kleiman E (2010) Stop! Définition nécessaire de l'estoppel entre faveur à l'arbitrage et droit d'accès au juge, JCP, doctr., No. 303

Kronke H (2004) Le cadre du projet ALI/Unidroit. In: Ferrand F (ed) La procédure civile mondiale modélisée. Editions juridiques et technique, Paris, pp 17–22

Mayer P (2001) L'utilité des règles transnationales de procédure civile: une vue critique. In: Fouchard P (ed) Vers un procès civil universel? Les règles transnationales de procédure civile de l'American Law Institute. Panthéon-Assas, Paris, pp 23–39

Mazeaud D (1995) L'expertise de droit à travers l'amicus curiae. In: Frison-Roche M-A, Mazeaud D (eds) L'expertise. Dalloz, Paris, pp 107–112

Mazeaud D (2006) La confiance légitime et l'estoppel. Revue internationale de droit comparé 58:362–392

Mc Lachlan C (2009) Lis Pendens in International Litigation. Martinus Nijhoff, The Hague

Mecarelli G (2004) Sanctions, frais et dépens, Les aspects financiers de la procédure. In: Ferrand F (ed) La procédure civile mondiale modélisée. Editions juridiques et technique, Paris, pp 139–148

Moréteau O (1990) L'estoppel et la protection légitime, Éléments d'un renouveau du droit de la responsabilité (droit anglais, droit français). Th. Dactyl. Lyon III, pp 96–97

Moussa T (2005) Le projet ALI/Unidroit, vue critique d'un magistrat. In: Ferrand F (ed) La procédure civile mondiale modélisée. Editions juridiques et technique, Paris, pp 47–71

Muir Watt H (1994) Pour l'accueil de l'estoppel. In: Loussouarn MY (ed) L'internationalisation du droit. Dalloz, Paris, pp 303–309
Muir Watt H (1999) Des conceptions divergentes du droit fondamental d'accéder à la justice dans l'espace conventionnel européen, Revue générale dés procédures, 4:747–761
Muir Watt H (2001) Quelle méthode? In: Fouchard P (ed) Vers un procès civil universel? Les règles transnationales de procédure civile de l'American Law Institute. Panthéon-Assas, Paris, pp 39–51
Murray P (2008) Reception and transmission of procedural law in the United States: a two-way street? In: Deguchi M, Storme M (eds) The reception and transmission of civil procedural law in the global society. Maklu, Antwerp/Apeldoorn, pp 321–346
Niboyet ML (2001) Quels litiges? In: Fouchard P (ed) Vers un procès civil universel? Les règles transnationales de procédure civile de l'American Law Institute. Panthéon-Assas, Paris, pp 51–67
Normand J (2001) La confrontation des principes directeurs. In: Fouchard P (ed) Vers un procès civil universel? Les règles transnationales de procédure civile de l'American Law Institute. Panthéon-Assas, Paris, pp 89–97
Normand (2004) Le rôle respectif des parties et du juge dans les Principes de procédure civile transnationale. In: Ferrand F (ed) La procédure civile mondiale modélisée. Editions juridiques et technique, Paris, pp 103–114
Pinsolle P (1998) Distinction entre le principe de l'estoppel et le principe de bonne foi. J du Droit Int 4:905–931
Rouhette G (1998) La procédure civile et la Convention européenne des droits de l'homme. In: Cour de cassation (ed) Le nouveau code de procédure civile: vingt ans après, Actes du colloque des 11 et 12 décembre 1997. Cour de cassation, Documentation française, pp 285–297
Sánchez-Cordero Dávila J (2006) Preface. In: ALI/Unidroit Principles of Transnational Civil Procedure. Cambridge University Press, Cambridge
Storme M (2001) Procedural law and the reform of justice: from regional to universal harmonisation. Unif Law Rev 4:763–778
Storme M (2008) Concluding remarks. In: Deguchi M, Storme M (eds) The reception and transmission of civil procedural law in the global society. Maklu, Antwerp/Apeldoorn, pp 353–358
Stürner R (2004) Anglo-American and continental civil procedure: the English reform as a model for further harmonization? In: Andenas M et al (eds) The future of transnational civil litigation. British Institute of Comparative Law, London, pp 9–13
Wijffels A (2005) French civil procedure (1806–1975). In: Rhee Van CH (ed) European traditions in civil procedure. Intersentia, Antwerp, pp 25–47

Chapter 18
Romanian Civil Procedure: The Reform Cycles

Sebastian Spinei

Abstract Modern procedural rules in Romania go back to the 1830s. A modern Code of Civil Procedure was adopted in 1865. Its source was the Civil Procedure Law of Geneva. The French-inspired Court of Cassation Law (1861) also regulated proceedings. During the early 1900s civil procedure was modified on several occasions. The first structural modification of the Romanian procedural system occurred in 1948–1950, when a Socialist model was introduced. The second batch of amendments was brought in during the 'transition' period in a quest to reform the justice system (with 1993 and 2000 witnessing the most substantial modifications). Finally, the new Code of Civil Procedure is now ready to enter into force. It has been said that the present Code is to be criticised mainly because it failed to provide the conditions to ensure speedy trial and enforcement proceedings, and the predictability of judgments. It was also argued that the present Code was the reason for the overburdening of the courts. The new Code modifies the system of jurisdiction, the technique for originating proceedings, the structure/phases of the trial, the regime of party-requested delays, appeals and appellate courts, arbitration, enforcement procedures and some special procedures. These special procedures include: the complaint for delaying the proceedings; the request for the opinion of the Court of Cassation on legal issues; small claims litigation; land registration in specific cases and eviction. However, even though it is a solid instrument and the result of a commendable effort, the new Code alone cannot mark the completion of justice reforms in Romania. Further steps will have to be made for the improvement of regulations concerning justice-related issues

Senior Lecturer, PhD, University of Sibiu

S. Spinei (✉)
University of Sibiu, Sibiu, Romania
e-mail: sebastian.spinei@ulbsibiu.ro

X. E. Kramer and C. H. van Rhee (eds.), *Civil Litigation in a Globalising World*,
DOI: 10.1007/978-90-6704-817-0_18,

including institutions, procedures, and the legal professions, in particular those regarding judges, prosecutors and justice personnel.

Contents

18.1 Precursors

Modern procedural rules in Romania go back to the 1830s, when they were introduced by the so-called Organic Regulations.[1] It was still the epoch of the distinct Romanian Principalities of Wallachia and Moldova (both remained under Turkish suzerainty, but the struggle to overthrow the Turks had started; Transylvania was part of Austria-Hungary at that time). The Organic Regulations were fundamental acts with (proto-) constitutional relevance. Some prescriptions also regulated procedural law and the judicial system. They sanctioned the principles of

[1] Romanian *Regulamentele Organice*. For earlier Romanian procedural legislation (going back to the 1700s), see Guţan 2008, 41–142, 153–155.

the separation and balance of powers, and the separation of Church and State. Furthermore, they articulated the judicial power.[2]

The precepts of permanent courts, professional and ethical standards, the irremovability of judges and professional incompatibilities, public hearings, the hierarchy and specialisation of courts and, surprisingly somehow, modern ideas such as reducing the duration of litigation and the number of court cases[3] can be found here, as well as rules concerning jurisdiction, evidence, extinctive prescription, time limits, expert opinions, procedural penalties, appeals and sequestration of goods, among other issues.

18.2 The Modern State

Eighteen fifty-nine was the year of the unification of the Principalities of Wallachia and Moldova[4] and the starting point of an elaborate process of internal reforms. New rules and institutions were required in order to rapidly consolidate the modern State. The 'importation' of legislation was one of the solutions at hand at that moment.[5] Against this background, a modern Code of Civil Procedure was adopted in 1865. Its source was the Civil Procedure Rules of Geneva. The French-inspired Law on the Court of Cassation (1861) also regulated proceedings. During the early and mid 1900s civil procedure was modified on several occasions with the intention of improving the existing regulations and speeding up trials.

The most significant amendments were those implemented in 1900, 1925, 1929 and 1943, which introduced the principle of the active role of the judge, institutions such as the court president's provisional orders for urgent circumstances, the application for a declaratory judgment, the rules on raising exceptions (procedural pleas) and of offering evidence *in limine litis* as well as of mentioning the name of proposed witnesses in the introductory request or in the statement of defence, the possibility of awarding a partial (and enforceable) decision upon a partial acquiescence to the claim, the obligation for the court to decide on exceptions before examining the merits of the case, et cetera. All of these institutions have

---

[2] See also Stanomir, '[the "Regulations" were] true fundamental documents, [even if they] did not include a "Declaration of Rights" or a "Bill of Civil Liberties"[; they] belonged to a historical process of constitutional modernization.... "The rule of law" is framed here... : the law can no longer be defined in terms of a loose absolutism, like the Prince's act of will, but it is defined as an agreement of will between the Ruler and the Assembly.' For the text of the 'Regulations,' see Negulescu and Alexianu 1944, 1–368.

[3] The 'Regulations' acknowledged the fact that one of the most frequent types of lawsuit of the time was the setting of landed property borderlines. The solution for reducing the number of such lawsuits was charging the Administration with the task of establishing the limits of all landed property in the country.

[4] The new State was initially named 'the Romanian United Principalities.' In 1881, it became the Kingdom of Romania (until 1947).

[5] The Civil Code (1865) and Commercial Code (1887) were adopted during that period. The first Code had the French Civil Code as a model; the second one, the 1882 Italian Commercial Code.

functioned in Romanian civil procedure up until now, and they are also maintained by the new Code. The sources of these modifications were some Western legal systems (one can identify here French, but also Austrian, influences). Ideas, initiatives and experiences of an already consistent tradition of national legal literature and practice were also largely employed.[6] The court system of that time was composed of the *Judecătoria*, the Tribunals (both were courts of first instance), the Courts of Appeal and the Court of Cassation.

18.3 The Communist Period

The first structural modification of the Romanian procedural system occurred in 1948–1950, when a Socialist model was introduced[7]: appeal[8] was suppressed and the Courts of Appeal abolished; cassation was replaced by a new devolutive type of recourse (in Romanian: *recurs*)[9] at the Tribunals (so not anymore at the highest court of the land) and the Court of Cassation by a Supreme Tribunal; judges were appointed by the Ministry of Justice, Supreme Tribunal judges by the legislator (the National Assembly); and the Prosecutor General obtained special powers (the right of supervision over the activity of the courts, the right to control any case record, and the right to order a stay of execution of a judgment against which he intended to file an appeal).[10]

Thus, the court system became composed of the *Judecătoria* (the courts of first instance), the Tribunals (courts having jurisdiction in matters of *recurs*) and the Supreme Tribunal (which issued 'guiding judgments'[11] and was competent to hear 'recourse for annulment' initiated by the Prosecutor General). This resulted in the destruction of a proven, functional system built up in Romania over almost a century. The peculiarity of these changes is that they were profoundly ideologically justified.

The new political regime also introduced drastic changes in society and the economy. The legal system followed the historical circumstances. It is shocking today to read some of the Romanian civil procedure tomes of the 1950s, in which legal, scientific and technical arguments are replaced by pure ideology. The distinguished Romanian proceduralist Graţian Porumb states, for example:

---

6 Păduraru 1943, 35–53. See also Hamangiu et al. 1930, *passim*.

7 See Stoenescu 1956, 703–707, 709, 715. See also, Hilsenrad 1956: 'a more profound knowledge *of the principles of USSR socialist judicial law* … determined these [Code of] Civil Procedure … modifications' (emphasis added).

8 Romanian '*apel.*'

9 'Recurs' is a final appeal *lato* sensu. It is a legal remedy heard by a lower court, and, in some cases, by the highest court; both the facts of the case and its legal aspects can be re-examined. Between 1948 and 1993 it replaced the previous 'appeal,' and from 1993 up to the present it has, in selected cases, functioned alongside 'appeal.'

10 Initially by way of the 'recourse in surveillance,' later the 'extraordinary recourse' and then the 'recourse for annulment.'

11 I.e. decisions in the interest of the law pronounced *ex officio*.

> [the previous system] did not … allow a better administration of justice, but it was maintained by the bourgeoisie because it provided an appropriate field for bureaucracy, whose labyrinth only those who disposed of sufficient material means to get the support of specialists could disentangle; maintaining appeal … is no longer necessary because, due to the active role of the judge and the assignment imposed to justice to discover the objective truth, conditions are created for the solid administration of justice in first instance courts.[12]

Ilie Stoenescu—prominent law professor and, intriguingly, a former judge (*Consilier*) at the previous Romanian Court of Cassation—also affirms[13]:

> cassation had a class character, and the Court of Cassation, a central State authority, helped the enforcement of laws through which oppression was exercised; appeal had only a formal nature, and uselessly led to slowing down the administration of justice, as there was no guarantee that the decision in appeal would be better than the one of the first instance judge.

Most of the previous Code of Civil Procedure texts and institutions, however, stayed unchanged until the fall of the Communist regime in 1989. Maybe this also contributed to the paradox that the image of that period, in retrospect, is an image of a better justice system than the present one. An explanation for this seeming paradox may be the fact that the judges feared the repressive regime of the time so they were most careful not to commit judicial errors. Another one is the fact that the tasks of the judicial system were not as complex as today. Indeed, it was the period when private property, commercial relations and instruments to challenge public authorities did not exist, when divorce was repudiated as contrary to Socialist morality, and so on. This meant that no litigation (or almost none) was carried out in these fields. Finally, the stability of the legislation during the Communist era can be another explanation.

18.4 After the Fall of the Communist Regime

Another batch of amendments was brought in during the 'transition' period in a quest to reform the justice system, with 1993 and 2000 witnessing the most substantial modifications. Modifications were introduced almost every year. Many of these were, unfortunately, characterised by hesitation and by a lack of vision, coordination and foundation. At times, the 'method' of the legislator was an unwilled *mélange* of principles and institutions from the previous (incompatible) periods.[14] This mixing can be currently observed in the structure and functions of the judicial system, which includes the *Judecătoria* (courts of first instance also having judicial control over some administrative jurisdictional acts), the Tribunals (courts of first instance but also of appeal and *recurs*), the Courts of Appeal—reintroduced in 1993 (these also function as courts of first instance for administrative complaints

---

[12] Porumb 1962, 14.

[13] See Stoenescu 1956, 714.

[14] Spinei 2010, 235–239.

against the central authorities) and the Court of Cassation[15] (which, paradoxically, decides ordinary cases where *recurs* has been brought in only a few matters; it is also competent to decide on cassation in the interest of the law).

18.4.1 Romanian Justice Before the Adoption of the New Code of Civil Procedure

In recent years, the level of trust Romanians placed in the justice system has been quite low. In fact, the average Romanian is significantly less trusting in this respect than the average citizen in the European Union, either in the new Member States or in the EU15.[16] For instance, the percentage of Romanians who trusted the justice system was 26 per cent in 2007,[17] and 28.7 per cent in 2009.[18]

18.4.2 EU Membership: Cooperation and Verification Mechanisms

The European Commission established a mechanism to cooperate and verify the progress made, *inter alia*, in the reform of the judiciary after accession, based on the commitments made by Romania[19] at the time of accession. Under this

---

[15] The Supreme Court was renamed 'High Court of Cassation and Justice' in 2003.

[16] See http://ec.europa.eu/public_opinion/archives/eb/eb69/eb69_ro_exe.pdf (last consulted in May 2011). The EU15 are the Member States of the European Union prior to the accession of the new candidate countries on 1 May 2004. In 2006, the level of trust in the judiciary was 34 per cent in the new Member States and 48 per cent in the EU15.

[17] See http://ec.europa.eu/romania/documents/news/eb_68-2_raport_national_validat.pdf (last consulted in May 2011). The level of trust only reached 20 per cent according to another survey (see http://www.alegericsm.ro/documentare-articole-etalii.aspx?articleId=8; last consulted in May 2011).

[18] See http://www.transparency.org.ro/politici_si_studii/studii/masurarea_perceptiei_coduri/OptiuniProcedura.pdf (last consulted in May 2011).

[19] And Bulgaria, both countries joining the EU at the same time. See http://ec.europa.eu/dgs/secretariat_general/cvm/index_en.htm (last consulted in May 2011): 'When they joined the EU on 1 January 2007, Romania and Bulgaria still had progress to make in the fields of judicial reform, corruption and organised crime. To smooth the entry of both countries and at the same time safeguard the workings of its policies and institutions, the EU decided to establish a special 'cooperation and verification mechanism' to help them address these outstanding shortcomings. In December 2006, the Commission set criteria ('benchmarks') for assessing progress made on these issues. The decision to continue assessing Bulgaria and Romania shows the EU's commitment to see the two countries develop the effective administrative and judicial systems they need to deliver on the obligations of membership as well as enjoying the benefits.' See European Commission Decision of 13.12.2006 establishing a mechanism for cooperation and verification of progress in Romania to address specific benchmarks in the areas of judicial reform and the fight against corruption, C(2006)6569 (December 2006).

mechanism, Romania agreed to report regularly on progress in addressing specific benchmarks, one of those being to ensure a more transparent and efficient judicial process. European Commission reports pointed out several problems: incoherence in case law, inconsistency and incoherence in the preparation of laws and in their application, which led to legal uncertainty.[20] Some other issues within the system were acknowledged by Romanian officials: the lack of speed in trials and enforcement proceedings, the lack of the predictability of judgments and the overburdening of the courts.[21] One of the responses from EU and Romanian authorities to these circumstances was the elaboration of new criminal and civil codes, and new codes of criminal and civil procedure.

18.5 The New Code of Civil Procedure

The new Code of Civil Procedure was adopted in July 2010.[22] It has not yet been decided when it will come into force.[23]

18.5.1 Drafting

The drafting was undertaken by a commission of academics, legal professionals and Ministry of Justice officials, constituted in March 2006.[24] In March 2008, the draft was ready for public debate. It was sent to the Government in February 2009 and to Parliament in March 2009.[25]

---

[20] European Commission, Key findings of the progress report on the Cooperation and Verification Mechanism with Romania (July 2007); European Commission, Report from the Commission to the European Parliament and the Council on Progress in Romania under the Co-operation and Verification Mechanism, COM(2008)494 final (July 2008).

[21] Minister of Justice—Statement of Grounds for the New Code of Civil Procedure.

[22] Law [*Legea*] No. 134/2010 regarding the Code of Civil Procedure, published in the Official Journal of Romania [*Monitorul Oficial al României*], Part I, No. 485 of 15.07.2010.

[23] A Law for the Implementation of the Code of Civil Procedure is awaiting Parliamentary debate.

[24] By Order of the Minister of Justice No. 829/C of 24 March 2006.

[25] See http://www.cdep.ro/pls/proiecte/upl_pck.proiect?idp=10395 (last consulted in May 2011).

18.5.2 Preparatory Research

According to the Preamble of the New Civil Procedure Code,[26] the underlying documentation comprised different sources, such as the 1940 Romanian Code of Civil Procedure[27]; foreign Codes of Civil Procedure (Quebec-Canada, France, Italy, Switzerland,[28] Germany, Finland, the Netherlands) and other legislative instruments; European Conventions, Directives and Regulations; the Storme Commission's work on drafting a European Judicial Code; the Model Code of Civil Procedure for Ibero-America; and the ALI/UNIDROIT Principles and Rules of Transnational Civil Procedure. The premise or design of such an exploration must be harmonisation, in other words, improvement through assessing and implementing proven solutions given by a comparative approach.

18.5.3 The Principles

For the first time, the fundamental principles of the civil procedure are explicitly and unitarily mentioned in the Code, within a dedicated preliminary section. Until now, even if most of them are traditional in Romanian civil procedure, they were, for the largest part, inferred from constitutional rules or disparate texts of the Code, theorised by scholars[29] and observed in legal practice.

The principles are proclaimed in Article 1–22 of the new Code[30]: justice is a public service; free access to justice; the right to a fair trial within an optimal and predictable time; speed; legality; equality; party initiative[31]; good faith; the right of defence; the contradictory character of civil procedure; oral and public debates; immediacy as regards evidence; debates in the Romanian language[32]; continuity[33]; and the judge's active role.

---

[26] *Tezele prealabile ale noului Cod de procedură civilă*, approved by Government Decision [*Hotărârea Guvernului*] No. 829/2007, published in the Official Journal of Romania, Part I, No. 556 of 14/08/2007. See also at http://www.just.ro/ (last consulted in May 2011).

[27] Also known as the Carol II Code of Civil Procedure, after the King of Romania who initiated its drafting. The Code was, however, never applied due to World War II-related and subsequent events.

[28] The new Swiss Code of Civil Procedure.

[29] Leş 2010, 39–65. See also Ciobanu 1997, 42–52 and Deleanu 2007, 20–35.

[30] Chapters I and II of the Preliminary Title. Chapter II also stipulates some procedural rights and duties of the participants.

[31] This refers to the parties' power to conduct proceedings—initiate the trial, determine its scope, withdraw the claim or settle the dispute, et cetera.

[32] National minorities and foreigners have the right to use their own language as well as translation.

[33] This means that the judges before whom the case has been argued should also deliver judgment.

18.5.4 The Structure

The new Code includes a Preliminary Title, seven Books and Final Dispositions, with a total of 1,119 articles. The Preliminary Title deals with the 'Domain and Principles of the Civil Process'. Book I (General Provisions, Articles 29–186) incorporates dispositions regarding The Action (Title I); The Participants (Title II); Jurisdiction (Title III); Procedural acts (Title IV: I. The claim; II. Summons and notification of documents; III. Nullity); Time limits (Title V); Fines and damages (Title VI). Book II regulates Contentious proceedings (Articles 187–519): The Procedure at first instance (Title I); Appeals (Title II); Provisions for ensuring uniform case law (Title III); The complaint for delaying the proceedings (Title IV). The remaining Books rule on Non-contentious proceedings (Book III, Articles 520–532), Arbitration (Book IV, Articles 533–612), Enforcement (Book V, Articles 613–902), Special procedures/specific provisions for certain subject-matters (Book VI, Articles 903–1049), and International Litigation (Book VII, Articles 1050–1118).

Modifications were made regarding jurisdiction, the techniques for originating proceedings, the structure of the trial, evidence, the regime of party-requested delays, appeals and appellate courts, arbitration, enforcement procedures, some special procedures (divorce, injunction to pay, declaration of absence and death), and other matters.

In relation to jurisdiction, a positive addition is a new set of rules destined to facilitate the determination of jurisdiction according to the amount of the claim (Articles 96–104). The plea of lack of jurisdiction can be raised only before courts of first instance and only at the first hearing date (Article 126). The new rule also concerns jurisdiction on the ground of 'public order,' which, until now, could be claimed in any stage of the process. The quashing of the proceedings based on lack of jurisdiction represented a source of delay, so a traditional principle of 'competence' was sacrificed in favour of the imperative of speed.

18.5.5 The Summons and Notification of Documents, the Trial Stages

Summons will be served and documents notified by judicial clerks and the postal service (the same as at present), but also through alternative means: by bailiffs and private couriers, and by fax or e-mail (Article 148 paras 5, 6). It will also be possible to carry out notification of documents between lawyers (Article 164). Once a party has received the summons, no further summons will be sent (Article 224). The proceedings are re-systematised, the trial being more clearly divided into stages: (*a*) a written pleading phase[34]; (*b*) a newly introduced intermediate

[34] This is the phase when the 'framework' of the case is configured through the claim and defence and counterclaim, as the case may be.

phase, when the claim is being considered by the court; the plaintiff will be notified if his claim is irregular, in order to rectify it; (*c*) an instruction phase, which will take place in the judge's council chamber; and (*d*) a final hearing, when concluding arguments will be presented.

The complaint for delaying the proceedings (Articles 515–519) can be addressed to the same court that judges the delayed case. If the complaint is admitted, the court will immediately take the necessary measures to eliminate the circumstances that caused the delay. The interlocutory judgment which dismisses the complaint can be challenged before the superior court.

18.6 Other Solutions

There are a series of provisions which are intended to restrain the possibilities of an unjustified prolongation of the process. Short delays (even of a single day only) will be ordered between hearing dates (Article 236). Delays given by the court when demanded by both parties or when no defence is established should be exceptional (Articles 216, 217).

Evidentiary rules have been unified,[35] both the admissibility and presentation of evidence being now governed by the Code of Civil Procedure. New types of evidence are subject to regulation (e.g. electronic documents). On the first hearing date, the judge will estimate, after listening to the parties, the duration of the instruction phase. This estimate can be reconsidered during the proceedings (Article 233).

The judge can impose duties on the participants, and he can perform any action necessary for resolving the case. The measures that have been ordered can be notified to the parties by phone, fax, or other means (Article 236 paras 3, 4).

Another source of delay and legal uncertainty were attempts to resolve cases without the participation of all interested parties. In the absence of procedures like the French *tierce opposition*,[36] the agreed solution was to allow the absent party to bring a new action. The new Code provides for the possibility for the judge to introduce a third party into the case (Articles 77, 78). Again, a traditional principle, i.e. party initiative,[37] was reduced in favour of a more fluid procedure.

The rule that the hearing should be recorded has also been introduced (Article 226) after some years since it was first proposed by lawyers. Hopefully this will function as a deterrent against potential abusive acts by judges and will countervail the new prescript of the instruction phase taking place in the council chamber.

---

[35] Until now, some of these rules could be found in the Civil Code.

[36] *Tierce opposition*, Arts. 582–592 of the French Code of Civil Procedure. See also Cadiet 1998, 698–704 and Vincent and Guinchard 1999, 995–1005.

[37] This signifies, among other things, that only parties can configure the 'subjective' framework of the process, i.e. establish who participates in the trial.

18.6.1 *Recourse Against Judgments*

Two principles are enunciated, *inter alia*, in this respect: the reinstitution of the Courts of Appeal as courts judging *appeals*; and the re-establishment of *cassation* (or at least its fundamentals). As regards the first goal, it can still be noticed that in reality many, if not most, of the appeals are heard by Tribunals. The devolutive effect of appeal will be reinforced, though, by reducing the possibility of quashing the decision and sending the case back to the first instance court. Instead, the appeal court will solve the case itself.

The second issue can be analysed, in my opinion, as the result of a compromise between the empathy of some of the drafters of the Code for the Romanian cassation system as it existed before the Second World War and the apprehension of most or many of the Supreme Court judges towards this institution.[38]

What resulted is a 'limited' possibility to introduce cassation complaints: most cases will end at the appellate stage,[39] and only a limited number will be subject to cassation proceedings; also the number of grounds for cassation are reduced. Another new rule regarding cassation is compulsory legal representation: the claim must be formulated and the party must be assisted by a lawyer or legal counsel. A preliminary 'filter' procedure will be introduced. Modifications are also introduced as regards other types of recourse against judgments—the 'complaint for annulment,' revision and cassation in the interest of the law.

18.6.2 *Mechanisms for Ensuring Uniform Case Law*

The previously existing cassation in the interest of the law will be accompanied by a request for the opinion of the Court of Cassation on legal issues.[40]

18.6.3 *Civil Enforcement*

Some innovations include: the introduction of advertising forced-sale auctions on the Internet; the rule that execution on immovables is not allowed for debts under the

---

[38] In 2003, a Government Ordinance, after receiving French advice and assistance, re-established cassation—all types of cassation should be heard by the Supreme Court, renamed the High Court of Cassation and Justice (the Ordinance also ruled that all *appeals* will be judged by the Courts of Appeal). Because the reform was not properly prepared and accompanied by logistical measures, the Supreme Court found itself flooded with cases. At times, the first date of hearing a complaint in cassation was scheduled after one year or more had elapsed and the same interval would separate the various court sessions (see http://www.scj.ro/Raport%202004.asp; last consulted in May 2011). Hence, the above-mentioned reluctance. In 2004 and 2005 the measure was abrogated.

[39] For the first time in the history of Romanian civil procedure.

[40] Similar to the French *avis de la Cour de cassation*.

equivalent of €1,250, unless no other assets are available (to avoid abusive executions and excessive costs); and the introduction of a simplified eviction procedure (the handing over of immovables) and of a special procedure for enforcing child custody orders. Positive clarifications have been made regarding the jurisdiction of the courts which monitor the legality of enforcement proceedings.

18.6.4 Special Procedures

Specific provisions are applicable to certain subject matters. Some existing ones, now regulated by special laws, are amended and introduced into the Code (the procedure regarding the protection of persons lacking legal capacity to act, the declaration of absence and death, the injunction to pay). Others are entirely new in Romanian civil procedure: the procedures regarding small claims; the acquisition by prescription and land registration procedure; and eviction procedures. Finally, modifications were made in order to simplify and re-systematise some procedures: divorce,[41] the action for partition in cases of joint ownership, and others.

18.7 Final Observations

Even with the new Code adopted, there is no justification for triumphant statements. The Code is a solid instrument and expresses a commendable effort designed to reorganise, systematise, reinforce and innovate. Romanian procedural traditions were largely preserved or restored. A number of new solutions, some of them revolutionary, were introduced. However, this was done too quickly without enough time for reflection which would be justified in the drafting of an Act, destined to last in order to ensure stability.[42]

On the other hand, the preparatory research looks not entirely comprehensive, since important sources were overlooked.[43]

---

[41] Divorce by mutual consent will be handled by the Notary Public, and no longer by the courts.

[42] In comparison, the work on the new Swiss Code of Civil Procedure started in 1999 with the commissioning of a group of experts; in June 2003 they issued a first draft and an explanatory report; after public debates, a second draft was submitted to Parliament in June 2006; the Code was adopted in December 2008 and entered into force in January 2011. See Baumgartner 2010; Draft of the Swiss Code of Civil Procedure 2007; Grob 2003. Comparable to the haste in the Romanian reform process is the haste in introducing the Spanish *Ley de Enjuiciamiento Civil*. In this case a commission started work in 1996; the draft was presented by the Government to Parliament in late October 1998; the Code was adopted in December 1999, officially published in January 2000 and came into force in January 2001. Thanks are due to Dr Christian Koller (University of Vienna) and Professor Antonio Maria Lara Lopez (University of Malaga) for the preceding information.

[43] In my opinion, such a survey should not have ignored, e.g., the Austrian, Spanish, Portuguese and British solutions. One would also have expected to see the experience of some other former Socialist European countries considered.

Some specific remarks can also be made.[44] The jurisdiction of the courts was supposed to be rearranged, so 'justice would be closer to the people and more predictable'—as stated in the Preamble of the Code.[45] In reality, the system does not look essentially different, since the *Judecătoria* is still the court of first instance for many matters (small or unproblematic claims) and is also competent as regards administrative jurisdictional acts,[46] whereas the Tribunal is the court of first instance, appeal and *recurs* (the latter is only the case if this is prescribed by a special legal provision).[47] The Courts of Appeal will still judge, as first instance courts, the administrative complaints against central authorities and, as appellate courts, appeals against the decisions of the Tribunals. If prescribed by a special provision, they will also hear *recurs*.[48]

The Court of Cassation will pass judgment, as before, on a limited number of issues, even if Article 477, para 3 enunciates that cassation aims at allowing the High Court to examine the challenged decision in order to decide whether it is in compliance with law. It will also judge cassation in the interest of the law.

Strictly personal opinions of some of the drafters found their place in the Code. One example are the provisions which affirm that not only the operative part of the decision[49] but also the grounds have the authority of *res judicata* and can constitute the object of an appeal.[50] Some dispositions seem to be bound to having inconsiderable efficiency in themselves or due to the way they are conceived: this is the case with, for example, the estimate, by the judge, of the duration of the instruction phase[51]; the complaint for delaying the proceedings[52]; and the removal of the possibility to make a counterclaim or to file a third-party complaint during an eviction trial (Article 1028).[53]

---

[44] See also, for an extended analysis of the new Code, Deleanu 2009, 25–52.

[45] See *supra* n. 26.

[46] Art. 92.

[47] Art. 93.

[48] Art. 94.

[49] According to the English version of the French Code of Civil Procedure (Art. 1054, at <http://195.83.177.9/code/liste.phtml?lang=uk&c=39&r=7343#art29853>), this would be the term for the French *dispositif* (*de la decision*). Romanian—*dispozitiv*.

[50] Arts. 418, 448. See, for a critical opinion, Leş 2009, para 11.

[51] Art. 233, mentioned in Sect. 18.6. Since this estimate can be reconsidered during the proceedings, it cannot really fulfil its proclaimed 'disciplinary' function.

[52] The complaint is addressed to the same court that is in charge of the case in which the delay has occurred. The interlocutory judgment which dismisses the complaint can be challenged before the superior court. According to some, it would make more sense to address the superior court directly. At the same time, it should be remarked that comparable instruments in other jurisdictions have proven to be ineffective. Such is the case of the Austrian *Fristsetzungsantrag* (application to set a time limit), directed to a higher court and requesting an order to an inferior court to perform a procedural act within a certain time limit. The application is rarely used, most likely because it generates further delay. See Van Rhee and Verkerk 2006, 120–134.

[53] It is true that the plaintiff will benefit, and the defendant cannot try to stall for time anymore, but justice will not gain, as instead of one lawsuit, there will be at least two.

Finally, it should be noted that other rules are fragmentary. Cassation, as stated before, is configured in such a way that only a limited number of cases will end up before the Court of Cassation. The nature and the amount of the demand is the norm for this restrictive policy. But the Supreme Court would have been in a larger measure able to perform its role of unifying case law if equipped with additional means. In Spanish civil procedure, for instance, cassation is also available when an 'interest to bring cassation proceedings' (*'interés casacional'*)[54] can be shown, regardless of the amount of the claim. A similar approach was also present in German law—the importance of the case functioned as an additional criterion for allowing proceedings before the highest court; since 2002, such proceedings must be authorised if the case 'poses a question of principle which must be clarified'.[55]

It must also be stated that, in any case, the Code alone cannot mark the completion of justice reforms in Romania; its adoption does not mean justice has been brought to the highest standards. Not even all four new Codes together can be credited with such an achievement. Further steps will have to be taken for the improvement of regulations concerning justice-related issues: institutions, procedures and the legal professions (particularly those of judges, prosecutors and justice personnel, and also including related recruitment and integrity policies).

Coherent, sustained, persistent positive action is needed in all these fields.[56] The Romanian legislature and administration are obliged to undertake such action; they owe it the Romanian people and to the new European project.

References

Baumgartner SP (2010) Civil Procedure reform in Switzerland and the role of legal transplants. In: Walker J, Chase O (eds) Common law, civil law and the future of categories. Available at http://ssrn.com/abstract=1677478 (last consulted in May 2011)

Cadiet L (1998) Droit judiciaire privé. Editions Litec, Paris

Ciobanu VM (1997) Tratat teoretic şi practic de procedură civilă. Editura Naţional, Bucharest

Deleanu I (2007) Tratat de procedură civilă. Editura C.H Beck, Bucharest

Deleanu I (2009) Consideraţii generale şi unele observaţii cu privire la Proiectul Codului de procedură civilă'. Revista Română de Drept Privat 2 :25–52

---

[54] Art. 477(2) point 3 *Ley de Enjuiciamiento Civil.* According to para 3 of the same article, there is sufficient interest in bringing cassation proceedings 'when the challenged decision opposes the case law of the Supreme Tribunal, concerns issues upon which there are contradictory rulings of lower courts (*Audiencias Provinciales*) or applies legal rules in force for less than five years without there being case law of the Supreme Tribunal on previous rules with identical or similar content.'

[55] Or if the intervention of the Court is necessary in case of the existence of a legal gap or divergent case law—Art. 554 *Zivilprozessordnung*, see Leş 2009, 11–39.

[56] Measures have already been taken for the immediate implementation of some solutions of the new Code into the present one and for amending the Law of the Constitutional Court. The latter eliminates the stay of civil proceedings during constitutional review (Law No. 177/2010, published in the Official Journal of Romania, Part I, No. 672 of 4/10/2010).

Draft of the Swiss Code of Civil Procedure (2007). Available at http://www.swlegal.ch/Publications/Newsletter/Draft-of-the-Swiss-Code-of-Civil-Procedure. aspx (last consulted in May 2011)

European Commission (2007) Key findings of the progress report on the cooperation and verification mechanism with Romania. Available at www.europa.eu/rapid/pressReleasesAction.do?reference=MEMO/07/262&format=HTML&aged=0&language=EN (last consulted in May 2011)

European Commission (2008) Report to the European Parliament and the council on progress in Romania under the co-operation and verification mechanism, COM(2008)494 final. Available at www.eur-lex.europa.eu/LexUriServ/LexUriServ.do?uri=CELEX:52008DC0494:EN:NOT (last consulted in May 2011)

Grob B (2003) Federal code of civil procedure, legal and tax news Switzerland. Available at http://www.swlegal.ch/downloads/memberspub/586.pdf (last consulted in May 2011)

Guţan M (2008) Istoria dreptului românesc. Editura Hamangiu, Bucharest

Hamangiu C et al (1930) Recursul în casaţie şi contenciosul administrativ. Editura Naţională S, Ciornei, Bucharest

Hilsenrad A (1956) Preface to Codul de procedură civilă. Editura de Stat pentru Literatură Economică şi Juridică, Bucharest

Leş I (2009) Dispozitivul hotărârii judecătoreşti şi procedura de filtrare a recursului în viziunea Proiectului noului Cod de procedură civilă. Dreptul 10:12–26

Leş I (2010) Tratat de drept procesual civil. Editura C.H Beck, Bucharest

Negulescu P, Alexianu G (1944) Regulamentele Organice ale Valahiei şi Moldovei, vol 1. Intreprinderile Eminescu S.A., Bucharest

Păduraru Gh D et al (1943) Accelerarea judecăţilor. Tiparul Românesc S.A.R, Bucharest

Gr Porumb (1962) Codul de procedură civilă comentat şi adnotat, vol 2. Editura Ştiinţifică, Bucharest

Spinei S (2010) Stadiul procedurii civile române în perspectiva adoptării Noului Cod. Revista Română de Drept Privat 1:235–239

Stoenescu I (1956) Curs de drept procesual civil. Litografia Învăţămîntului, Bucharest

Van Rhee CH, Verkerk R (2006) Civil procedure. In: Smits JM (ed) Elgar Encyclopedia of comparative law. Edward Elgar, Cheltenham, pp 120–134

Vincent J, Guinchard S (1999) Procédure civile. Editions Dalloz, Paris

Chapter 19
Closing Comments: Harmonisation or Globalisation of Civil Procedure?

Marcel Storme

Abstract This chapter brings the subject of this book to conclusion. It recalls the work of the Storme working group and the political developments thereafter. It argues that further harmonisation within Europe should (1) start from the notion of equal access to justice, (2) not narrow the application of instruments to cross-border cases, (3) be based on horizontal harmonisation instead of vertical harmonisation, and (4) make a clear choice as to its interaction with national civil procedures with the so-called 28th model being the most feasible. It gives an overview of the contributions in this book and offers some concluding proposals. The author is of the opinion that the process of harmonisation and unification of procedural law on a European level appears to be an irreversible trend.

Contents

Honorary President of the International Association of Procedural Law; Professor Emeritus of Civil Procedure at the University of Ghent.

M. Storme (✉)
University of Ghent, Belgium
e-mail: M.Storme@storme-law.be

X. E. Kramer and C. H. van Rhee (eds.), *Civil Litigation in a Globalising World*,
DOI: 10.1007/978-90-6704-817-0_19,

19.1 Introduction

Throughout my career, I have cherished the ideal of a universal code applicable throughout the world. As long ago as 1949, one of my masters at Ghent University announced that a worldwide system of law would only come about when we came under attack by extraterrestrials. However, since then we have witnessed various ventures into outer space which have demonstrated the non-existence of such creatures, thus removing the opportunity to create a new world order on this basis. Nevertheless, I have kept alive my dream of harmonising the law. Although I may have toyed with the notion of a code of law which would apply on a worldwide basis, I have gradually come to cherish the notion of a European code, more particularly in the field of civil procedure.

Twenty-four years ago in Milan, I made a plea for the unification of procedural law throughout the European Union.[1] This was the first time anyone had dared to challenge the taboo which hitherto had killed stone-dead any such project in the field of civil procedure, i.e. the notion that procedural law was the law which applied to the courts—which, in turn, could only be regulated by the sovereign domestic legislation of the EU Member States.

The rest, as they say, is history. A working group was set up consisting of twelve experts—one for each of the Member States of that day. Once the European Commission had announced its support for this initiative,[2] we started operations in 1987. The resulting report[3] was, in the course of 1993, submitted to the Commission. It was only at a much later date that the realisation dawned that Europe should start to develop an interest in civil procedure. But, it also emerged later that the Treaty of Amsterdam of 2 October 1997, and more particularly Article 65 thereof (currently Article 81 TFEU), would represent a significant breakthrough in this regard.

Since the turn of the century, the EU law-making authorities have been far from inactive, adopting as they have, *inter alia*, many procedural regulations which resulted directly from the conclusions drawn up by the European Council at Tampere (15–16 October 1999). These conclusions emphasise the importance of improving access to the courts by the introduction of, amongst other techniques, common minimum standards for cross-border disputes, as well as the enhanced mutual recognition of court decisions by harmonising legislation and adopting new rules of judicial procedure.

In this connection, it is quite remarkable that the report which I submitted to the Commission in 1993 had remained apparently unnoticed, until, unexpectedly, the Green Paper on a European order for payment procedure, dated 20 December 2002, made reference to the Storme Report in the following terms:

---

[1] Storme 1986, 293 et seq.

[2] This support was restricted to the travelling expenses of the steering group members for every meeting.

[3] Storme 1994.

In 1993, a working group of experts on procedural law, presided by Professor Marcel Storme, presented to the Commission a draft proposal for a directive on the approximation of laws and rules of the Member States concerning certain aspects of the procedure for civil litigation (the so-called Storme Proposal).[4] This first comprehensive attempt at addressing the most fundamental features of civil procedure, clearly based on an internal market rationale, comprises a section setting up detailed rules of an order for payment procedure, thus recognizing the particular importance of harmonisation in that area. Although this proposal was never converted into a legislative initiative of the Commission, it is a valuable point of reference and source of inspiration.

It would seem that this was the starting point for a system of truly uniform procedural rules throughout Europe, and therefore also for the harmonisation of judicial procedures.

The first real set of uniform procedural rules was the European Community (EC) Regulation No. 1896/2006 (applicable beginning 12 December 2008) which created a European Order for Payment Procedure, followed by the EC Regulation No. 861/2007 (applicable beginning 1 January 2009) which established a European Small Claims Procedure.

It is therefore fair to say that 2009 represented the definitive breakthrough for a European system of civil procedure—an outcome which I, and the members of my working group, had dreamed of back in 1987.

This is why I believe that the time has come to examine whether this initial exercise in harmonising court procedures in Europe has been a success, or whether it should be described as a false start.

19.2 How Should European Procedural Law be Regulated?

1. The elaboration of a European system of procedural law was not inspired by harmonising dogma, but by the very essence of the European Union, which is to give all European citizens equal access to the courts.

   There should not be any discrimination in areas such as court costs or trial duration.

   As matters stand at present, such discrimination is only tackled where it takes place within a Member State. Discrimination as between citizens of different Member States is, wrongly, missing from the agenda.

   Neither of the regulations under review removes such discrimination. Thus, for example, no domestic payment order procedure is available in the Netherlands, whereas most EU Member States do make provision for such a procedure.[5]

---

[4] Storme 1994.

[5] Freudenthal 2009, 205.

2. It is clear that both regulations (order for payment and small claims) have, wrongly, attributed a narrow interpretation to the notion of 'cross-border implications.'

   Article 81 of the Treaty on the Functioning of the European Union (TFEU) reads as follows:

   1. The Union shall develop judicial cooperation in civil matters having cross-border implications, based on the principle of mutual recognition of judgments and of decisions in extrajudicial cases. Such cooperation may include the adoption of measures for the approximation of the laws and regulations of the Member States.
   2. For the purposes of para 1, the European Parliament and the Council, acting in accordance with the ordinary legislative procedure, shall adopt measures, particularly when necessary for the proper functioning of the internal market, aimed at ensuring:

      (a) the mutual recognition and enforcement between Member States of judgments and of decisions in extrajudicial cases;
      (b) the cross-border service of judicial and extrajudicial documents;
      (c) the compatibility of the rules applicable in the Member States concerning conflict of laws and of jurisdiction;
      (d) cooperation in the taking of evidence;
      (e) effective access to justice;
      (f) the elimination of obstacles to the proper functioning of civil proceedings, if necessary by promoting the compatibility of the rules on civil procedure applicable in the Member States;
      (g) the development of alternative methods of dispute settlement;
      (h) support for the training of the judiciary and judicial staff.

   3. [family law]

It is abundantly clear that the term 'matters having cross-border implications' has the broadest possible meaning and, in essence, concerns all types of dispute. The differences between the Member States as regards their rules governing dispute settlement constantly have—at least potentially—cross-border implications (*l'incidence transfrontière)* within the European Union.

Thus, if the rules on dispute settlement are better in one Member State, this will cause a distortion if less effective rules apply elsewhere.

When dealing with provisions of this nature, it is also appropriate to apply an interpretation which views each rule against the background, or better still the policy objectives, of the entire legal system.

It cannot seriously be maintained that the effective operation of civil procedures should only be a requirement for so-called cross-border disputes—a contention which is all the more fanciful when comparing the number of cross-border disputes with the abundance of domestic disputes occurring within the Member States. And I quote B. Hess: 'Those instruments are of little practical relevancy.' It might be appropriate in this context to apply the old legal method rule devised by Von Jhering, to wit, his *Durchbruchspunkte* theory: legislators make laws for situations as they present themselves at the time, without, however, necessarily excluding other situations which have yet to arise. It is not possible to deny altogether that the drafters of former Article 65, now Article 81 TFEU, initially had in mind the occurrence of cross-border disputes.

However, discrimination would indeed arise if one were to restrict oneself to a narrow interpretation of Article 81, since this would entail that the object was to devise a more efficient set of procedures for cross-border disputes, thus ignoring the various domestic civil procedures.

This would mean that the intention was to create a paradoxical situation. Initially—and this was undoubtedly the objective pursued by the 'Approximation of Judiciary Law in the European Union' working group—the object was to achieve a degree of approximation which would enable the citizens of all the Member States to have the benefit of similarly efficient procedural rules. Now, a narrow interpretation of Article 81 would restrict improvements in litigation only to citizens involved in cross-border disputes.

Finally, there has been an important decision by the European Court of Justice (ECJ) which entirely supports the line of argument taken above.[6]

The Court of Appeal (England and Wales) had requested the ECJ to give a preliminary ruling on the question whether the Treaty of 27 September 1968 (Regulation No. 44/2001 of 22 December 2001) could be applied to a national dispute between two British citizens. Although the defendant, as well as the British government, claimed that Brussels I did not apply to internal disputes, the Court held that the Treaty was in fact applicable.

In a significant passage of the decision, the ECJ ruled that the uniform rules on jurisdiction contained in the Brussels I Treaty were not intended to apply exclusively to situations which have a real and sufficient link with the operation of the internal market—which would imply a requirement of connecting factors with other signatory States to the Treaty.

3. The fundamental criticism I have of the law-making process in the European Union on the subject of procedural law concerns the issue of vertical harmonisation, under which a wide range of loose procedures—such as those covered by the regulations mentioned above—are simply dumped alongside each other in the storage room of EU legislation.

   We urgently need to find our way towards horizontal harmonisation, under which a coherent set of procedural rules could be drafted in accordance with the model which we designed in 1993.

4. Essentially, any policy choice to be made will remain at the level of the twin-track approach, to wit, the relationship between the European and the domestic rules of procedure. In my view there are three possible options here:

[6] ECJ 1 March 2005, Case C-281/02, ECR I-1383 (*Owusu v Jackson*).

(a) we follow the (bad) example set by the regulations I have discussed, and we allow both the European and the national procedural rules to exist side by side, each with their own different field of application;
(b) we impose a European system of procedural law, to replace the national procedural law of each of the Member States. This is a proposition which is, in my view, totally unrealistic.; or
(c) we give the citizen—even when operating within the national legal order—a choice between the national and the European rules of procedure. In other words, we 'let the best win.' When the best practice ultimately wins, we will experience a new era in which the European citizen will succeed in creating the most satisfactory system of procedural law. This will be the so-called 28th model of procedural law.

19.3 Overview of Chapters

This was indeed an excellent and inspiring colloquium, since it gave us an original approach to the globalisation and harmonisation of civil procedure. So let me, on behalf of the reporters and participants, first of all congratulate and thank the organisers of the colloquium Professor Xandra Kramer and Professor C.H. (Remco) van Rhee, and of course all those who helped with the preparations, as well as the eminent scholars who wrote and reported on the different topics.

It is not my intention to repeat or to summarise the excellent reports of this two-day colloquium. Let me just highlight some striking ideas and provocative statements.

May I remind you of the introductory lecture by Neil Andrews in which he stressed the value of Integrity, which is at the root of all of the rules of conduct for the actors of Justice. Since we became conscious that the conduct of the actors is more important than the procedural rules, the requirement of Integrity could be considered as a kind of filigree for this colloquium.

One cannot understand harmonisation without knowledge of the historical and comparative perspective brought by one of the most excellent legal historians in the field of procedural law, Remco van Rhee, beginning more than a decade ago with his inaugural lecture 'Adam, ubi es?'[7]

I am very happy with the criticism *vis-à-vis* vertical harmonisation as it was explained in the reports of Gerard Walter and Burckhard Hess. We need indeed a horizontal and more functional harmonisation, which will facilitate access to justice and ensure procedural fairness.

Gerhard Wagner stated that alternative dispute resolution gives no access to justice and that it is strongly developed in Scandinavian countries, and rather weakly in Mediterranean countries. And it was an original idea to examine the

[7] Van Rhee 1999.

interaction of civil procedure with private international law and also with private law, as Xandra Kramer and Matthias Storme did. Normally we limit ourselves to a relationship between these branches of law. Those branches can indeed help towards harmonisation or even generate harmonisation. Sometimes harmonisation makes private international law obsolete. And that procedural law can have a great impact on private law is clear. But we have to look for an adequate and correct terminology.

Our Croatian colleague Alan Uzelac gave us again the sometimes stunning figures collected by the European Commission for the Efficiency of Justice. Some of these figures can explain the divergences between European procedural systems and help us to improve our strategy of harmonisation. Can we suggest a comparative analysis of the workload of the judges? Can we also have figures about the results of first instance proceedings? If my feeling that 75 per cent of the claims are well founded is correct, one can imagine putting the burden of proof on the shoulders of the defendant.

Our good friend Michele Taruffo explained to us again that the principles and rules of transnational civil procedure can help us in the harmonisation of procedural law in Europe, and not only for transnational litigation.

As we all know in the debates pro and contra harmonisation, one of the arguments which are probably more convincing than the economic ones, is the reference to federal States which do not have a federal Code of Civil Procedure, as, for instance, the United States of America. So we were very happy to hear the report of Tanja Domej, telling us that on 1 January 2011 the unified *Schweizerische Zivilprozessornung* has entered into force. We were also told that the Lugano Convention had a big influence on the new Swiss Code. And that the federal courts in the United States do help to unify the procedural law in the state courts which is a very hopeful evolution.

From among a beautiful set of national reports on the United States, Switzerland, Scotland, the Netherlands, Germany, Belgium, France and Romania, as I did for the other reports, I will only highlight some original ideas and illuminating statements.

Paulien van der Grinten gave us critical insight into the relationship between the Member States and the European Commission in the field of procedural law.

The German code is in my opinion one of the best codes of civil procedural law and has inspired many such codes abroad. This appreciation probably explains why I was shocked by the information of our colleague Stefan Huber about the introduction of English in court proceedings in Germany '[to make] German law more attractive in commercial transactions.' This means that 'legal service' has become 'legal business.'

All of this explains why I was so glad to hear my young Belgian colleague Benoît Allemeersch who reacted critically *vis-à-vis* this German evolution during the conference. Justice is not a product.

For all of us it was a pleasure to listen to the report of our French colleague Frédérique Ferrand. The Association of Procedural Law has for ten years succeeded in bringing together eminent colleagues of the country, where the *Code de procédure civile* was drafted more than two centuries ago (1806), the mother of so many codes in the international academic family. And it was extremely interesting to see how some common law institutions (estoppel, anti-suit injunction, freezing order, et cetera) were remodelled and incorporated into the civil law culture. France is not lost in translation!

Finally, the Romanian reporter Sebastian Spinei revealed a fundamental problem in procedural law, which is probably the most political branch of law. Transitional justice is indeed not an exception all over the world. In that sense the Romanian example is an extremely interesting model for the study of transitional justice and its problems.

19.4 Concluding Proposals

Procedural law has become an autonomous branch of law and the unique scope of procedural law is to legitimise the intervention of a judge. How can we convince private persons to submit their conflicts to a State authority? We can only succeed when we give them the feeling of a fair trial. This means that we should try to give the same feeling of legitimacy to all the citizens of the EU.

How do we get there from here? One option could be to operate on a regional basis—the Baltic States, the Benelux, the Scandinavian countries, et cetera. There could also be a civil law-common law split.

I would be inclined to take it as a defeat if we did not involve all 27 Member States in this process. However, I am willing to contemplate the stages set out below.

First of all, a group of experts from all the Member States, drawn from the ranks of both academics and practitioners, should develop a global vision for European procedural law and set out the ways and means in which this can gradually be translated into concrete legislation.

Subsequently, a new group should proceed to draft a general section, which would contain fundamental principles, rules on the normal conduct of civil proceedings, and a number of necessary special procedures.

All this should result in the adoption of a *Codigo Tipo Europeo*, or a framework which would follow the model developed for the European Contract Law Project.

In my opinion the process of harmonisation and unification of procedural law on a European level appears to be an irreversible trend. We will have to shift the attention of science and practice away from purely national (egocentric) items. I make mine the conclusion of Burkhard Hess: 'In the long run, the emergence of a genuine and coherent European procedural law appears to be possible.'

And finally we have got here new ammunition to continue our battle in favour of a harmonised or unified or globalised procedural law, since we are convinced that this could help to find Justice, not only in Europe, but all over the world.

References

Freudenthal M (2009) Grensoverschrijdende erkenning en tenuitvoerlegging. Sdu, Den Haag

Storme M (1986) Perorazione per un diritto giudiziario Europeo. Rivista di diritto processuale 41:293–307

Storme M (ed) (1994) Rapprochement du droit judiciaire de l'Union européenne/Approximation of judiciary law in the European Union. Martinus Nijhoff, Dordrecht

Van Rhee CH (1999) Adam, ubi es? Het burgerlijk procesrecht als juridische wetenschap met Europese allure. Kluwer, Deventer

The manufacturer's authorised representative in the EU is Springer Nature Customer Service Centre GmbH, Europaplatz 3, 69115 Heidelberg, Germany. If you have any concerns regarding our products, please contact ProductSafety@springernature.com

Printed and bound by CPI Group (UK) Ltd, Croydon, CR0 4YY
25/09/2026
02222839-0004